Ajmer Sharif

Awakening of Sufism in South Asia

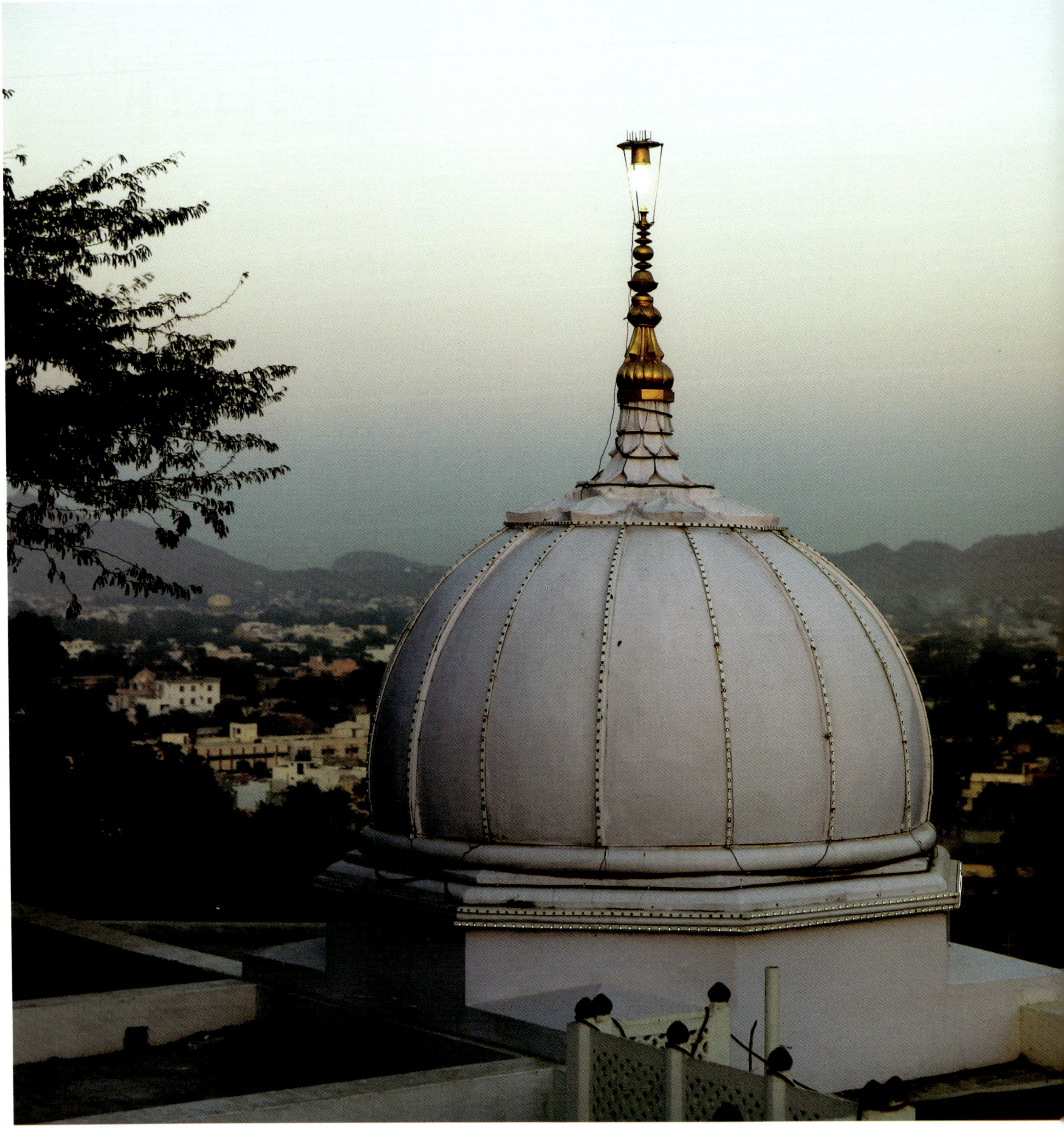

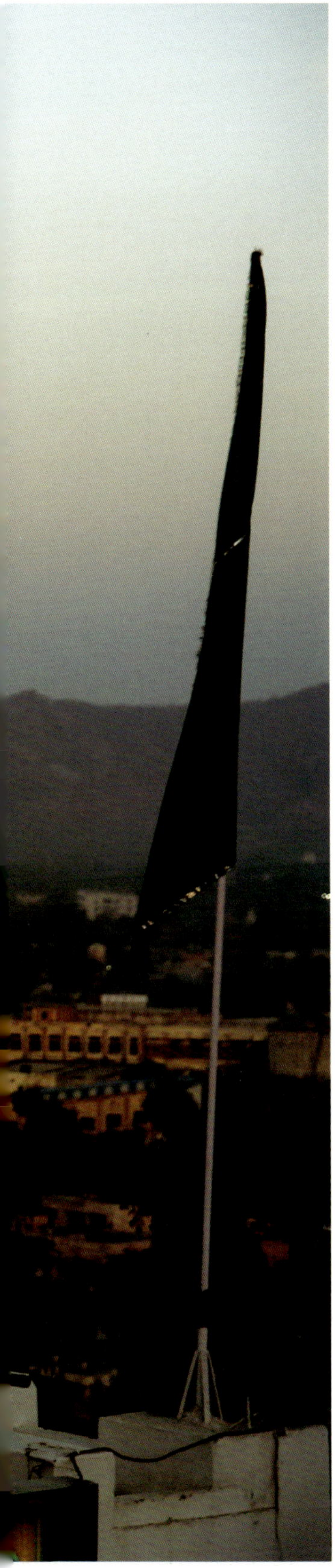

Ajmer Sharif

Awakening of Sufism in South Asia

REEMA ABBASI

FOREWORD BY

Mehru Jaffer

FACILITATION

Shaykha Amat un Nur, Pakistan

Syed Salman Chishty, Director,
Chishty Foundation, Ajmer Sharif, India

NIYOGI
BOOKS

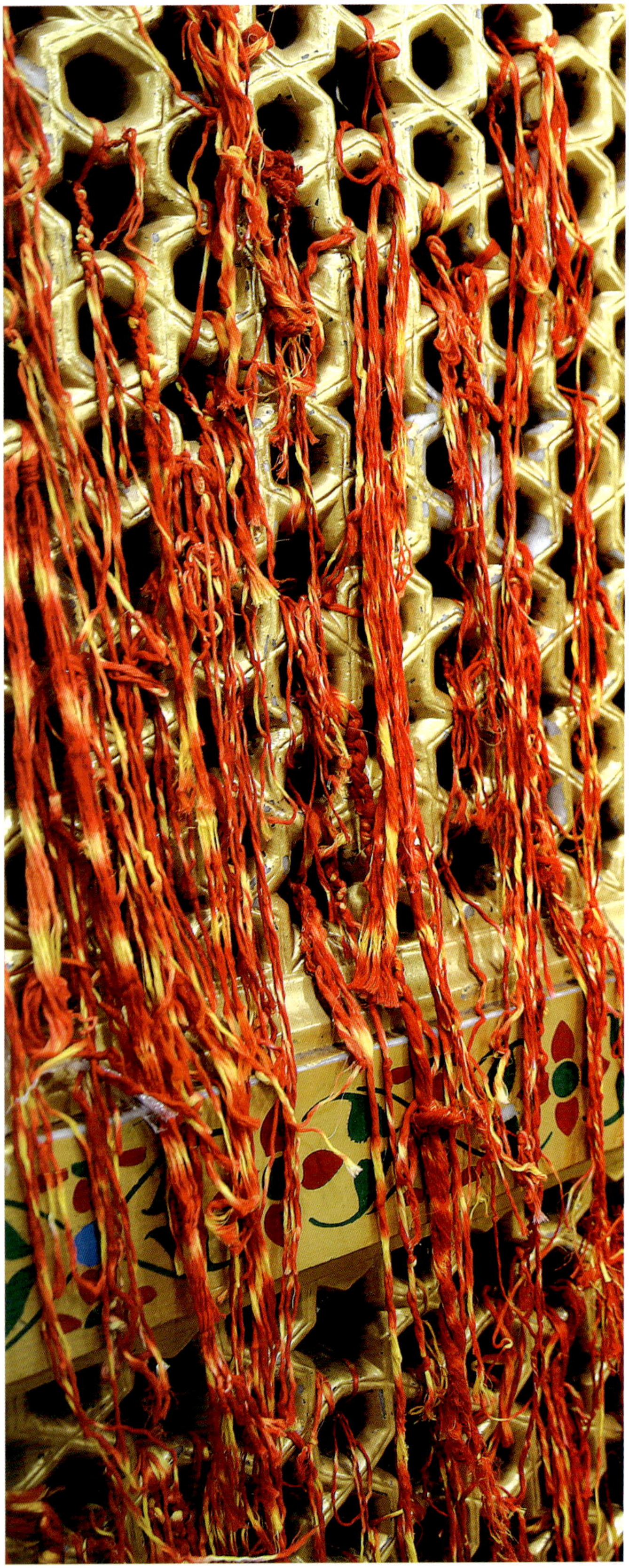

Previous page: The light of faith and hope radiates from the dome of Ajmer Sharif

Left: Sacred threads denote wishes made by worshippers at Ajmer Sharif

Published by

NIYOGI BOOKS

D-78, Okhla Industrial Area, Phase-I
New Delhi-110 020, INDIA
Tel: 91-11-26816301, 49327000
Fax: 91-11-26810483, 26813830
email: niyogibooks@gmail.com
website: www.niyogibooksindia.com

Photographs: Syed Salman Chishty, Gaddi Nasheen, Ajmer Sharif, and Director, Chishty Foundation (except where otherwise indicated)

Editor: K.E. Priyamvada
Design: Shraboni Roy

ISBN: 978-93-85285-64-6
Publication: 2017

Printed at: Niyogi Offset Pvt. Ltd., New Delhi, India

To

Khwaja Muinuddin Chishti

'Not Christian or Jew or Muslim, not Hindu
Buddhist, sufi, or zen. Not any religion

Or cultural system. I am not from the East or the West, not out of the ocean or up
from the ground, not natural or ethereal, not composed of elements at all. I do not exist,

am not an entity in this world or the next,
did not descend from Adam and Eve or any origin story.

My place is placeless, a trace of the traceless.
Neither body or soul.

I belong to the beloved, have seen the two
worlds as one and that one call to and know,

first, last, outer, inner, only that
breath breathing human being.'

Only Breath, Mevlana Rumi

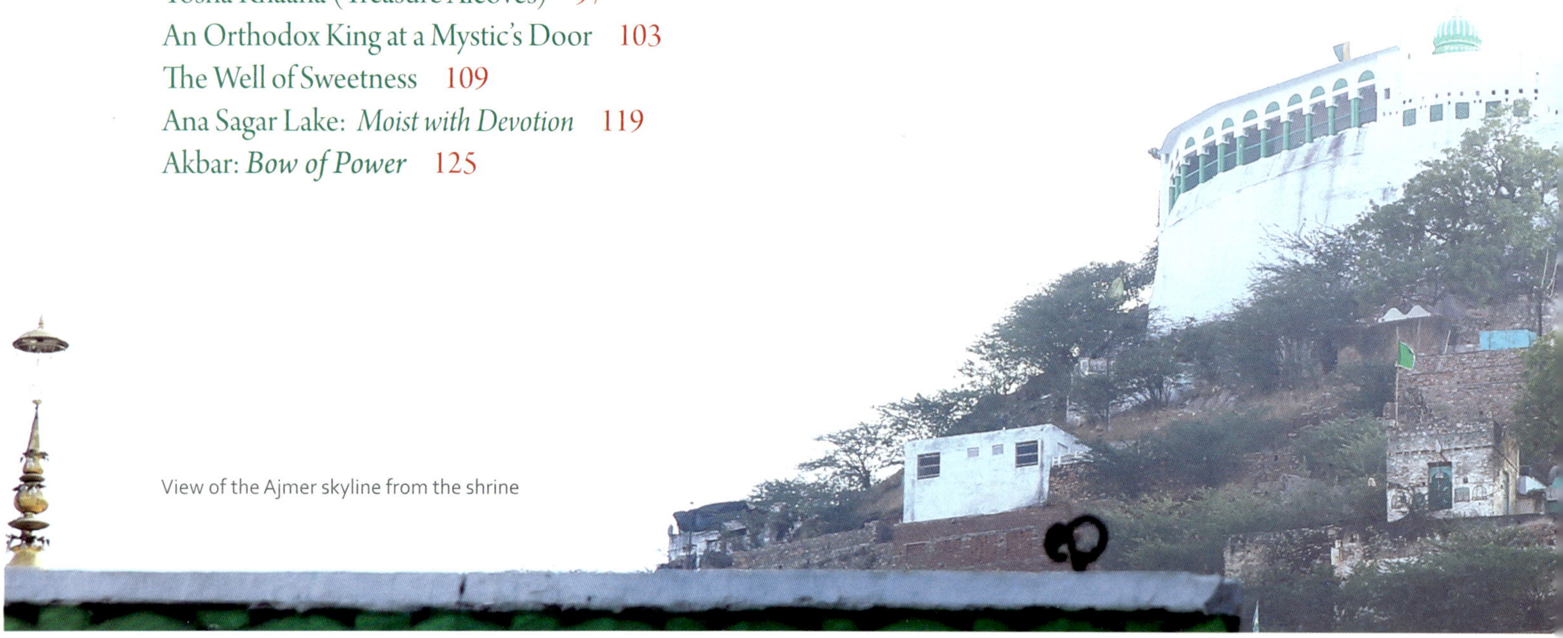

View of the Ajmer skyline from the shrine

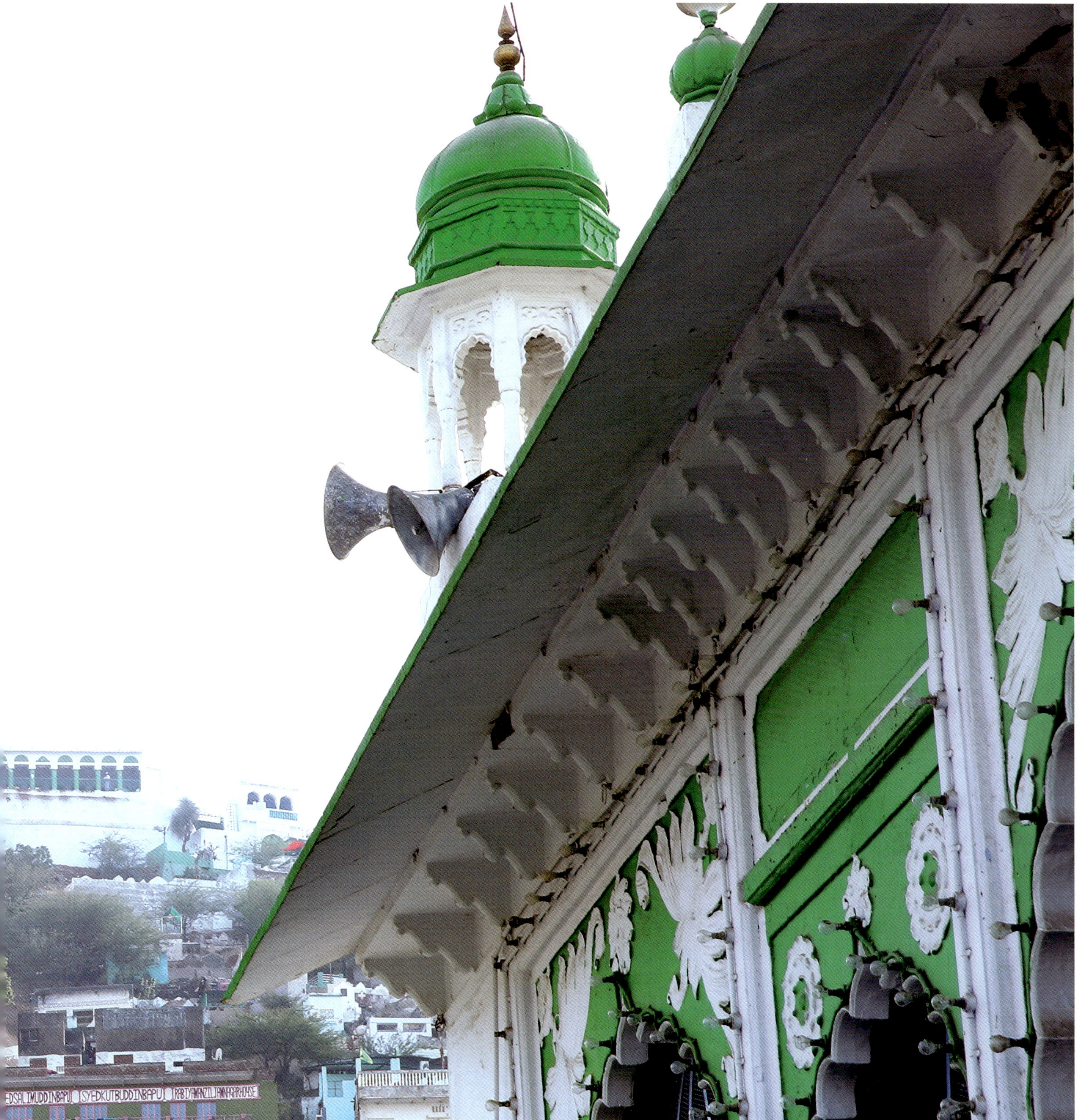
EDSALIMUDDINBAPU
SYEDKUTBUDDINBAPU

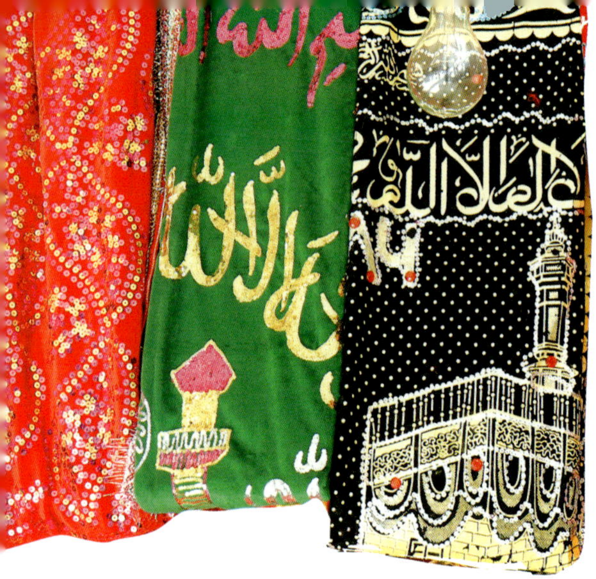

Foreword

Any moment is *mubarak* to remember Muinuddin Chishti. However, when war and violence become routine, as they seem to be these days, then repeating the story of Muinuddin Chishti also becomes a responsibility.

To know Muinuddin Chishti better is to glimpse the poetic side of Islam, especially when it seems so difficult for the world to appreciate Muslims today. The life of Muinuddin Chishti, founder of the Chishtiya mystical order in South Asia is a glowing example of how to practise love in times of hate. What Muinuddin Chishti did was to conquer fear, suspicion and the religious divide of the day with poetry, music and a simple philosophy of love that appealed most to the majority of people who were tired of war waged upon them by others.

Because of his open house lifestyle in Ajmer, in the heartland of the Indian subcontinent, Muinuddin Chishti was able to initiate a cultural dialogue amongst people belonging to different cultures and religions, at his doorstep. This naturally earned him more friends, even amongst total strangers.

In medieval days the responsibility of improving understanding between the Hindu and Muslim communities was assumed by mystics who showed great interest in local people, their religion and cultural traditions. This appreciation of the other, immediately opened communication and people felt even closer to each other after they found similarities between the teachings of Islam and the Hindu philosophy of advaita vedanta.

Muinuddin Chishti was born in 1141, about two decades before the birth of Genghis Khan—founder of the Mongol Empire—and witnessed

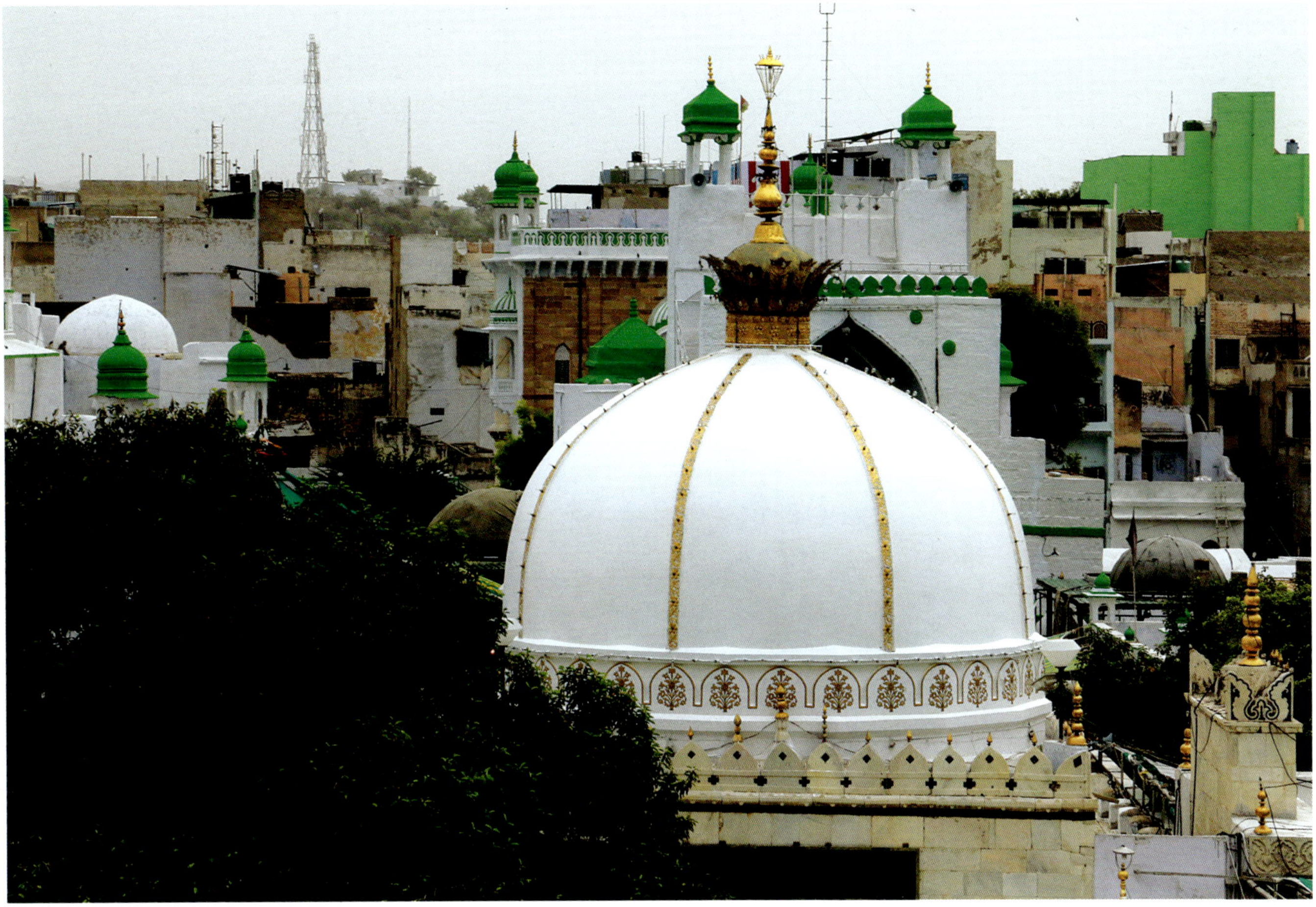

the Mongol military genius's obsession for world conquest. The result was a chain of brutal attacks on places and populations that ruined the peace and quiet of mostly ordinary folk and made migrants of people like Muinuddin Chishti.

Those were times of immense strife. The wealth of the great Silk Road was contested by armies from different parts of the Arabian Peninsula and Persia as well as by newly empowered people of several Turkic and Mongol tribes.

Above: The dome rises like a symbol of hope and grace

Facing Page: Ritual offerings at Ajmer Sharif

To add to his suffering, Muinuddin Chishti was orphaned while still a teenager. Sistan, his place of birth on the border of modern-day Afghanistan, Iran and Pakistan had become a battleground for many a military incursion.

Muinuddin earned his last name from Chisht, once a peaceful town near Herat in modern-day Afghanistan. The scholar Abu Ishaq Shami had fled, some two hundred years before Muinuddin to Chisht, away from the political shenanigans of 10th century Baghdad and Damascus. Here Shami spent time in a humble hut to meditate upon the state of the human condition. The many like-minded visitors who flocked to his home became a fraternity that soon expanded into a people's movement called Chishtiya.

By the end of the 12th century strife had caught up with Chisht as well. It was no longer possible to live and to love in Chisht. The hermits of the Chishtiya order were forced to disperse and to wander, mostly around the Muslim world, in search of calm.

In Nishapur, in modern-day Iran, Muinuddin Chishti met Usman Harwani and received his first lesson in the philosophy of the Chishtiya. Harwani remained Muinuddin Chishti's guru for 20 long years. His succession to Harwani made Muinuddin Chishti the eighth mentor after Abu Ishaq Shami Chishti, founder of the Chishtiya School of Islamic mysticism.

After Harwani bid him goodbye, Muinuddin Chishti was left on his own to practice the Chishtiya way of life, and he never forgot that respect for other human beings is the most obvious manifestation of a person's devotion to god.

More wanderings finally brought Muinuddin Chishti into South Asia through Multan, Lahore, Delhi and Ajmer. Throughout his life he had fought hate and now he faced fresh hostility in a new land, amongst strangers practising a different religion and speaking a different language.

Following in the footsteps of most Chistiya masters who stayed away from cities that were a hub of political power, Muinuddin Chishti did not tarry long in Lahore or Delhi. He made a home in Ajmer close to Pushkar, a city that was already a place of pilgrimage for local mystics.

Inspired by Muinuddin Chishti's brief stay in Lahore, hundreds of years later, Muhammad Iqbal—a 20th century Urdu poet from the same city—wrote verses praising his visit to the shrine of al-Hujwiri, one of the first Islamic mystics in the region, who lived during the 11th century:

A young man, cypress tall,
Came from the town of Merv to Lahore.
He went to see the venerable saint,
That the sun might dispel his darkness.
'I am hemmed in,' he said, 'by foes,
I am as a glass in the midst of stones.
Do teach me, o' sire of heavenly rank,
How to lead my life amongst enemies!'

It is a tradition to bury the mystic close to where he had lived. In the mind of a believer, the place of burial of a great soul converts into a sanctum sanctorum, suggestive of a place of communion of the mystic with the concealed nature of the creator of the world.

It is the habit of many a pilgrim to journey to a shrine in the mood of a lover who looks forward to opening gates, climbing steps, bending below lintels and crossing many a threshold—all symbolic of stepping out of this world and into the sacred world of the beloved in desperate desire to experience spiritual ecstasy in this life, in this world, here and now.

The mystic is revered for being a bridge between the seen and the unseen world. But the large majority of people who flock to a shrine feel close to the mystic because they believe he is a miracle maker and bearer of divine bliss. Before the arrival of the Muslim mystic, South Asia already had an ancient tradition of pilgrimage and it did not take much for the

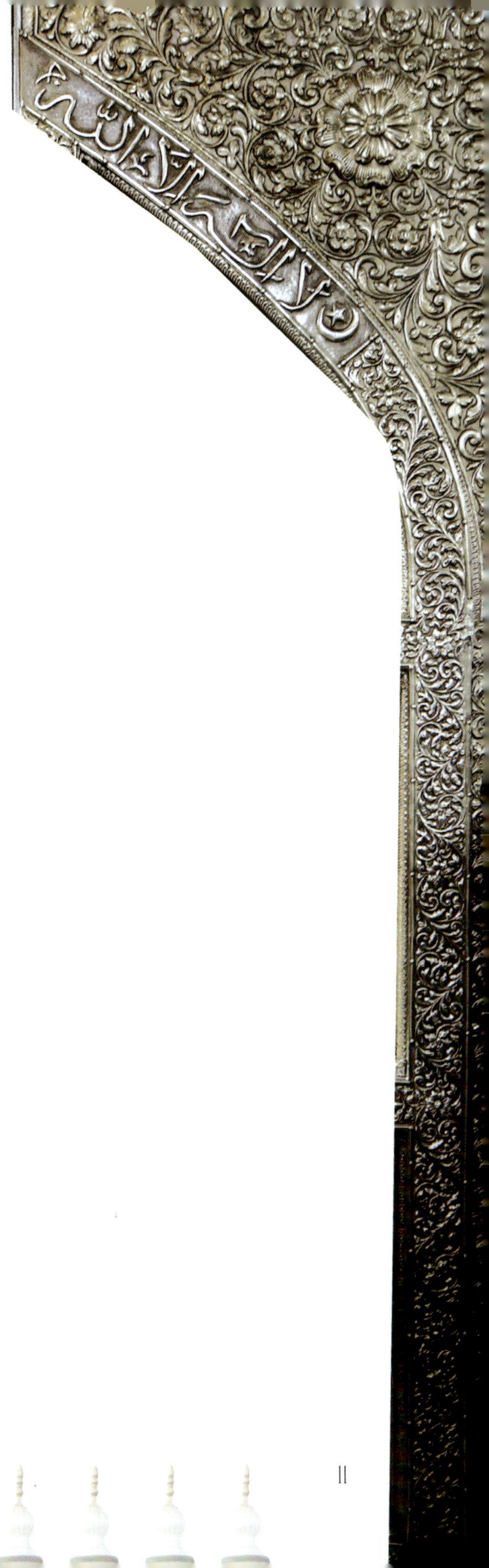

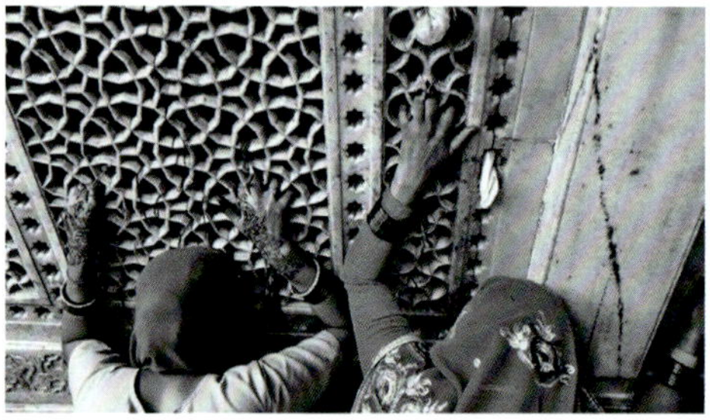

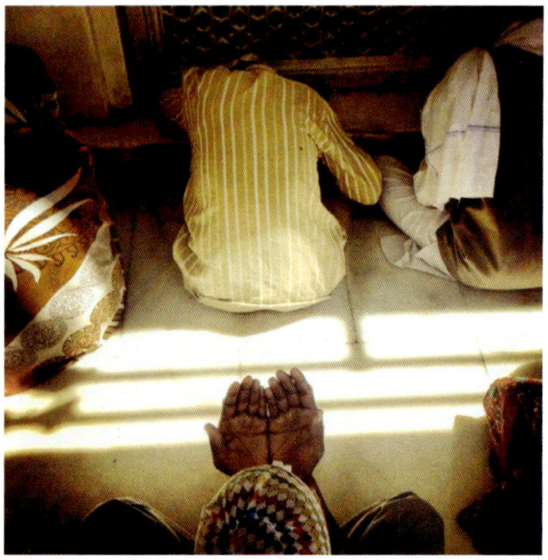

practice to blossom around the shrine of a beloved mystic as well, even if he was a Muslim.

The one and only reason why the people of Ajmer allowed Muinuddin Chishti to live in their midst was because they grew to love the man. And people loved Muinuddin Chishti because they felt loved by him. Visitors to his home in Ajmer multiplied because everyone was welcomed here without prejudice.

In times of intense hate amongst human beings, love was assured at the doorstep of the dervish whose worship included listening to the distressed, helping the helpless and providing food to the hungry. Soon Muinuddin Chishti earned the name of *Gharib Nawaz* or friend of the poor for his oceanic generosity.

Yet Gharib Nawaz was even forgotten for a while, despite all his good deeds. There is no mention of him in any record soon after his death. For almost a century later he seems not to have existed. Even Nizamuddin Auliya of Delhi who died in 1325 and was a Chistiya mentor does not say a word about Gharib Nawaz in his book *Fawaid al-Fuad* or *Morals for the Heart.*

The spiritual significance of Gharib Nawaz was resurrected only in the 16th century and ever since countless roads from around the world continue to lead to Ajmer Sharif, the shrine of Gharib Nawaz that is perpetually adorned by the wealthy, and adored by the poor.

Now Reema Abbasi, a Karachi-based journalist and author, has put together this book on Ajmer Sharif, maybe as a reminder that to love other human beings like Gharib Nawaz did, is so easy.

It may also be the hope of the author to make readers realise that the only path to happiness for all human beings is to appreciate, and not to attack, each other.

Mehru Jaffer
Lucknow, October 2016

Top: Scenes of deep devotion

Above: Pilgrims at prayer

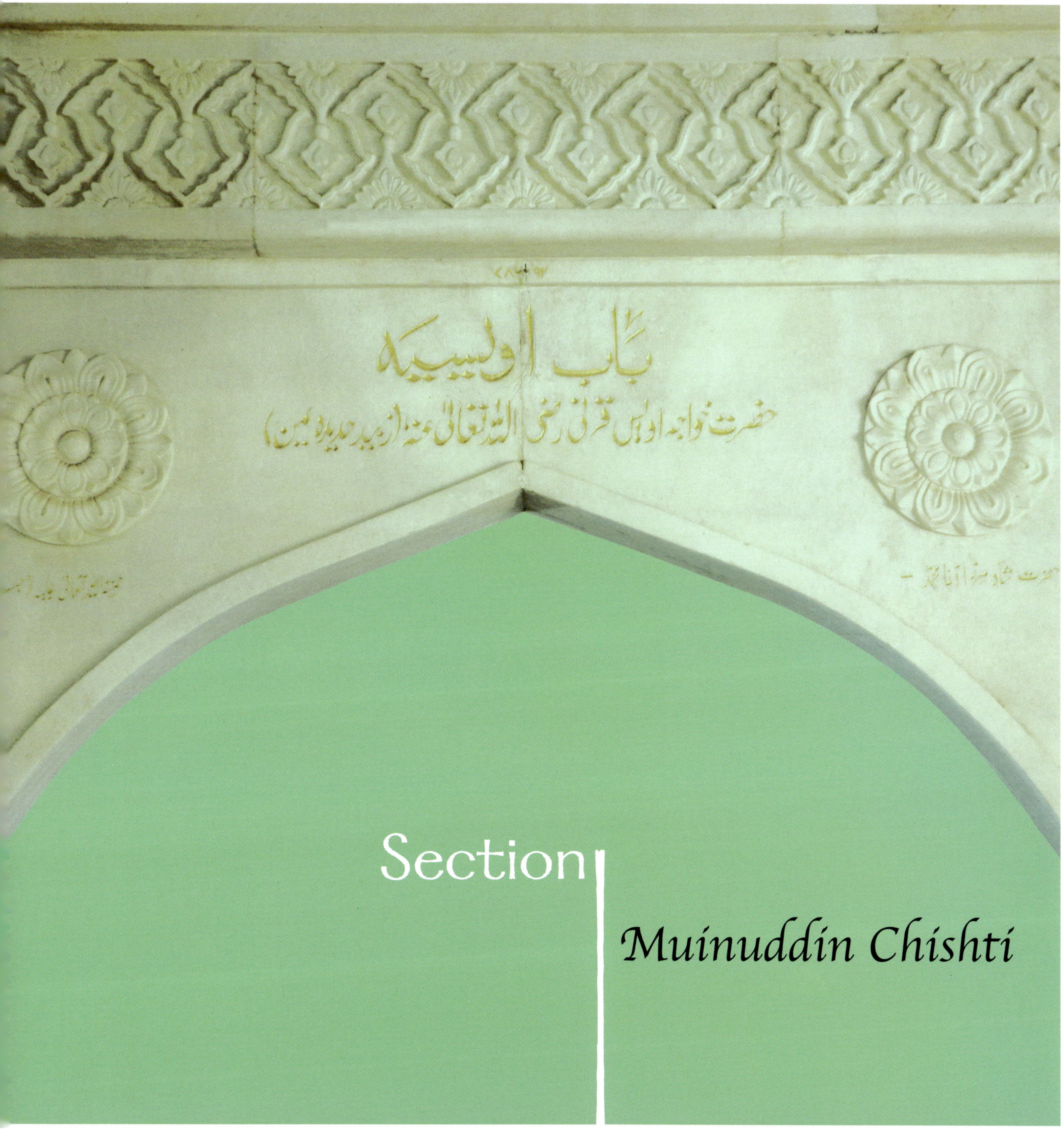

Section

Muinuddin Chishti

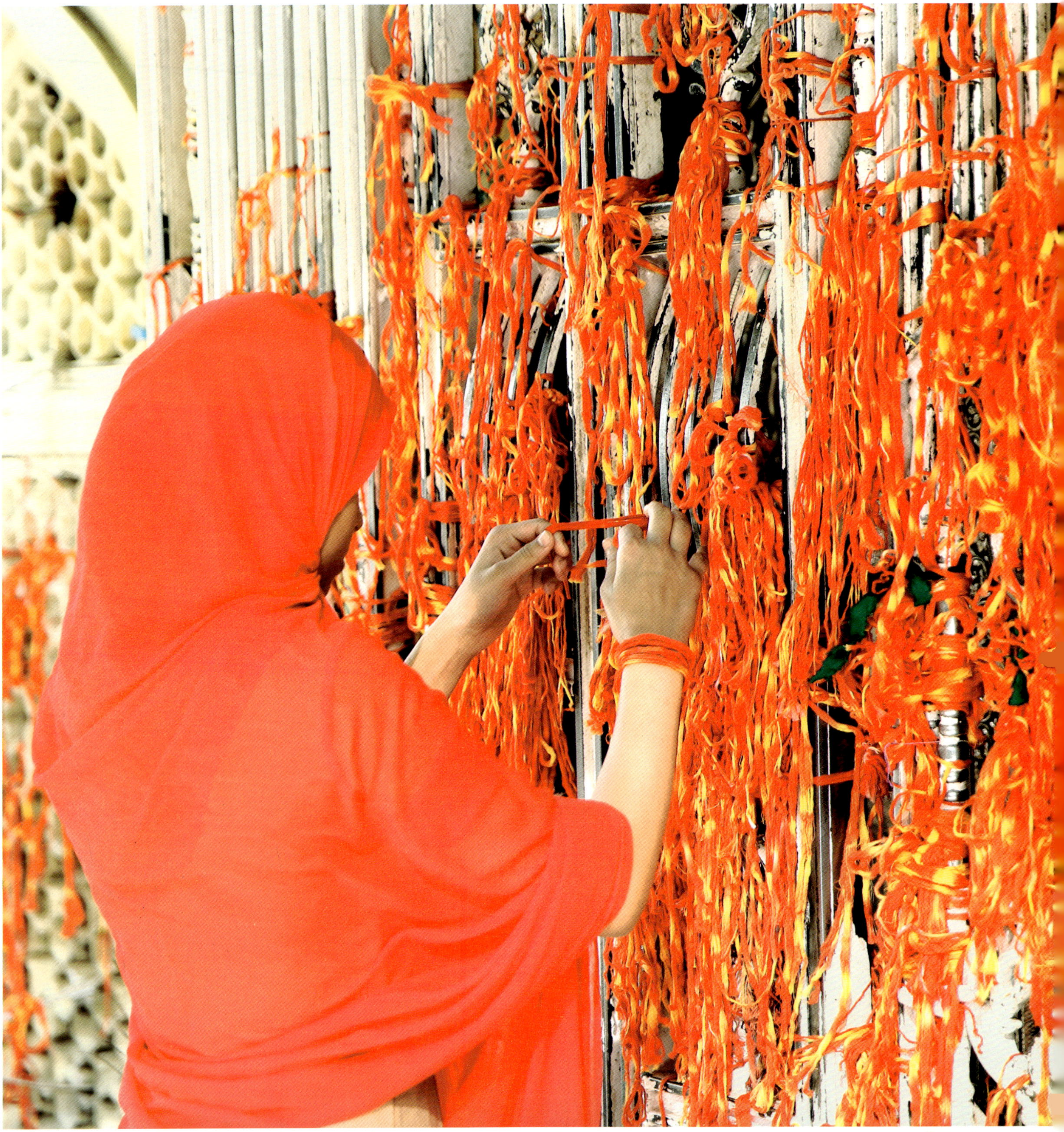

Man and Monument

'The heart of a lover is set ablaze with love.
Everyone who enters the domain of love is scorched.
It should not be avoided, since there is no loftier fire than the fire of Love.'
Khwaja Muinuddin Chishti

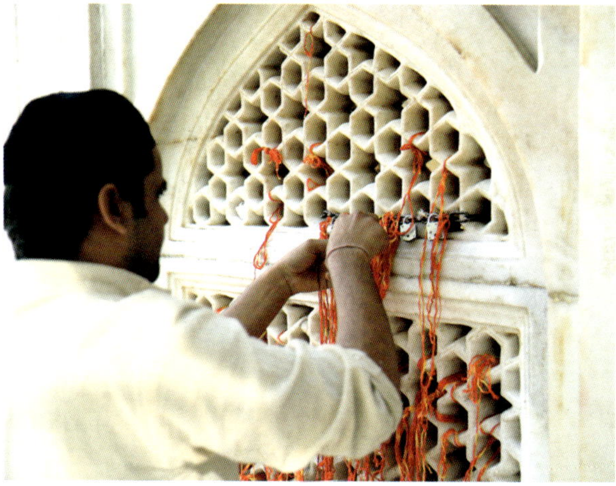

Above and facing page:
Ties of hope and relief

It was an extraordinary Monday when I died. The summons, over many months, were overwhelming. They fell on a spirit caged in the din of orthodoxy by self-styled defenders of 'real' faith.

In my person, I was a believer with a fascination for the pagan; everything of the mortal who had sullied many vows, many times. Stories of belief from my family, awe of people beholding and living miracles, and my own dreams, the search for peace and wishes, sent me on this road.

Even so, the pull of a place, felt in another land, remains mythical. However, this road made me a seeker of destiny, faith, an anchor. On this particular Monday, as one travelled on instinct to the ancient desert shrine of Ajmer Sharif, one knew the answer was bigger. It would untangle religious obscurity that at once deepened and confused my bond with Islam.

All this, and many prayers in the heart were enough to carry a pilgrim to the fold of Khwaja Muinuddin Hasan Chishti. An 805-year-old enigma of acceptance, who placed hunger above any creed and caste. Although, without a solid theological reason to make the journey, since that first step on the soil of a spiritual saviour, Monday has brought Life.

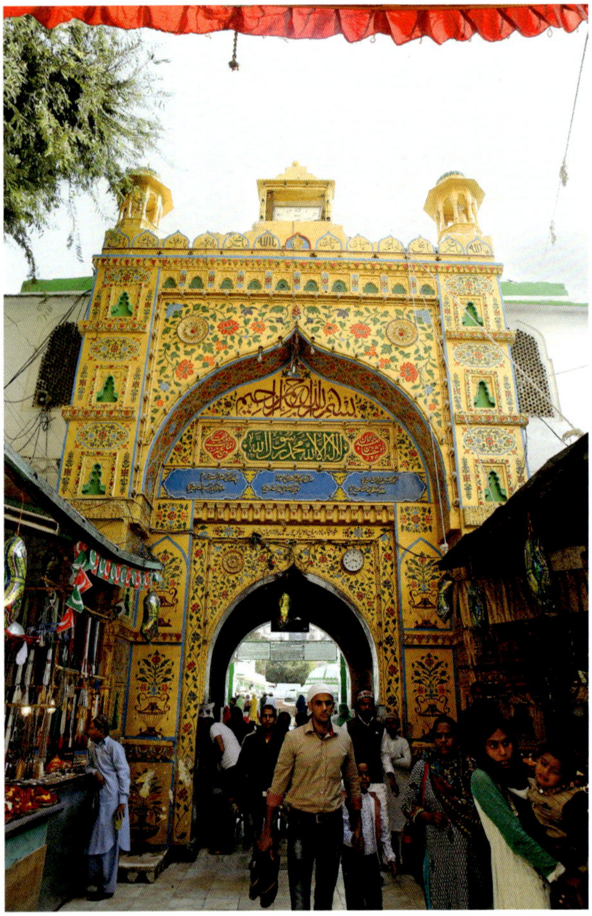

It comes with hope, and the wonder of spiritual zeniths that ordinary humans are capable of. So, call me a storyteller and listen. This is a divine tale—a mystic's life wrapped around his legacy, now an eternal refuge for humanity.

It must have been springtime in Paradise. The walk through the Dargah Bazaar was intense. Strangely, it is the nearest one has ever come to what Greek mythology and ancient scriptures see as 'man's first condition'—pure and sinless. In this small, cramped alley of sounds, sweat and fumes, Oneness did set in.

Impassioned devotees jostled past beggars, the disabled and various sellers to reach the majestic Nizami Darwaza. The gate, designed by British engineers in 1911 and crafted at a cost of 50,000 rupees was a bequest from Mir Osman Ali Khan, the Nizam of Hyderabad in the Deccan. An archaeological record puts the width of its intricate, scalloped arch at 16 feet; the gateway towers at 70 feet and extends to 76 feet.

Drum or Orchestra Pits (*Naqqaarkhana*) flank its clock tower and the town sways to drumbeats and strains of the shehnai that emanate from these chambers at five appointed hours throughout the day.

One deposits shoes, thoughts and the outside at its steps to enter the most venerated, medieval monument from the 13th century—the tomb of the founder of South Asia's paramount Chishti Sufi order.

In the alabaster oasis, custodians (*khuddaam* [plural], *khadim* [singular]) in crisp white, await to guide one through the complex. Saturated in the fragrances of sandalwood and rose, the entrance platform undulates in emerald, saffron and cherry, with streaks of gold on stalls of prayer offerings.

Like the mystic mesmerised by the image of a pattern on a snowflake, one moves in a trance through a valley of senses—every sight, a stamp on a captive soul. As classical Islamic mysticism blends with folk traditions and customs of ancient faiths, boundaries in humanity break down in tenderness. Some cling to him, others to hope.

Above: Devotees walk through the grand Nizami Darwaza

Facing page: Ornate chandeliers brighten Khwaja's doorstep

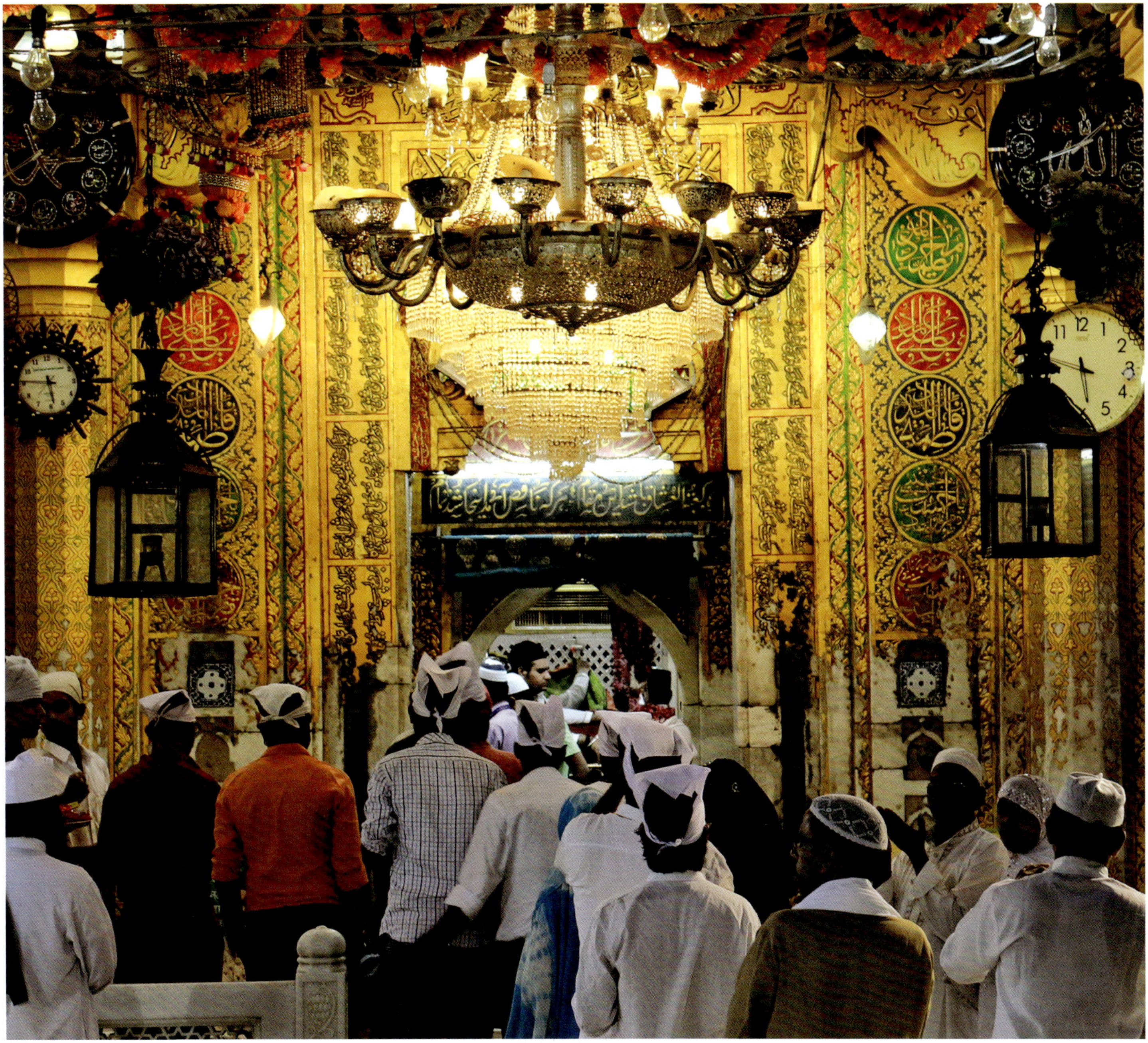

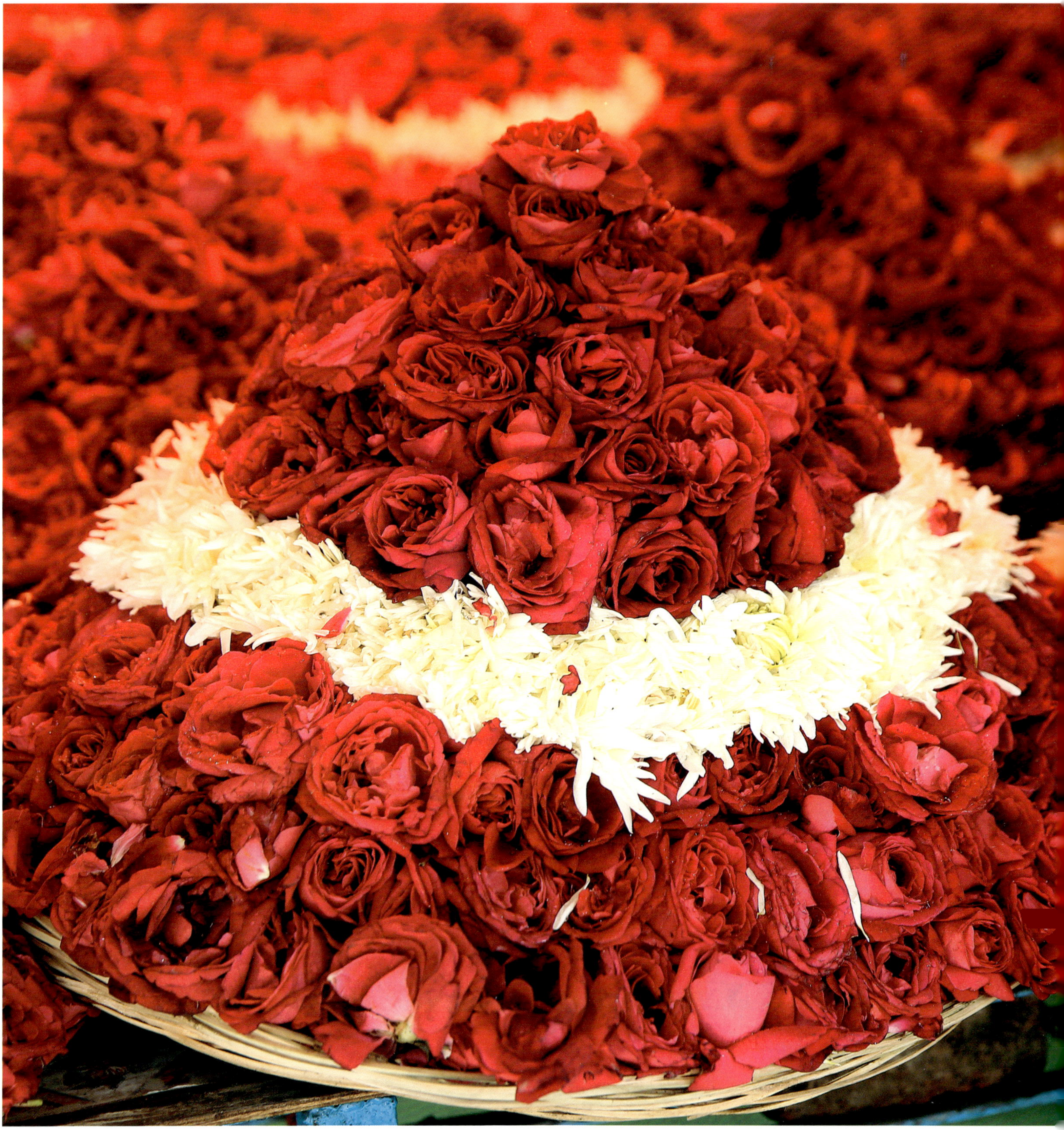

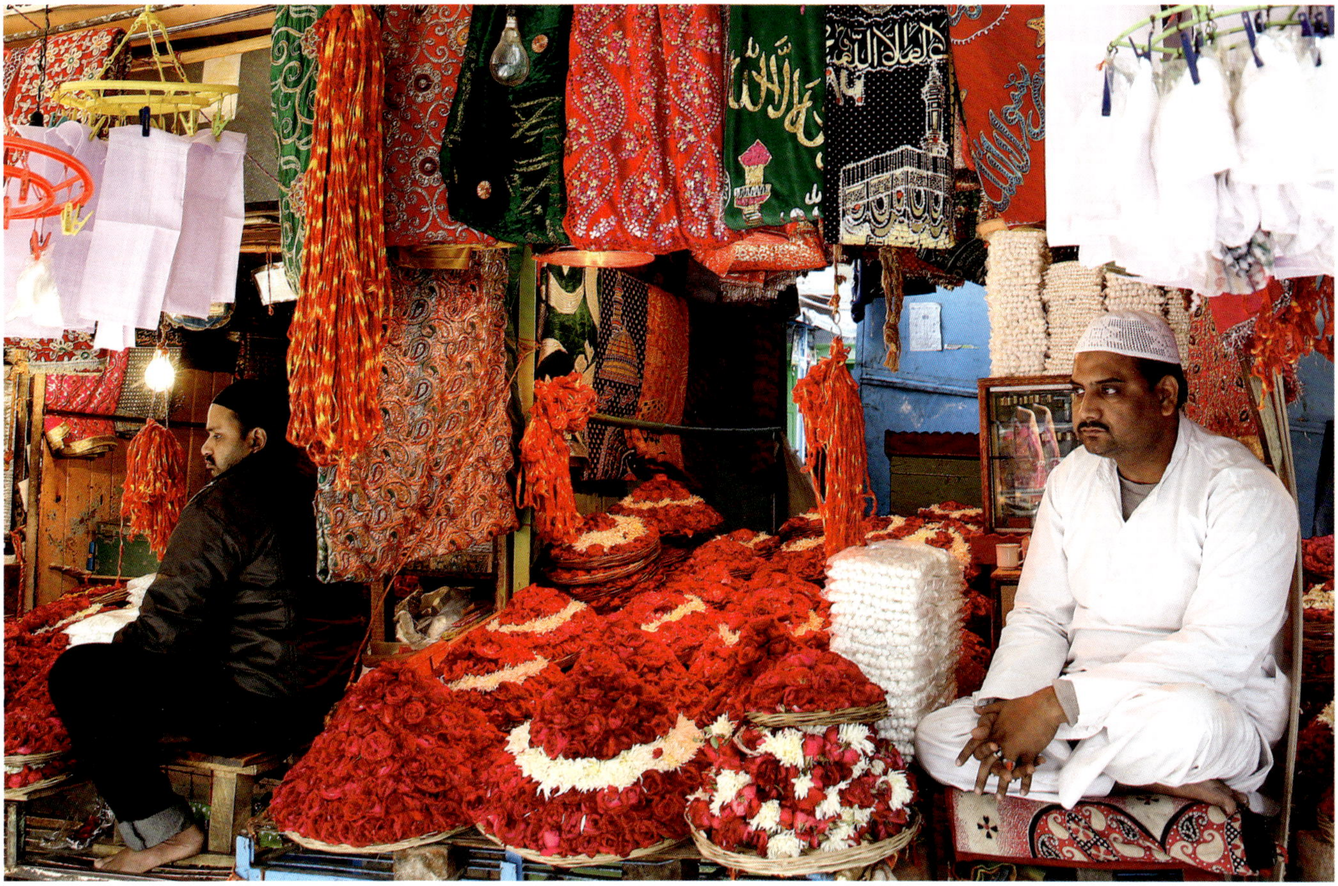

A tapestry of human devotion, this expanse is marked by mostly Mughal mementoes. Imposing structures, arches, columns, corbels, niches, domes and pavilions etched with filigree, calligraphy and geometric, floral or natural motifs outline the Muslim architecture of the Delhi Sultanates.

But swept by impulse, one begins with areas touched by the saint. Further down, to the north-west of the premises lies the second courtyard from the Nizami Gate.

Above: Stalls with prayer offerings on the way to the shrine

Facing page: Floral tributes to the Sufi saint

Next page: Radiant spirituality lights the pilgrims' path

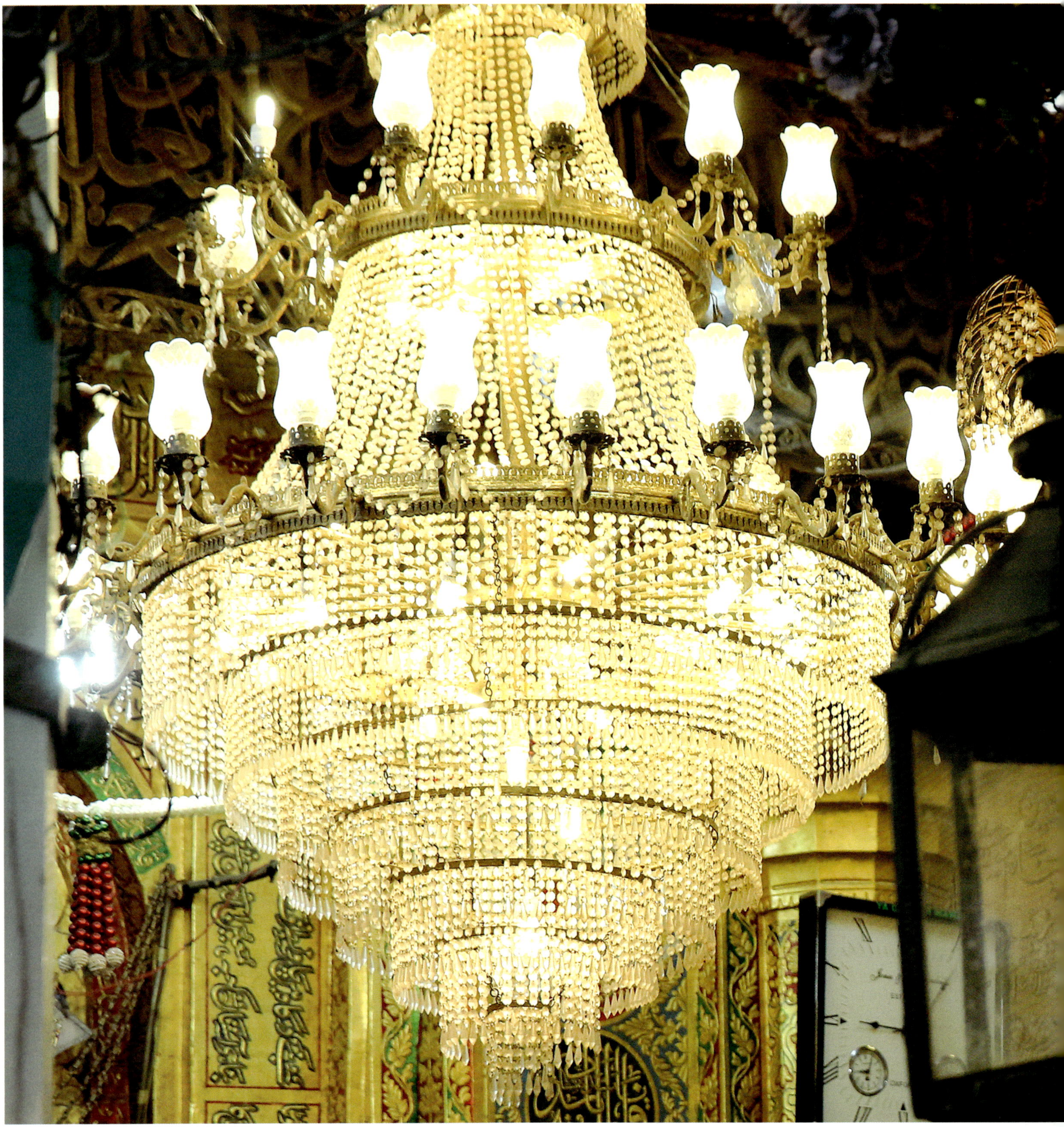

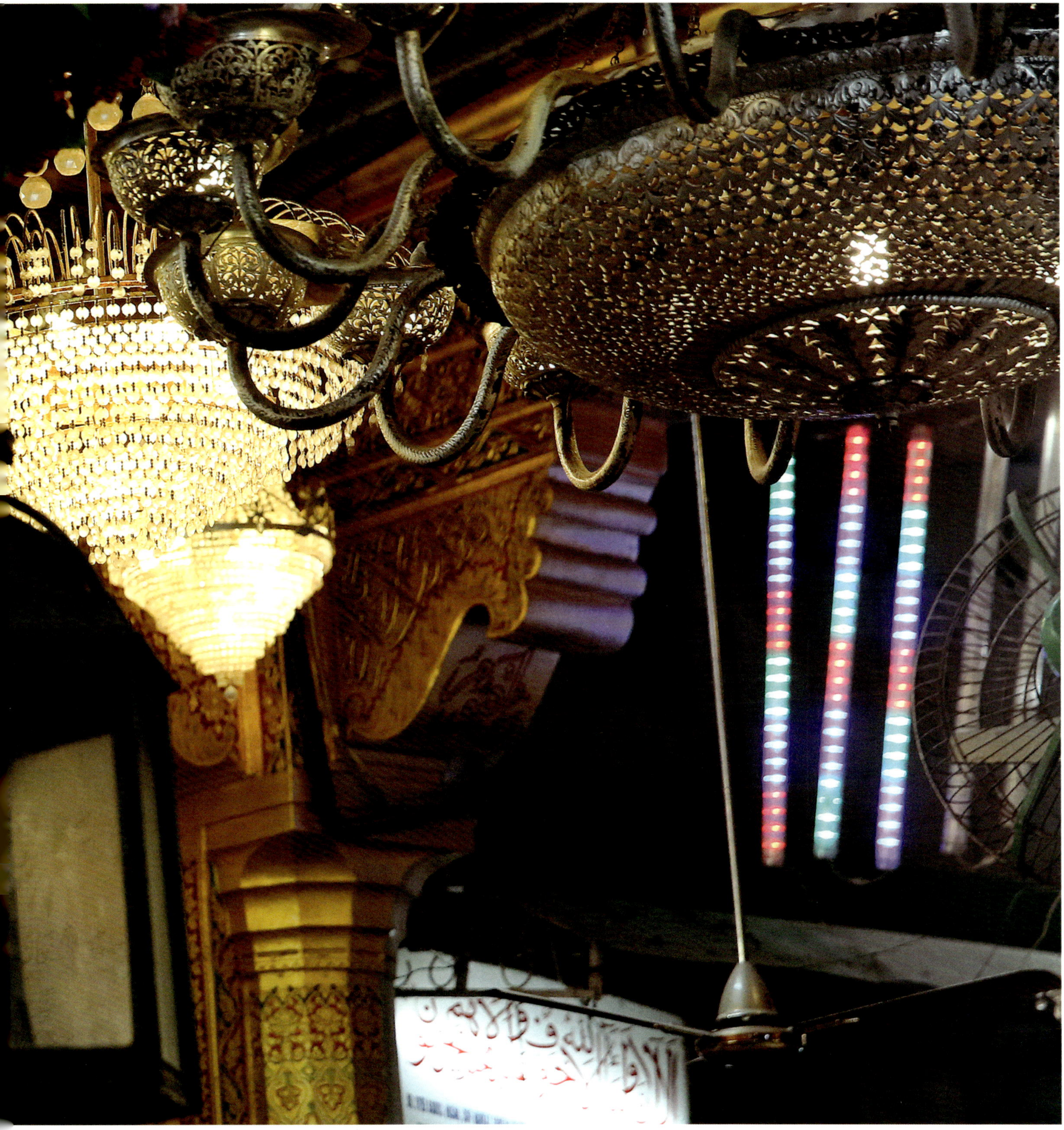

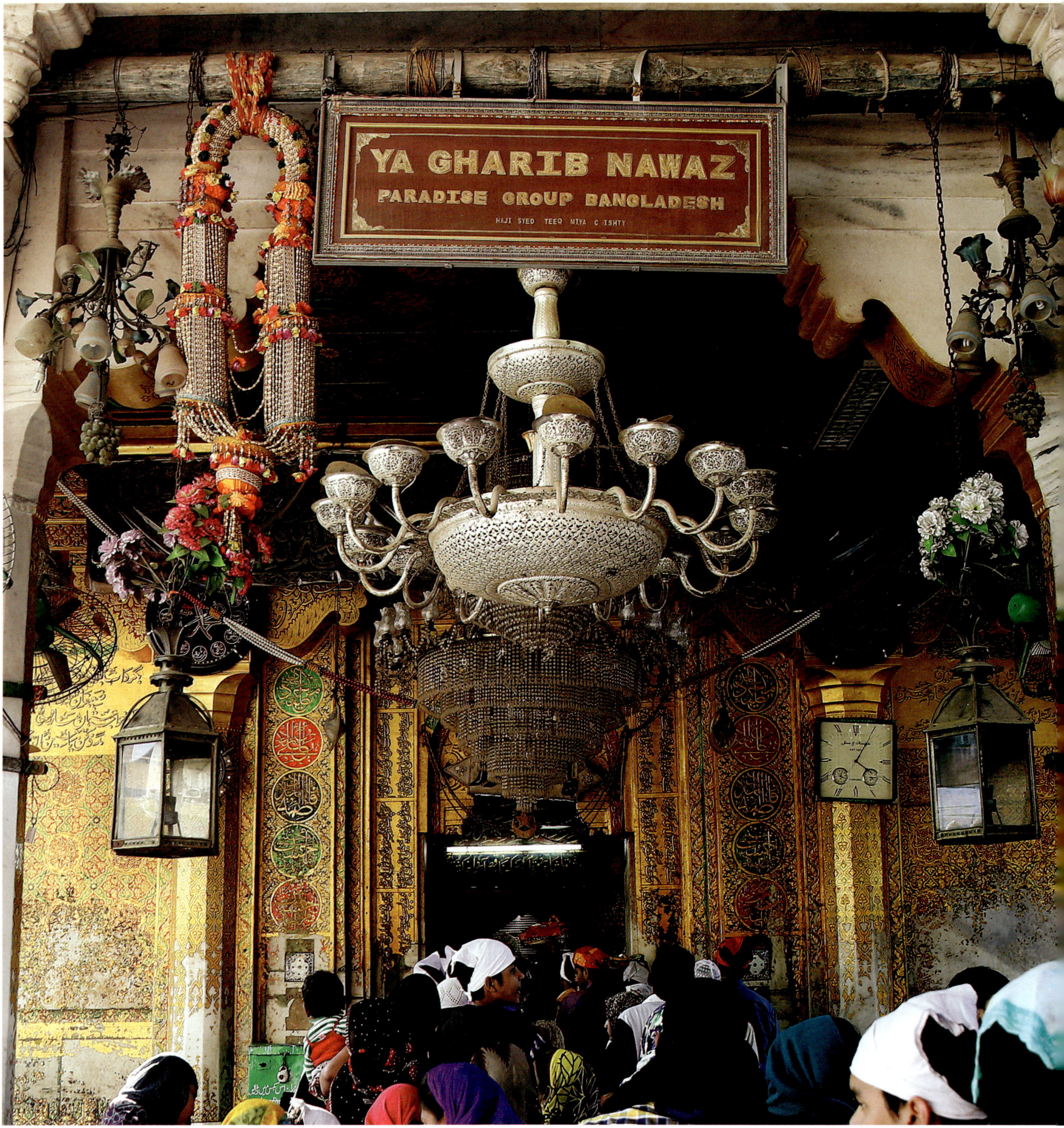
YA GHARIB NAWAZ
PARADISE GROUP BANGLADESH

The Sanctum

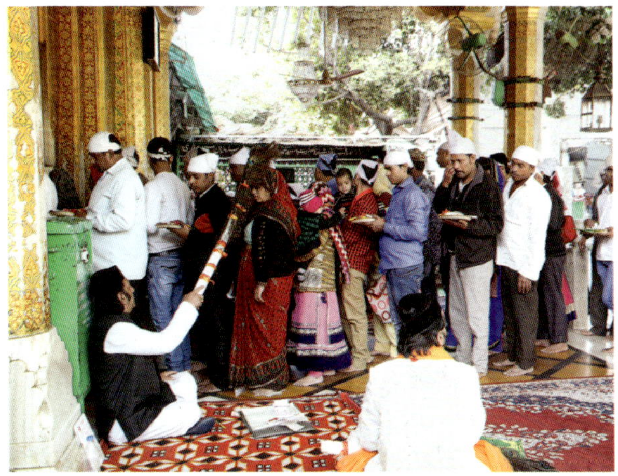

Ehaata Noorani (the Quarter of Light) is partly covered by a marble roof, rich with an inlay of silver rosebuds. From here, two doors open into the cenotaph sanctum. Many saints once stood in this courtyard to pray for the Khwaja.

His hallowed chamber, on the side of the platform extends into Ehaata Astaana (the Sanctum Quarter). Outlived by his children, Muinuddin passed away at the age of 95 in 1236 CE (633 AH).

Scholar Anna Suvorova, in *Muslim Saints of South Asia*, mentions that he was buried in his home, which then began its journey from a haven to a universal seat of mysticism. Sufism researchers refute the claim and document this chamber as his place of worship.

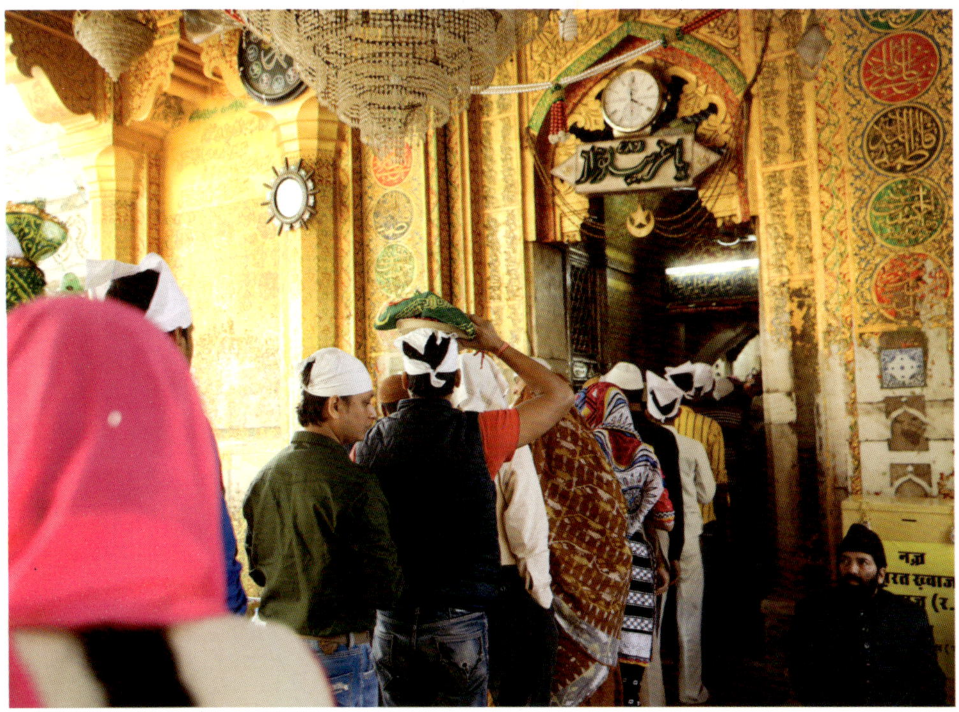

Above right: A Khadim blesses pilgrims as they enter the shrine

Right: The faithful come bearing gifts of devotion

Facing page: Grand chandeliers decorate the entrance to Muinuddin Chishti's tomb

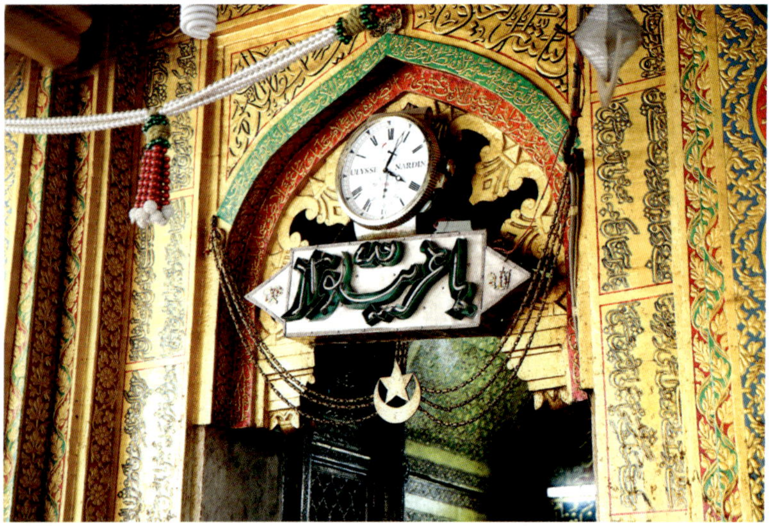

Left: Ya Gharib Nawaz (O Redeemer of the Poor) inscribed on the main door

Below: The author and Haji Farrokh in the main portico as Karka (Closing Ceremony) preparations begin

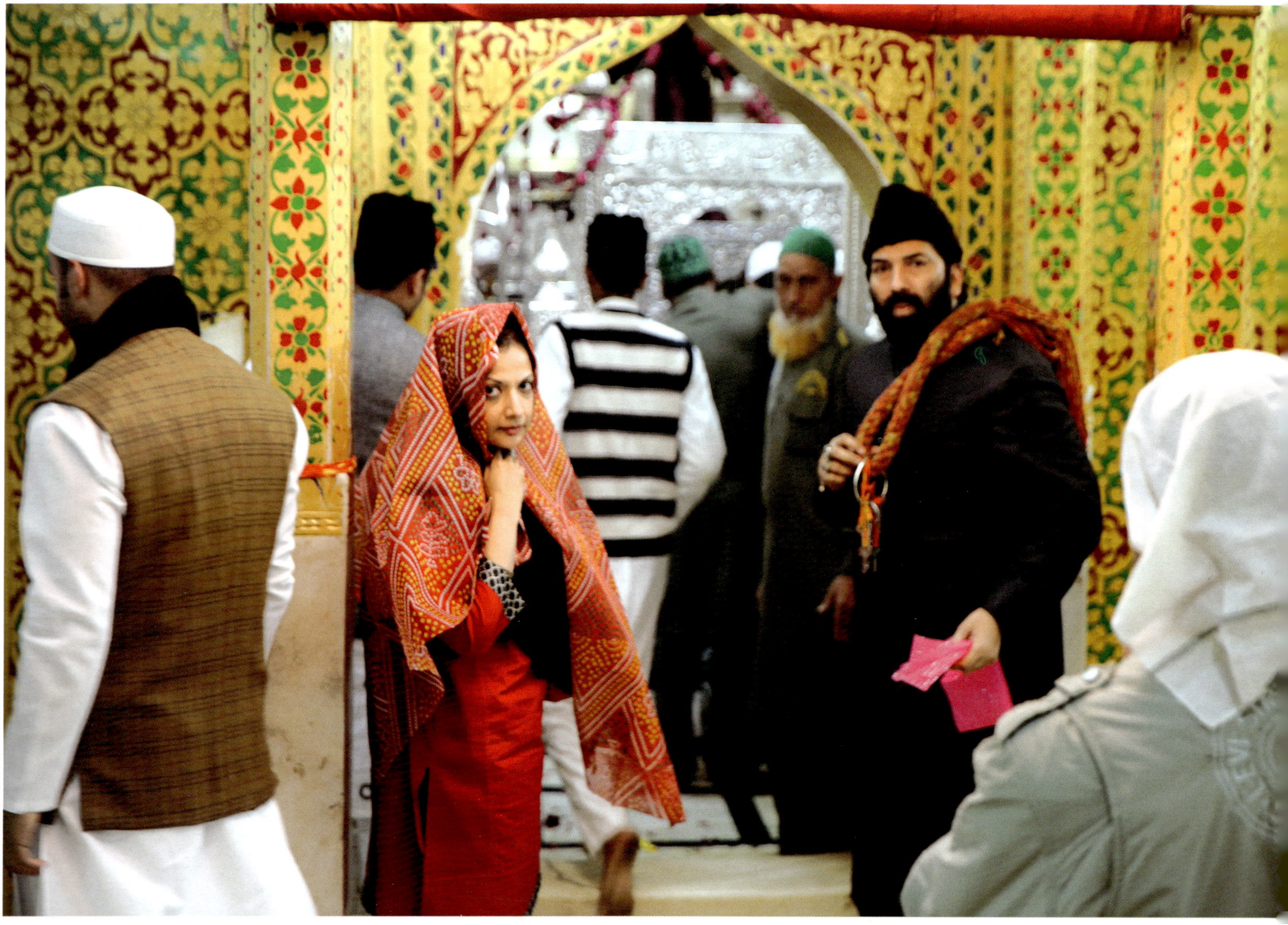

They state that he delivered his last sermon:

Love all and hate none.
Mere talk of peace will avail you naught.
Mere talk of God and religion will not take you far.
Bring out all the latent powers of your being
and reveal the full magnificence of your immortal self.
Be overflowing with peace and joy,
and scatter them wherever you are
and wherever you go.
Be a blazing fire of truth,
be a beauteous blossom of love
and be a soothing balm of peace.
With your spiritual light,
dispel the darkness of ignorance;
dissolve the clouds of discord and war
and spread goodwill, peace, and harmony among the people.
Never seek any help, charity, favours
from anyone, except God.
Never go to the court of kings,
Never refuse to bless and help the needy, the poor,
the widow, and the orphan, if they come to your door.
This is your mission—to serve people.

Then, retired to his room after evening prayers and forbade any interruption of his seclusion.

Muinuddin's chanting rose as the night aged and closer to dawn, the room fell silent. When the door was forced open, followers saw that he had relinquished life.

The burial rites, led by his eldest, Fakhruddin, saw the arrival of almost all saints of renown in the region. Khwaja's early resting place

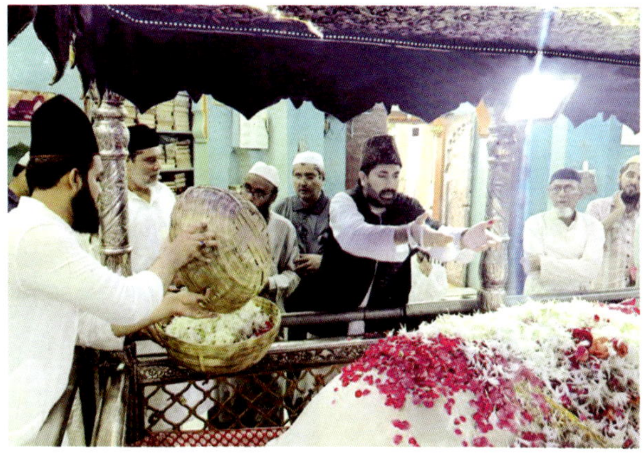

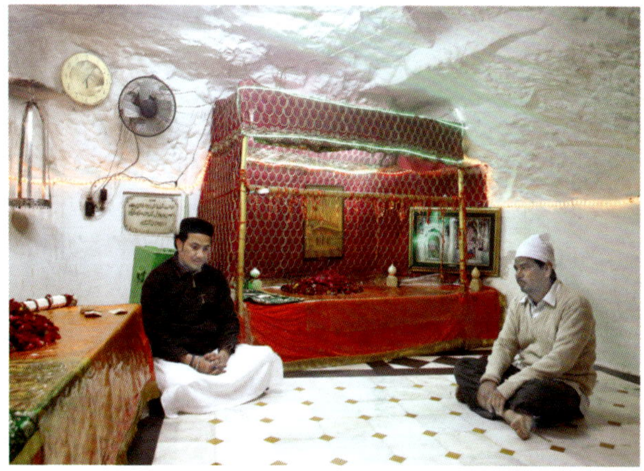

Top: Syed Salman Chishty offers floral tributes at the tomb of the saint

Above: Devotions at Gharib Nawaz's cave in the hill

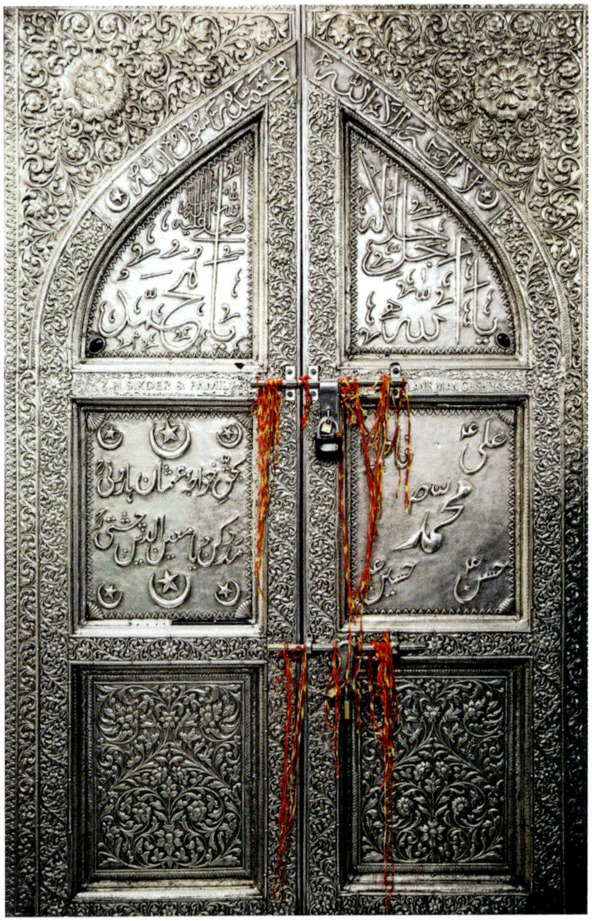

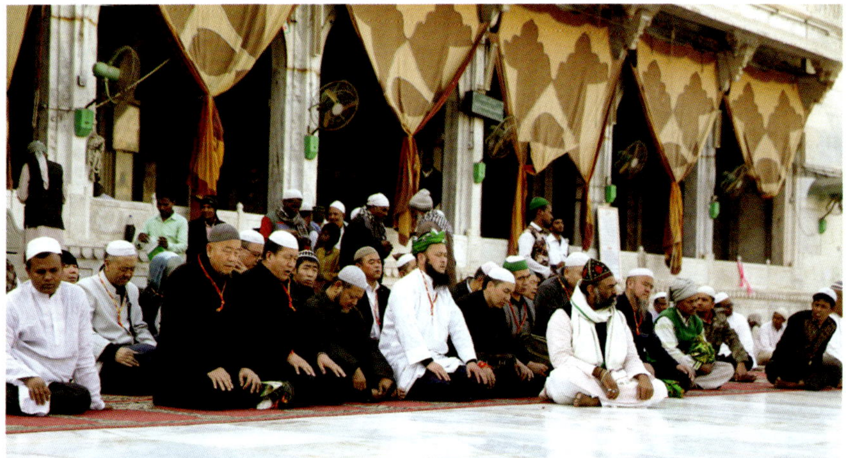

under the sprawling canopy of a pomegranate tree was of baked bricks. For over two centuries, it remained unaltered by splendour.

In *Sufi Martyrs of Love*, Carl W. Ernst and Bruce B. Lawrence write that his first tomb was in wood, and then a stone canopy was built to protect it. Khwaja Hussain Nagauri provided the earliest construction over his master's tomb.

In the 15th century, the Sultan of Malwa created a cenotaph in milky onyx, laying the first foundation for future trappings of gratitude. However, as the prime sanctum stands today, it is an intensely filigreed, columned porch of polished marble with chandeliers, as gold and silver panelled, heavily inlaid doors lead to where Muinuddin Chishti, the dervish who once lived in a mud hut, rests.

So I go towards the side where a quieter door, by his feet, opens into the same room. Intimate, a little less touched by flashy gestures of recognition from ancient emperors and nobles, the doorway has small, enclosed prayer patios in white granite on either side.

In 1579 CE, the Mughal Emperor Akbar reconstructed the sanctum, crowning it with a flamboyant dome. Its keystone is stone pasted in lime,

Above: Silver doors protect the sanctity of the shrine

Above right: Devotees pray in the courtyard of Ajmer Sharif

Facing page: The soaring dome above the tomb with its inverted lotus and gold *kalasha*

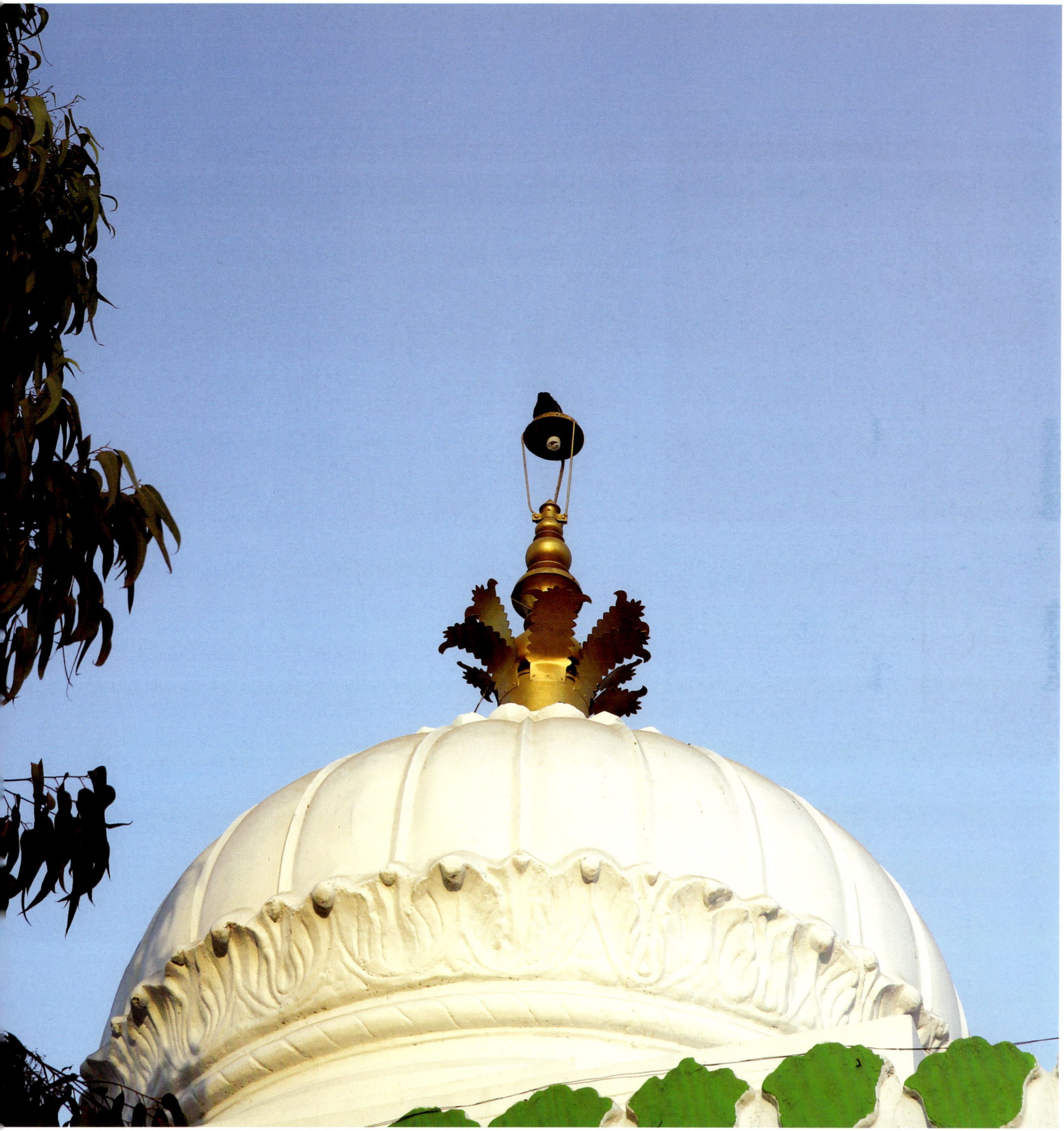

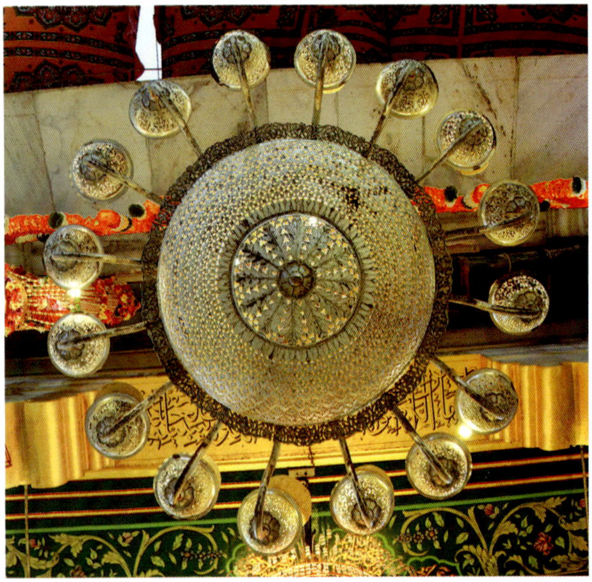

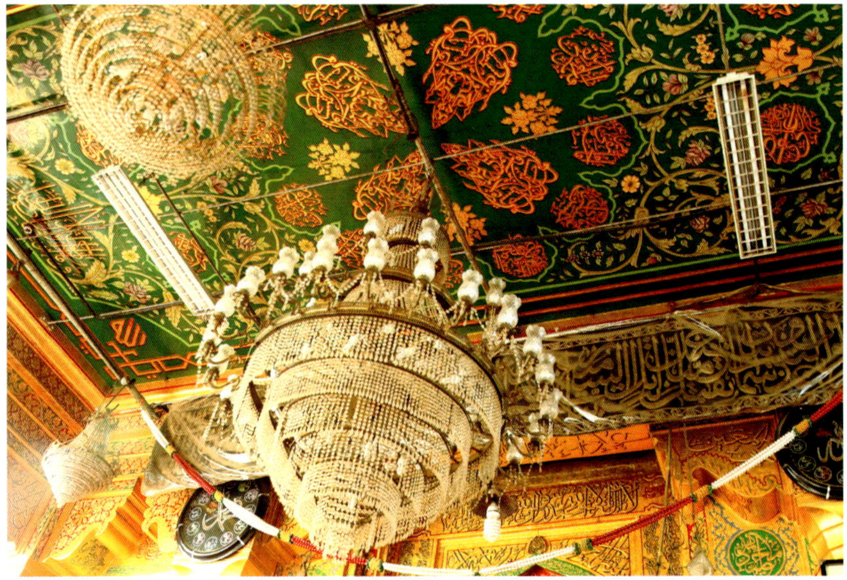

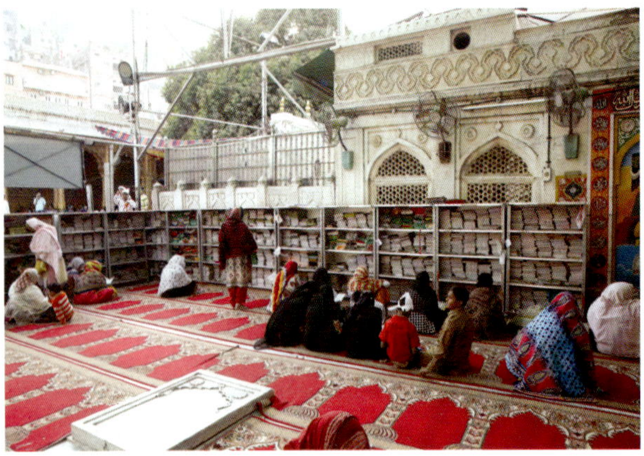

Above left and right: Opulent chandeliers light paths of love and hope

Above: Ladies' prayer terrace near Bibi Hafiza Jamal's grave

with a baked brick cone. Silver filigree from Nawab Mushtaq Ali Khan of Rampur adorns it.

Presently, the inner ceiling wears a spread of Kashani velvet and brocade held up by metal chains with silver orbs, each priced at 50,000 rupees. A historic handwritten Quran is kept in one of the niches and is removed during his *Urs* (death anniversary) festivities.

Khwaja's circular white cupola topped with an overturned lotus has a cylindrical drum. A *kalasha* (finial) of gold, from Nawab Haider Ali Khan of Rampur, rises to jab into the sky. It is said that a donor, Alam Banjaara, installed the first, humbler kalasha, fashioned with a quarter gram of gold.

This threshold is consuming. The air, moist with sweat and tears, resonates with rushed, desperate murmurs and the reluctant shuffle of hundreds of feet amid directions from keepers.

Few moments can create a similar inner vortex. The custodian says that prayers offered at the mausoleum, after invoking God and His Prophet, are steered by the saint.

Every inch of the lattice is tied in hope—threads with bells, tiny cradles, keys, scraps of paper or a plain knot. I too relayed wishes; the custodian asks me to write them on a piece of paper and then tucks it beside the cenotaph, under myriad drapes.

Sadly, there is no time to gaze at the grave beneath the souvenir gifted by the Mughal Emperor Jahangir (lived 1569–1627 CE; ruled 1605–1627 CE)—a silver and mother-of-pearl canopy atop four silver posts, valued at 110,000 rupees at the time. Flowers and shrouds cover the crypt, hemmed in with a patterned silver fence.

The present railing is a mark of devotion by Jahanara, (lived 1614–1681 CE) the eldest daughter of the Mughal Emperor Shah Jahan (lived 1592–1666 CE; ruled 1628–1658 CE), who gifted its predecessor.

More than his architectural flourishes, Akbar's Persian inscription in gold on three sides of the dome's rim has captivated kings, devotees and scholars.

Supreme saint of saints, Muinuddin
Most noble of saints that walked the earth,
The sovereign on the space of belief.
What to say about his faultlessness?
It is apparent from forts impenetrable.
Thy threshold is the heart of followers.
The sun and the moon bow at thy doorsill.
Thousands of kings; the ruler of China
Come to touch thy floor with their foreheads
Keepers of Heaven, custodians of your doors
Your tomb as sacred as Paradise
Its dust, fragrant
Its moisture, holy water
Oh Allah, let the Chishti lamp spread light
Till the sun and the moon illuminate thy universe.

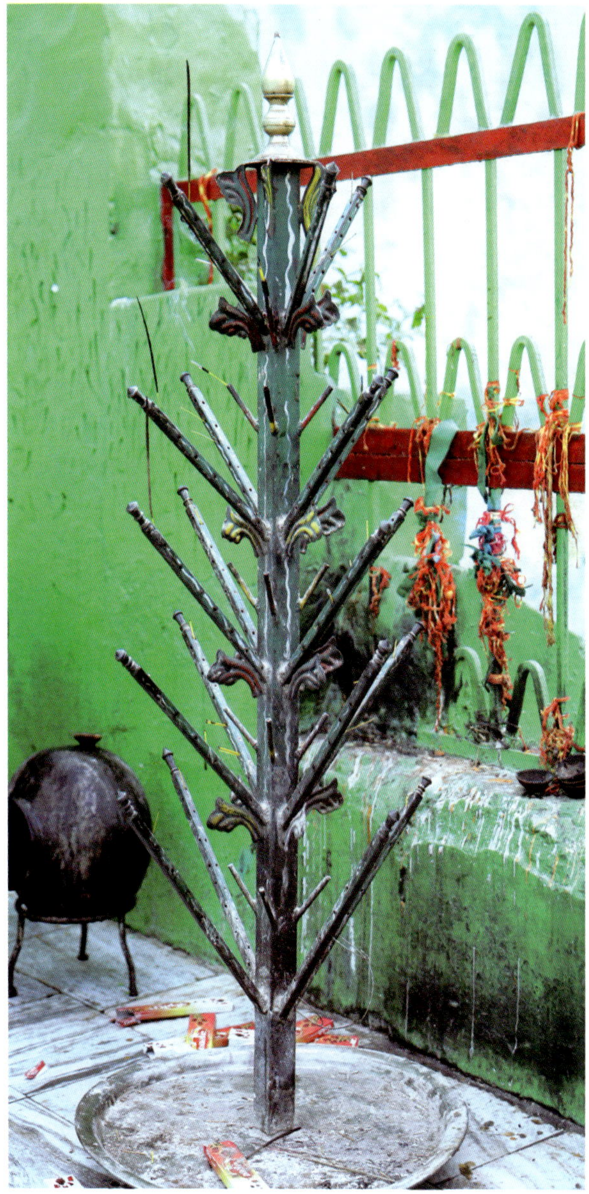

An incense stand for various rituals seen at many places in the shrine complex

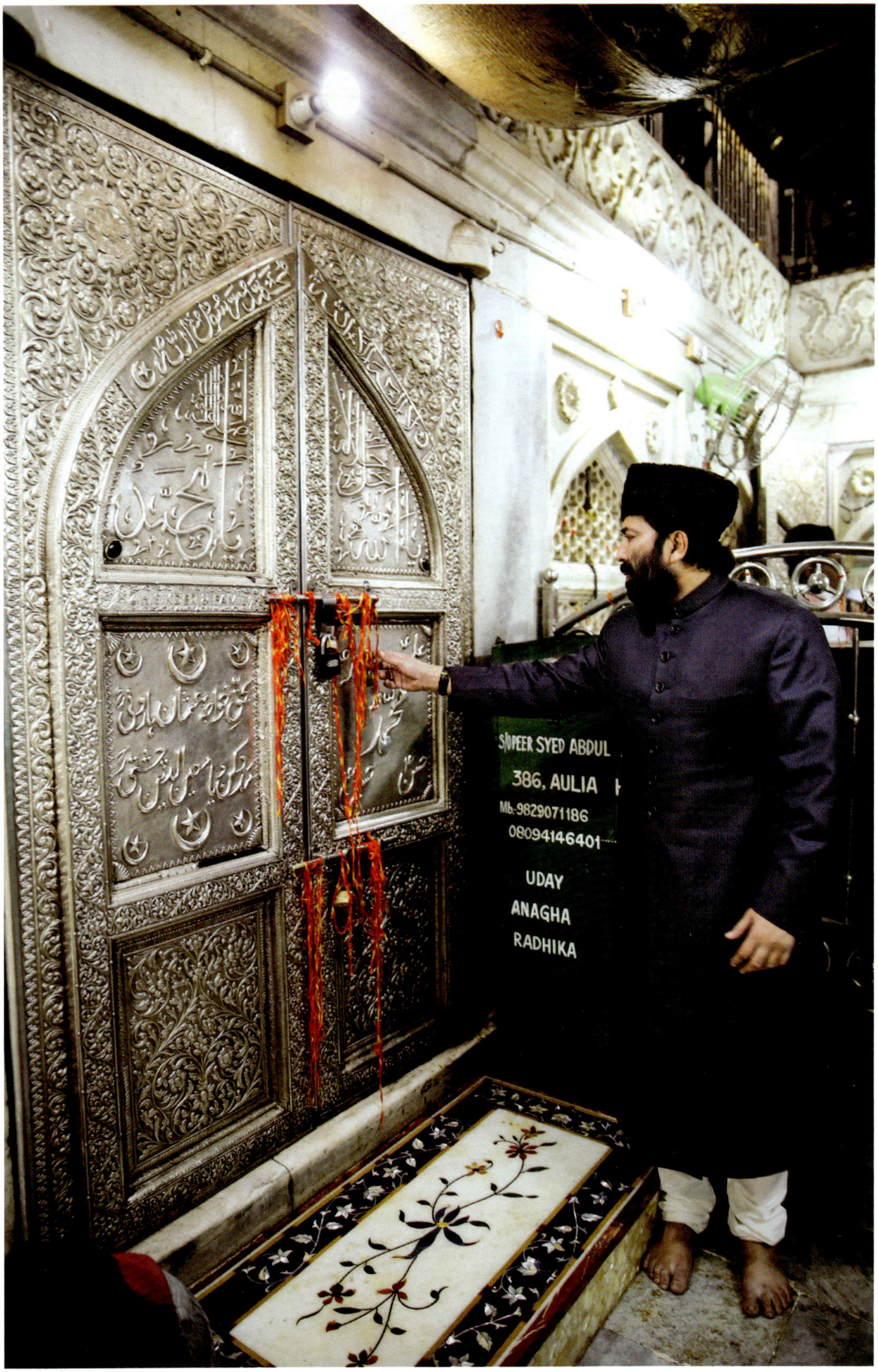

The custodian of the shrine at the rear door to the sanctum, Payanti Darwaza

I turn to a Hindu lady, dressed like a bride, to ask what she finds here.

'You cannot see Allah. We don't know Eeshwar, but Gharib Nawaz knows God. He can take our prayers to Him. Can't you feel the power?' she replies.

Haji Farrokh, an eminent custodian, elegant in a black sherwani and black cap, says that more than 65 per cent of Khwaja's visitors are non-Muslims. Haji believes that his son, an only child born after 15 years of marriage, is the fulfillment of his pleas at the shrine.

Few aspects are entirely unique to the most consecrated shrine in South Asia.

> *'In all other shrines, the real taweez (grave) is in the basement. Our Sarkar's grave was given a customary boundary and covered because all the saints of the time sprinkled dust on him as they recited holy verses. So it was hardly suitable to build over it. You are at the actual site,'*

explains Mohammed Khalid Hashmi, a prominent khadim.

Hashmi says that it is the only memorial where prayers are ceaseless. I look around and see people in deep meditation, others on a prayer mat, some chanting from holy books and a group of Sikhs huddled around the *Guru Granth Sahib*. The pilgrims are an intriguing assortment—many wild-eyed with passion, some smiling at the night sky; legions of pained foreheads against walls and pillars.

Then there is the frail Khateeb sahib, the respected calligrapher, who carries a small steel urn, and wanders in white cotton garb, red socks and an old-fashioned cap. Khateeb Abdul Qayyum Hoja has spent over 40 years at the shrine and says nothing of his belongings or family. However, he holds his peacock feather pen close to his heart.

Most of the calligraphy on the mausoleum walls is his immaculate artwork, as are the inscriptions at the Bakhtiyar Kaki and Nizamuddin memorials in Delhi.

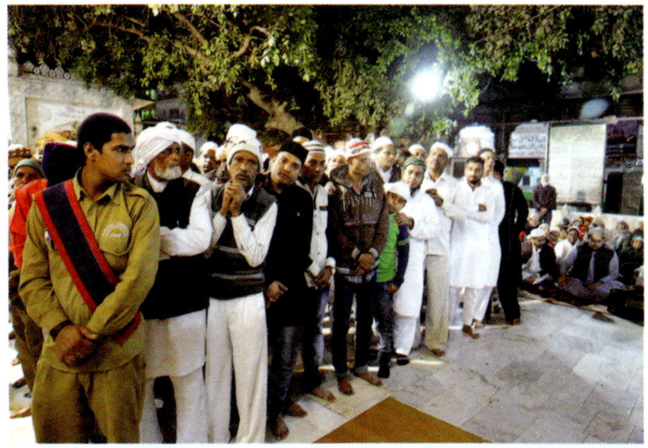

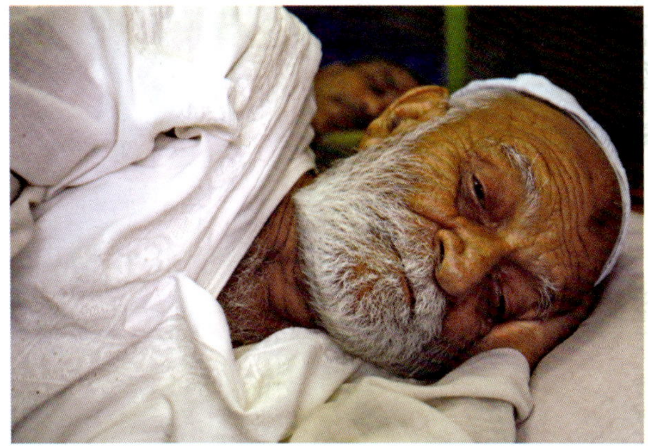

Top: Trails of faith—pilgrims await their turn to enter the shrine

Above: Khateeb sahib, the elderly master calligrapher and linguist

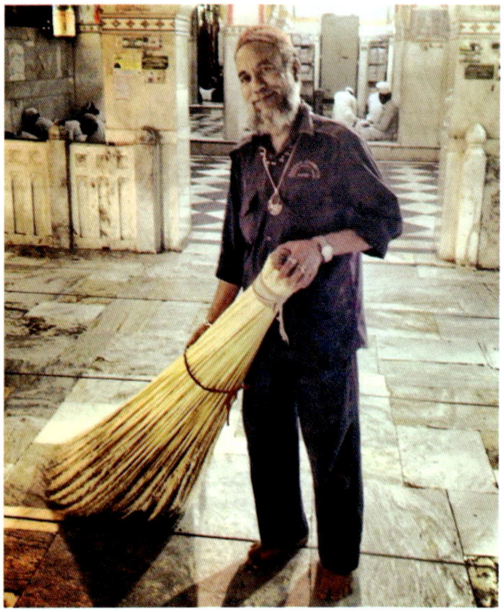

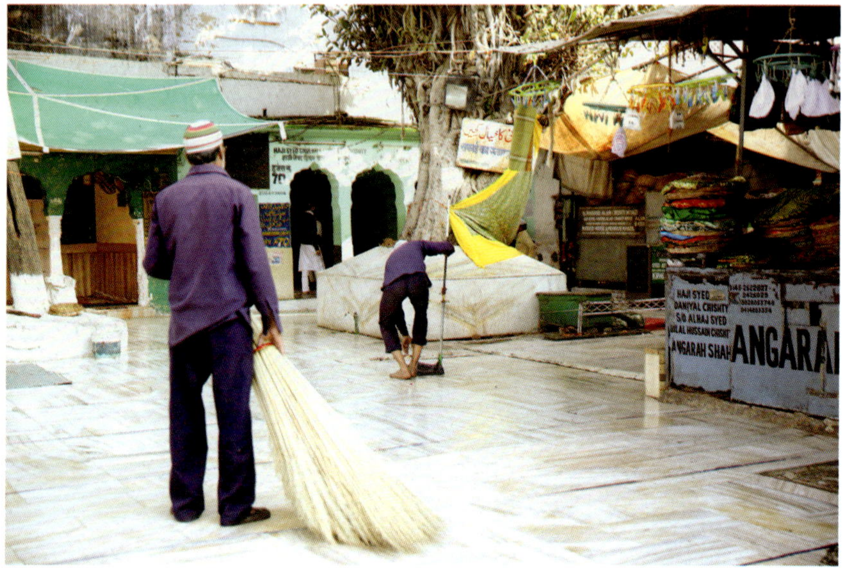

Hoja is fluent in Arabic, Persian and Urdu; an old hand at herbal medicine and an ace chef. A small room has been allotted to him in Faizzan Manzil, an old residential block near Akbari Masjid.

'Khateeb sahib is like the wind but not for Gharib Nawaz. He stays put through Ramadan, the time of fasts, and in the month of the Urs,' says Hashmi.

Another old-timer and avid devotee is Rahman bhai, in charge of cleaning the sanctum terrace at night. He labours away in the dark, leading a band of cleaners with long, bushy handmade brooms, till the floor glows to his satisfaction.

I look at the mausoleum from the courtyard, blinded by light dancing on its ivory surfaces. Sheathed in luminous calm, it repeatedly strikes me as the abode of a pearl.

Above left: Rehman bhai, head of the cleaning crew at Ajmer Sharif

Above right: Afternoon cleaning with the specially woven brooms of the shrine

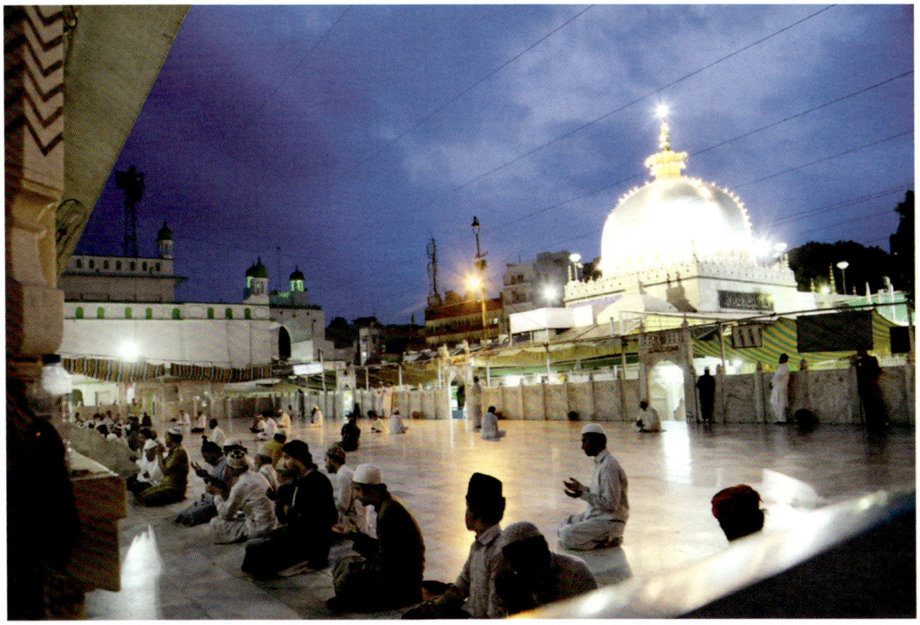

Right: The radiant dome—a pearl of peace...

Below: Pilgrims in Shah Jahan's vast courtyard

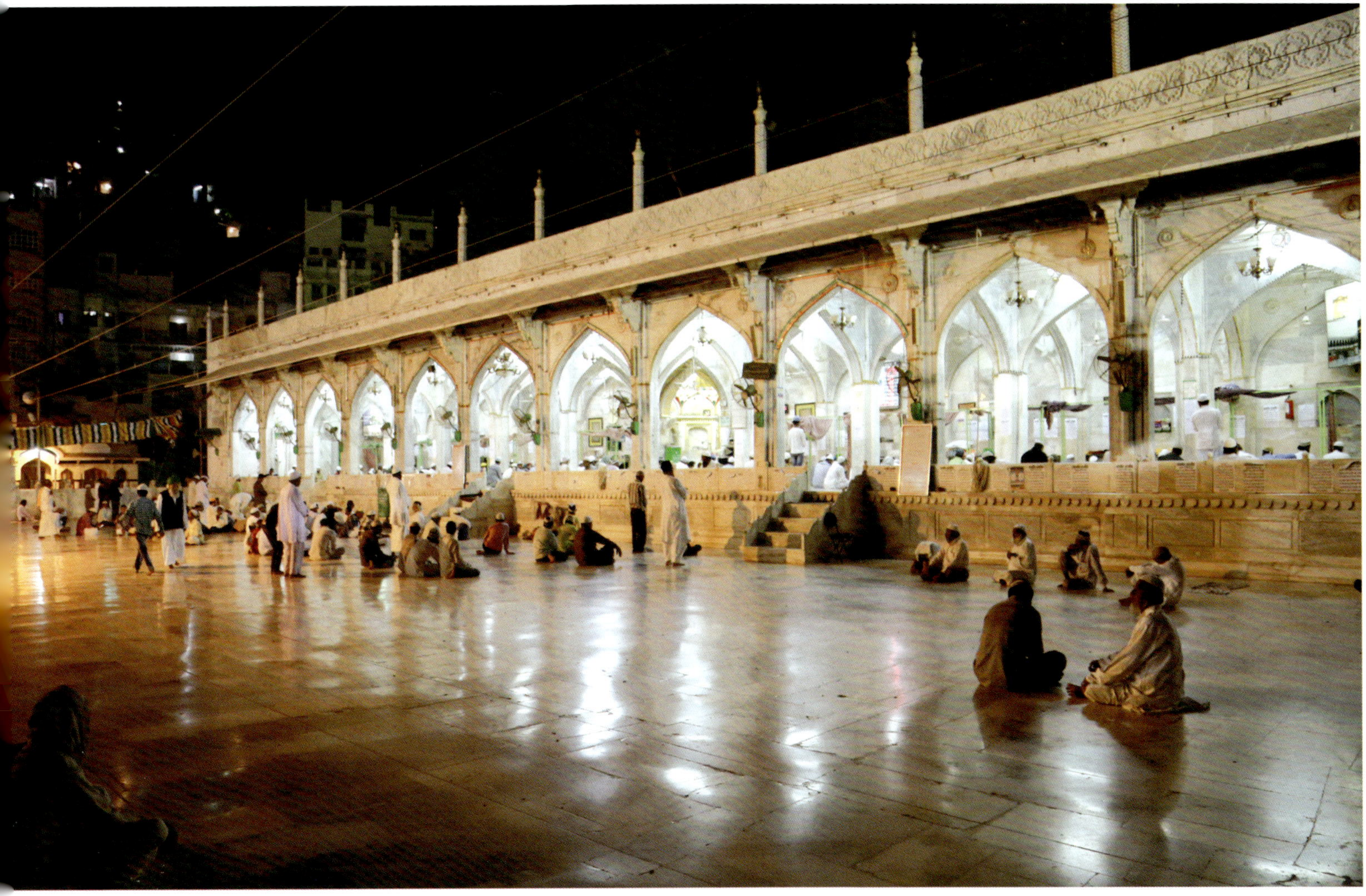

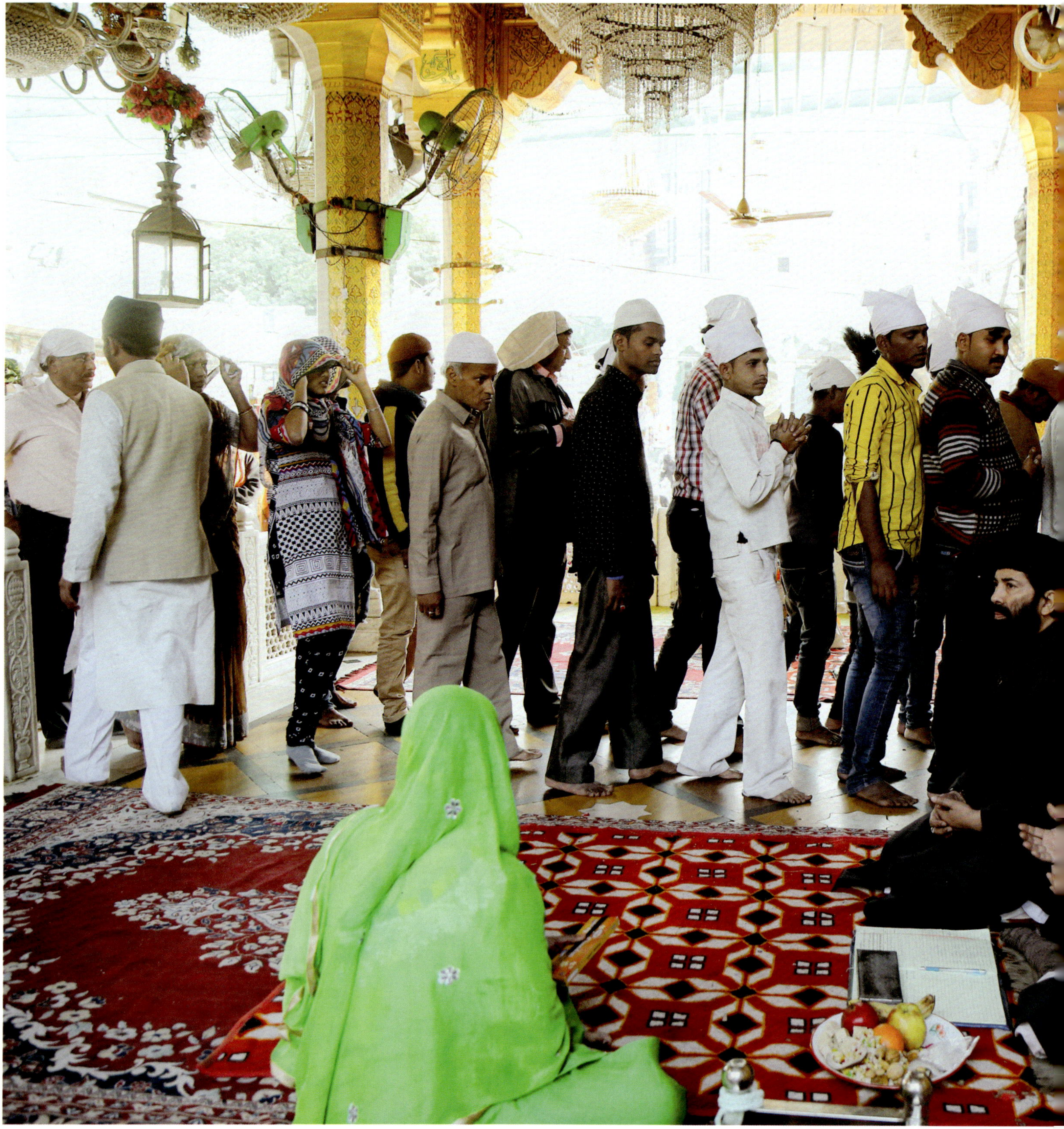

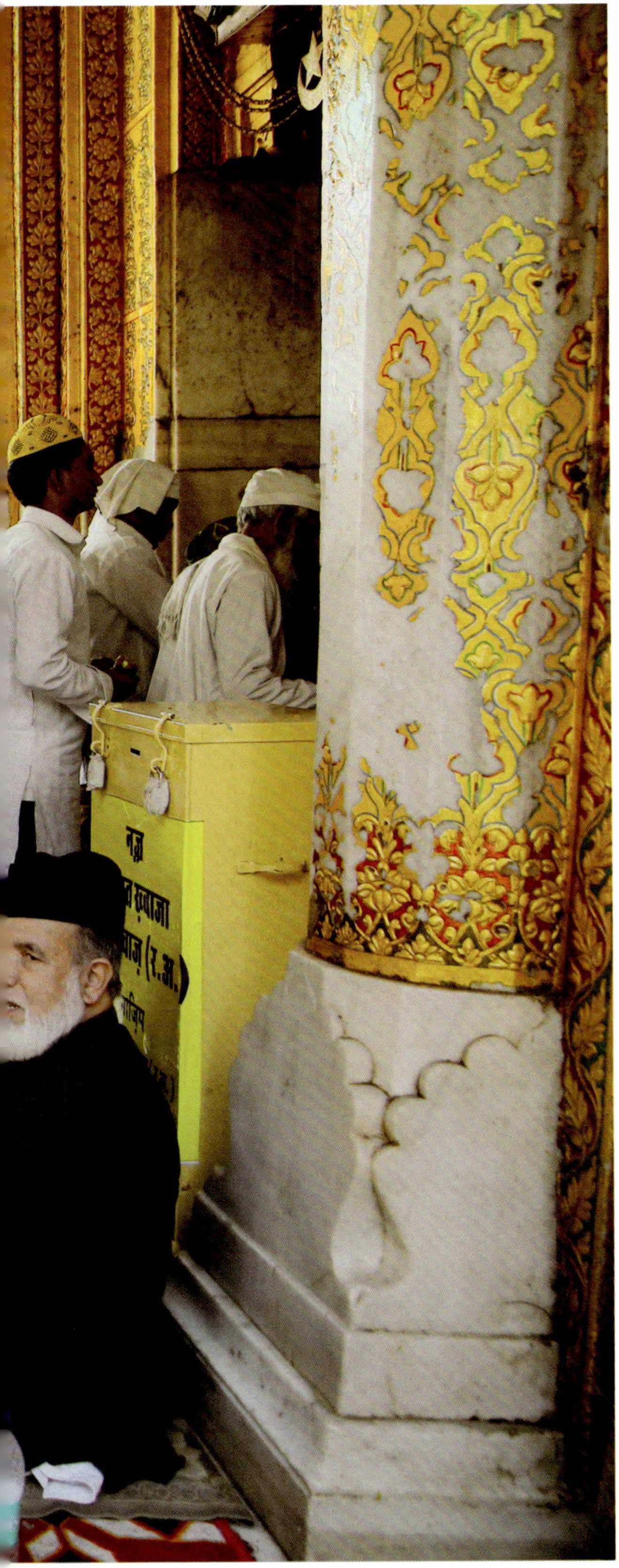

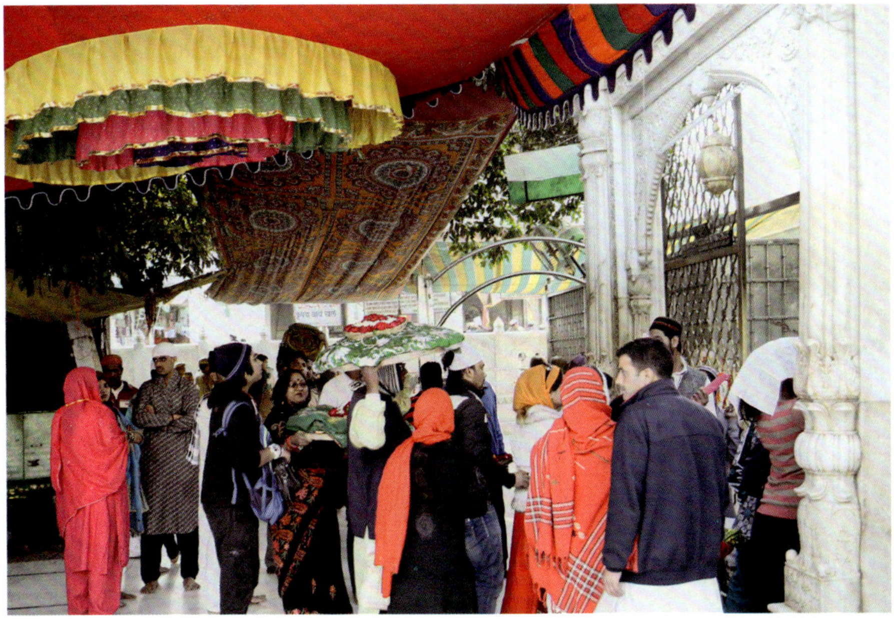

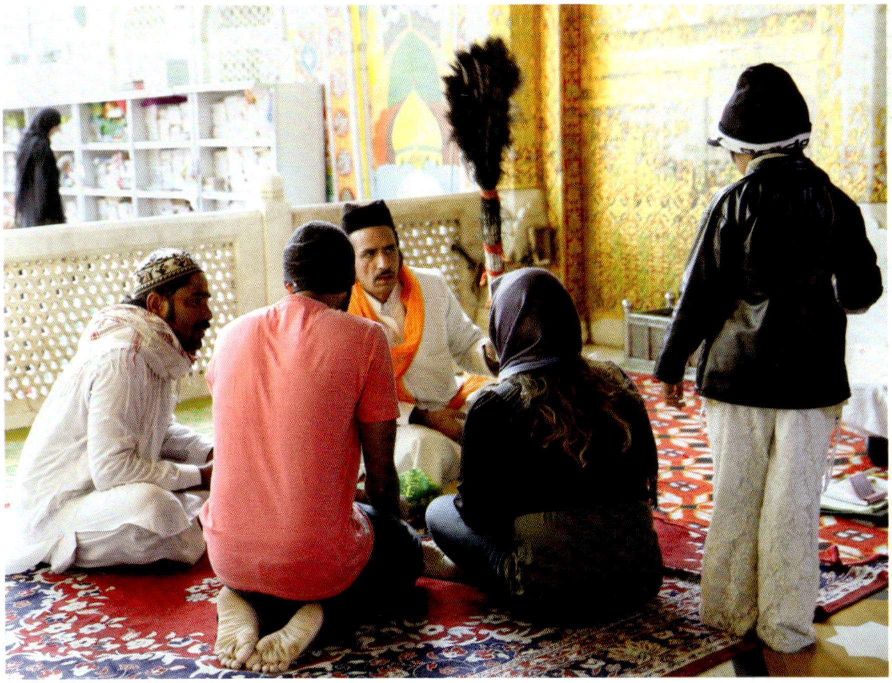

Top: Seekers of the saint's grace carrying submission fare

Above: Pilgrims seek a Khadim's blessings

Left: Pilgrims entering the shrine

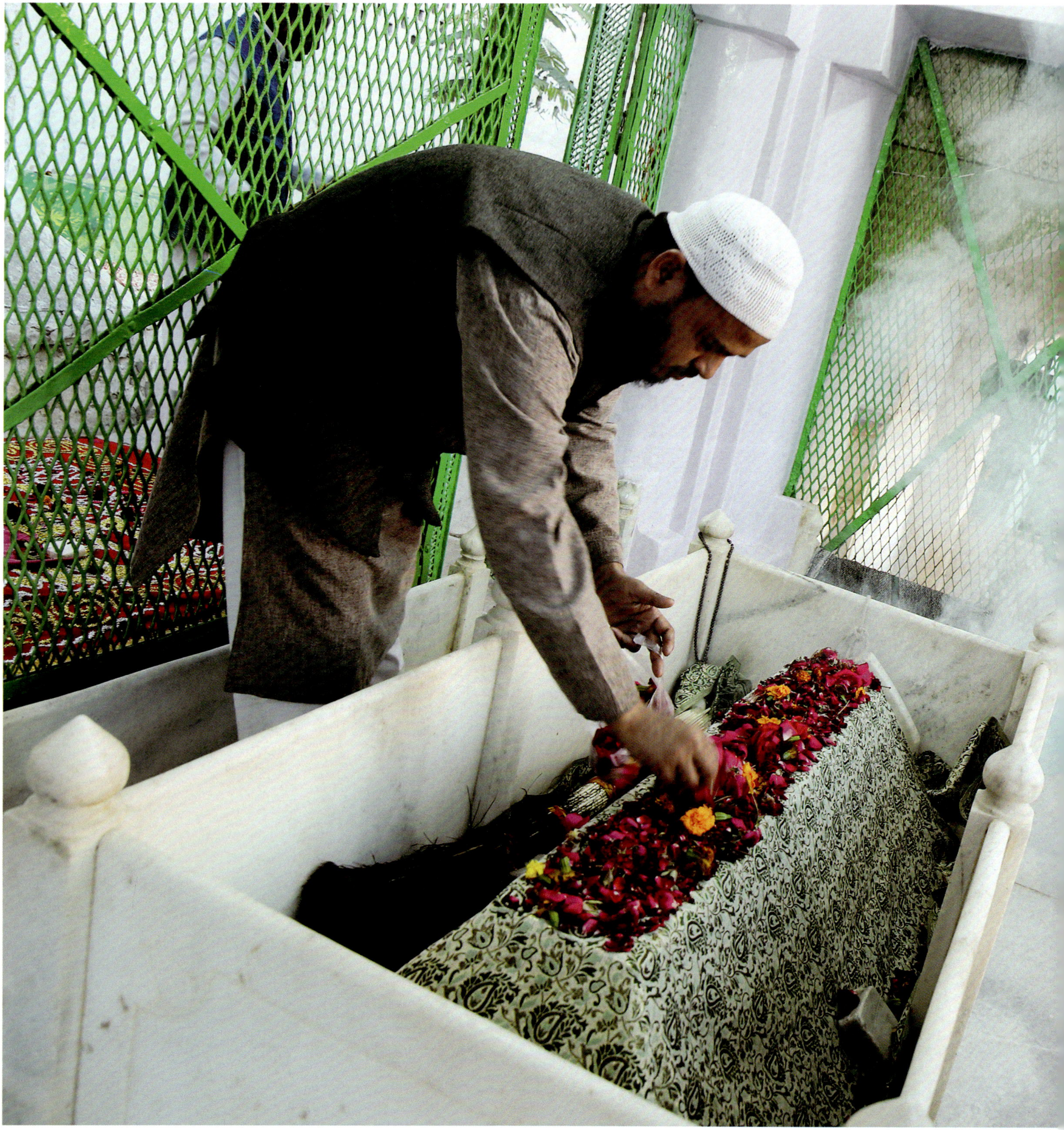

The Beloveds

Bibi Ummatullah, Bibi Asmatullah

A saint's legacy often dehumanises and imprisons him in perfection. However, during his lifetime, Muinuddin Chishti was a husband and a father, as well as a saint.

In the same quarter as the mausoleum is a grill-covered enclosure where Khwaja Muinuddin Chishti's two wives lie, its lattice ablaze with wish lists in saffron and red.

Some 30 years and three children after his first marriage, Muinuddin married for a second time at around 80 years of age. Ainslee Embree presents detailed accounts of the two betrothals in *Sources of Indian Tradition.*

He cites the incident when Syed Wajihuddin Mashadi, the Commissioner of Ajmer, recounted his dream to Khwaja—an ancient caliph, Imam Jafar, had recommended Chishti for Bibi Asmatullah, Mashadi's young daughter. Muinuddin alluded to his years, the controversial nature of such an event and then, seeing it as a sacred order, gave his consent in 1223 CE.

Bibi Asmatullah came to him after she attained puberty and their relationship grew with affection. Yet, all folklore pales before his first love. It happened in a time of pain and tumult—strands of strife were a permanent backdrop to Muinuddin's life.

According to legend, Jaichand, the sovereign of Benares and Kannauj at the time, was consumed by jealousy for the powerful Prithviraj Chauhan who loved, and was loved by, Samyukta, Jaichand's daughter. A vengeful father, Jaichand positioned Chauhan's statue at his doorsill to denote his condescension. Then he summoned eligible kings and princes

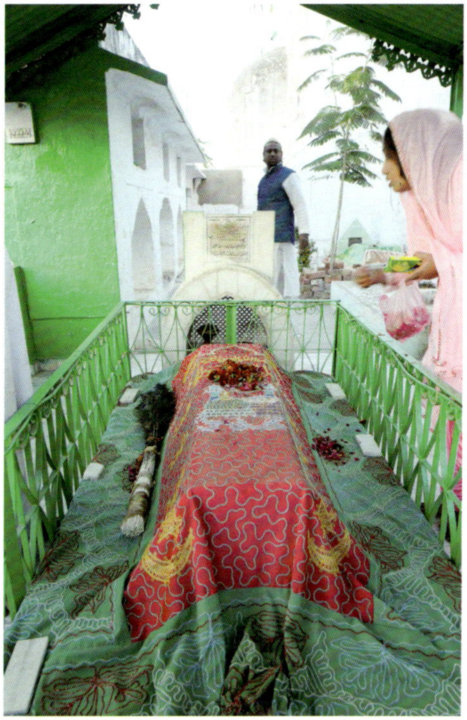

Above: Remembered with reverence

Facing page: Ritual offerings at the graves of the beloved

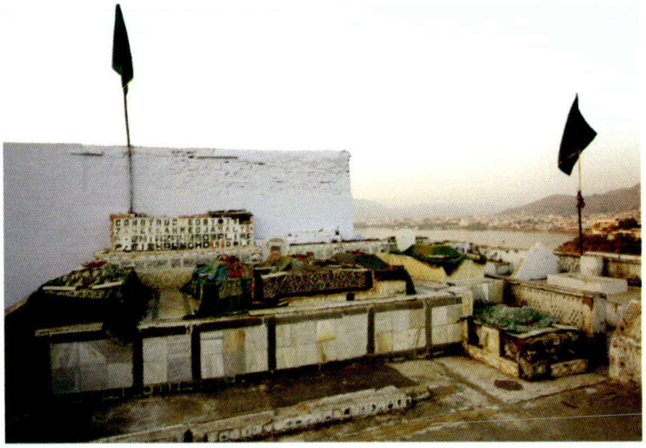

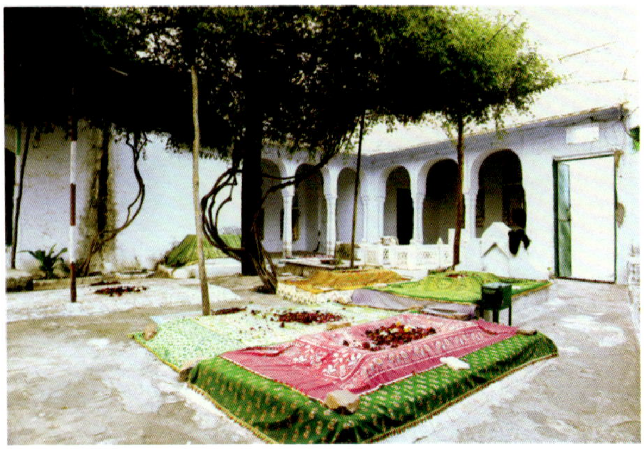

from across Hindustan for a swayamvar (a ceremony where a princess chooses her husband).

When it was time for his nubile princess to pick her companion, Samyukta emerged from the inner recesses of the palace, before Jaichand's court. Iridescent in royal regalia, she swished passed the lineup of princes and placed a garland around Prithviraj's statue. At that moment, her prince came into view on a horse and swept her away.

Singed by betrayal, Jaichand joined Muhammad Ghori and launched an attack on Chauhan's capital of Ajmer in Rajasthan. In Ajmer, Muinuddin awoke not to an inky quilt of stars, but to wails and blood. Speared into the ground, layered with blood, he writhed at the rivers of vermilion. His own agony deadened by scenes of flesh letting go of carcasses, he slid into unconsciousness.

When he emerged from a long coma, Muinuddin recalled his nightmares—corpses piled in heaps and saints with powers to change fates and time. He had seen divinities concealed in the skies. Sermons, served by the special, on the quest for truth and wisdom, unclear in scripture.

Perhaps, these were subliminal answers to the guilt in him as he saw himself as a harbinger of destruction. Bereft and plagued by these visions, breath no longer came easy to Muinuddin. He also learnt of Ghori's triumph over North India. The conqueror had marched back to Kabul; Aibak, his warrior successor, rose to power. The sand turned a sad shade of scarlet as he slaughtered Jaichand. Gujarat and Gwalior gave way, Ajmer stood dismissed and subjugated.

North India's crown jewels—Prithviraj Chauhan and Jaichand, had been vanquished. The desert mourned with stories of Chauhan's valour that brought Delhi into his empire. Prithviraj and Samyukta's bond was ephemeral. However, another hope was beginning to stir in the arid devastation of Rajasthan.

On one night of gasps, as hard reality thrashed around him, Muinuddin woke up to a woman cleansing his wounds on the banks of

Top: The final resting place of a saintly soul

Above: The Chaaryaar Courtyard, Ajmer Shrine

a river. In an unknown lady's care, he began to take feeble steps and sporadic syllables made for fractured conversations. In these dialogues, he learnt of her background—she was Rajput royalty and the daughter of the family that rescued him from chaos and insanity.

This was a moment when his soul recognised trysts with destruction as affirmations of powers of creation. And he confessed his lifelong mission to her—the quest for justice and his station in it. As her care and desire to spend all her years with him swelled, she proposed to him when his sight returned and he could put words together. Muinuddin took her hand in marriage and requested her to become Bibi Ummatullah.

It is said that she was immersed in him; in the conviction that he was her redemption. A title from him became her identity. Embree cites that Vaishnavism had Bibi captive and she would often read Vedic records and ancient chronicles of theoretical disbelief. Khwaja reminisced about his betrothal to Bibi Ummatullah as a most heart-warming moment. At 51, a late stage in life, he was with one who shared his mission and passion.

The couple returned to Ajmer where his beloved land was still bleeding and bodies festered like gangrene. It reeked of congealed blood and destitution.

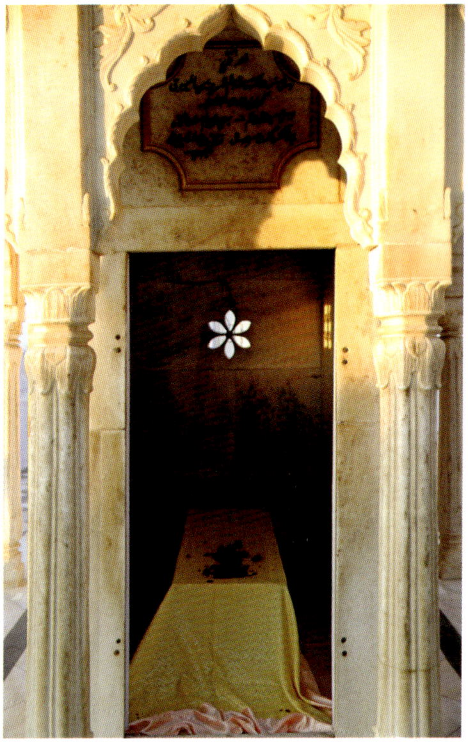

Above: Detail of a tomb near Ana Sagar

Next page: At peaceful rest, a tomb beside Ana Sagar Lake

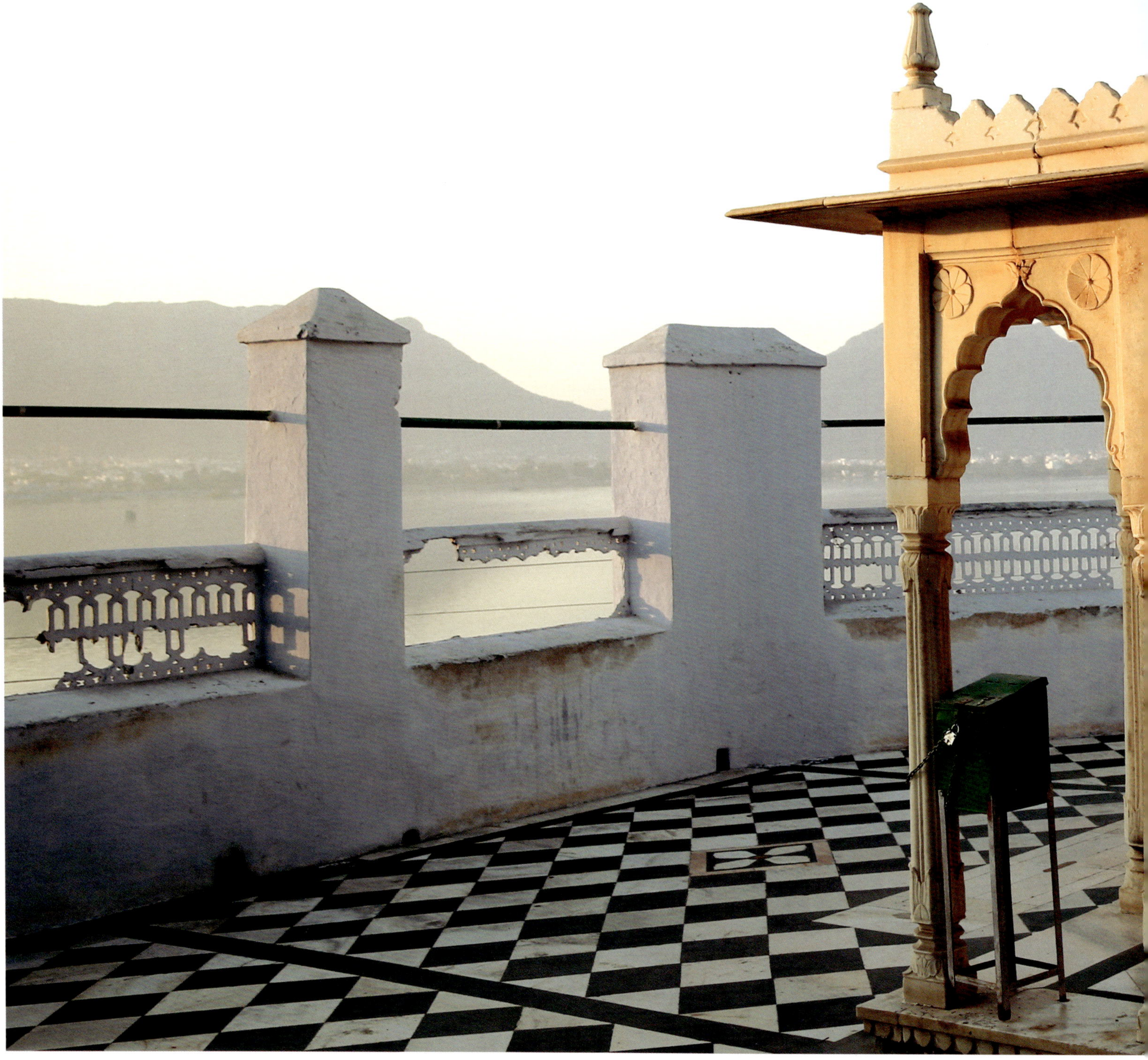

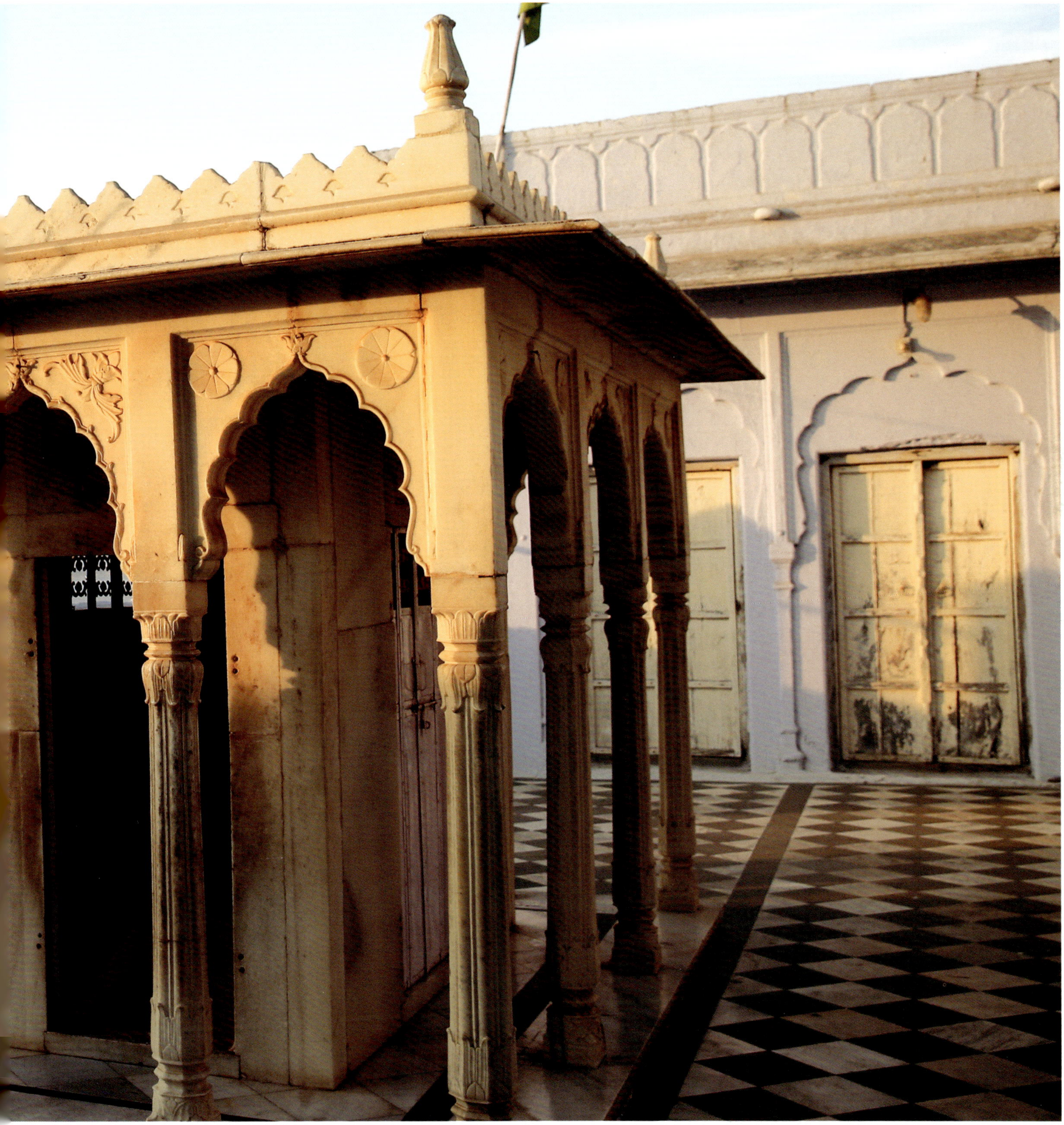

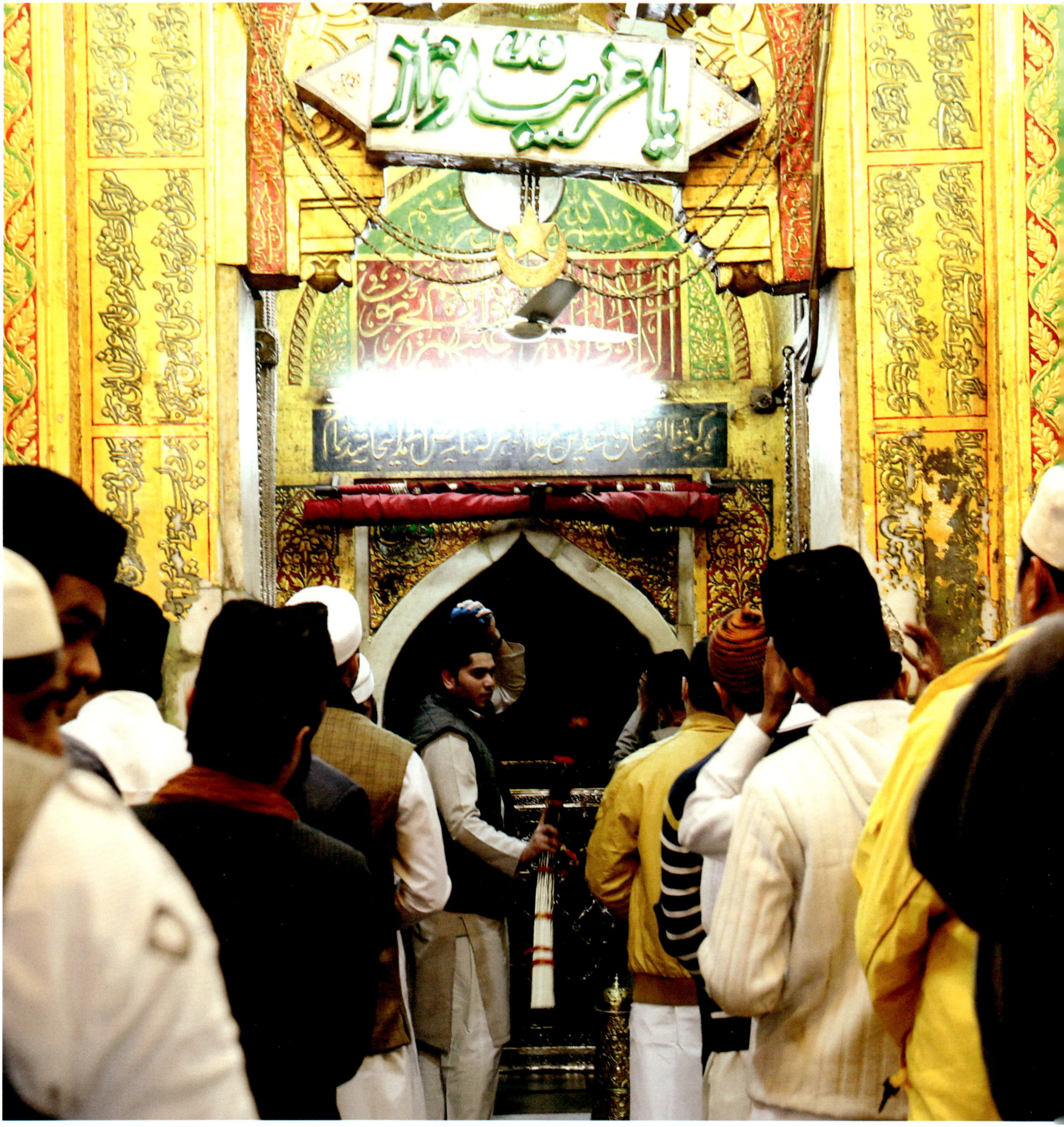
یا غریب نواز

Birth of Gharib Nawaz, Redeemer of the Poor

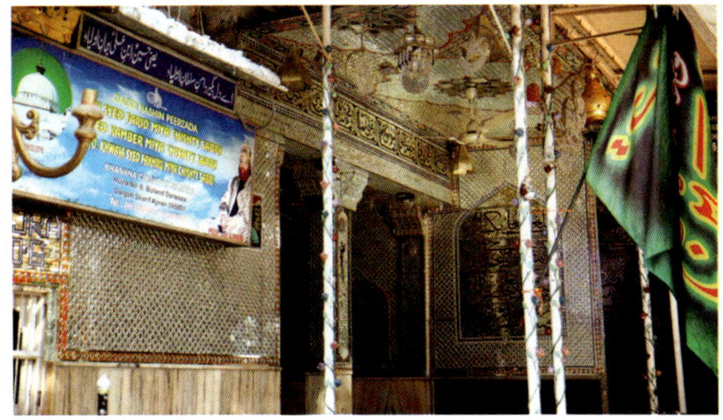

Despite the desolation, Muinuddin renounced the safe and palatial maternal home of his wife. He built a mud hut as their haven. In this act he had followed the merits of a story he had heard in Balkh—in the 8th century, the Prince of Balkh lost a night's sleep to sound of a stranger's footsteps on his roof. When arrested, the stranger—a shepherd—was admonished by the regal scion: 'The palace roof is not the place for you to search for your camel,' he said.

'I know, but neither is a king's room the place to discover the divine,' replied the shepherd.

As Shiva, Vishnu, Rama and Krishna became favoured cults, Bibi Ummatullah narrated tales of freedom to Muinuddin, seeking bliss in devotional music. Social injustices were the ethos of her songs, which challenged the clergy. Their humble hutment soon turned into a caravanserai for the hungry or homeless or travellers. Bibi ran a communal kitchen to free humanity from hunger. Solace and relief sans prejudice absorbed the pair; they embraced this lifestyle as their faith and calling.

Khwaja would spend his time as a vehicle of catharsis for the weary, letting them seek respite in dance, song and verse. Such indulgences to heal souls led to organised gatherings (*mehfil-e-sama*) harking back to eras predating Islam, when dance of rapture was a norm. Some Sufi scholars suggest that Khwaja Muinuddin introduced qawwali to draw more people to Ajmer; most would turn towards Pushkar for its lyricism. But the basis of qawwali lies in Khwaja Muinuddin's passion for music.

Above: Where faith shines supreme

Facing page: The path to peace and blessings

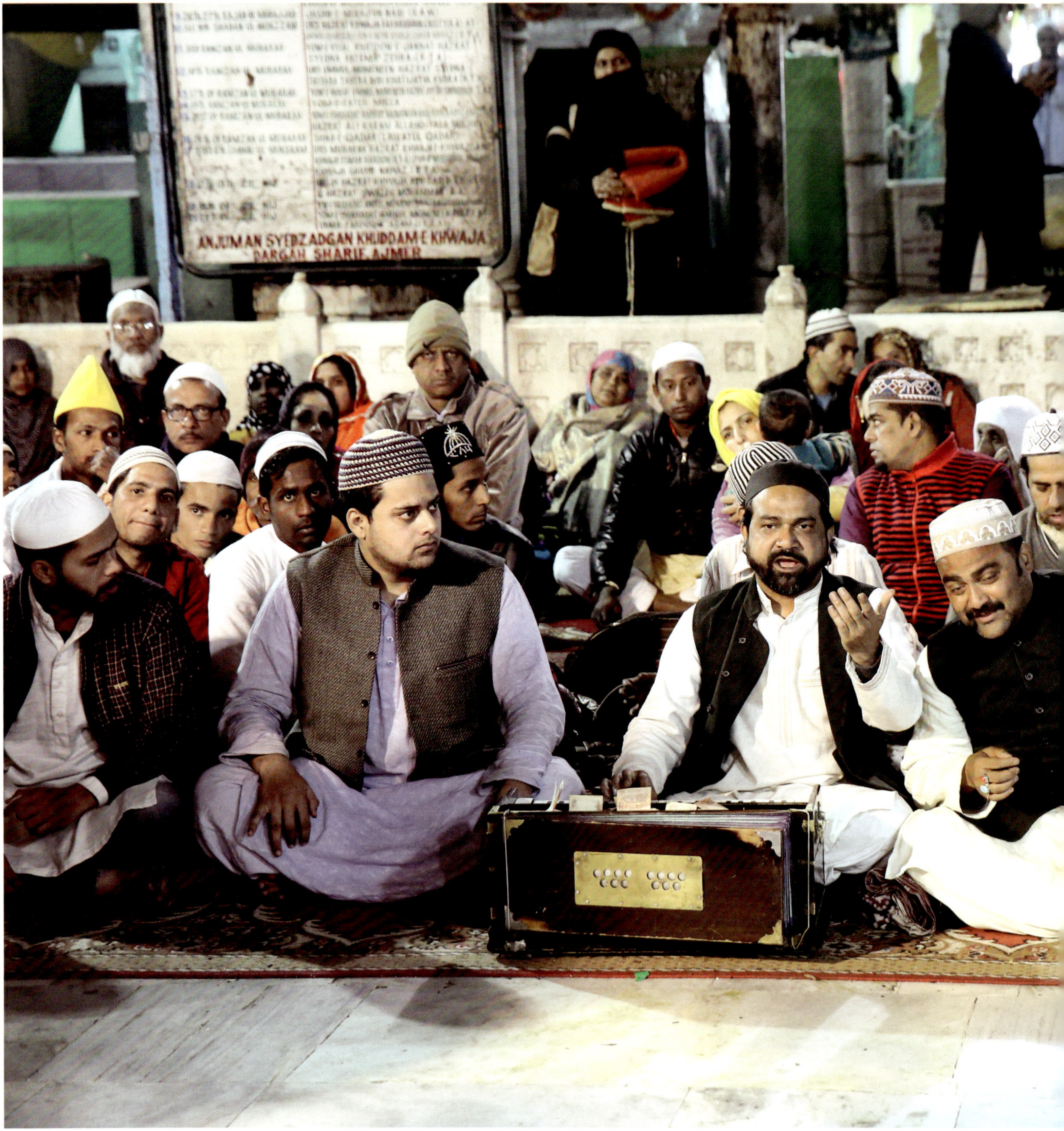
ANJUMAN SYEDZADGAN KHUDDAM E KHWAJA
DARGAH SHARIF AJMER

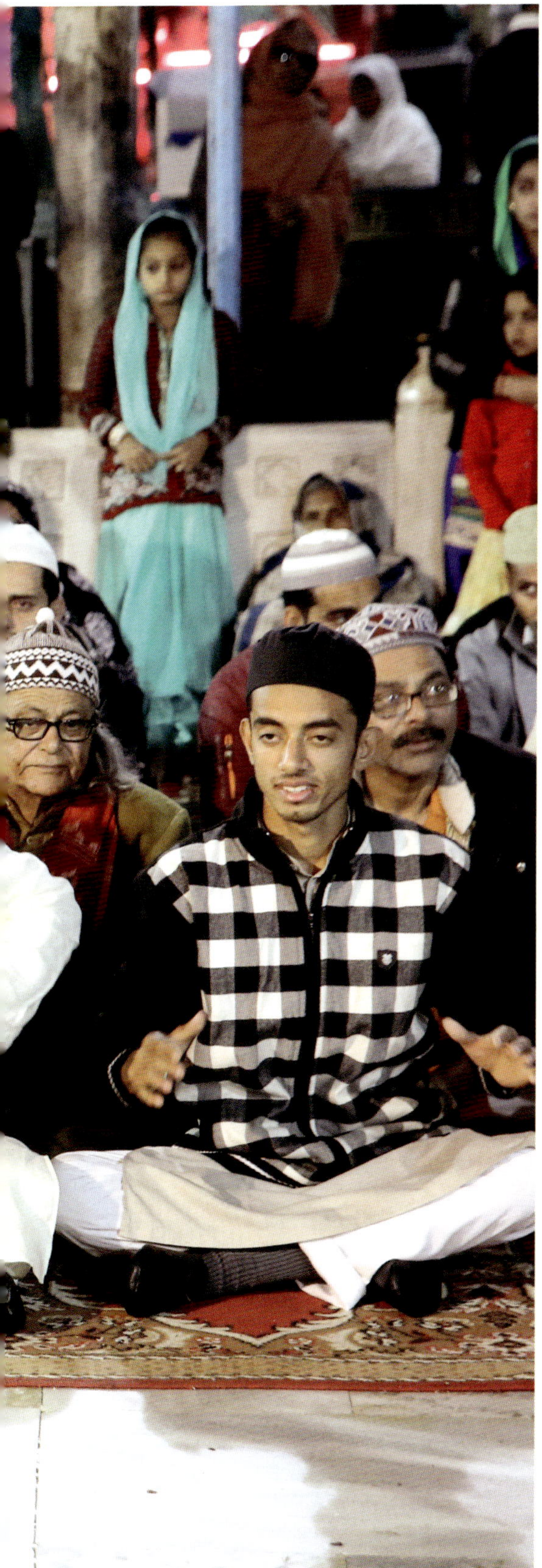

Risalai-sama, an exposition on the flair for music, which was compiled by Hamiduddin Nagauri on the behest of his master, serves as evidence of such an attachment. Thus, in these moments the ancient art of qawwali, unique to the Chishti Sufi Order, came to life.

The modern qawwali maestro, Nusrat Fateh Ali Khan attributed his success to God and to his performances at Ajmer Sharif. Another legendary troupe that performed at the annual Urs was that of the Sabri Brothers. The slain Pakistani qawwal, Amjad Sabri, carried his family's flame of Chishti passion with devout zeal. His avatar of a qawwal was born after the death of Farid, his celebrated father, and with Amjad's first recital at the front portal of Muinuddin's sanctum.

Left: Music of devotion—a qawwali performance at Ajmer Sharif

Next page: The grand interiors of the shrine

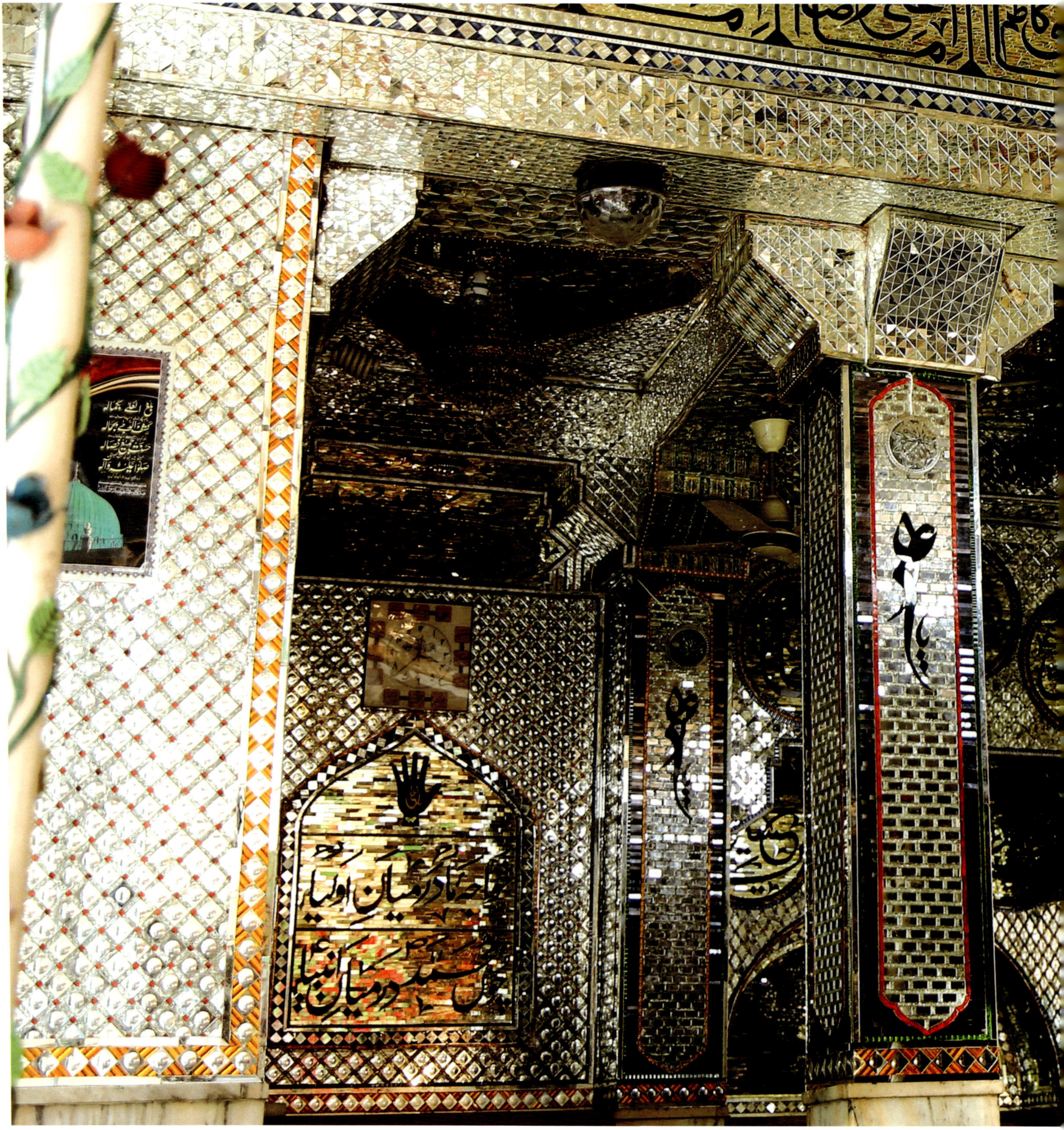

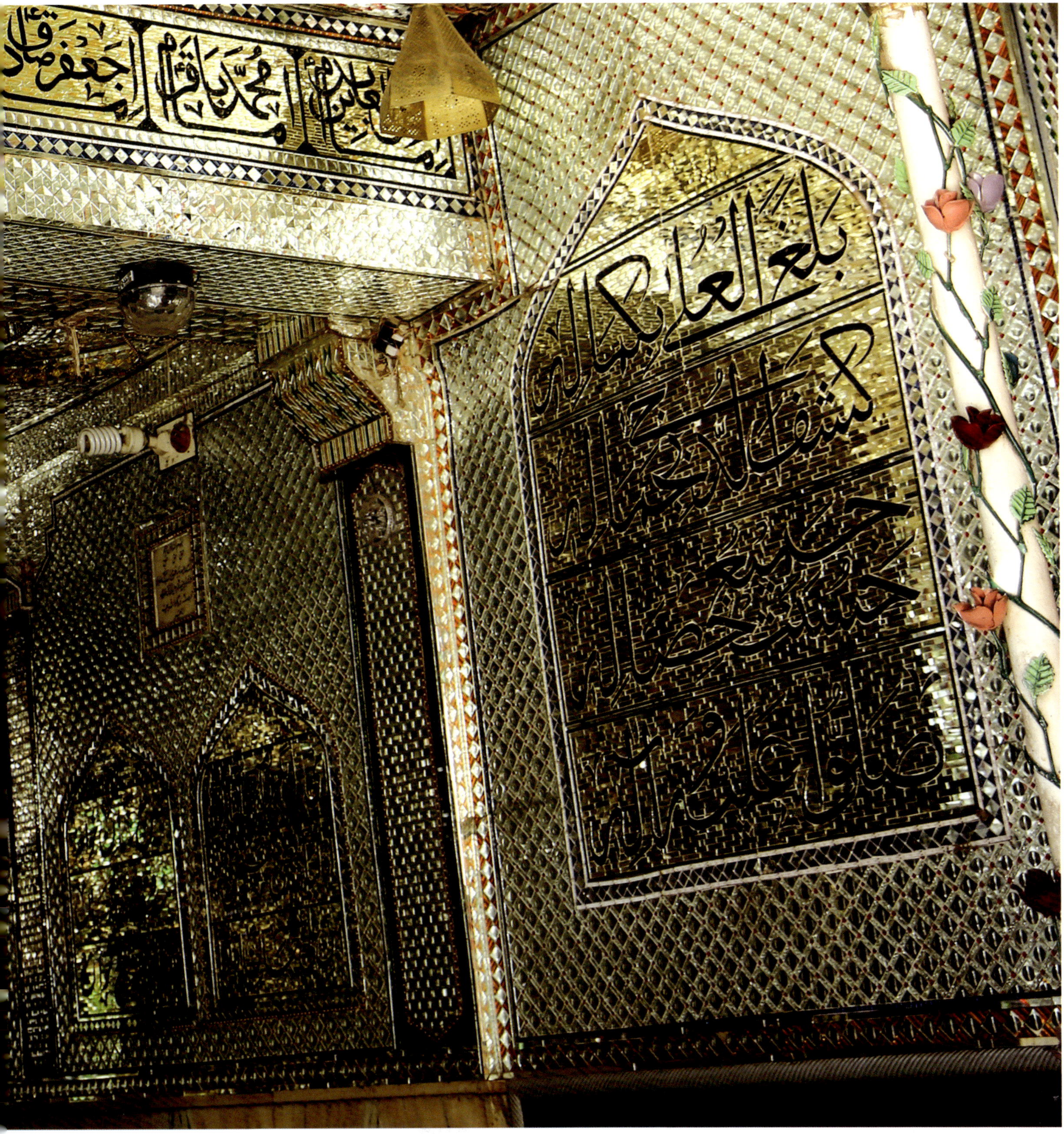
بلغ العلى بكماله
كشف الدجى بجماله
حسنت جميع خصاله
صلوا عليه وآله
محمد باقر
جعفر صادق

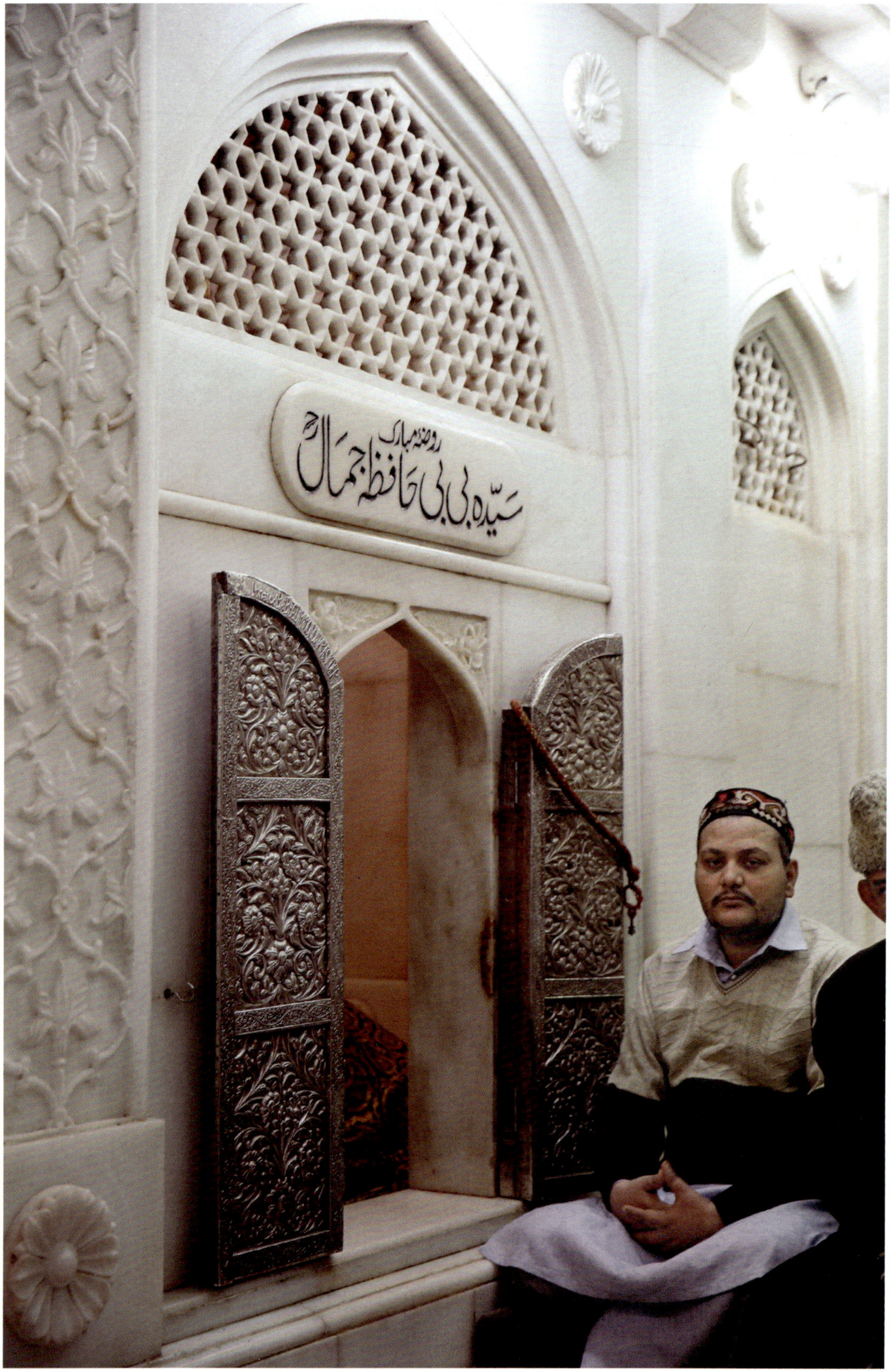

A small window into Bibi Hafiza Jamal's room from the Princess Courtyard

Chishti Inheritors

As settlements mushroomed around them, Bibi and Khwaja's abode persisted as a love-spring. They were blessed with two sons and a daughter. Fakhruddin was their first born who, as years rolled by, took to mysticism. A celebrated dervish of his era, spiritual reflection was his pastime. Agriculture was his livelihood and he lived in the nearby village of Mandal.

Hisamuddin, their second son, passed away at the age of 50 in 1255 CE and is buried near Jhalra in the precincts of Khwaja's shrine in Ajmer. Also known as Shahi Ghat, the graves of Khwaja Wajihullah, one of Mashadi's sons and Muinuddin's brother-in-law, Abu Saleh, are also in the same area.

Meanwhile, Khwaja's only daughter, Afifa, later christened Bibi Hafiza Jamal, was deeply spiritual and his favourite offspring. She married Raziuddin, son of her father's avid disciple, Hamiduddin Nagauri. Bibi Hafiza also lived in a house of mud with her husband, a poor agriculturist—her parents' beginnings casting uncanny shadows on hers.

Muinuddin appointed Hafiza as one of his caliphs and in death, she is entombed with her two sons in a small marble vault to the south of her father's prime sanctum. Other crypts outside her door belong to Sheikh Muinuddin Kurd and Khwaja Qayamuddin Babar Yal.

After the bathing rituals of Khwaja's cenotaph, his drapes and flowers come to her tomb as a special ritual for his favourite child.

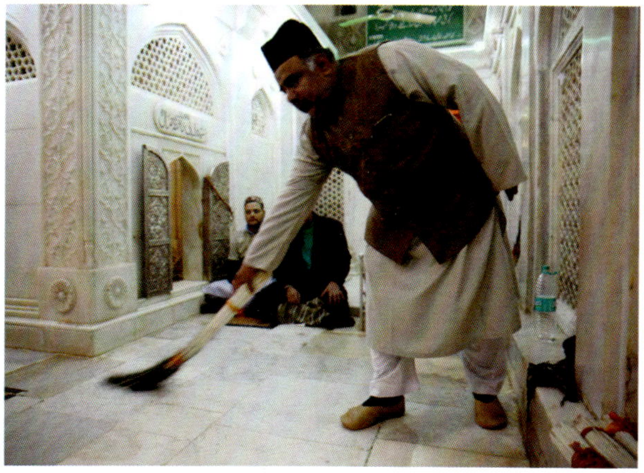

Above: Ritual cleaning around the sepulchre of Gharib Nawaz's most beloved child, Bibi Hafiza Jamal

Next page: Serene silence—the still waters of the Ana Sagar Lake

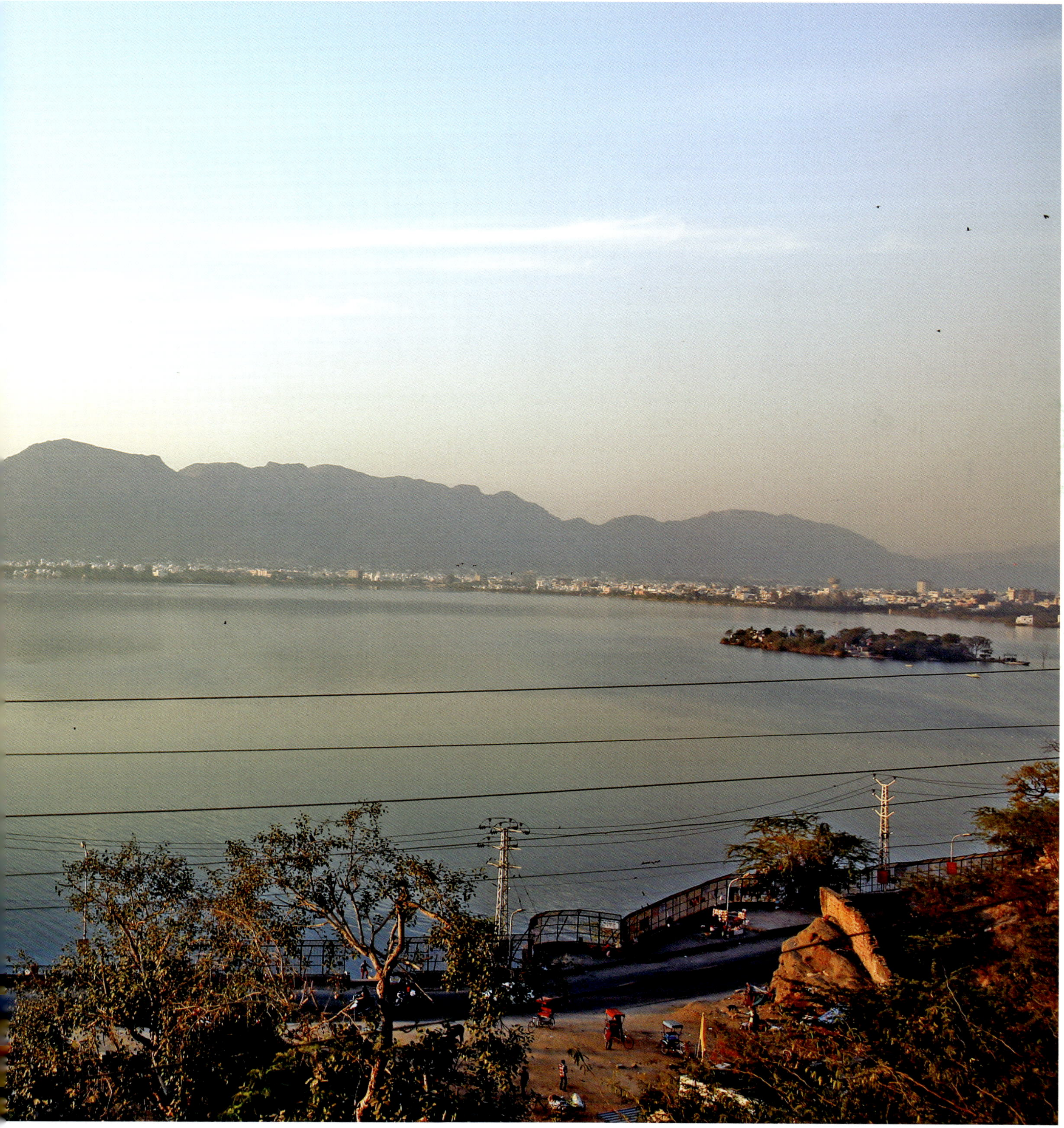

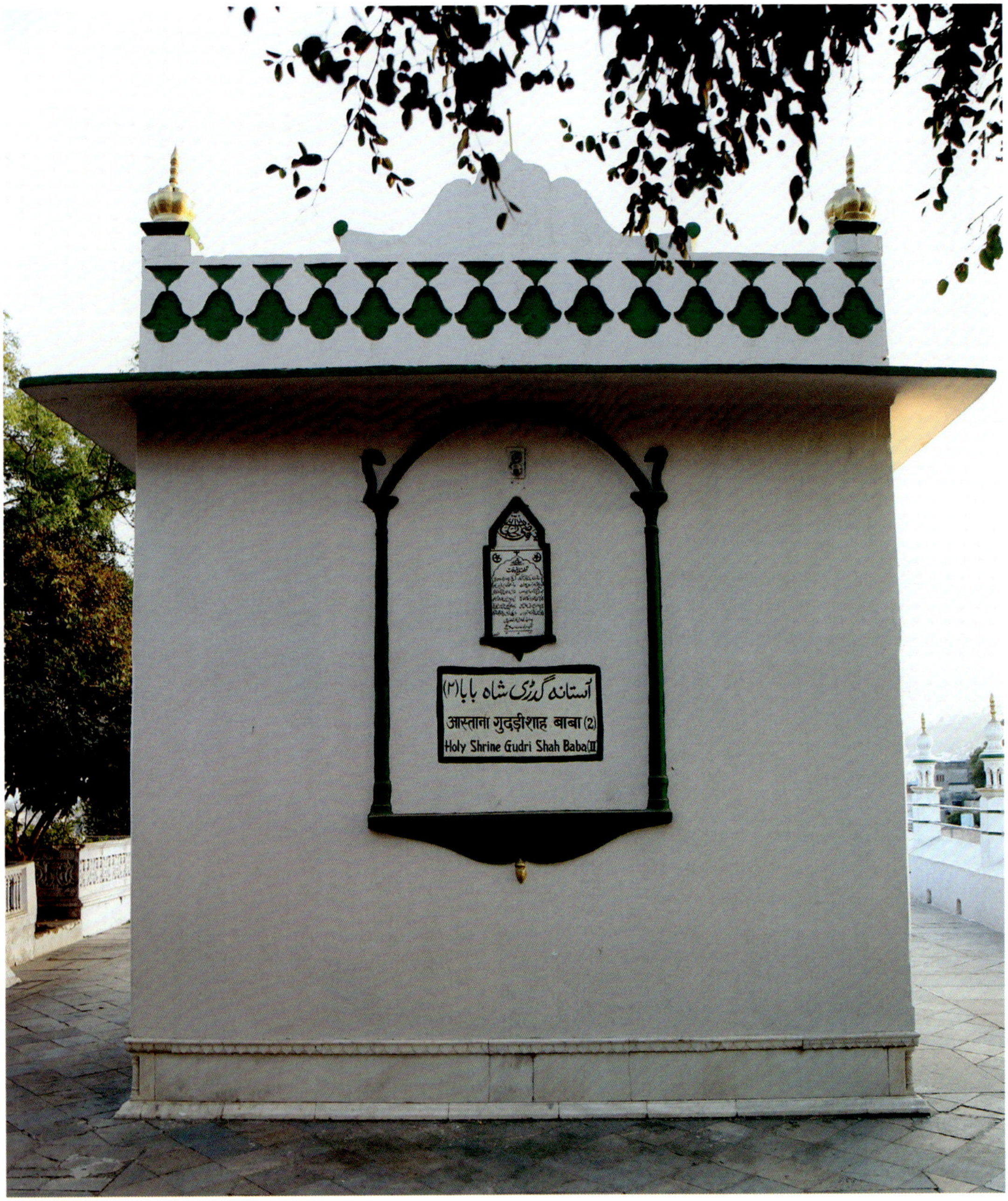
آستانہ گدڑی شاہ بابا(۲)
आस्ताना गुदड़ीशाह बाबा (2)
Holy Shrine Gudri Shah Baba(II)

The Lost Son

Ziauddin Abu Saeed was born from Khwaja's second marriage to Bibi Asmatullah. Zia, in Sufi terms, became an *abdaal*, one who disappears from this world but is within its realms.

Hamiduddin Nagauri, instrumental in the diffusion of the Chishti code in Indian culture, renounced material pleasures to live among mendicants as a vegetarian. *Akhbarul Akhyar*, penned in 1641 by a leading Sufi biographer, Abdul Haqq Muhaddit Dehlvi, quotes the time when Hamiduddin Nagauri asked the saint about the saddest truth of his life.

'Your son has been taken away by a caravan of dervishes because he was not of this world. There is not a day that you do not cry for him. As one of God's chosen few, have his whereabouts not been revealed to you?'

'My Lord has not kept me in the dark. But to mourn this eternal parting is the custom of Prophet Jacob. I must follow it for as long as I breathe,' explained Khwaja.

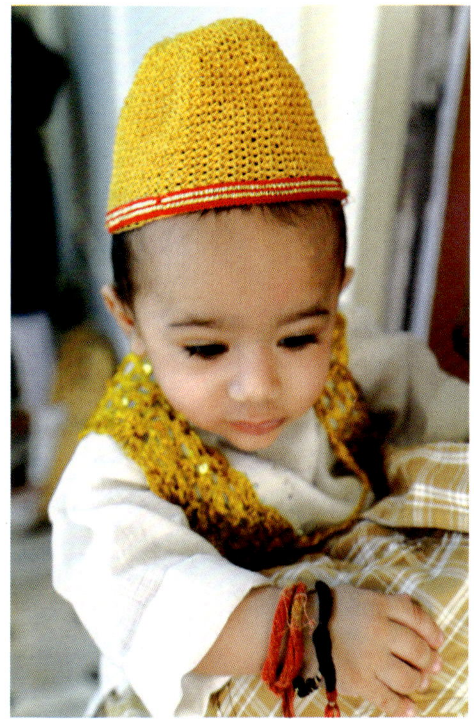

Above: A young pilgrim at the shrine

Facing page: A peaceful shrine in Ajmer Sharif

Next page: The scent of love

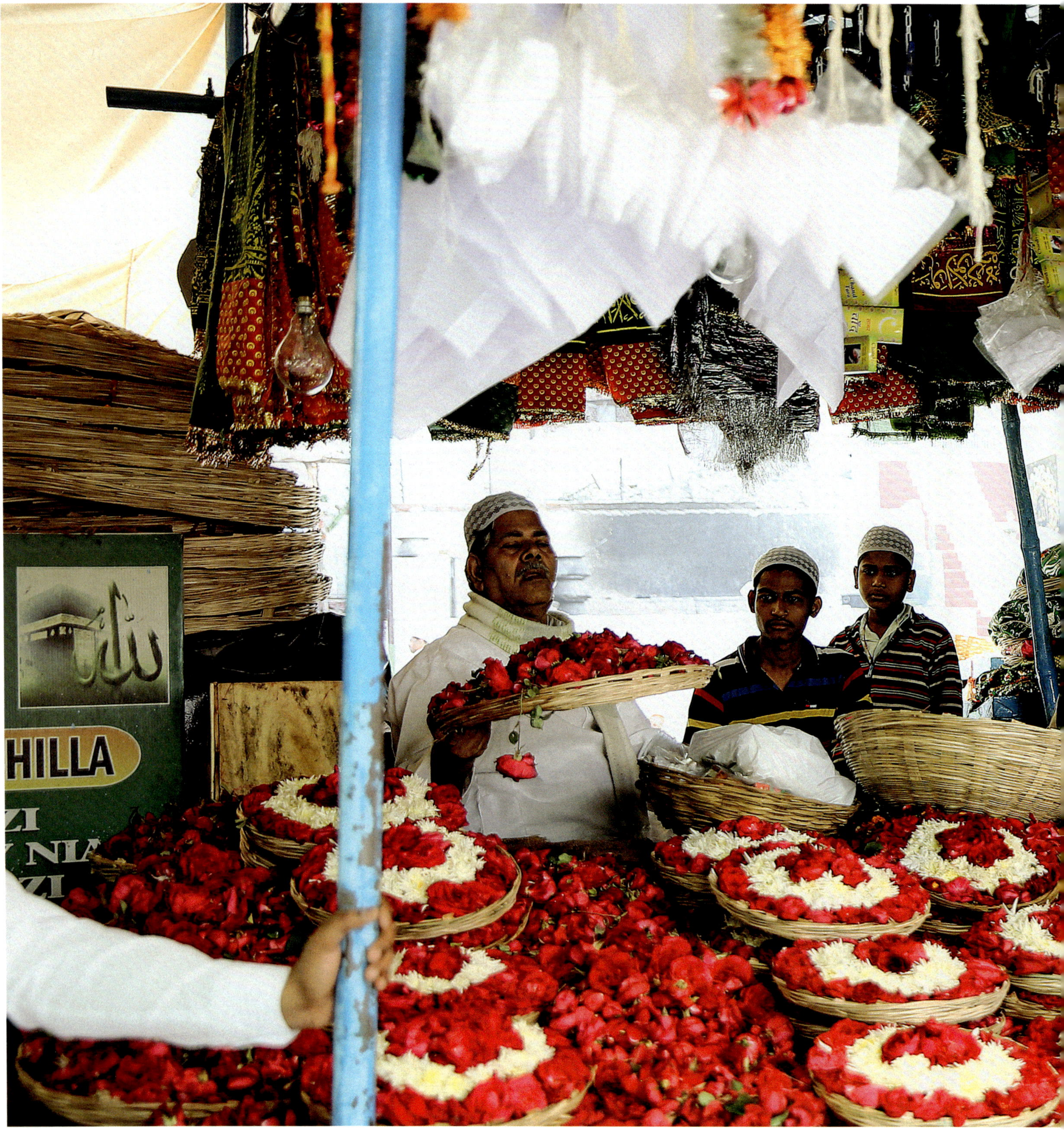

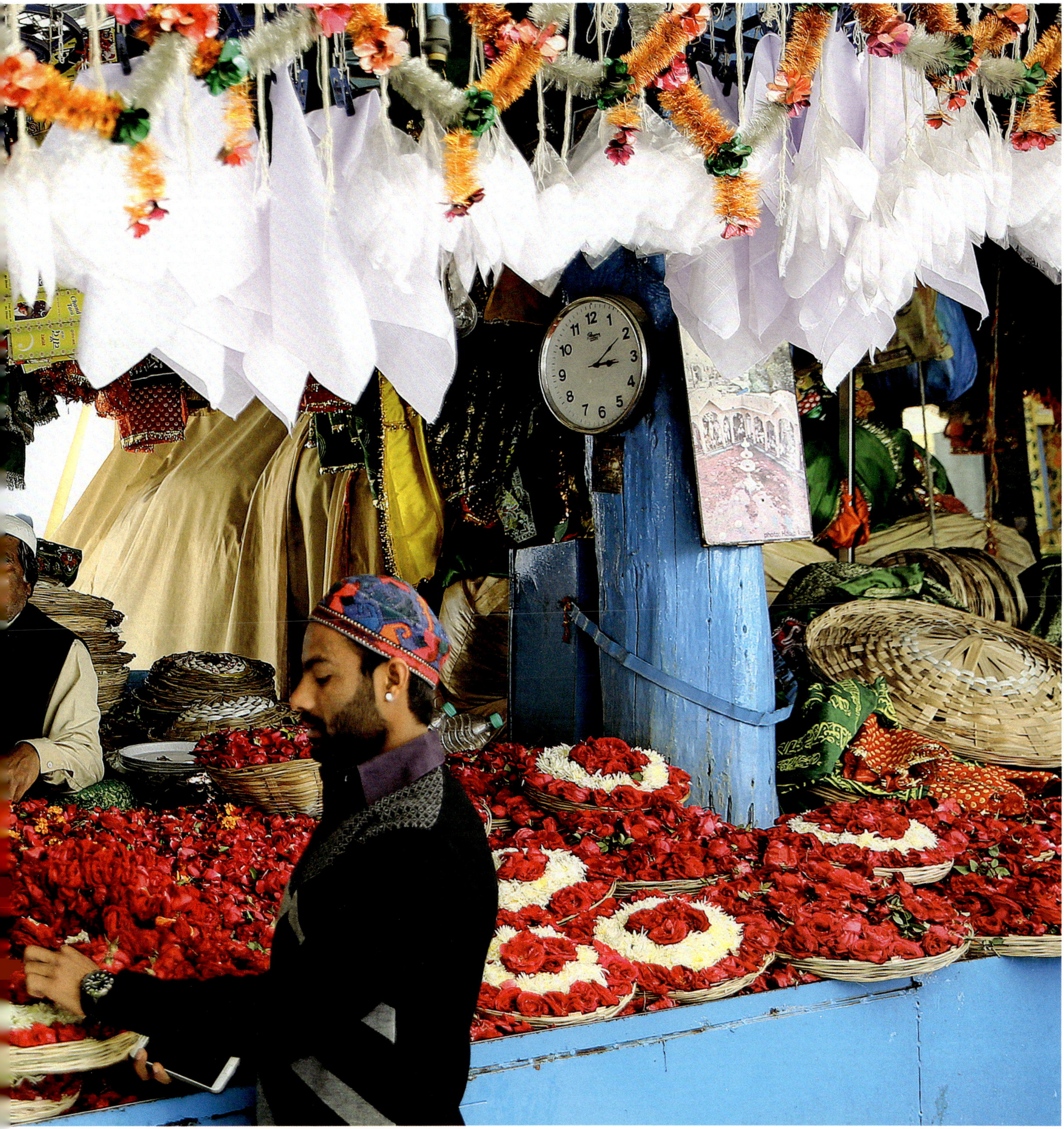

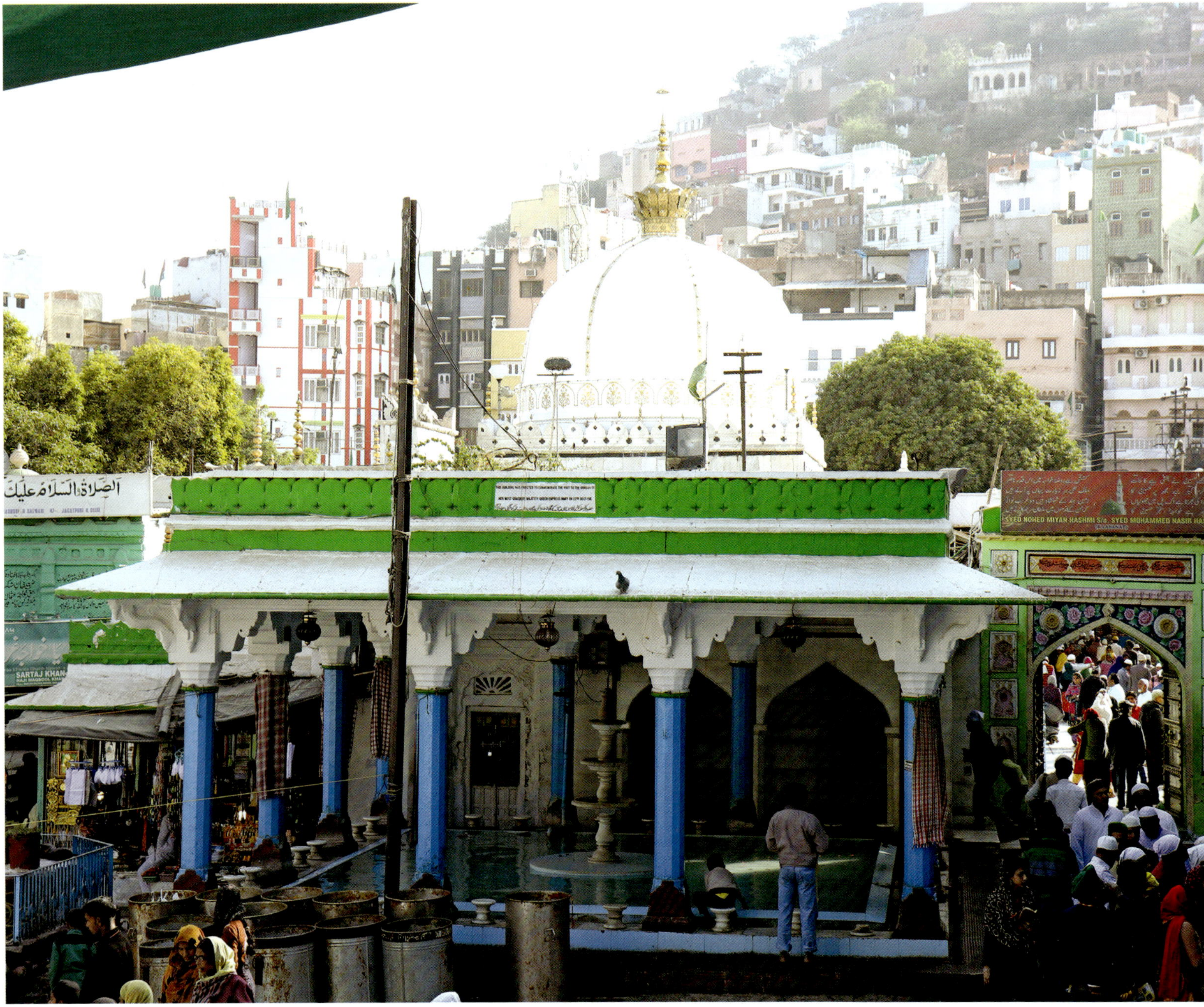
الصلاة والسلام عليك
SARTAJ KHAN
SYED NOHED MIYAN HASHMI S/o. SYED MOHAMMED NASIR HAS

The Saint and the Orphan

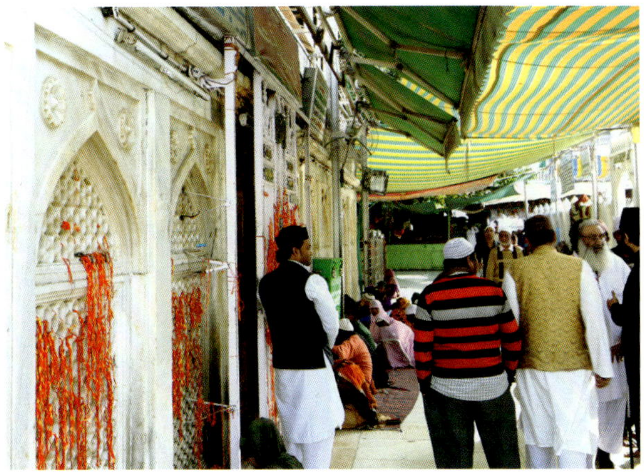

A destination, such as Ajmer Sharif Dargah, is rooted in the journey. Therefore, Muinuddin's dawn period must provide the context for his institution in India.

Born in Sistan in 1141 CE, he arrived in Ajmer in 1192 CE, when he was over the age of 50, after navigating Multan and Lahore, where he confronted unsettled environments; Lahore, no longer the Ghazni of India, was entering the Delhi Sultanate.

Muinuddin spent 40 days in devotional seclusion at the renowned Data Darbar, mausoleum of Data Ganj Baksh Ali-El-Hujwiri. *The Revelation of the Veiled (Kashf-e-Mahjub)*, a treatise on Sufism and its orders in the 11th century, was penned by Hujwiri, who died in 1063 CE. Khwaja's seclusion chamber is preserved to date as one of his first footprints on the subcontinent.

Some 500 years before his time, Persia had produced a number of the first empirical sciences and was the citadel of cultural growth. But by 1135 CE, its lustre had diminished. As the Seljuk Turks crumbled into self-proclaimed princedoms and fiefdoms, Persia disintegrated into lawlessness.

Mesopotamia was unraveling in the absence of a core identity. The Mongolian warlord and sovereign of the Qara Khitai, Yelu Dashi was on a rampage there, and the Assassins had become a clear threat. The heart of philosophy, sciences and the arts was a wasteland of turmoil.

The Sufi giant, Muinuddin Hasan al-Husaini Sijzi Sanjari Ibn-e-Khwaja Ghiasuddin Hasan, was born in 1141 CE (536 AH) to Ghiasuddin

Above: Pilgrims wait and pray outside the shrine's marble walls

Facing page: The dome rises above Queen Mary's fountain and a gate to the shrine

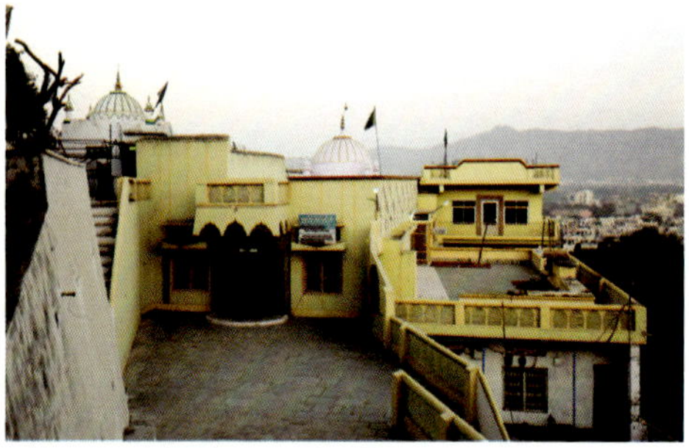

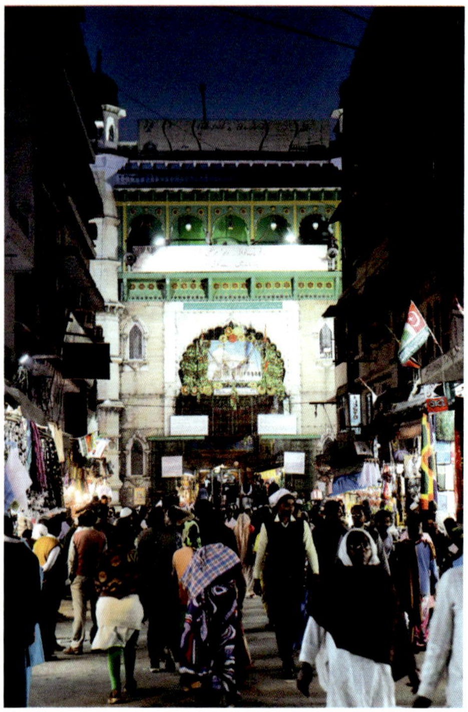

Top: View of the hills from the roof of the shrine complex

Above: Pilgrims pass through the Nizami Gate

and Bibi Mahnoor in Sijh, near Sanjhar, now in Afghanistan. Records such as *Sehrul Al-Aqtaab* claim Isphahan to be his birthplace.

A descendant of Prophet Muhammed's grandson Hasan, he was raised in Khorasan and left to subsist on the proceeds from his family orchard and a windmill, when he was orphaned at the age of 15. The tormented setting of a clash of ideology and tribalism set the mood and pattern of his life.

An ancient account, *Seeratul Muin*, states that at the orchard in Nishapur, young Muinuddin spent his days distributing the daily yield to the forlorn—perhaps, a subconscious act of rebellion in his brutal, acquisitive environment. A child pitted against wild polarisation was fated to cross paths with destiny.

His defining moment arrived in the guise of an elderly dervish, Ibrahim Qandozi. Worn out by travel, the dervish stopped to rest at the orchard. He saw a wistful boy tend to his garden and as was his habit, Muinuddin served grapes and bread soaked in water to Qandozi. Surprised by the child's nature, the mystic brought out some bread from his own satchel and the two began to converse over a meal.

Qandozi spoke to him about the search for an alternate world, of a pursuit of Truth to counter his destructive surroundings, and of the call of his heart. After the visitor returned to the road, Muinuddin knew his path had diverged. The orchard, windmill and his grinding stone were given away to the less privileged. The boy then set out on a trail that was to end in Eternity. Each place presented its own strain of civil war and plunder. Battling varying conflicts, he read the Quran in Khorasan, moved on to Samarkand and met Hisamuddin Bokhari in Bukhara where he spent years as a student. Muinuddin was educated in religion, philosophy and language by Bokhari and then embarked on a pilgrimage of shrines.

His desire for a spiritual guide took him through the treacherous terrains of Iraq and the Arab deserts, till, as a 20-year-old, he found his spiritual father closer to home, in the Persian town of Harwan. Usman

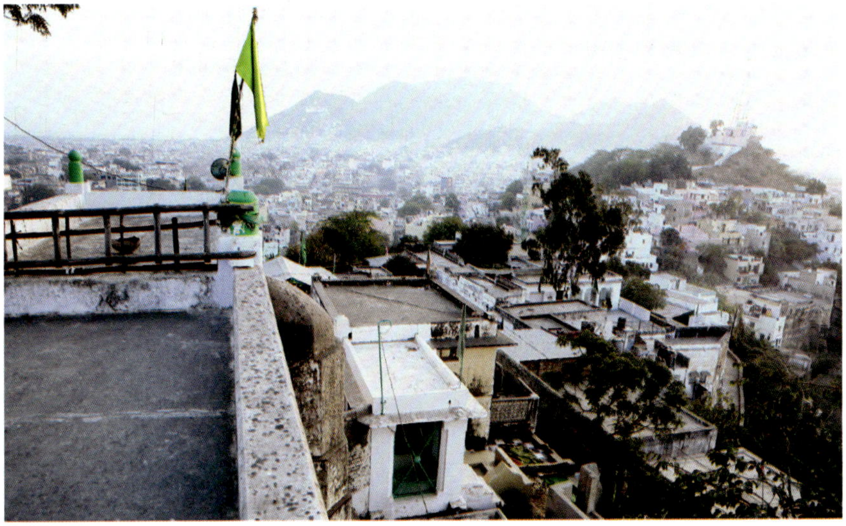

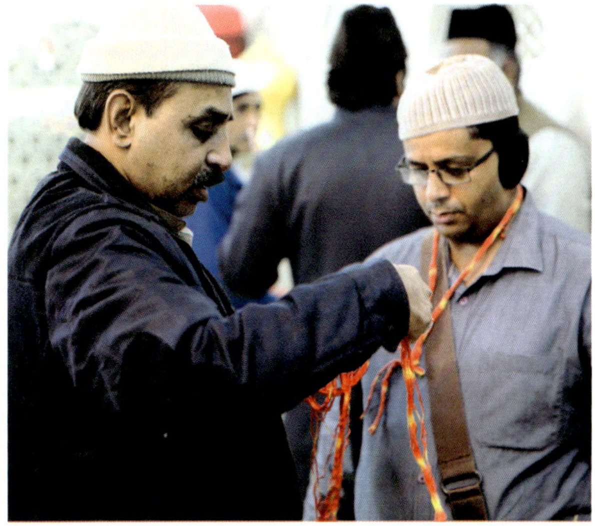

Harooni, also called Harwani, took Muinuddin into his spiritual fold. As per the custom of Harooni's own mentor, he cut Muinuddin's hair, placed a cap on his head and explained the cryptic meanings in the four sides of the headgear.

Muinuddin then spent the next two decades of his life with his master and travelled to remote places; to Damascus, Cairo, crossed the Arab dunes to Mecca and spent time with spiritual leaders. It was in Baghdad that the day came when Harooni put a special patched robe on Muinuddin, presented him with his personal belongings, bestowed upon him the title of Chishti and honoured him with the status of a caliph.

Above left: The many paths of the faithful all lead to the shrine

Above: Pilgrims garland each other with holy threads

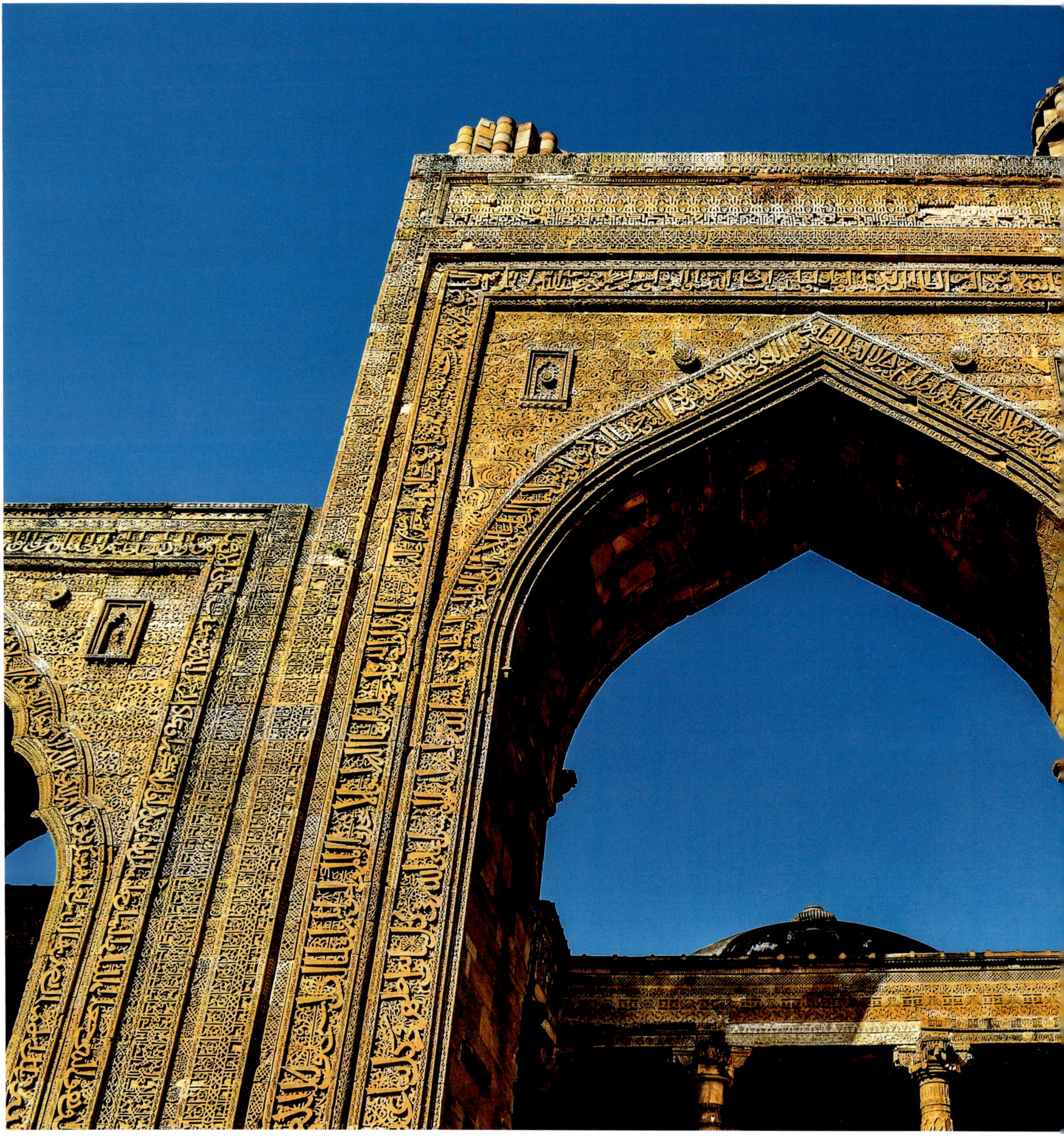

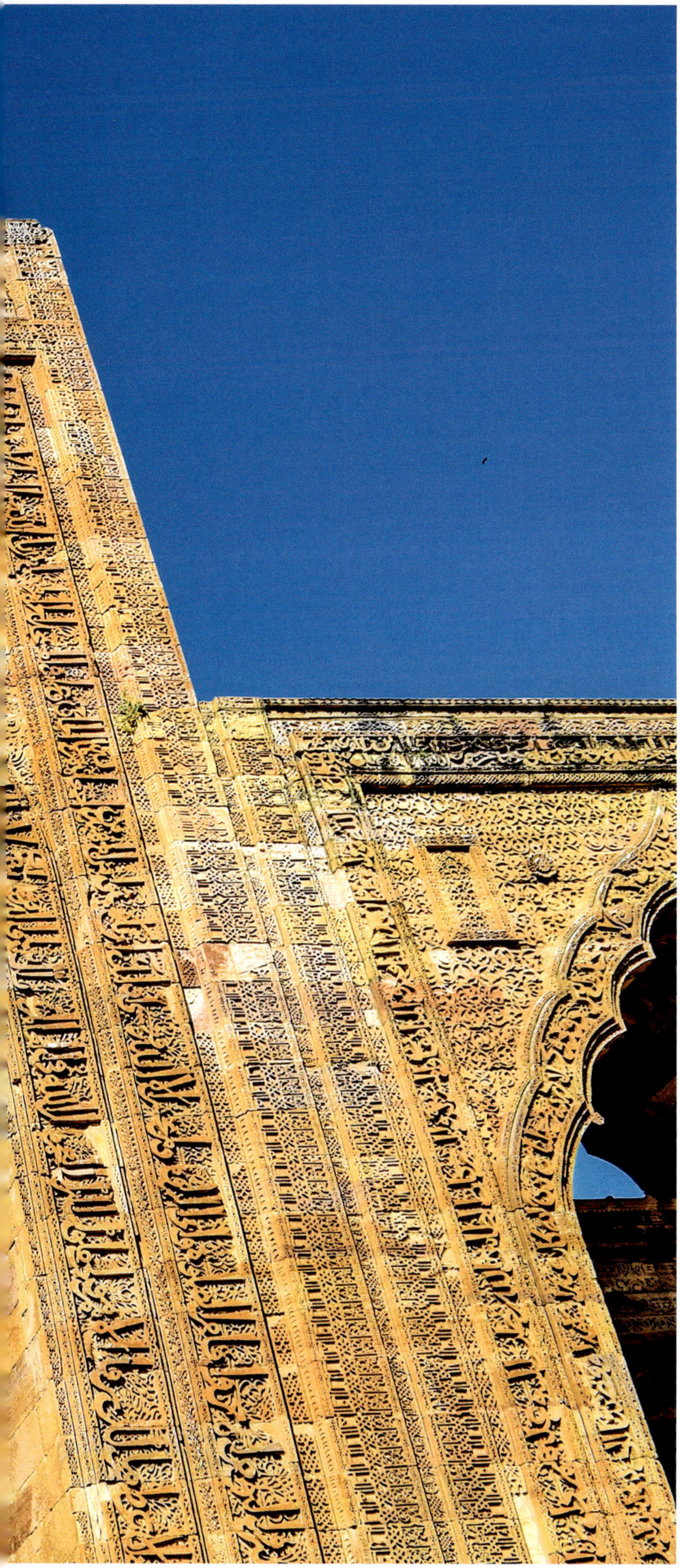

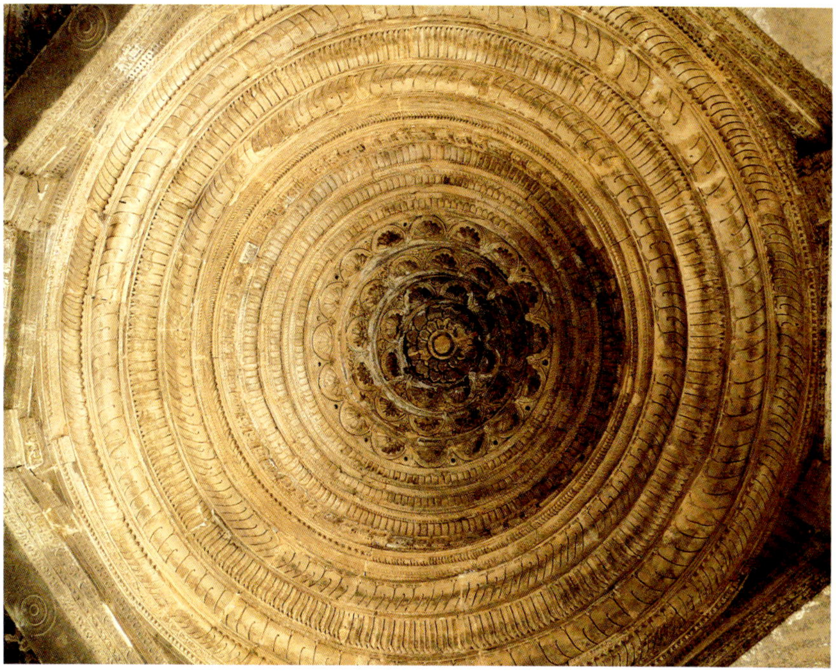

Above: The high arch of the screen wall at Adhai din ka Jhonpra, Ajmer

Left: The interior of the mosque's dome at Adhai din ka Jhonpra, Ajmer

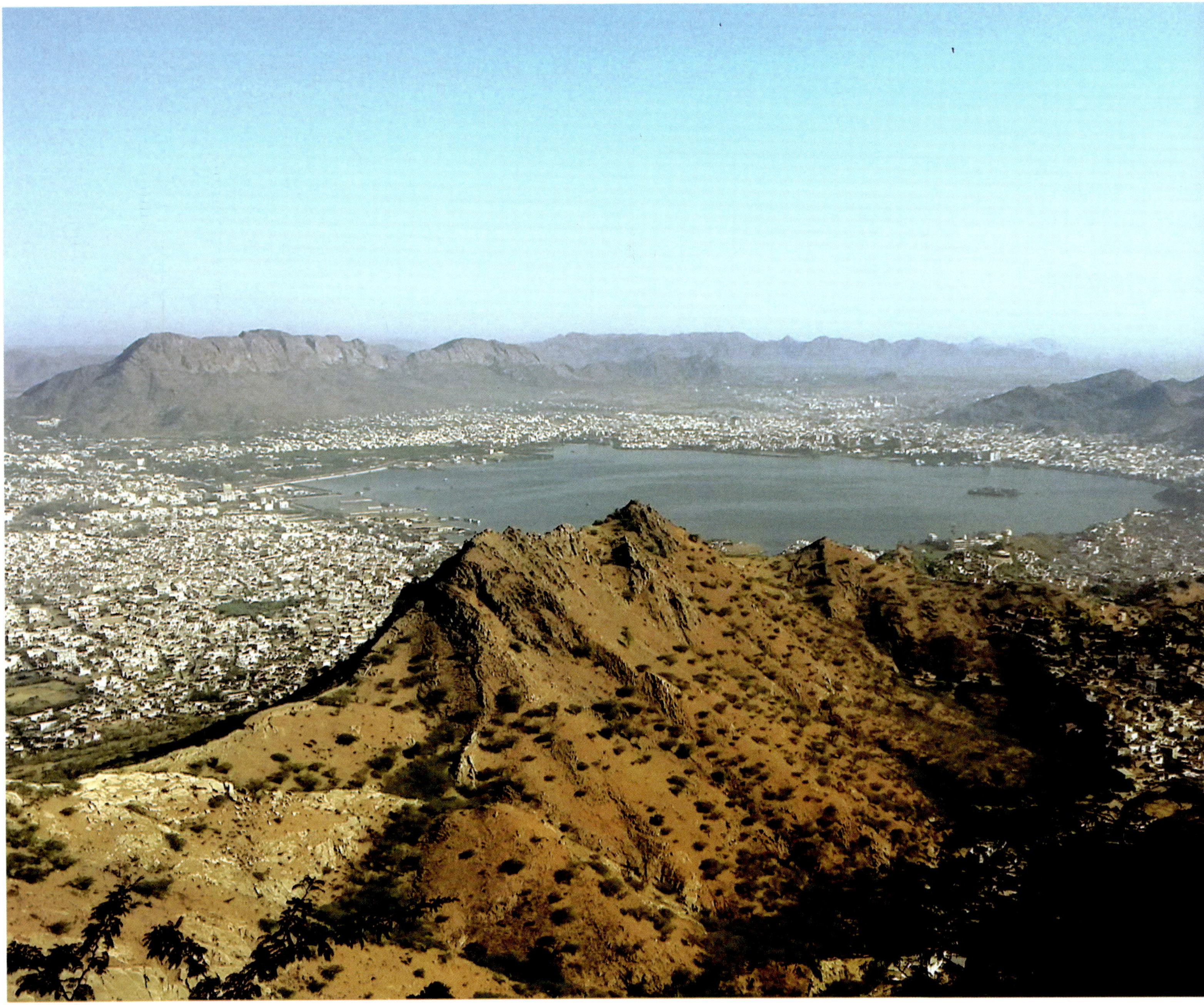

Path to Hindustan

Harooni sent Khwaja out into the world with four instructions—to travel, abstain from greed, forsake expectations, and to camp away from settlements.

Accompanied by a few friends, Muinuddin made his way through Sanjar, Baghdad, Hamdan, Tabrez and Kharqan, where he spent two years. He then chose Astarabad, north-east of Tehran, for an extended stay under the guidance of Khwaja Nasiruddin Astarabadi.

Khwaja Fakhruddin joined him in Herat and they came to Balkh, which was under Seljuk and Qara Khitai rule. After a few months in Balkh, Ghazni was the last pause before India. With a caravan of 40 companions Muinuddin arrived in Hindustan aged around 50 years, in 1192 CE. Khwaja Qutubuddin Bakhtiyar Kaki, whose feted sepulchre is in Mehrauli, Delhi, was his closest ally.

Some accounts refer to a sacred dream where Muinuddin was directed to this region. Others point to his education in Nishapur and to his study of ancient Indian scriptures as the catalyst of his migration. They came up the ancient Aravalli Hills to reach Ajamir or Ajameru; his first station is now commemorated as the Auliya Masjid (Mosque of Saints) where he continued to pray in later years.

Qalandari Masjid honours the site where his disciples meditated. However, the oldest monument that connects Muinuddin to Ajmer, is Adhai Din Ka Jhopra (Hut of two-and-a-half days); he meditated, chanted and prayed with fervour here. Popularly known as Jamia Iltutmash, it was begun by Qutb-ud-Din-Aibak (ruled 1206–1210 CE) and completed by

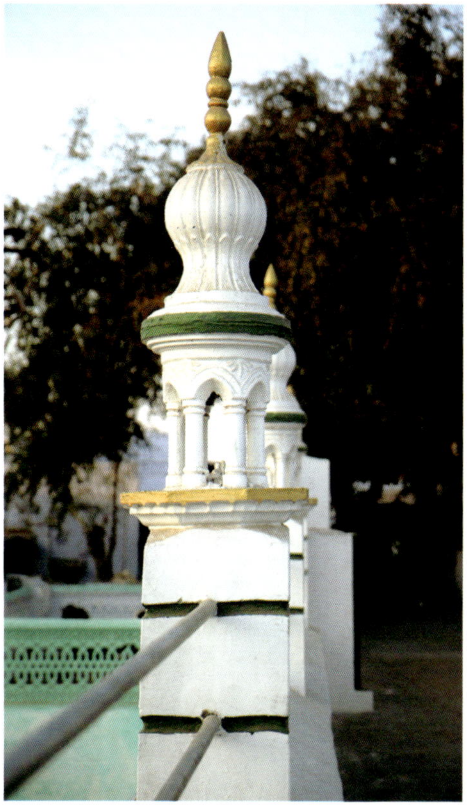

Above: Ornamental pillar at Ajmer Sharif

Facing page: Ajmer—a silver lake nestled amidst rocky hills

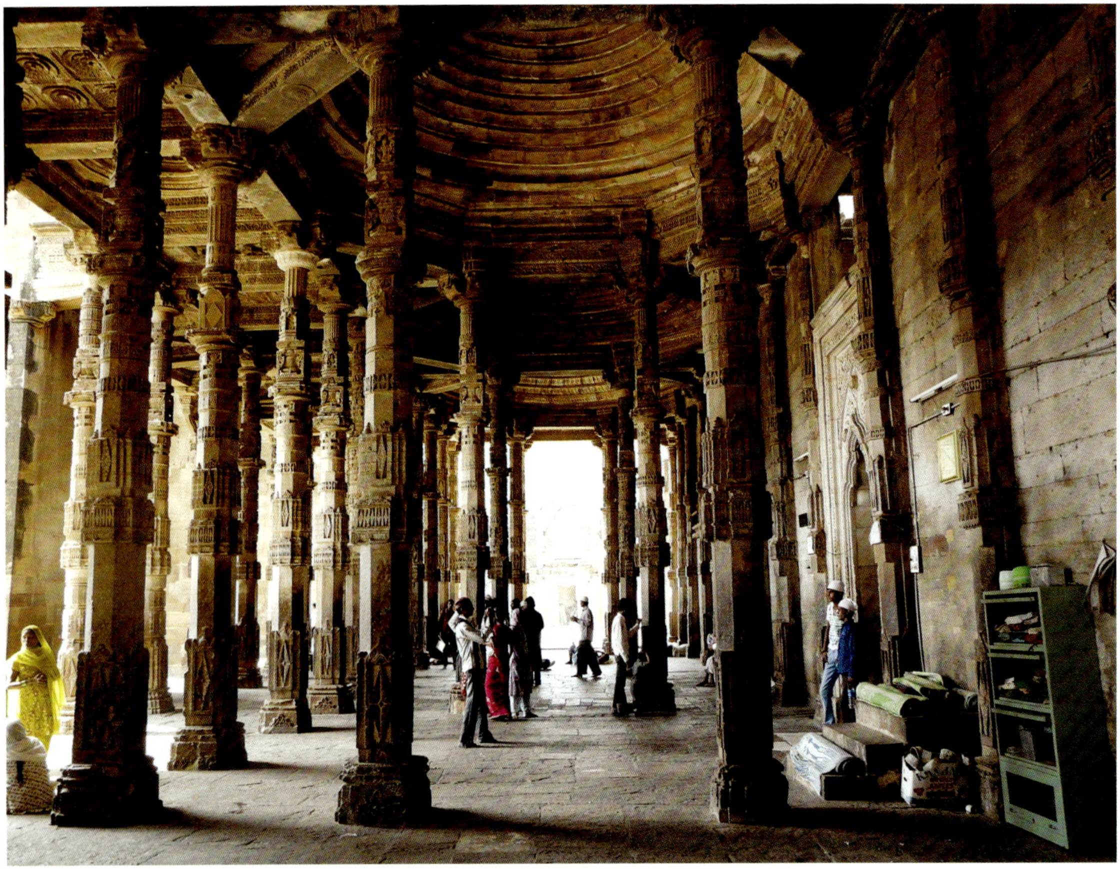

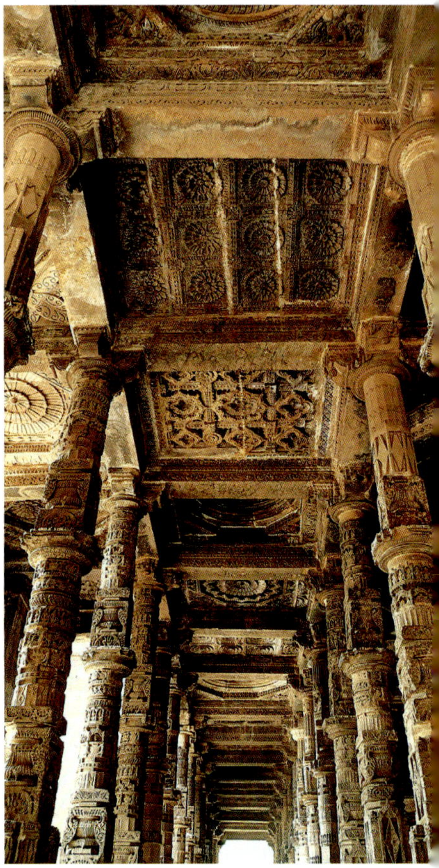

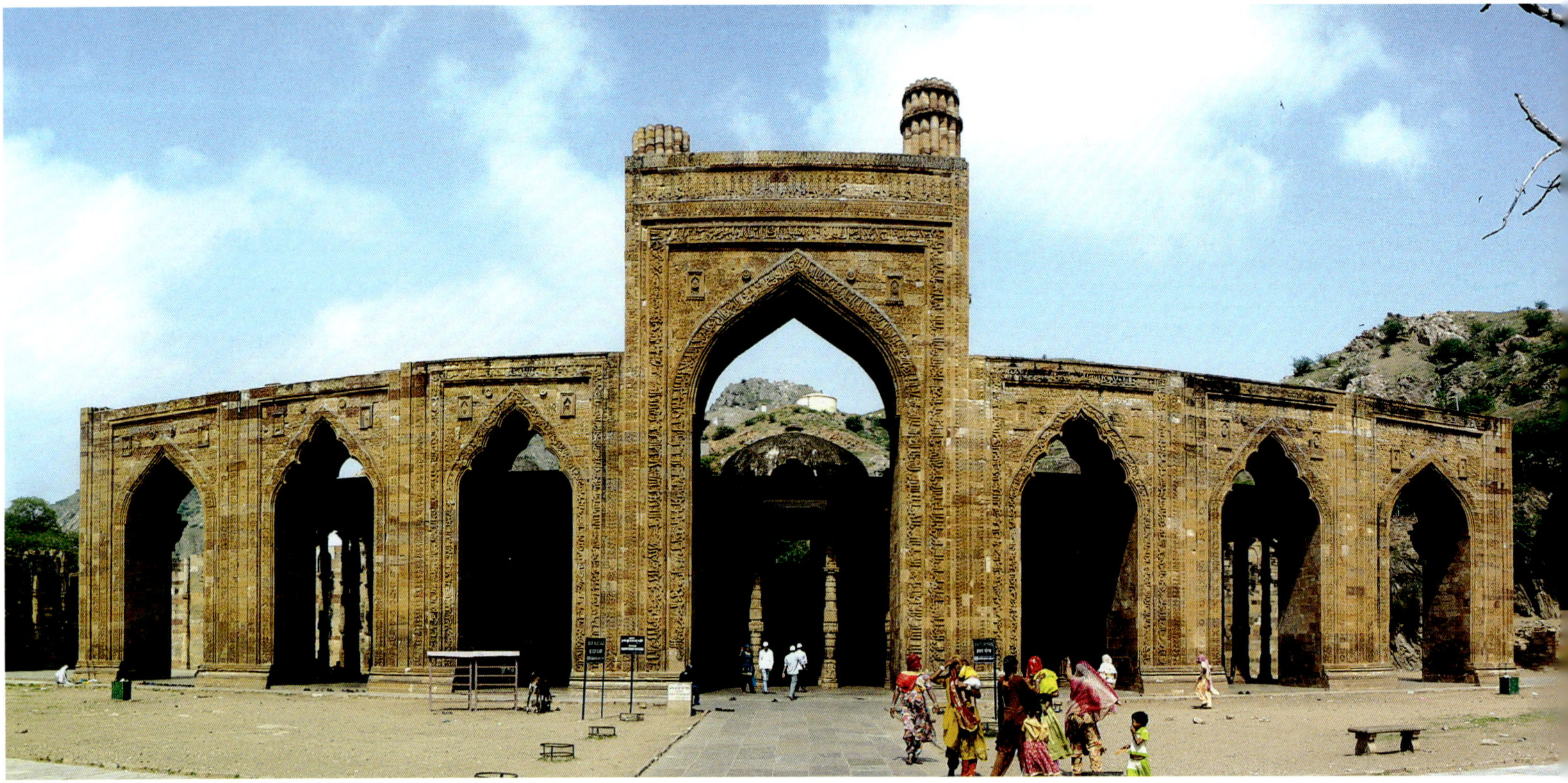

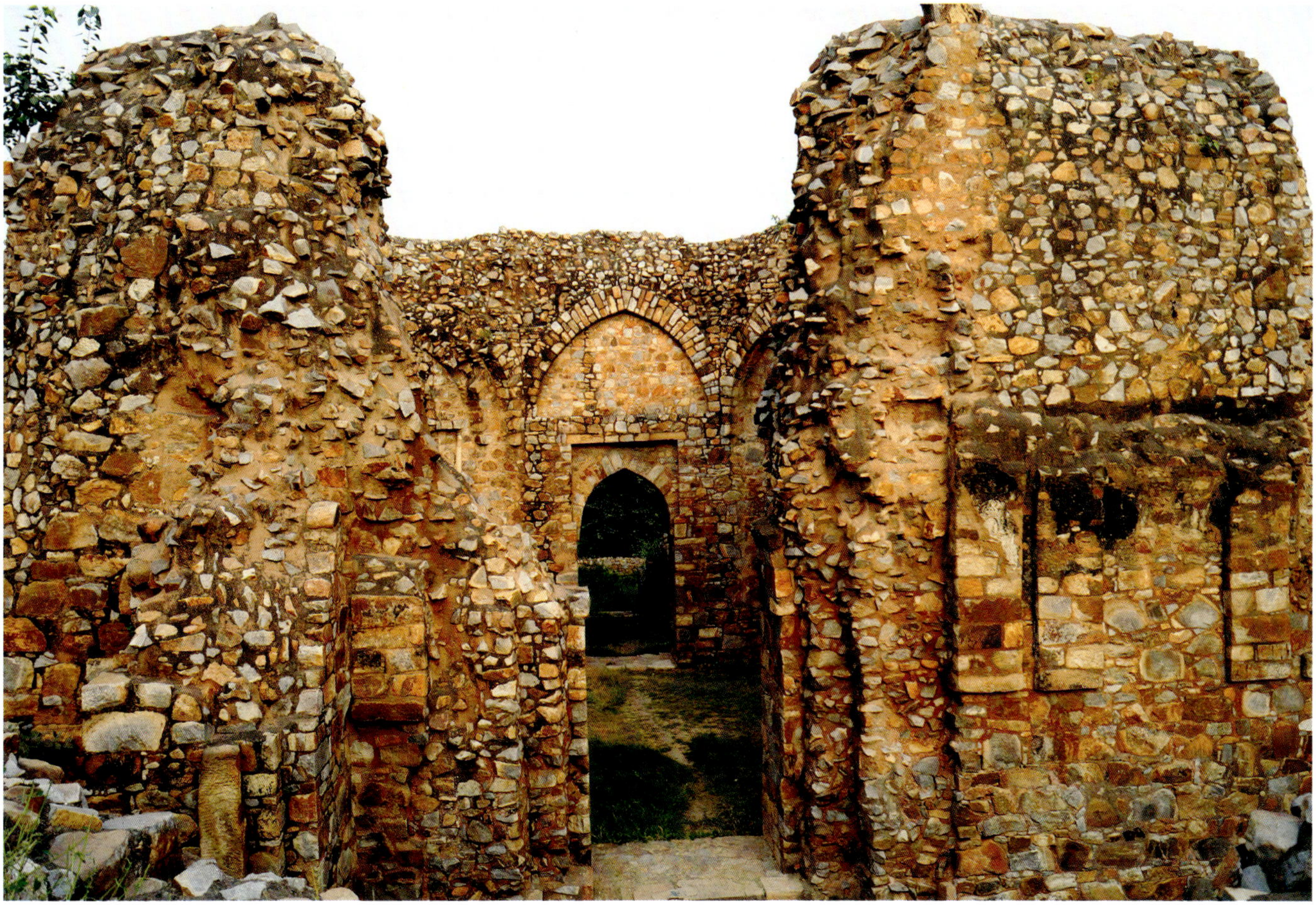

Sultan Shamsuddin Iltutmish (ruled 1211–1236 CE). Built in 1199 CE, archaeologists suggest similarities to the Delhi mosque—an angular dome with spandrels and arches shaping the corridor around it. Consisting of a quadrangle with a front screen of seven sharp arches, the mosque was a masterpiece of Islamic and Indian architectural harmony.

The 40 intricately embellished columns that hold its roof are entirely different and the mosque's calligraphy is another aspect of immaculate fusion in Kufic and Nashq lettering. Archaeological studies of its minarets indicate that it is likely to have been the prime mosque at the advent of Islam in the subcontinent. Whereas, the earliest sign of a classical Indian arch is claimed to be the one in the debris of the tomb of Balban (ruled 1266–1286 CE).

Above: Tomb of Balban at Mehrauli Archaeological Park, Delhi

Facing page top left: Mihrab dome and arcade at Adhai din ka Jhonpra, Ajmer

Facing page top right: Decorated ceiling of the mosque arcade at Adhai din ka Jhonpra, Ajmer

Facing page below: The screen wall at Adhai din ka Jhonpra, Ajmer

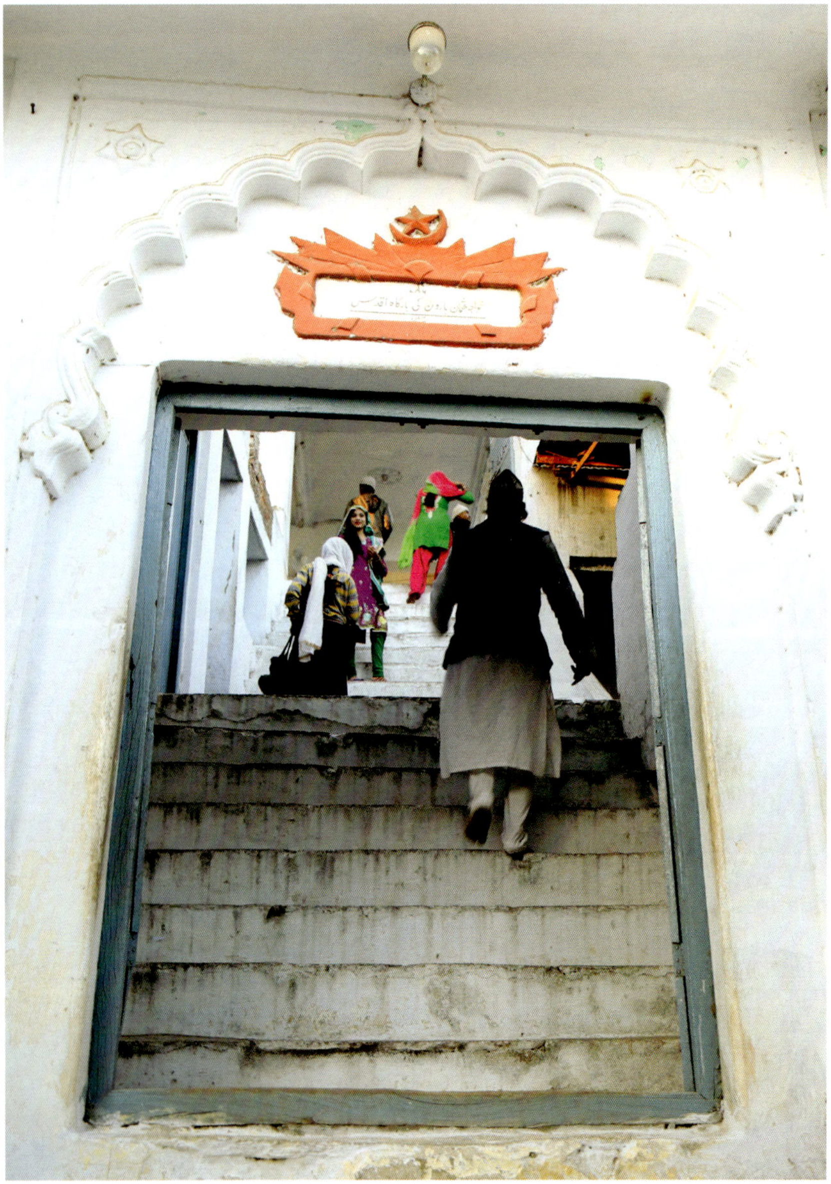

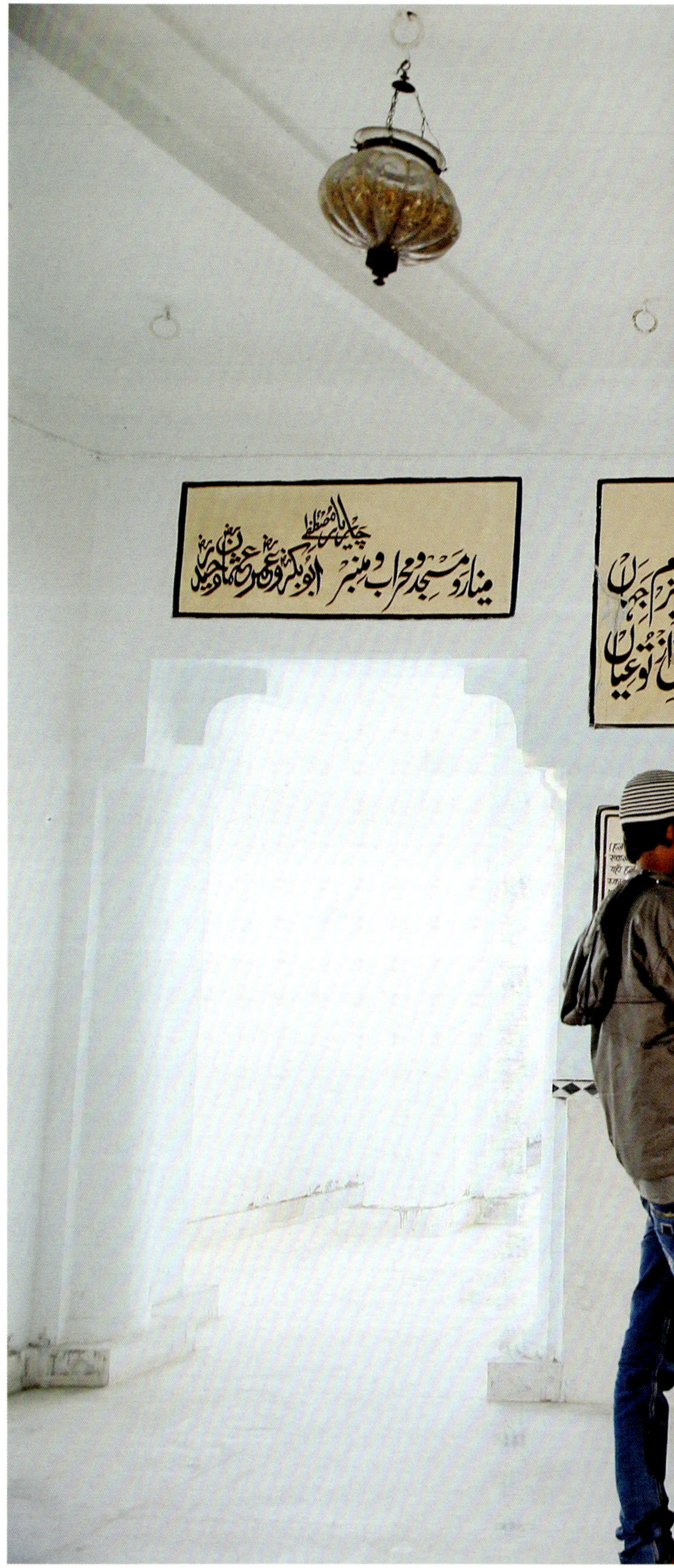

Above: Stairway to the chamber dedicated to Usman Harooni's mementoes

Right: Visitors view Usman Harooni's belongings at the shrine

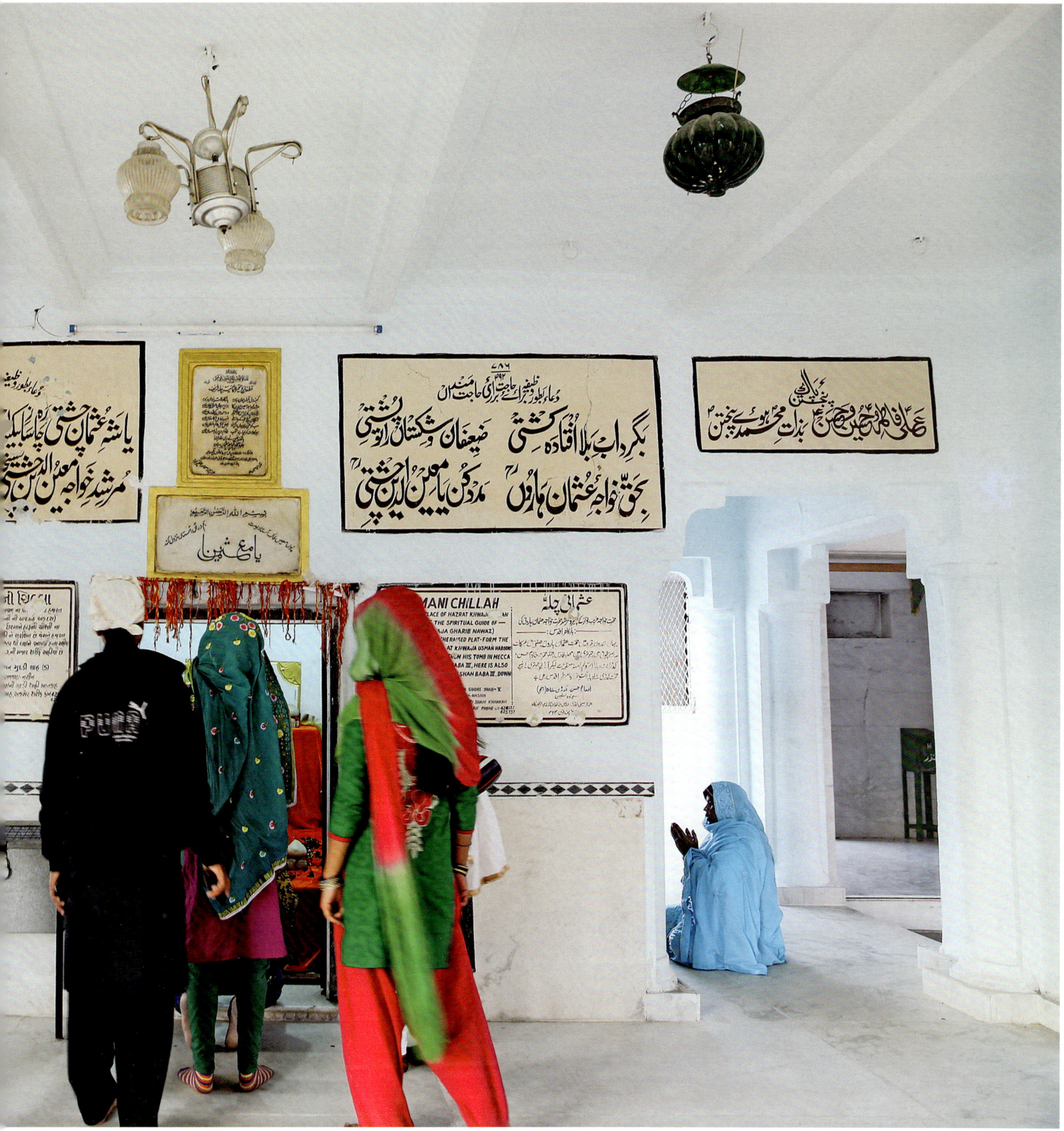

بگرداب بلا افتادہ کشتی
ضعیفان و شکستاں را توئی پشتی
بحق خواجہ عثمان ہارونی
مدد کن یا معین الدین چشتی
MANI CHILLAH

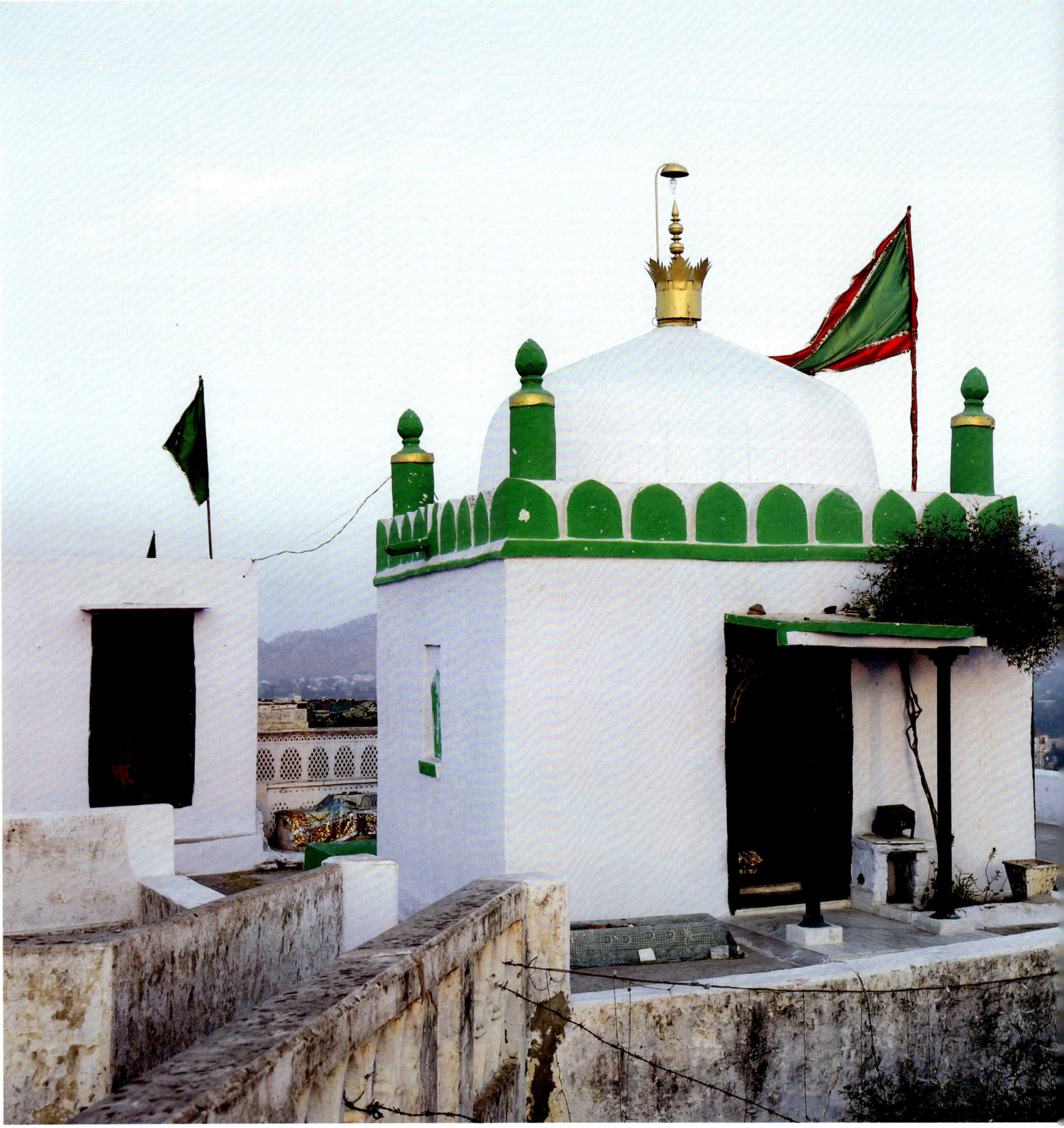

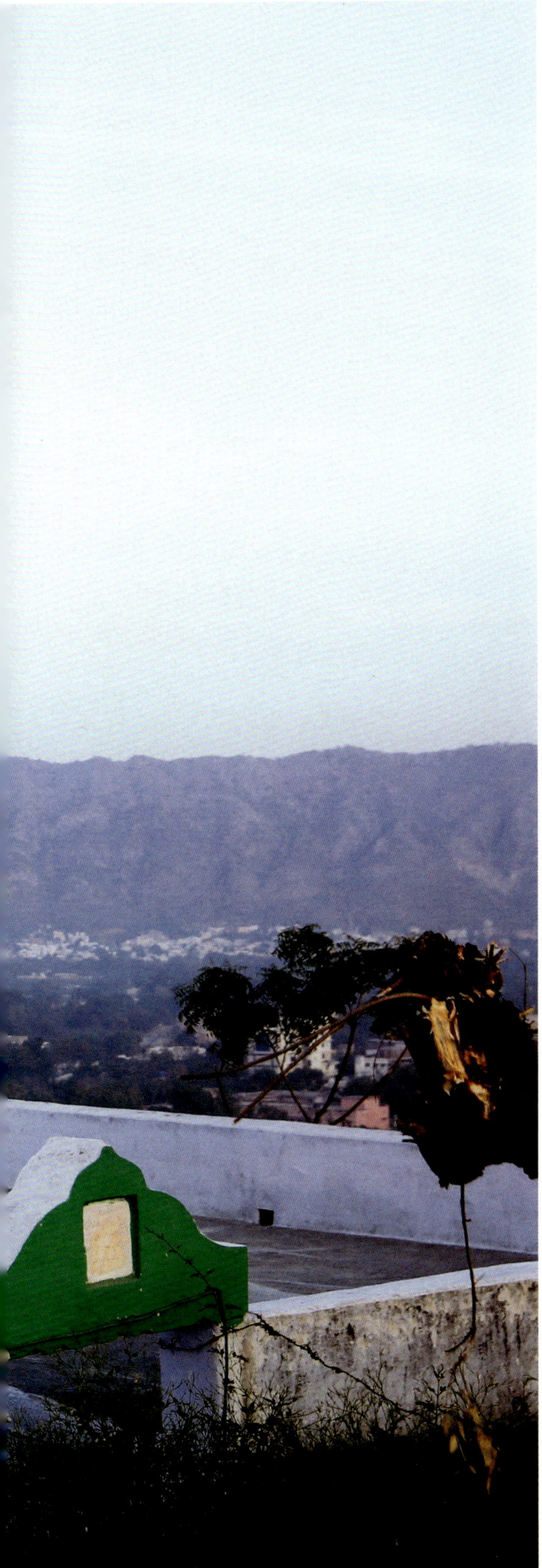

The Chishti Bloodline

Fakhruddin, the Saint of Sarwaar, the eldest offspring of Khwaja Muinuddin, died in 1265 CE. His body lies entombed in a shrine at Sarwaar Sharif, some 40 miles from his father's town of Ajmer.

His death anniversary is a three-day celebration, alive with qawwali, communal meals and multitudes of devotees. A congregation sets out from Ajmer to place a special shroud on his tomb at sunset. Records state that Iltutmish allotted Sarwaar to the ascetic on the recommendation of Bakhtiyar Kaki, the ruler's patron saint.

A serene shrine on the rooftop of the Ajmer Sharif complex

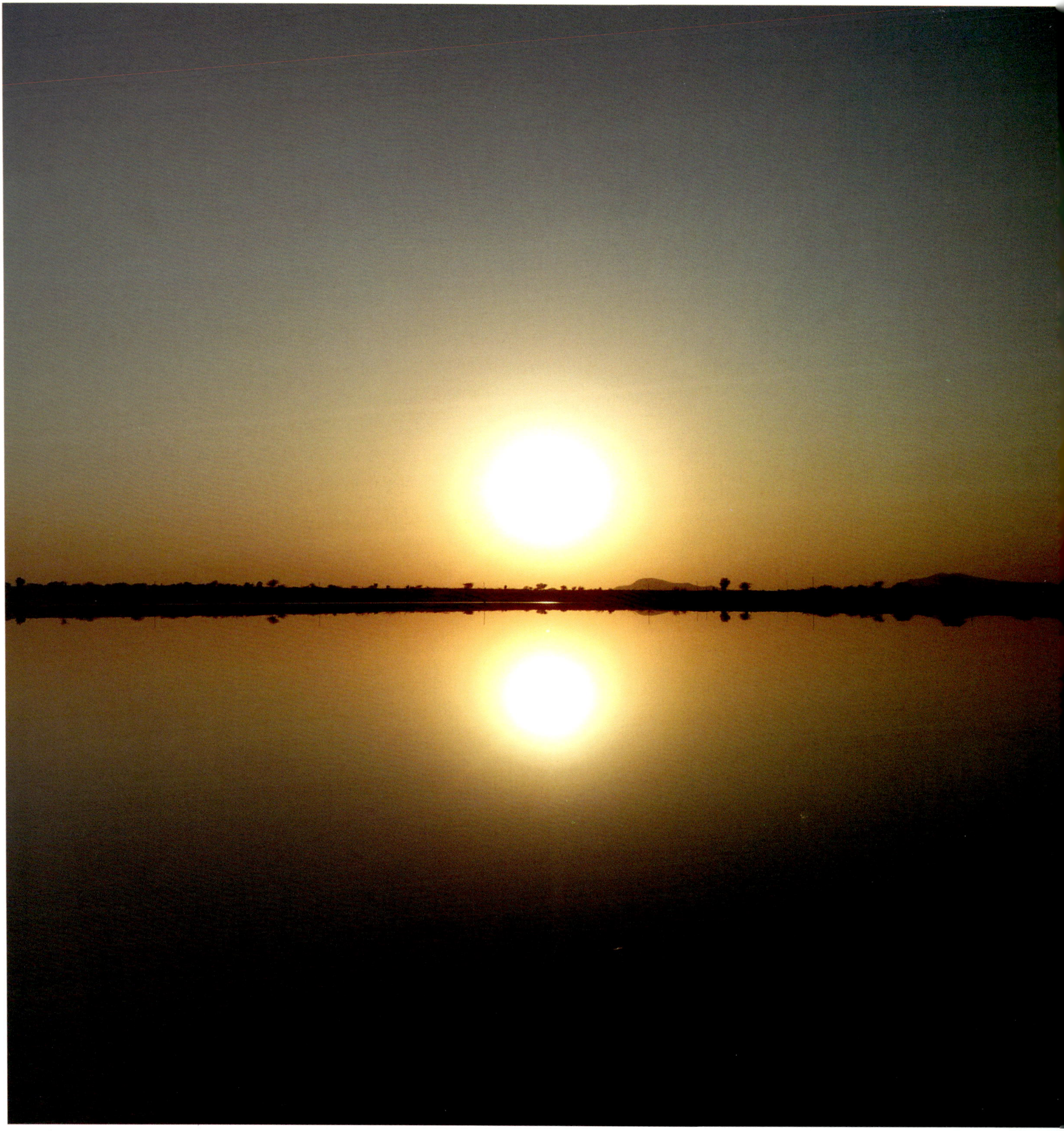

Sambhar Sharif

Fakhruddin's heir, Khwaja Hisamuddin Sokhta Sambhari also slipped into the ancestral ascetic mantle and his tomb stands by a lake at Sambhar, in Rajasthan. Another son rests in a large memorial on Tonk Road, near Jaipur. Other burial chambers belong to Fakhruddin's grandsons. The first, also named Muinuddin, became a disciple of Naseeruddin Chiragh Dehlvi, prime caliph of Nizamuddin Auliya, a revered saint of the Chisti Order in Delhi. Khwaja Qayamuddin, the second grandchild, is noted as Nizamuddin's pupil. According to *Seeratul Muin*, his burial place is undetected.

In the 15th century, Khwaja's direct descendents left Ajmer for Mandu, Delhi and Gujarat. Consequently, Qayamuddin's progeny, Ahmed and Wahid, are believed to be buried in the neighbouring areas of Hyderabad in the Deccan. Hence, Muinuddin's bloodline ends with the fourth generation.

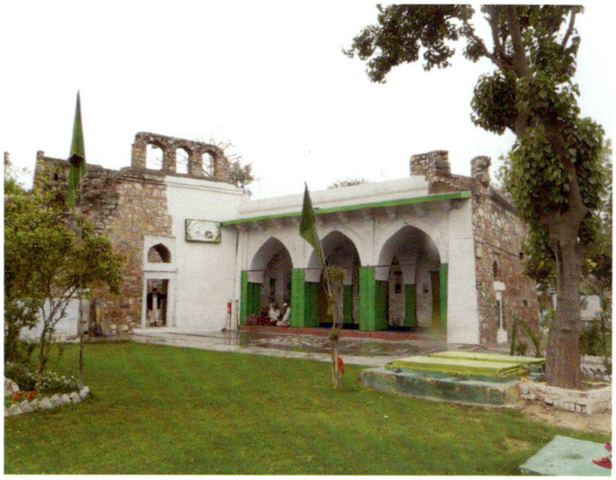

Above: Chilla Nizamuddin, the residence of Nizamuddin Auliya, in the Humayun's tomb complex, Delhi

Facing page: The fire of faith—sunset over Sambhar Lake, Rajasthan

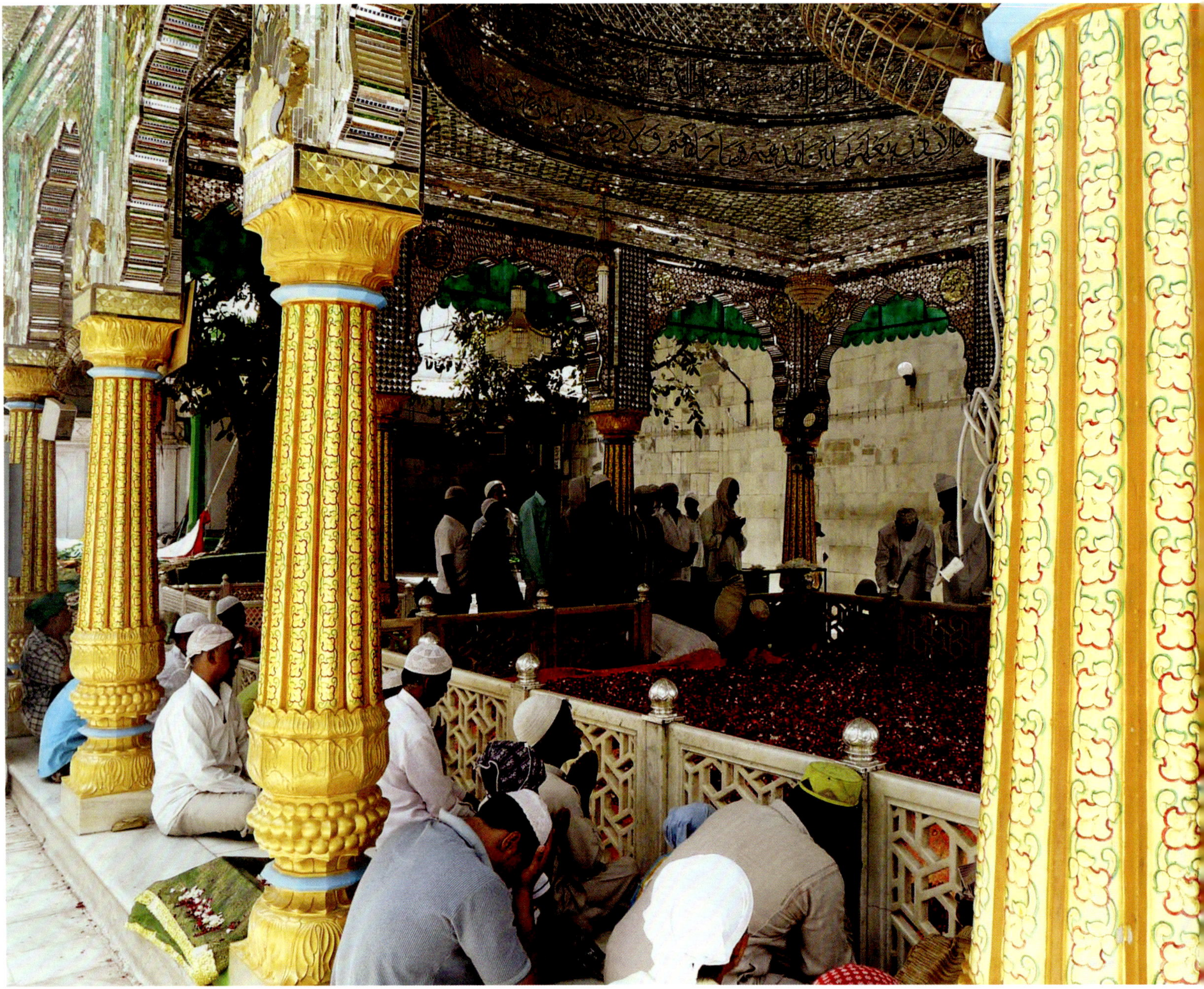

Mystic Lineage

In his lifetime, Muinuddin Chishti selected a mere five primary spiritual successors:

- Khwaja Qutubuddin Bakhtiyar Kaki
- Hamiduddin Nagauri
- Sheikh Sulaiman Qazi
- Ziauddin Hakim
- Sheikh Ahmed Chishti

So, along these unflagged trails is the tale of an instinctive direction of the heart.

Now, one knows from experience that revered spaces and saints are sacred signposts to find one's way around life. As the early Buddhists said, 'Walk on', for there are no better words to propel a pilgrim or a discoverer onwards.

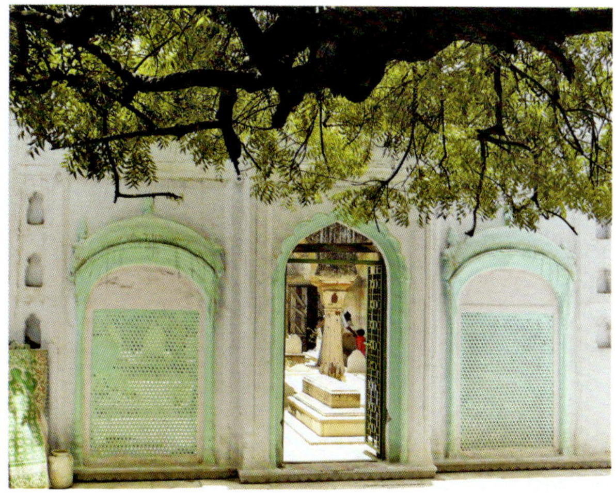

Above: Entrance to the grave enclosure in Qutbuddin Bakhtiyar Kaki's tomb

Facing page: Devotees at the tomb of Qutubuddin Bakhtiyar Kaki

Next page: The many faces of faith

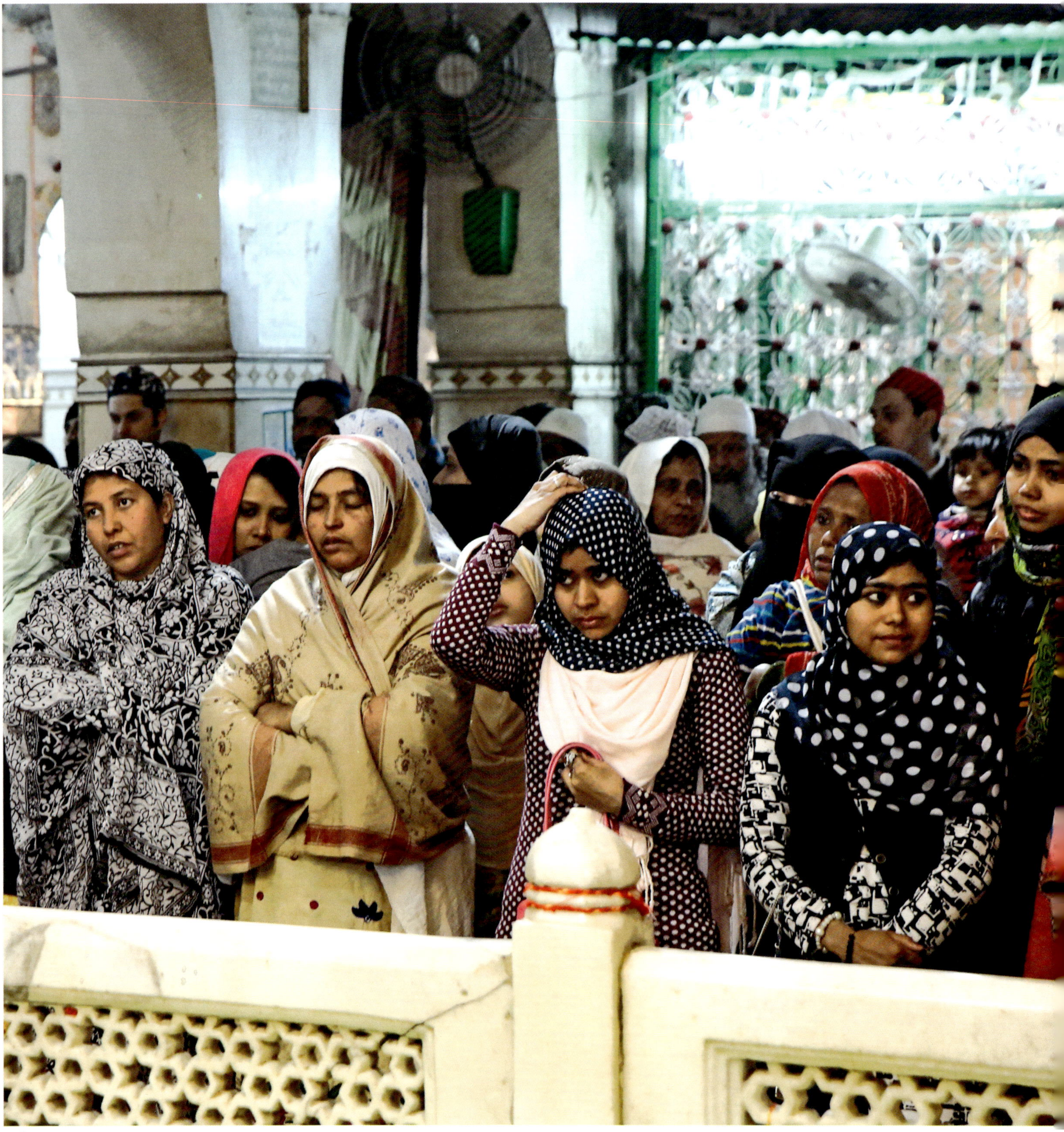

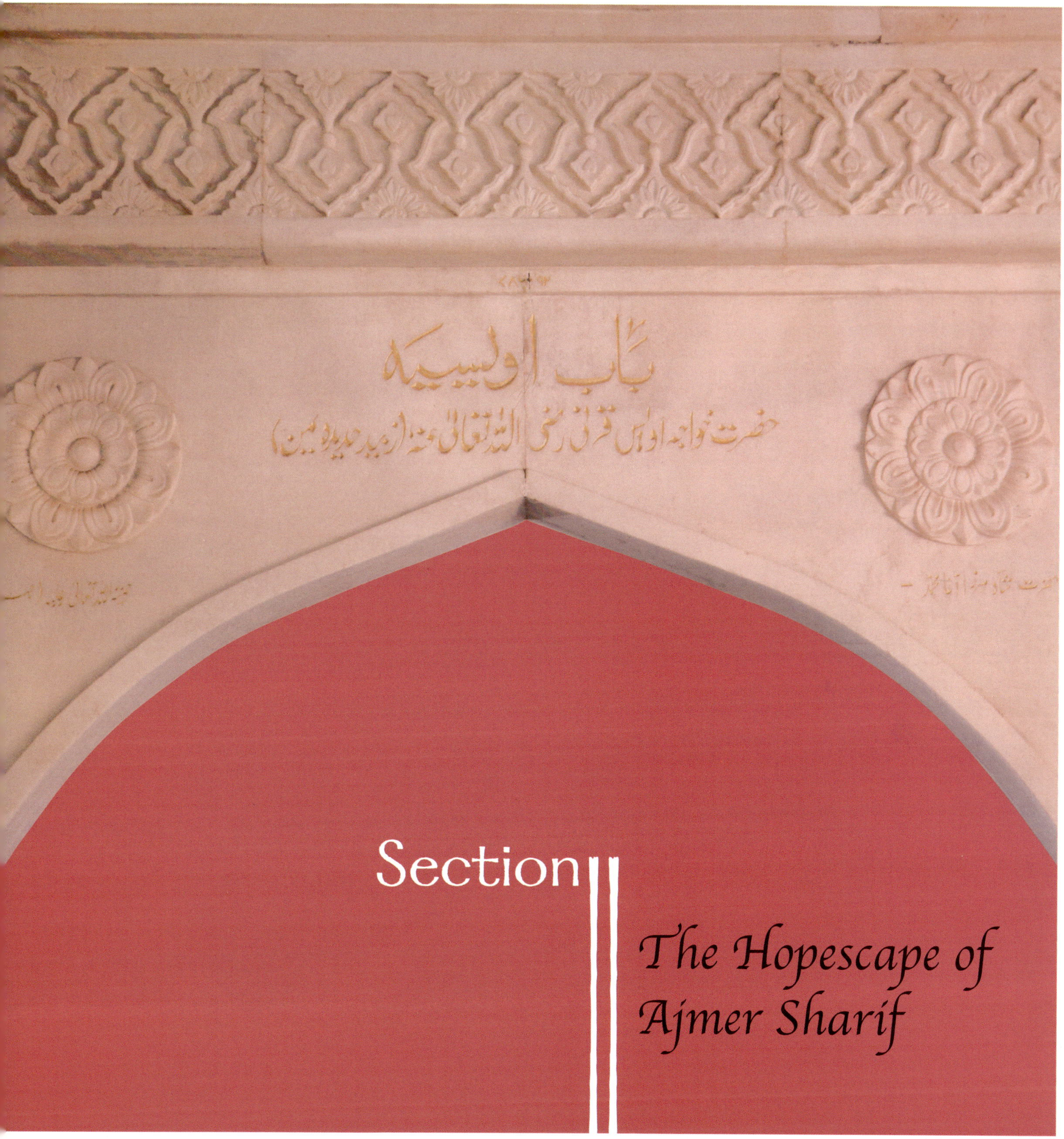

Section II

The Hopescape of Ajmer Sharif

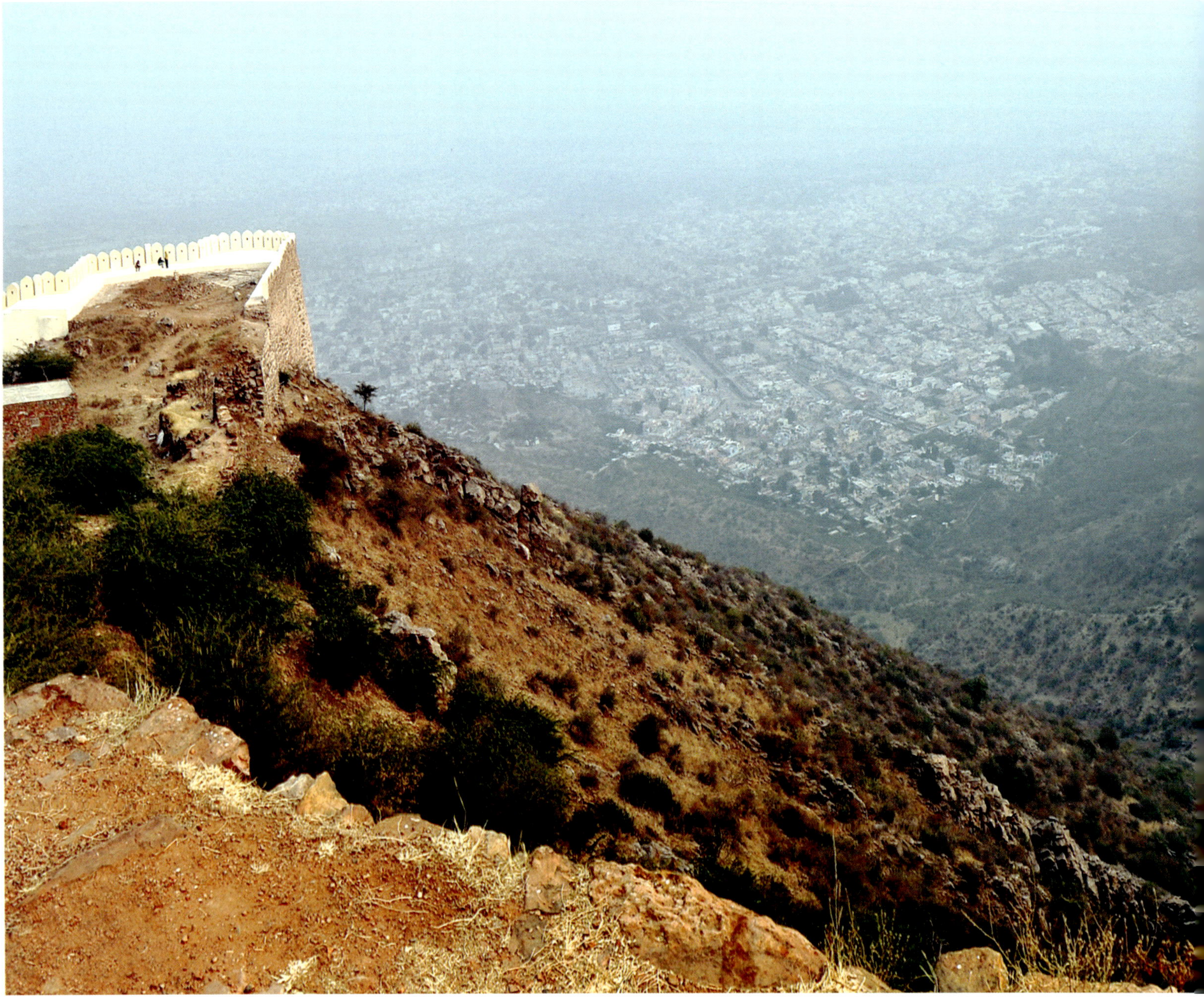

Introduction

'Listen to the voice from the incoming waves; it is loud.
But when the tide goes out, the voice becomes silent.'
Khwaja Muinuddin Chishti

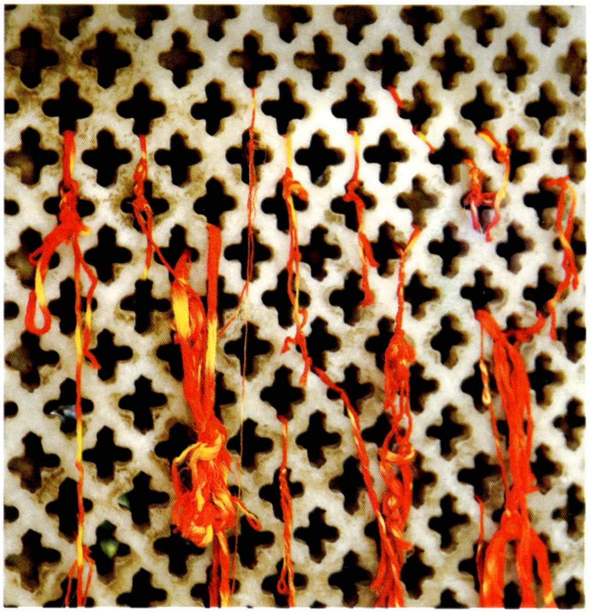

The shrine, central to the human geography of Sufi belief in South Asia, is lodged in a sweeping bend of one of Ajmer's rocky hills.

In *Ajmer: Historical and Descriptive*, Har Bilas Sarda writes that in the early seventh century, Ajaipal gave a human face to the city of Ajmer. Its original appellations, Ajameru, the supreme mountain, or Ajamir—*Mir* is Persian for mountain—find their roots in his name.

Sada Bahaar Pahari (The Evergreen Hill), rolls along the banks of the Ana Sagar Lake to Ajmer's north. Ruins of the ancient Taragarh Fort are scattered to the south, with the Kokla Hills rising on the east. To the west lies the lesser-known Alif ke Ghanaywali range of hills.

Muinuddin Chishti spent 46 years of his life in Ajmer. India was a more spiritually conducive refuge than the politically volatile environs that he traversed on his journey to his final abode. At that time, tribalism was the subcontinent's prevailing social mode. As structural systems of knowledge fell to pieces, the possibility of an inspiration altogether different from them gained credence.

Muinuddin's universe was fragmented; Islam was a diluted version of the Arabs. It had absorbed numerous cultures spanning Byzantine to Mesopotamian. Therefore, he could only depend on intuition and

Above: Hope hangs on fragile threads at Ajmer Sharif

Left: Taragarh Fort stands proudly over the city of Ajmer

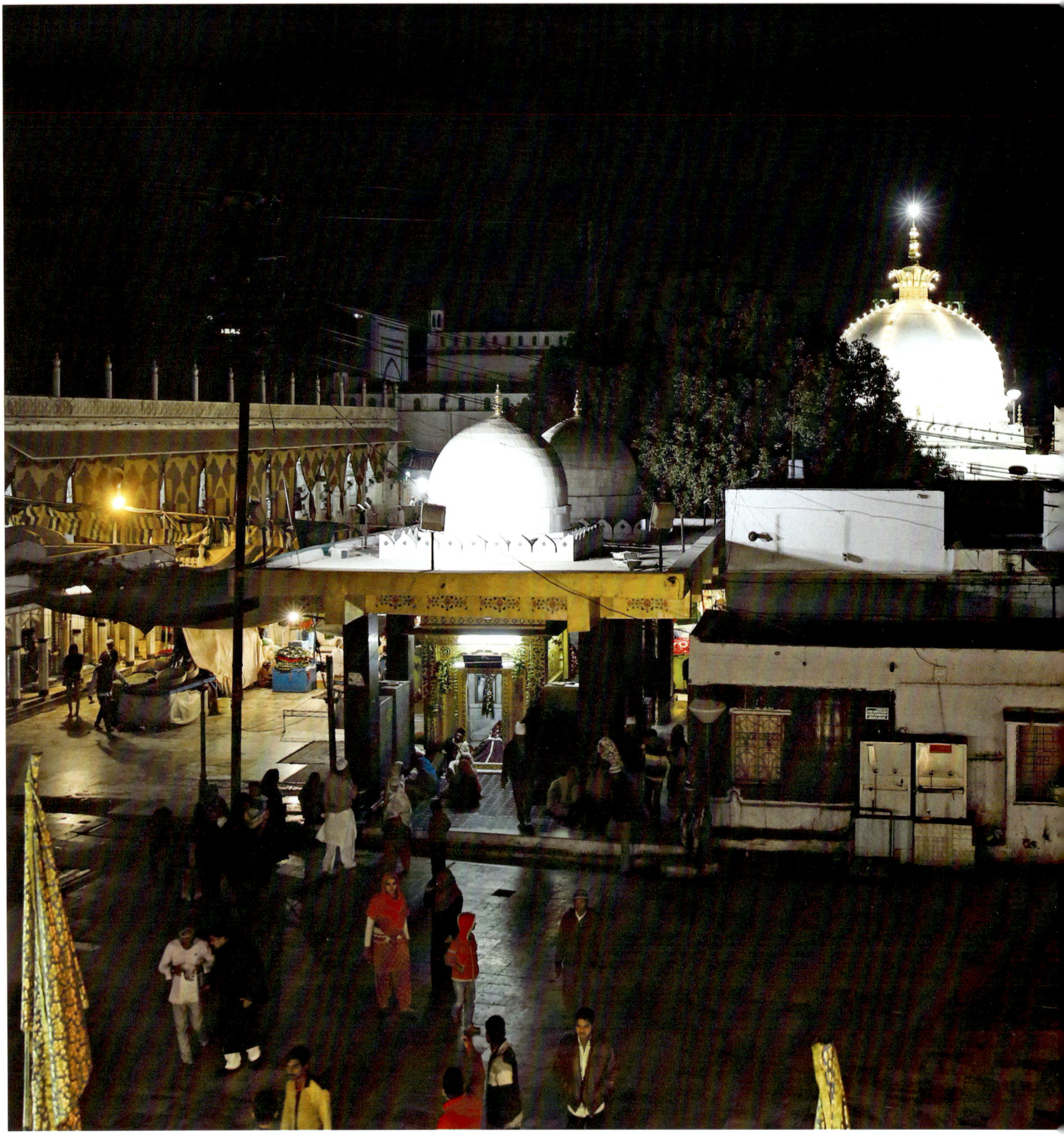

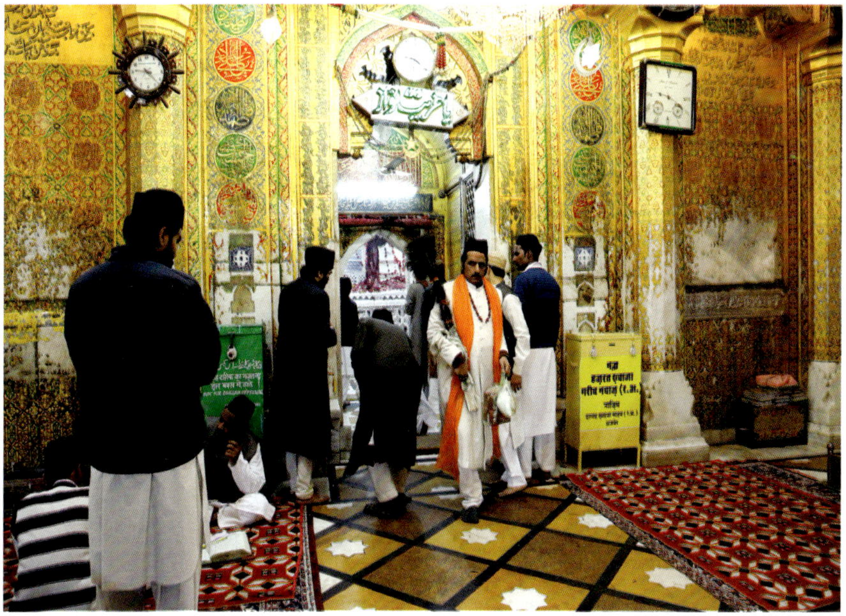

a synthesis of observations, not rationale and logic. The aim, then, was to rise over and above the temporal struggles around him. The tide of change in this land, a fight against Islamic and Hindu orthodoxy, had room for mystic dialogue.

Today, eight centuries on, after a star-soaked night, the Ajmer Dargah glistens at first light in ivory serenity. Archival records say that its topography of deference is mapped into four quarters and its monuments precede the downfall of the Delhi Sultanates, after which it stayed forsaken for many years.

Right: Poetry in stone around the tomb of the saint

Above left: A khadim guards the entrance to the Khwaja's tomb

Facing page: Radiand domes dispel the dark

Next page: The glistening courtyard of Akbari Mosque

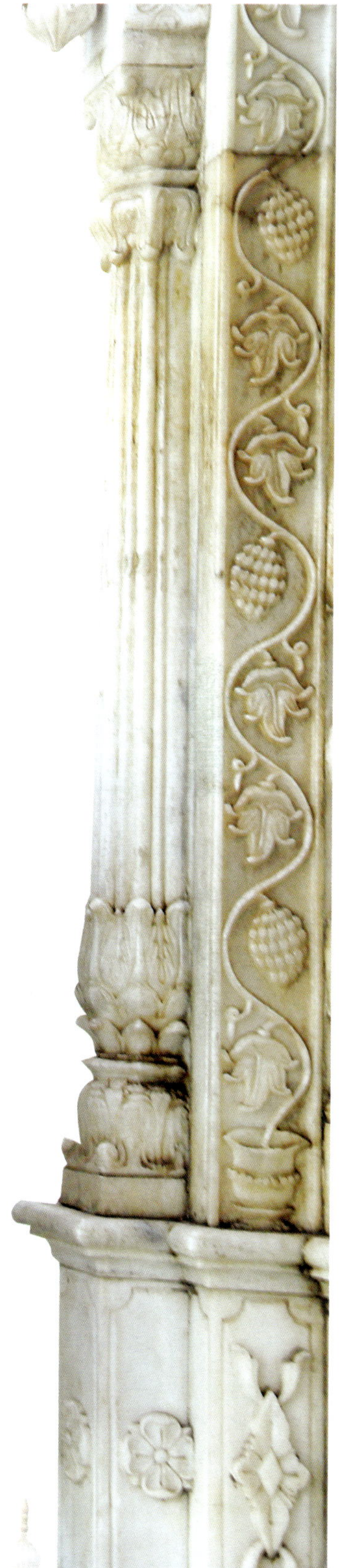

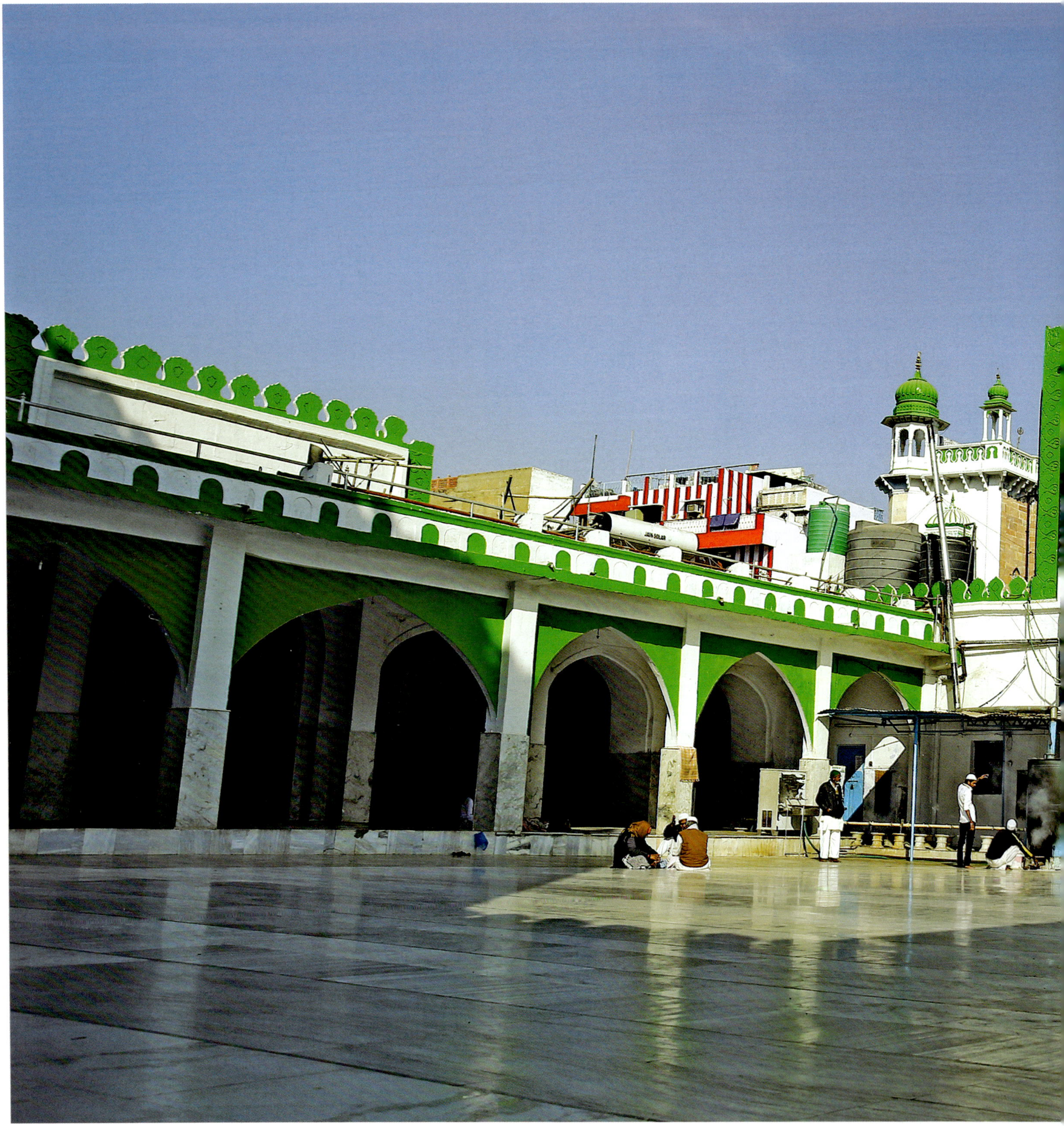
JAIN SOLAR

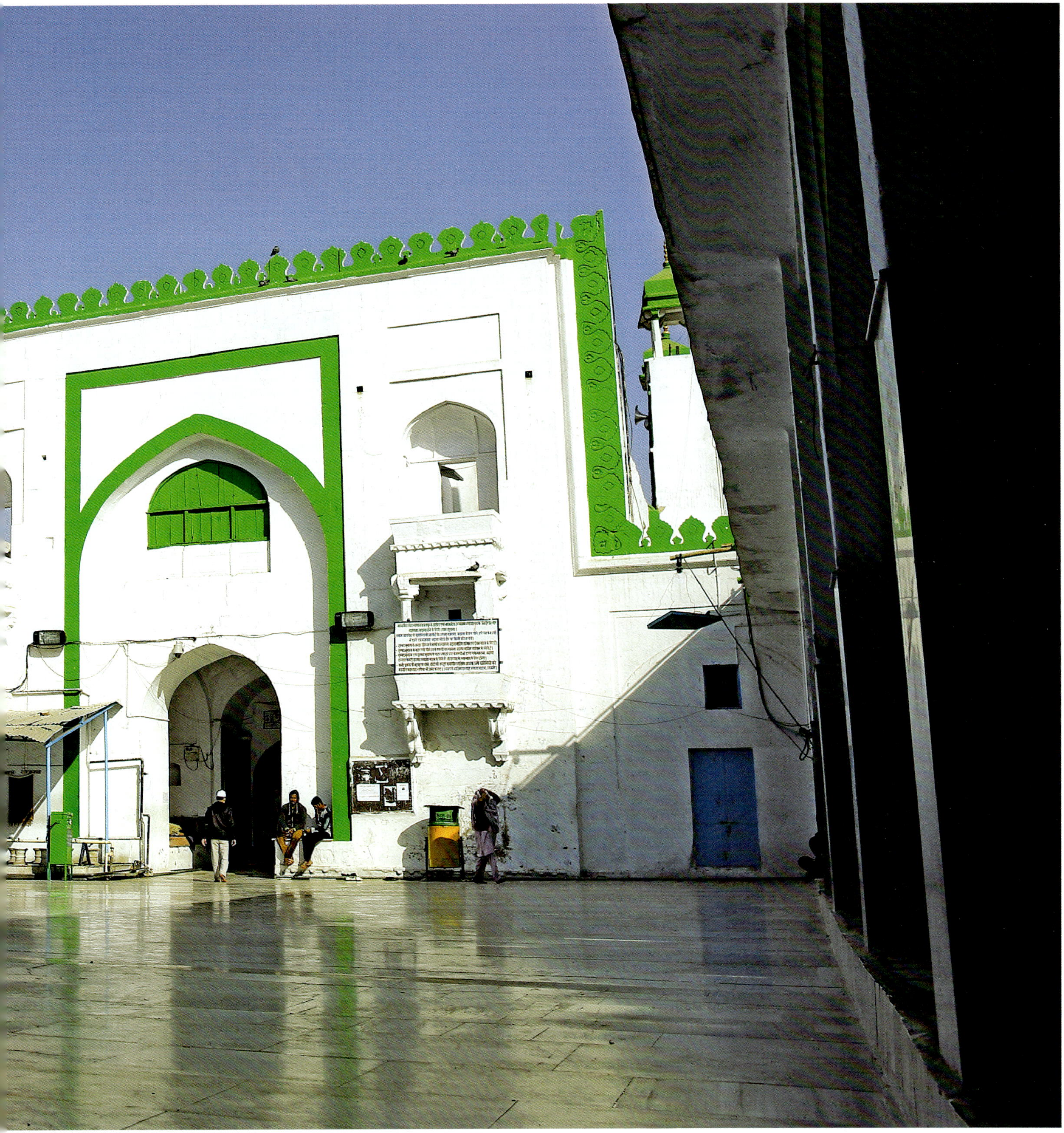

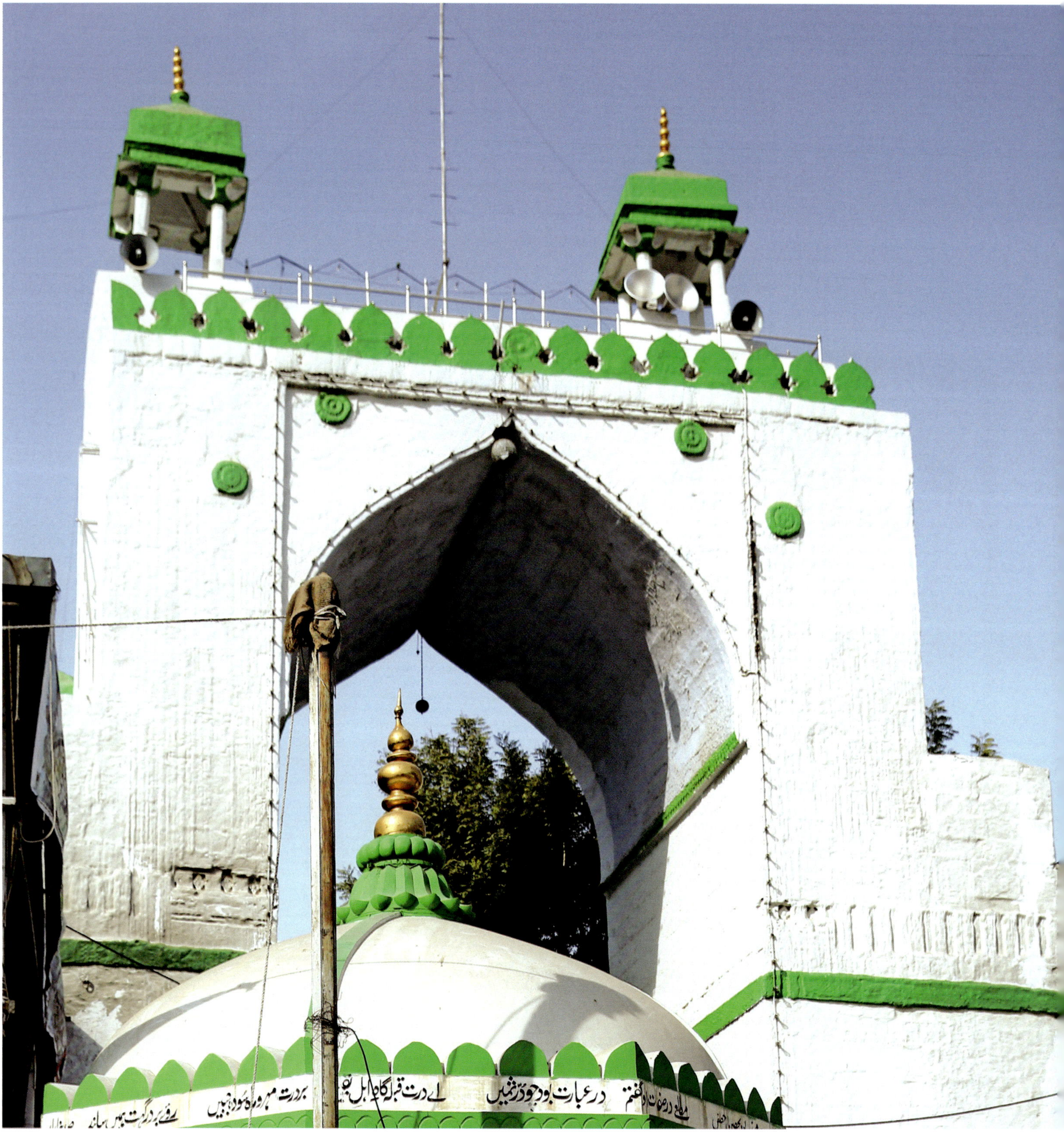

Inheritance of Belief

'The head must bend and the neck obey
For whatever a just prince does is right'
Abul Fazl, Akbarnama

As I cross the Osmani Gate, to the north of the expansive complex, is the Shahjahani or Kalima Gate. One halts for a few fleeting moments and a childhood memory whispers the precise moment when the Ajmer Shrine began to occupy my subconscious.

I recall the days when restrictions and caution were scarce. After spending some time in Delhi, my mother, on a scorching summer afternoon, had hailed a taxi on a whim and asked to be taken to Ajmer Sharif. This was neither the first nor the last time that she would give in to the impulse of traveling to Gharib Nawaz. Various images somersaulted in my mind as I crossed over from personal memory into imperial history.

The Mughal Prince, and later Emperor, Shahabuddin Shah Jahan, in keeping with the beliefs of his predecessors, was convinced that Dara Shikoh came to him as an answer to his prayers at this sanctified doorsill. His young prince too grew up to be a mystic thinker and an undeniably more favoured son.

Considered the foremost patron of Mughal architecture, Shah Jahan's structures were ceremonial and distant. He also made the first grand shift in material—filigreed marble took over from red brick.

In the 30 years that Shah Jahan held sway over Hindustan (1628 –1658 CE), he ventured five times to the Ajmer Sharif shrine. The first

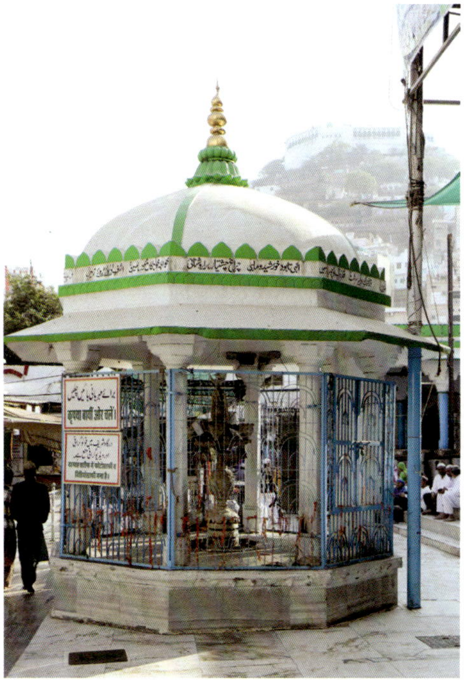

Above: Akbar's Sehan Chiragh (Lamp Terrace)

Facing page: The imposing Buland Darwaza, with its twin pavilions

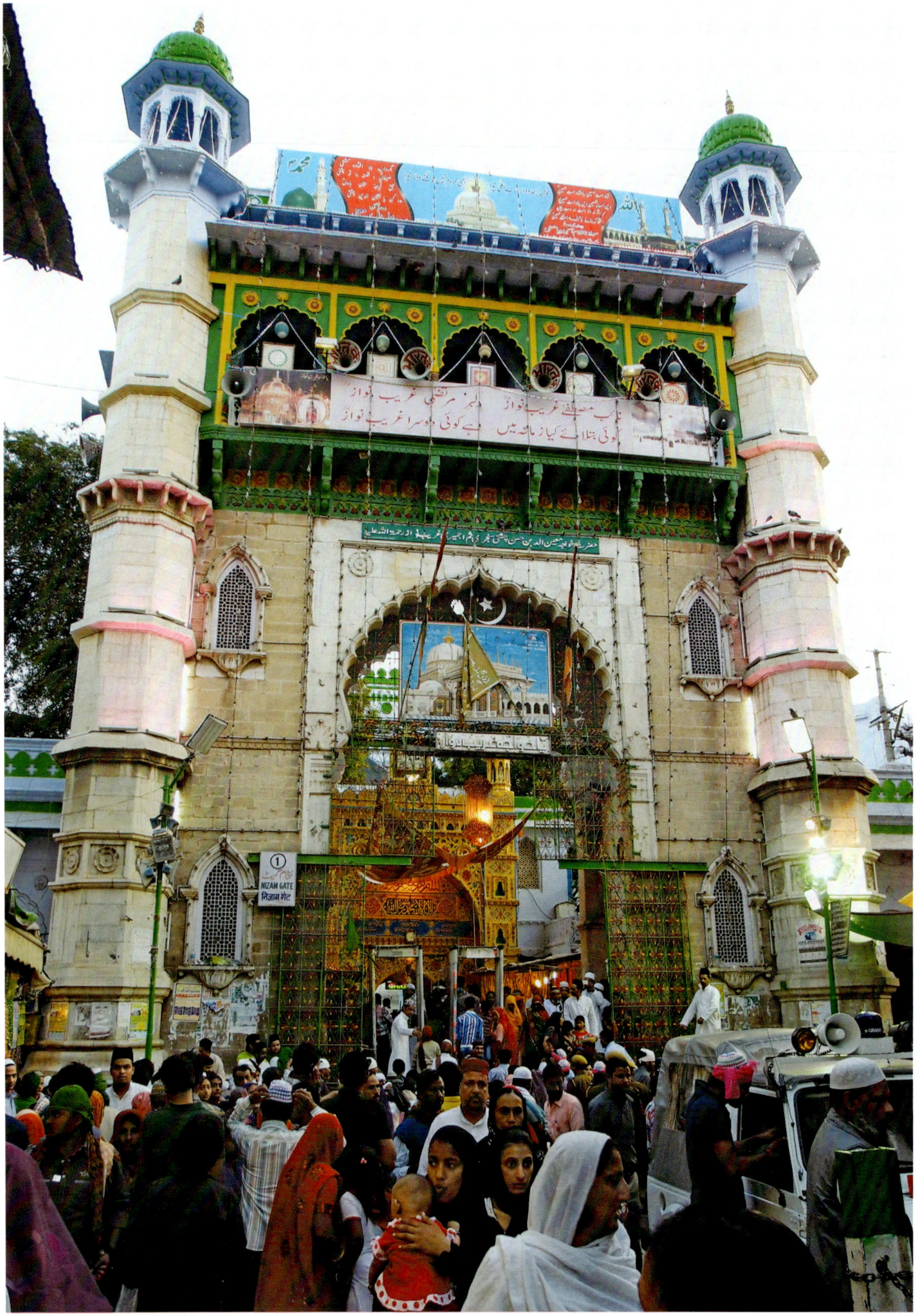

Grand gates lead into the shrine complex

homage is recorded in the first year of his rule. In the second instance, Shah Jahan and his caravan billetted down by the beatific Ana Sagar Lake; he walked to the mausoleum where he made a donation of 10,000 rupees, followed by prayers at the Akbari Masjid.

The monarch's third visit was on the insistence, and in the company, of his daughter, Jahanara. He was to perform these rites of devotion for a fourth time, also with Jahanara. Daulat Bagh, by the Evergreen Hill along the becalming channel, served as their resting place on that occasion. Shah Jahan's fifth journey on foot from Agra to Ajmer was his last. However, his imprints of everlasting mementos remain undimmed by eras, regimes, and the ravages of time.

The construction of the Shahjahani Gate began in 1654, during the Emperor's last arrival at the shrine, and was completed in 1655. Two drum pavilions (*chhatris*), crown both ends of its white marble trellis with the *kalima* and a Persian verse by Shah Jahan in silver.

In front of the tallest gate, the portal is the first point of entry into the mausoleum. Arced by a sharp parabola, it conforms to the design of the Buland Darwaza. Panelled in wood, with a granite floor dulled by age and footfalls, *naubat* brings it alive five times a day. Today's version of the entry is white with touches of pale aqua on the rims, corbels and lattice panes.

Akbar, after his victory over Bengal, bequeathed two *niqaare* or large drums, which were placed by this doorway. The beat of the largest, with a circumference of 10 feet, announced the ruler's arrival in the Chittor Fort; it was wrenched out of its home by the emperor. These, with eight others, were in red stone, now coated in stark lime. A small primeval enclave of the Unani Shafakhana (Herbal Clinic), stands before it, by the staircase of the grand Akbari Mosque.

In 1638 CE, the Shahjahani Mosque, west of the shrine, marked the sovereign's gratitude for his triumph over Udaipur. The edifice took nine long years to complete at the cost of 240,000 rupees. Easily the most

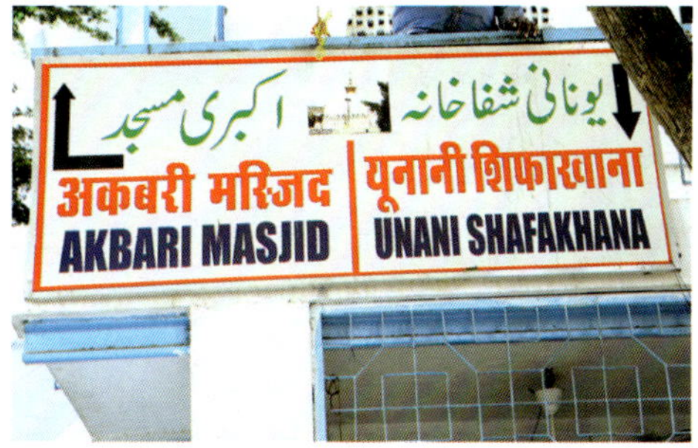

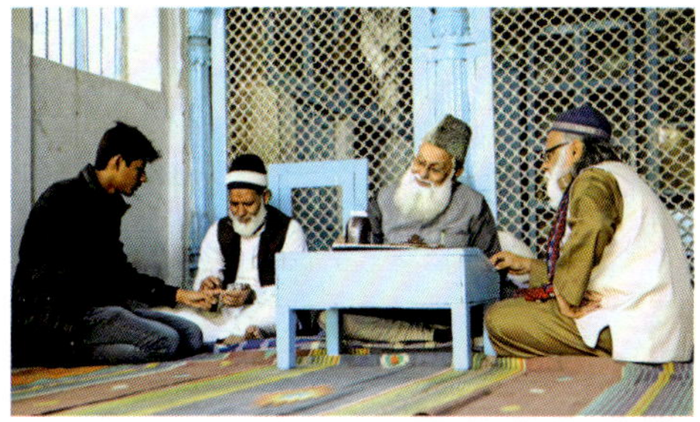

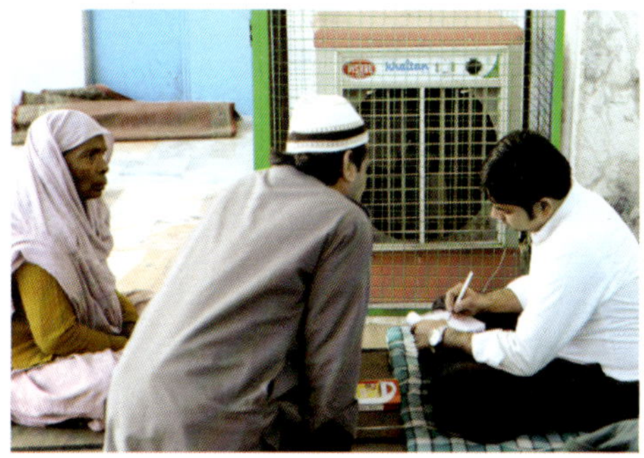

Top: Abodes of prayer and healing

Middle: Experienced physicians at the Unani Shafakhana

Above: Patients consulting a physician at the herbal clinic

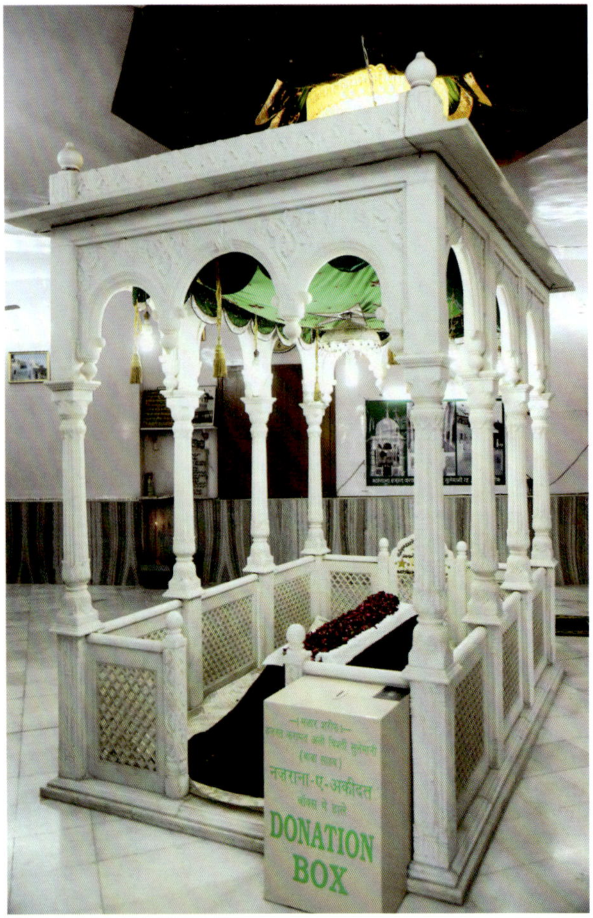

Tranquil tomb of a favoured one

intricate spot, carved entirely out of the finest alabaster from Makrana, the mosque is laid out in a rectangular frame—97 feet in length with a width of 67 feet. It has five entrances and two aisles of slender posts divide its space. The central *mihrab* (priest niche), in ornate gold and inlay, with net arcs, is deep-set in three cleaves or tripartite design. The inner ceiling is inscribed in silver with the *kalima*, and 99 names of God adorn the outer minarets.

The Shahjahani Mosque or Jama Masjid's 11 arches on slight berths shape its eastern facade, their corbels meeting in the centre. Under the top eaves is a detailed dedication from Shah Jahan, which also affirms the king's childhood intention to build a mosque at Ajmer Sharif. In this instance, such a detailed dedication on the exterior of a Mughal Mosque is unique. Interestingly, from here on, such epigraphs became an almost persistent feature in Shah Jahan's ensuing religious structures.

The monument is altogether unique, and different from other mosques due to the absence of a dome—an attempt by the king to ensure that the shrine remained a most pronounced feature. A four-gun salute resounds around it at specific moments during Friday prayers.

The Sola Khamba (Sixteen Pillars), is an imposing antiquated edifice with ornate workmanship of sharp, scalloped curves and towering colonnades in ageing alabaster. An intensely arcuated structure, cleaved and patterned borders supported by designed corbels comes into view as one crosses a diminutive, heavily painted entrance of spindly pillars and green arcs. Inside, in a chipped and worn enclosure in pale blue and green, lies the grave of Ahmed Bakhtiyar.

Revered by the custodians, Bakhtiyar was sent by Emperor Akbar to tend to the shrine. But he strayed, began to stake claim to Muinuddin's bloodline and misused donations. As word spread through Rajasthan, Akbar banished him into exile for more than two decades. Once forgiven, Bakhtiyar returned to live in Ajmer.

A decaying white dome in stone stamps Sola Khamba with the title of the Mausoleum of Shaikh Alauddin, an avid disciple who passed away here at 75. Alauddin is also honoured with a mention in Shah Jahan's decree.

The Chaaryaar (Four Companions Quarter), unfolds along the northern wall of the Shahjahani Mosque. A snug walkway cased in a plain stone arc runs to a pergola of sarcophagi. White, personal and minimal, it harbours many lives.

Forty Sufi elders who accompanied Muinuddin Chishti on his journey into Hindustan are interred in the verandah. Shaded by a bottle-green awning and trees, other graves here belong to devoted sages, dervishes, custodians, followers and scholars.

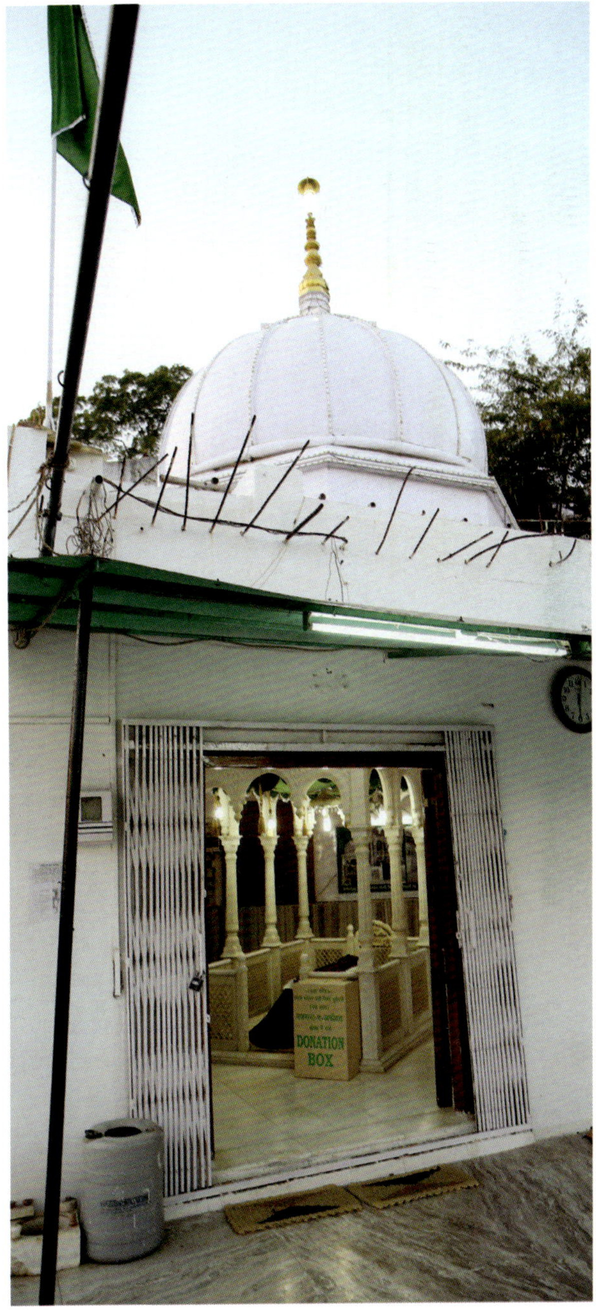

Right: A dome shelters a resting soul

Next page: Past the Door of Paradise, into the sanctum

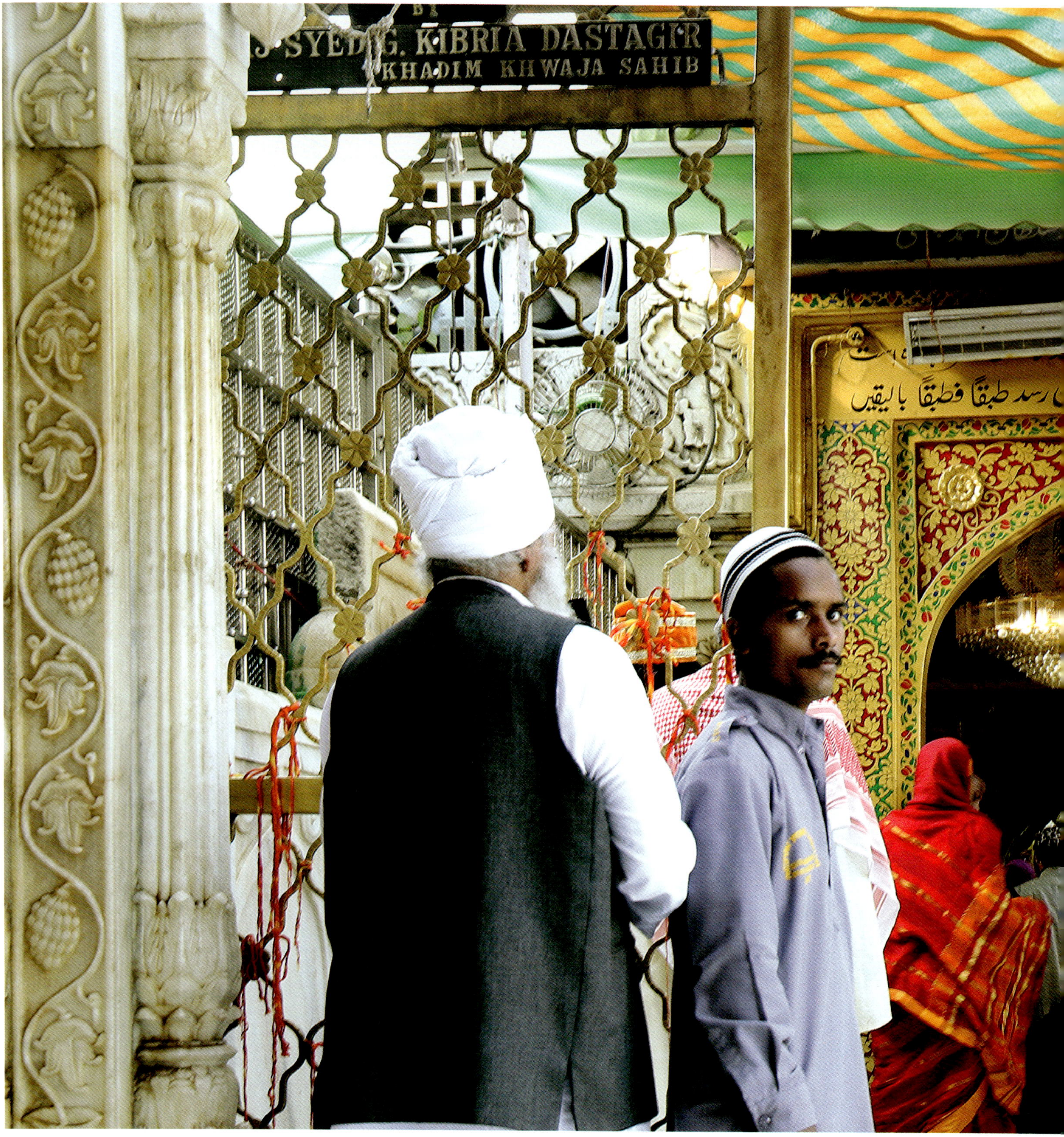
BY
SYED G. KIBRIA DASTAGIR
KHADIM KHWAJA SAHIB

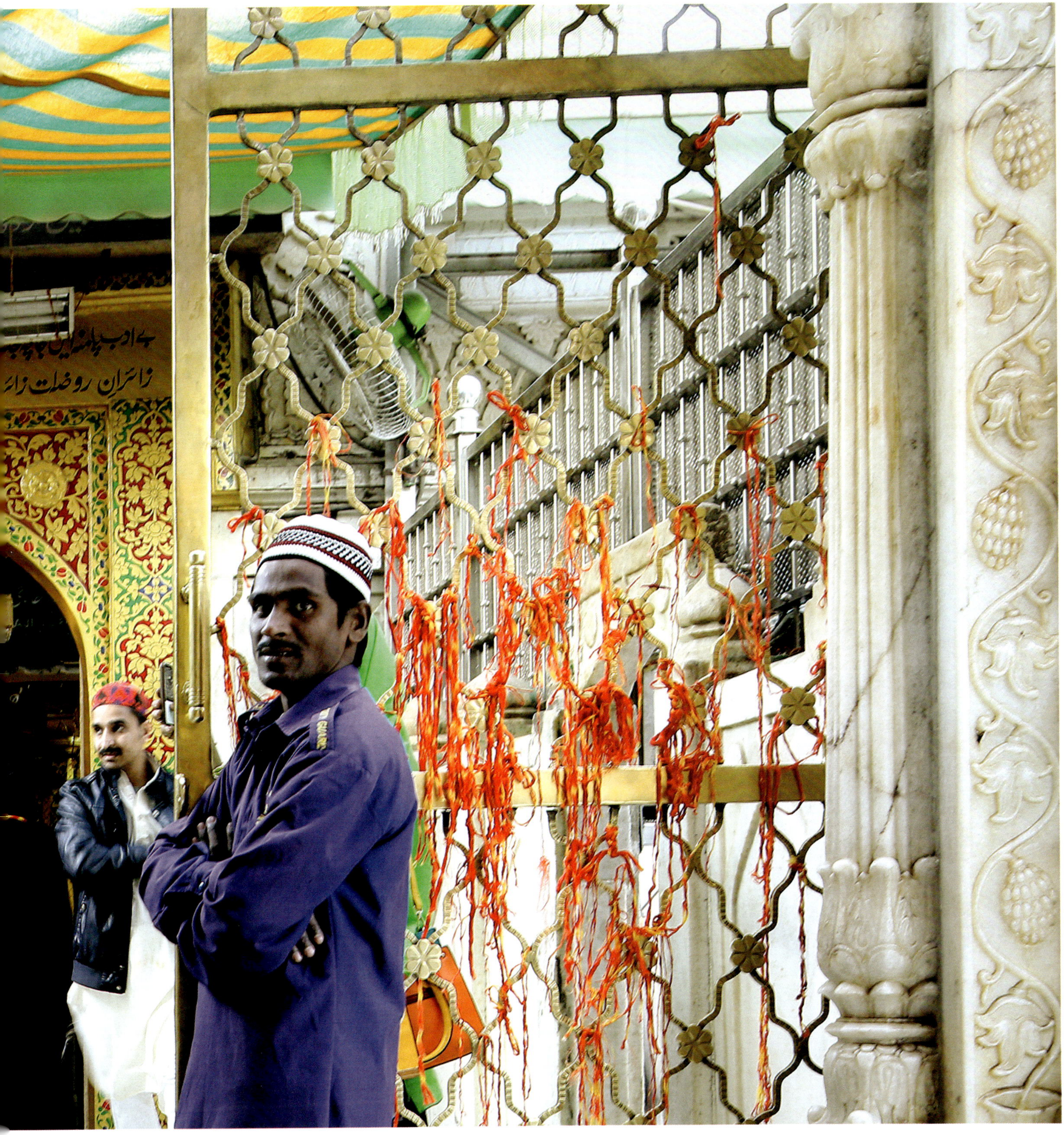

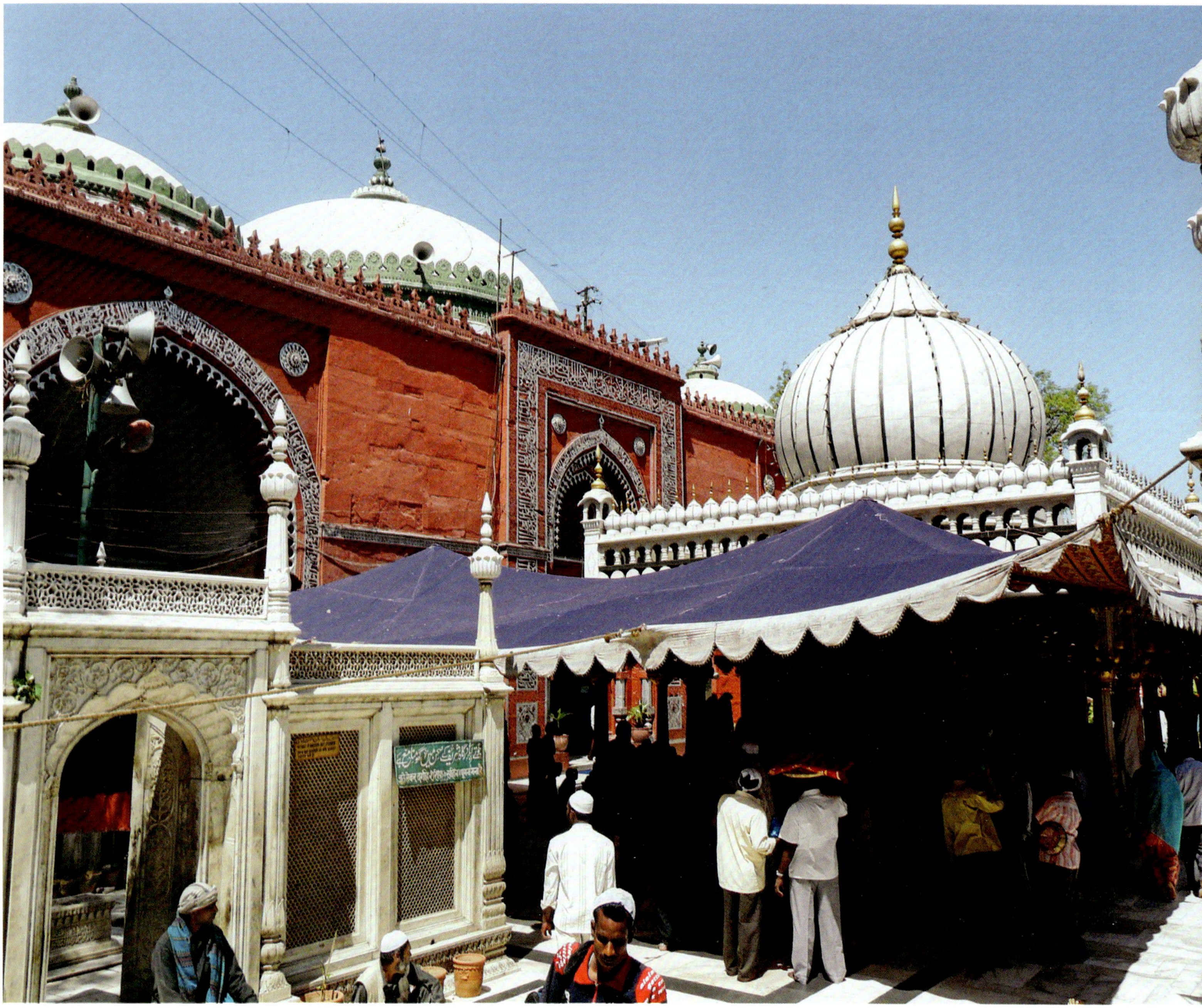

The Ascetic Princess
Jahanara

'He is the Living, the Sustaining.
Let no rich canopy cover my grave,
For this very grass suffices as a tomb cover for the poor.
The annihilated fakir Lady Jahanara,
The disciple of the lords of Chisht,
The daughter of Shah Jahan, the Warrior'
Epitaph, 1681 CE

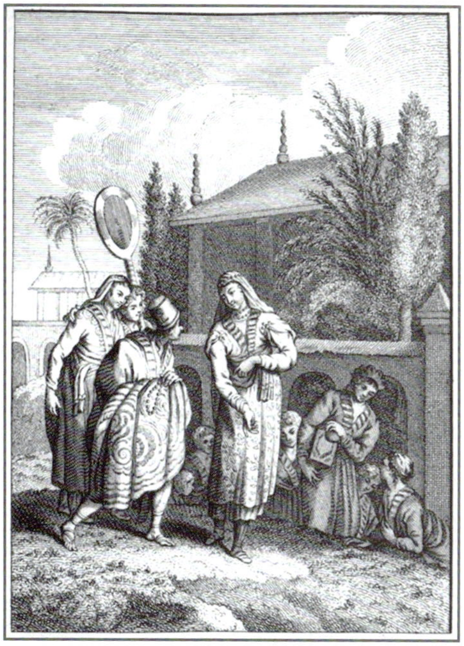

Shah Jahan's eldest daughter, Princess Jahanara was a devout follower of Muinuddin Chishti, who was her patron saint. In her biography of the saint, *Mu'nis al-Arwāḥ*, she refers to herself as *faqira*, to illustrate her own mystical calling as a Sufi. In the same chronicle, she also reminisces at length about her Sufi guide, Mulla Shah.

To her, Muinuddin was the supreme saint of Hindustan, and the master who brought her into the Chishti fold, four centuries after he breathed his last. In 1643 CE, the princess came on her first visit to the shrine, which coincided with the saint's birthday.

She says in *The Confidant of Spirits* by Carl W. Ernst:

> *I went to the holy sanctuary and rubbed my pale face on the dust of the threshold. From the doorway to the blessed tomb I went barefoot, kissing the ground.*
>
> *Having entered the dome, I went around the light-filled tomb of my master seven times, sweeping it with my eyelashes, and making the sweet smelling dust of that place, the mascara of my eyes.*

Above: Princess Jahanara depicted in an 18th-century text

Facing Page: Princess Jahanara's tomb (left foreground) at Nizamuddin Dargah complex, Delhi. Also seen are Nizamuddin Auliya's tomb (right) and Jamaat Khana Masjid in the background

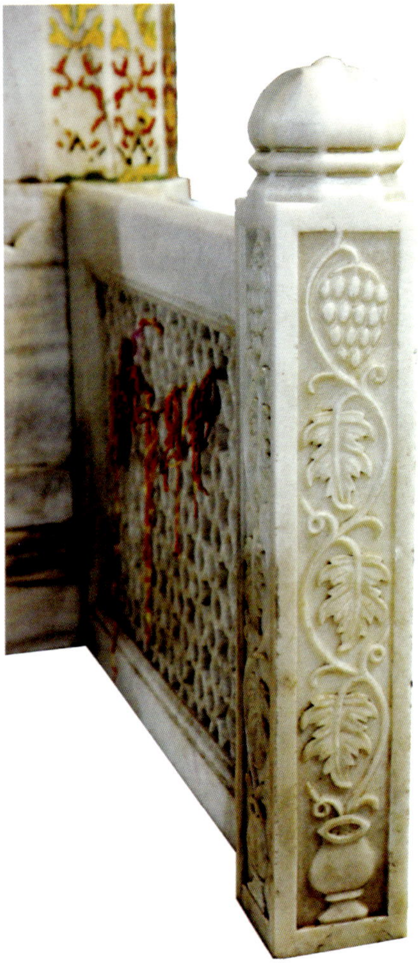

The marble legacy of Jahanara

Jahanara, in other chronicles, says that through the course of her first ride to the saint, she halted her caravan to pay her respects at each post. Perhaps she refers to the stone *kos minar*s, milestones of the Mughals, which marked the route from Delhi and Agra.

She stayed at the pavilion built by her father along the shores of the Ana Sagar Lake in Ajmer; slept on its bare, cold floor, not on the customary leopard skin, and never turned her back towards the mausoleum.

Jahanara spent her hours in meditation at the cavern dedicated by Khwaja Muinuddin to his cousin, an exalted saint and founder of the Qadiria Order, Abdul Qadir Shah Gilani. An hour before sunrise, she took the path to her spiritual nucleus. In the sanctum, she made seven rounds of the cenotaph; her tresses and lashes swept its ground; she smeared essence on the crypt and laid her own rose scarf over it.

After her dusk prayer at the Shahjahani Mosque, she returned to the sanctum's threshold to recite devotional verses. With the mythical waters of Jhalra spring and a lament in her heart, the princess broke her fast. Jahanara confessed that had she been unfettered, her remaining years would have passed at Khwaja's abode as a *faqira*. Her devotion knows no better description than the one in her own words:

'The Beloved has placed a noose on my neck,
And he pulls me wherever he wishes.'

After donating the present fence around the sage's tomb, Begami Dalaan (The Princess Courtyard) was Jahanara's second bequest in 1643.

The verandah wears a silver sheen in the shadow of the magnificent dome, and sprawls out before the Light Quarter, on the eastern side. Its lofty, bevelled columns in white onyx stand on a vast marble carpet. Pristine and intricate, arched passageways in white lead to it from two sides—beneath a pearly archway, the checkered arcade of the main entry stretches to the south. Two marble-trellised casements of Bibi Hafiza Jamal's chamber, with motifs, under a finely cut, patterned border, face this terrace.

The plateau's cover was etched by Nawab Mushtaq Ali Khan of Rampur; each rosebud in the design is said to be dedicated to a person. In 1948, Nawab Ghulam Kibria (Jalpaiguri, Bengal) undertook the renovation of a section of its decaying roof. The oldest Moulsari tree (*Mimusops elengi*) in the complex also spreads over a large portion of the platform.

Stories are strewn all over—on epitaphs, edifices, in eyes, and creased foreheads. In the tight grips on railings, in the twirls of the consumed and the abandon of the tousled. All lore of annihilated egos.

Shah Jahan's daughter, Hurun Nisa, succumbed to smallpox in 1616 and is buried on one side in a tight chamber, with a small white dome and a pane in marble lattice, in a side wall. Its access is rich with ornate silver panels. The Mughal Emperor Jahangir's most beloved grandchild Hurun Nisa's commitment to the mystic giant was honoured by him. He ordained that she be buried beside the western wall of the saint's sanctum.

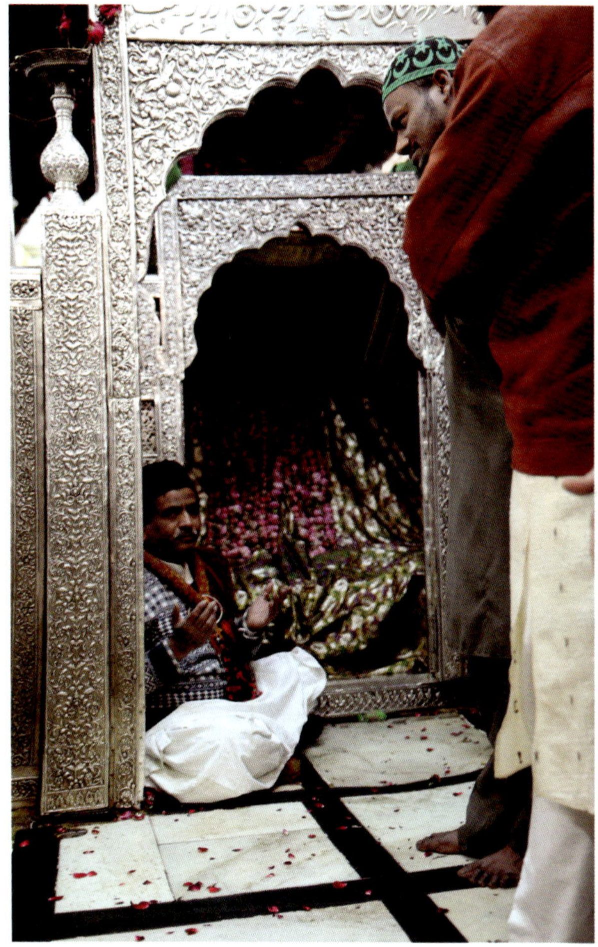

Above: Shah Jahan's younger daughter Hurun Nisa's silver-panelled enclave

Next page: The sun rises where peace reigns supreme

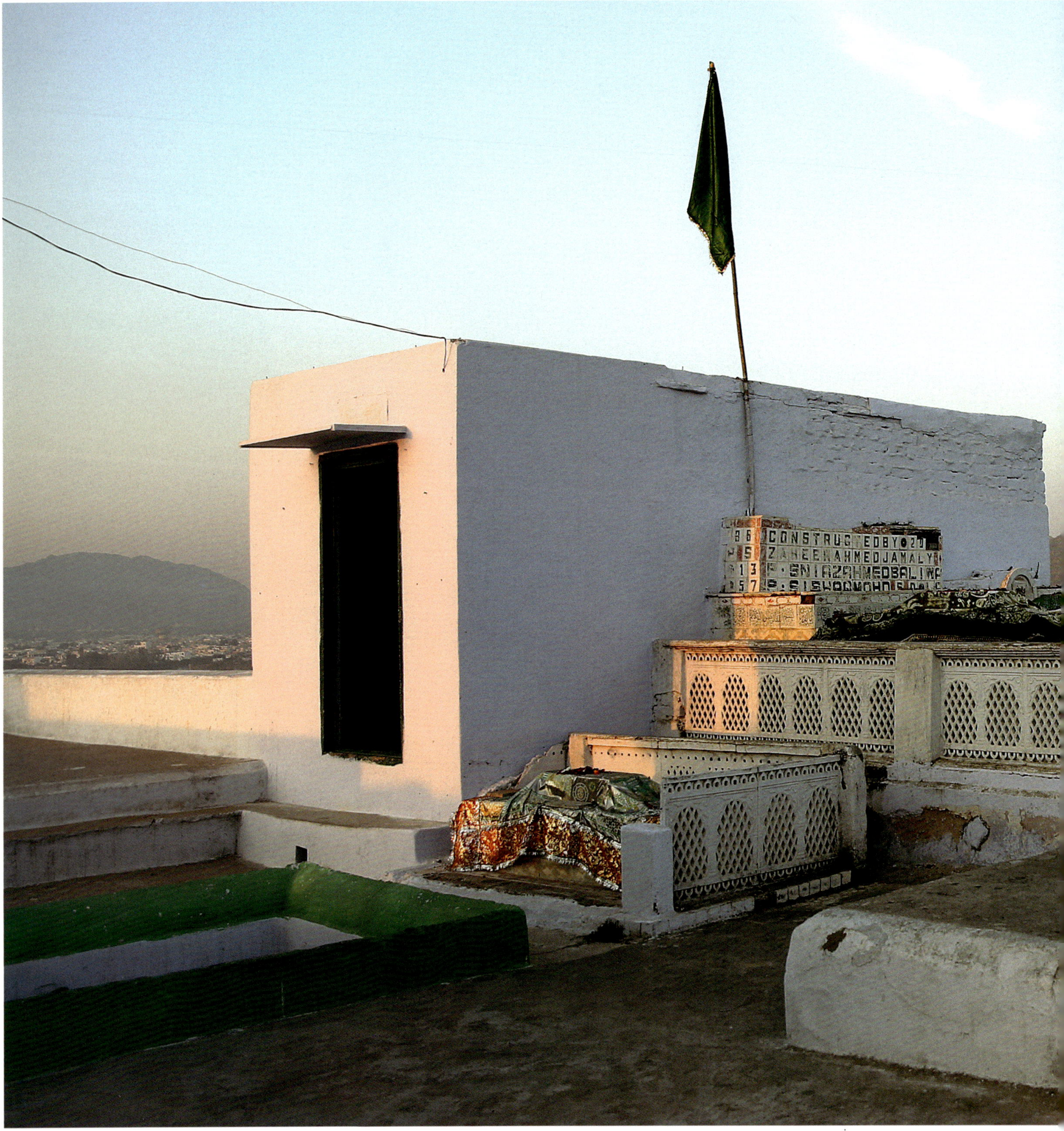

36 CONSTRUC EDBY 20
5 ZAHEERAHMEDJAMALY
13 F. SNIAZAHMEDBALIWA

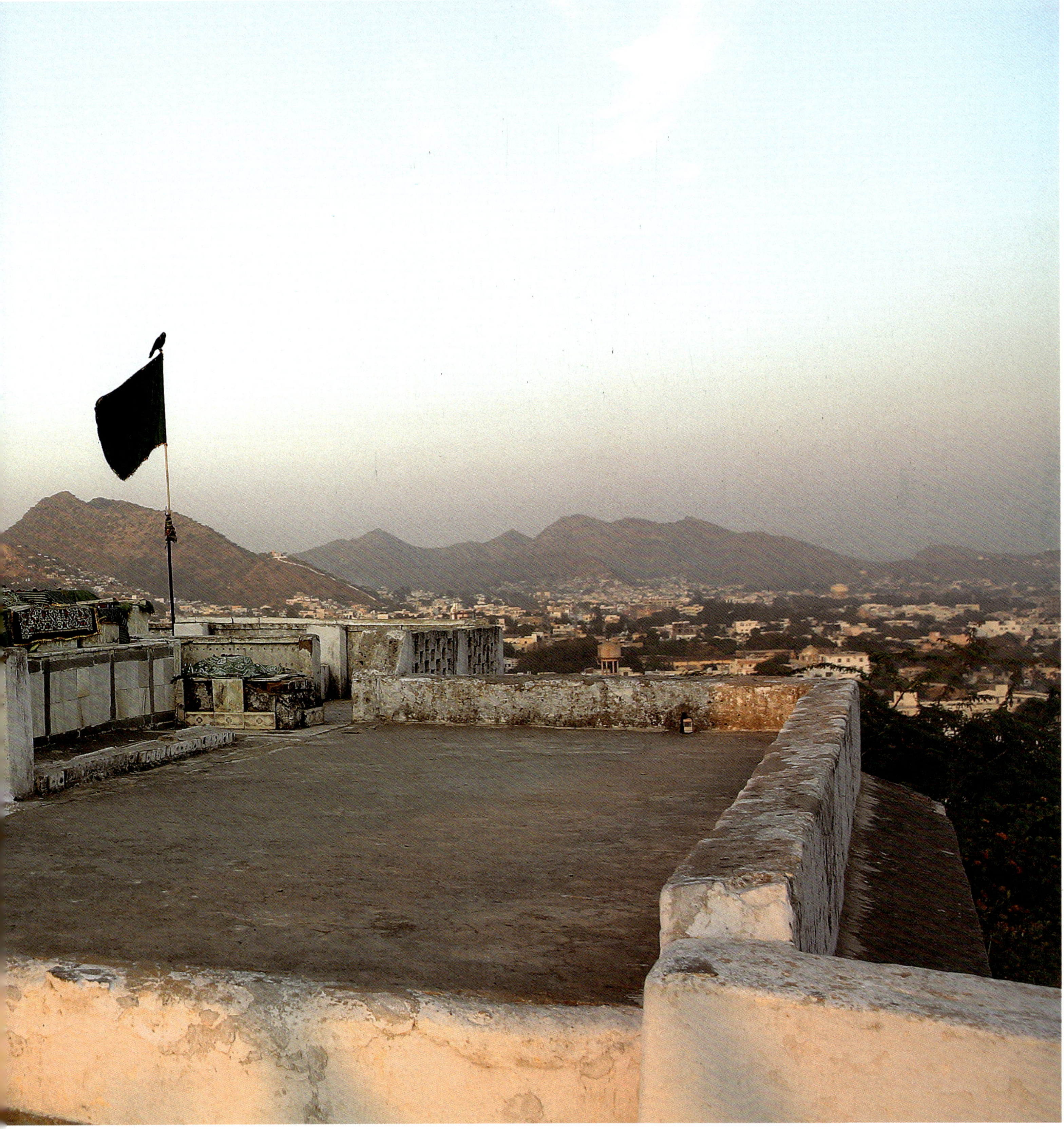

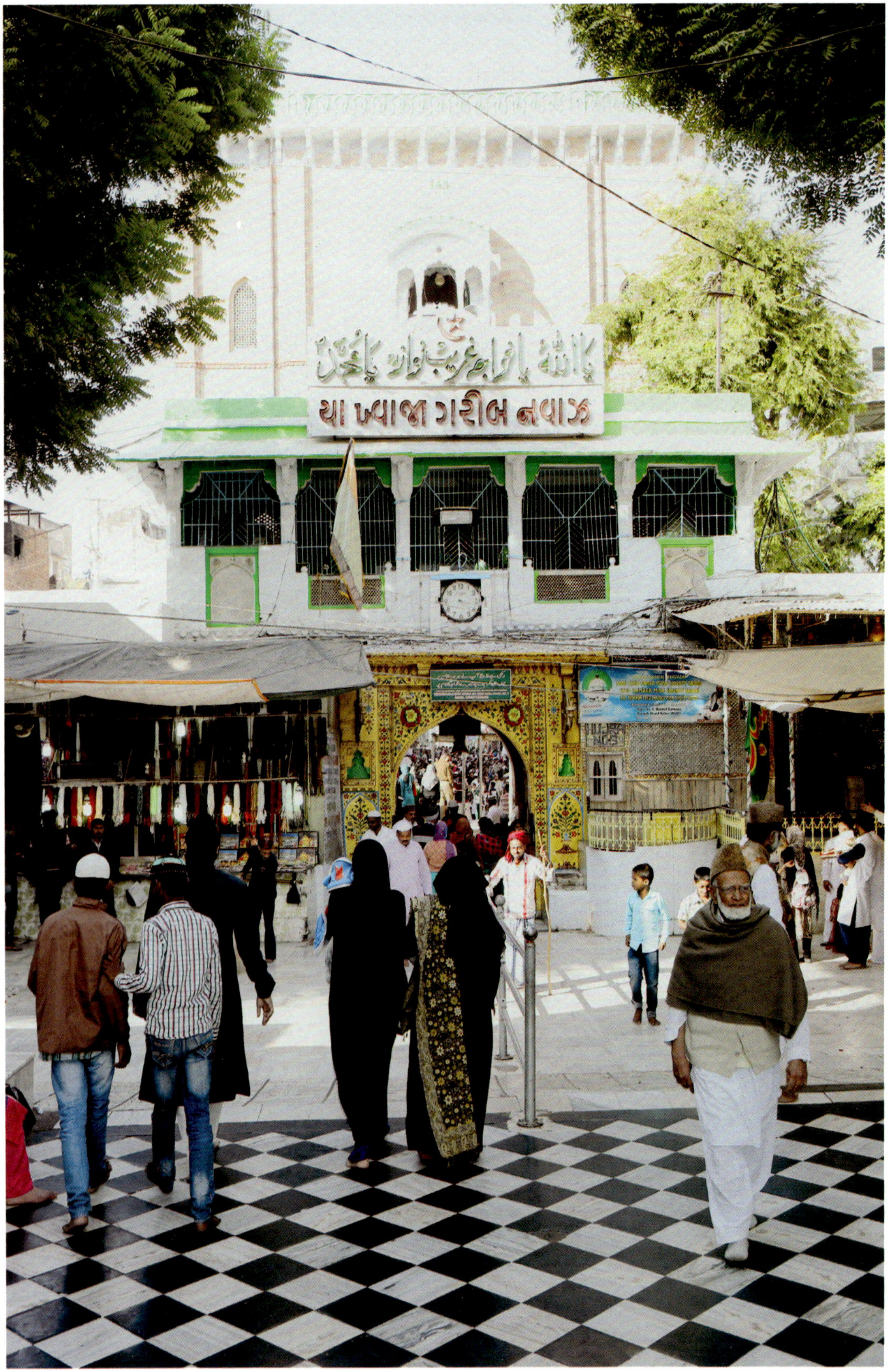

Pilgrims pass through
the Chattri Darwaza
to the Begami Dalaan

Tosha Khaana (Treasure Alcoves)

A striking, flamboyant cellar door opens into two rooms overlooking the Begami Courtyard. While one holds the daily ritual fare; precious, historical ornaments, including *Farmaan-e-Shahjahan* (Shahjahan's Declaration) aired on annual celebrations, lie in the other. This small door has seven locks, each belonging to one of the seven custodians.

The Princess Courtyard, the third patio, is passed through the Chhatri Darwaza (Pavilion Door). A smaller access, surrounded by cubicles of custodians, is now maintained with black polished stone on the pillars and a new floor of black and white mosaic. The entryway closes in the evening except on the festival of Urs. However, its panels stay open into the night.

Time has seen the Chhatri Darwaza expand in size and grandeur; its floor concealed with carpets as chandeliers brighten new gloss. Funerals and mourning ceremonies of keepers' families are carried out at this gate. Small memorials rest on either side of the Khirki Darwaza (the Skylight Door). The forecourt holds the grave of Shaikh Mir, slain by Aurangzeb Alamgir's forces at Taragarh Fort.

Beside him is a famed soldier, Shahnawaz Khan, killed by Dara Shikoh's army.

The two combatants in elegant crypts of untarnished granite, were interred in the ground here on Alamgir's directives.

Hameedia Courtyard unfurls between this approach and the Begami Dalaan. Lustrous in marble, an archway of inlaid onyx frames the entrance; flower vendors' baskets heaped with yellow and red petals tint it with flashes of ebullience. The inner arcs and pillars are now edged with

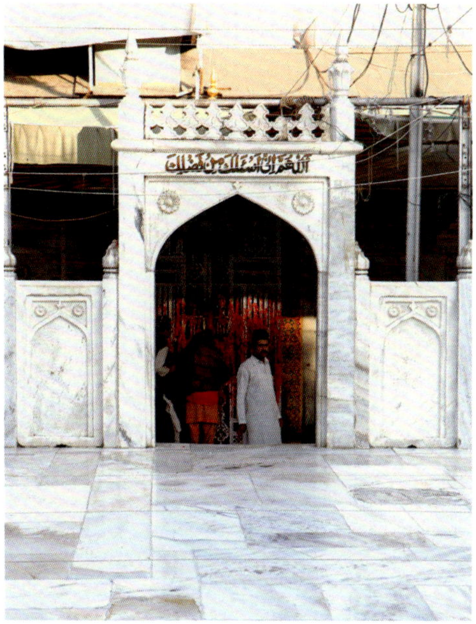

The marble purity of the Kalima Gate

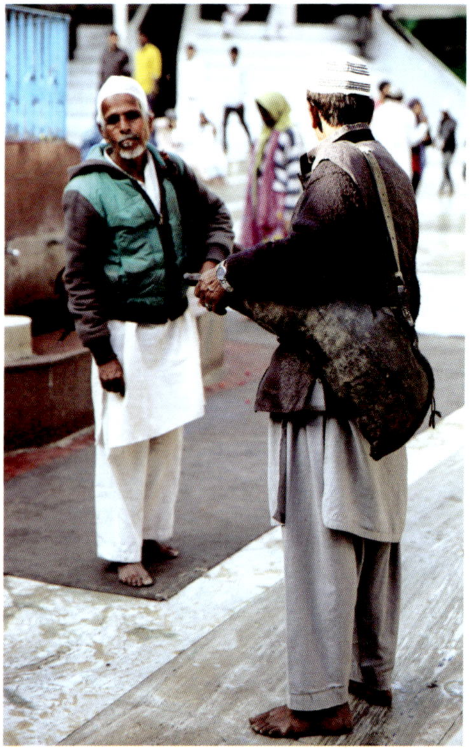

shades of blues and emerald. In the soft hours before the sun sinks, an ancient tree, Jahanian Jahan Gasht Darakht, casts wide, circling shadows over the courtyard.

Many narrow, pointed lamp-stands in pale stone dot the terrace. Stained by soot, miniature oil lamp niches run in circular rungs across their length. The porch fills with women during the *Punjshamba* (fifth evening or night) ceremony.

On a marble pier, near Hameedia Courtyard, encircled by a lattice fence and edged with fine filigree is Nizam Saqqa's grave. A water carrier during the reign of the Emperor Humayun, legend has it that once, as Saqqa filled his bag made of animal skin with the waters of the Yamuna, he heard cries for help. Saqqa looked up to see a man drowning in the choppy river. The hapless mortal was none other than Emperor Humayun, who was waging a war against Sher Shah Suri. Saqqa inflated his bag with air and helped the Emperor float across the river using it as a flotation apparatus.

After his triumph, Humayun summoned Saqqa and asked him about his preferred reward for saving a king's life. The water carrier requested to rule Hindustan for one day. His wish was granted and Nizam Saqqa, the water man went down in history as ruler of India for a day. Small wonder then, that this, after the saint's sanctum, is the most venerated place for the Bahishti (Water Carrier) community.

Above: Dargah Bahisti's or water carriers

Below: Sabeel Sanjari, where the shrine's water carriers fill their sacks, in the Jasmine Courtyard

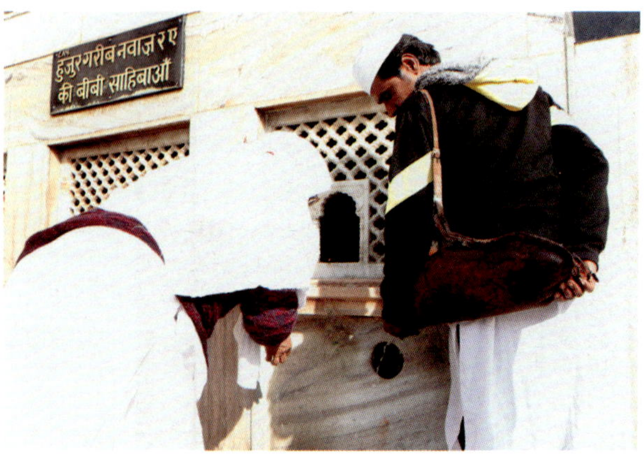

The book *Ageless Mind and Spirit* records a conversation with one of Saqqa's last descendants.

'We have descended from Nizam Sattar, the bhishti (traditional water carrier) who had rescued Mughal emperor Humayun from drowning while crossing a river. Humayun was fleeing from a battle and his horse sank under the weight of the armour it was wearing. Nizam, who was collecting water, inflated his mashaq (waterbag) with air to rescue the drowning emperor. He was later rewarded by being made the emperor of India for six hours and he commemorated his short tenure by issuing special coins made of leather instead of silver, as was the norm in those days.

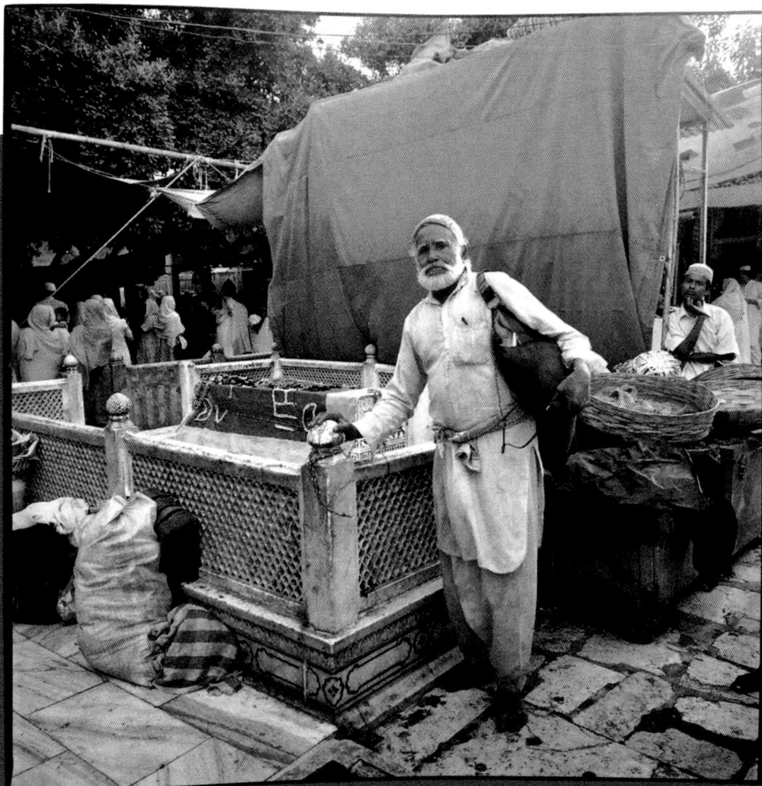

Hafeez Abbasi, last of the bhishtis, born in Ajmer, 1921, standing next to the tomb of the water carrier who saved the Mughal Empire.

Our mashaqs are made of goat skin and can hold up to 40 litres of water. We have been pursuing this line of work for generations and I don't find it hard at my age because I have been doing this since the age of 12. As long as there is life in my body, I will continue. At one time in India, we were the most important water suppliers for people living away from water sources, but then with the coming of pipelines and water tankers, our utility was totally finished. It is only in dargahs and mosques that you will still find us working.

I have five children who are all married. There is not enough of this type of work and the earnings are low, so my children have opted for other professions like furniture-making or welding. They help me out by taking turns on holidays. Thus we ensure that someone is doing this duty each day of the year.

I make an average of Rs 40 to 50 daily, but earnings are always fluctuating. If we make Rs 500 on some days during Urs festivities, we may go home with Rs 25 on other days. The langar (communal meal) at the dargah is what sustains us at all times.'

(Text by Vijay Jodha, Photograph by Samar S. Jodha)

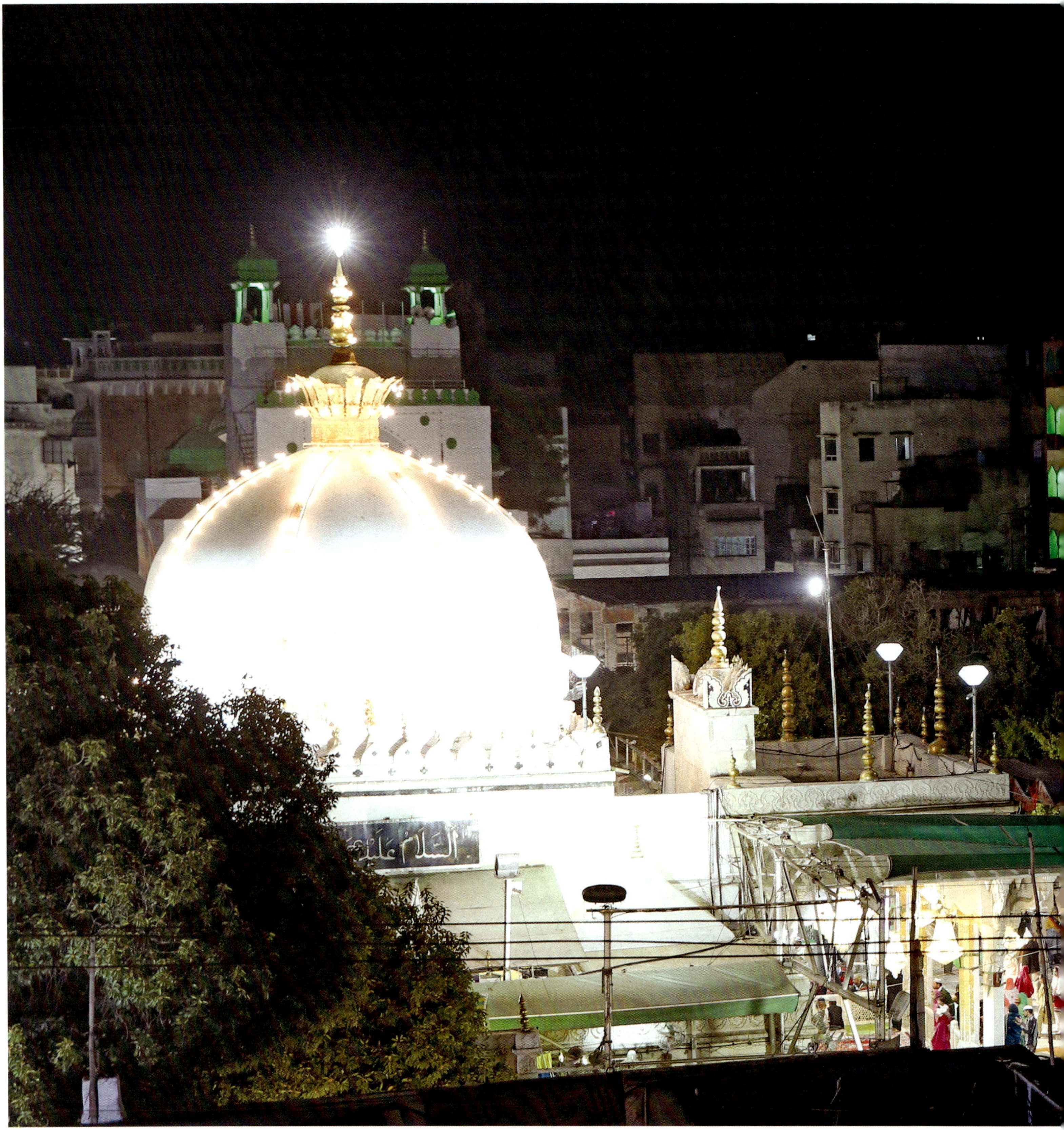

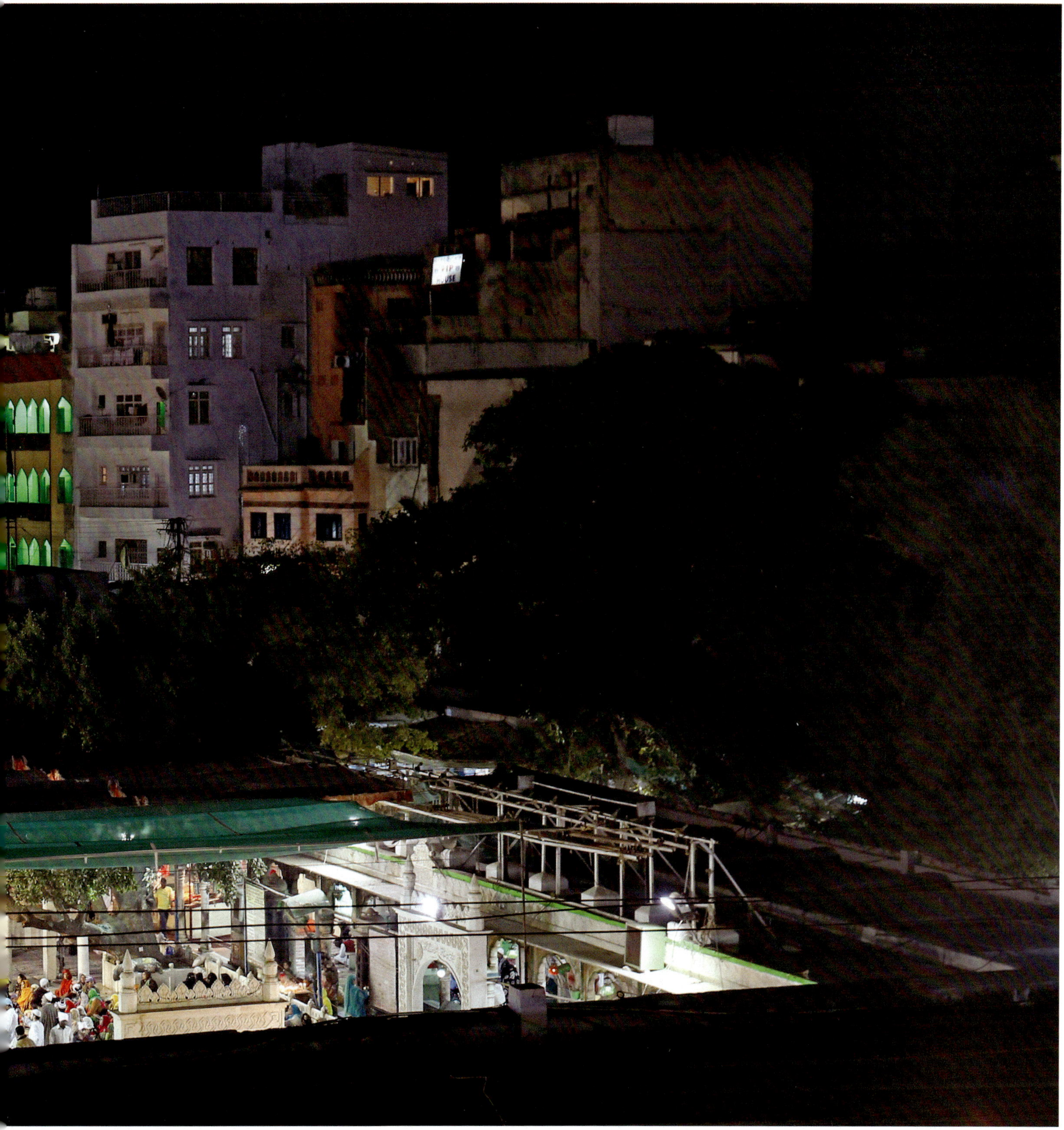

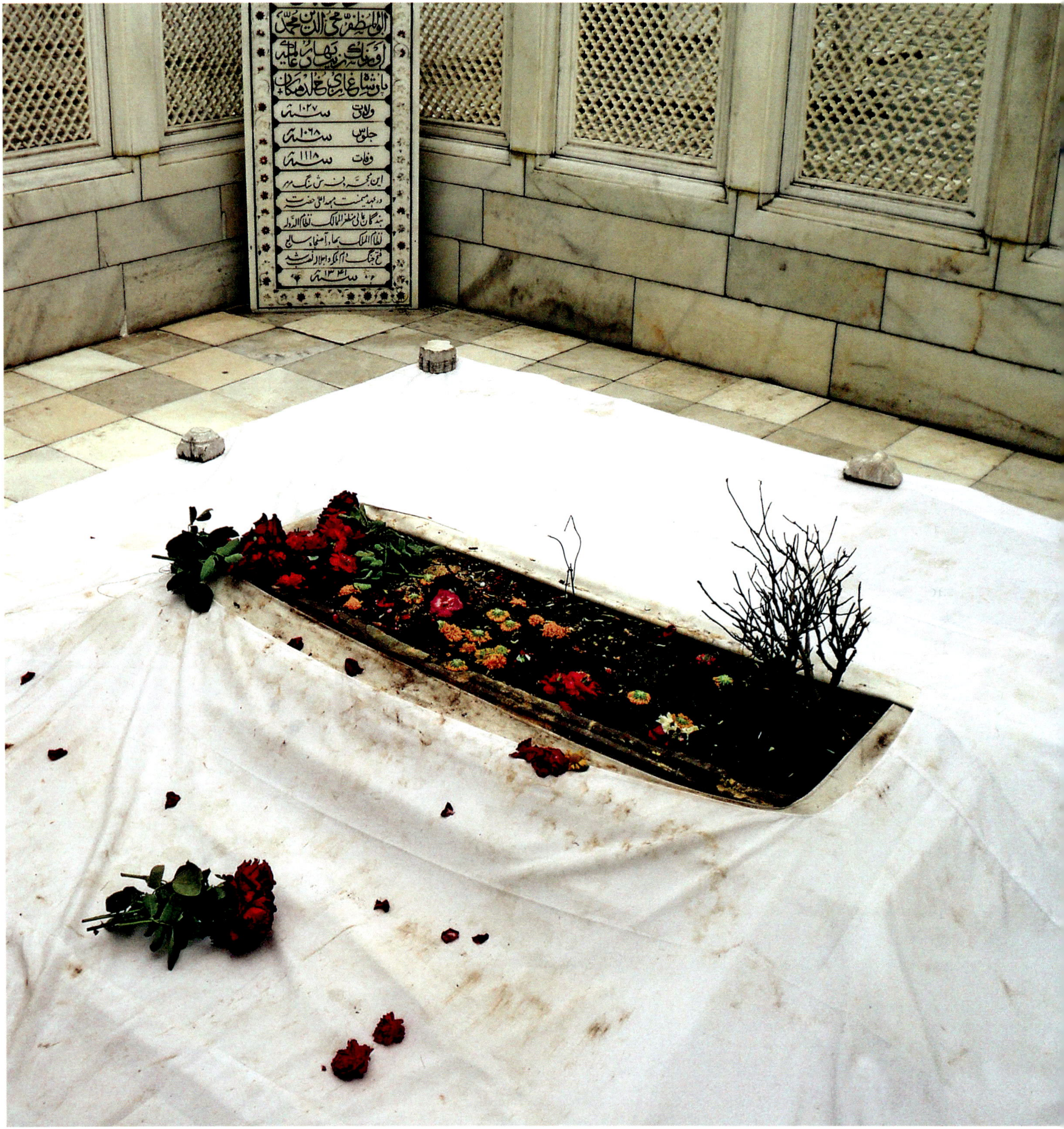
ابوالمظفر محی الدین محمد
اورنگ زیب بهادر عالمگیر
بادشاه غازی خلد مکان
ولادت سنه ۱۰۲۷
جلوس سنه ۱۰۶۸
وفات سنه ۱۱۱۸

An Orthodox King at a Mystic's Door

'A foreigner I came into this world and a foreigner I leave it. The moment which passed in power has only left sorrow. I did not become the guardian and protector of the empire. My time has been spent in vain...'

From Alamgir's letter to Azim, his son.

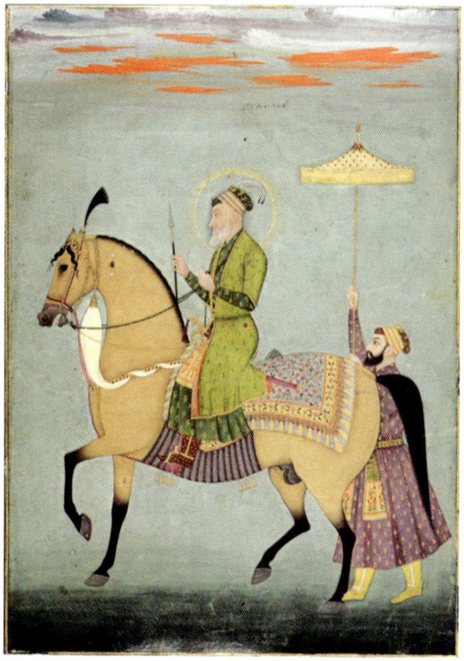

Above: Emperor Aurangzeb on horseback (ca. 1690–1710)

Facing Page: Aurangzeb's tomb, Khuldabad, in the courtyard of the Sufi shrine of Shaikh Burhanuddin Gharib Chisti

Previous page: Peace radiates from the luminous dome

Abul Muzaffar Muhi-ud-Din Mohammad Aurangzeb Alamgir (lived 1618–1707 CE; ruled 1658–1707 CE) could hardly resist the auspicious trail traversed by his ancestors and siblings. A rigid adherent of Islamic law, sadly his first step on Muinuddin's ground, was after he executed his brother, Dara Shikoh in 1659 CE.

He too marched on foot to the sage, and on one of his visits, according to *Seeratul Muin*, donated 5,000 rupees to custodians in appreciation of a qawwali recital. An annulment of his embargo on music in the shrine also followed the orthodox monarch's visit.

In 1469 CE, following Sultan Shahabuddin Khilji's visit to the humble shrine, Sultan Ghiyasuddin Khilji constructed the Sandal Khana Mosque by the side of the headstone and other monuments. Khilji's tribute after his victory over Ajmer, was the modest, three-door Mehmoodi Mosque. Later, Alamgir restored and expanded the ancient site, adding space and splendour. Alamgir added four doorways to the Sandal Mosque. It then became known as Alamgiri Mosque. Hence, centuries after Khilji's original three-door place of worship, it has seven entries to the present day.

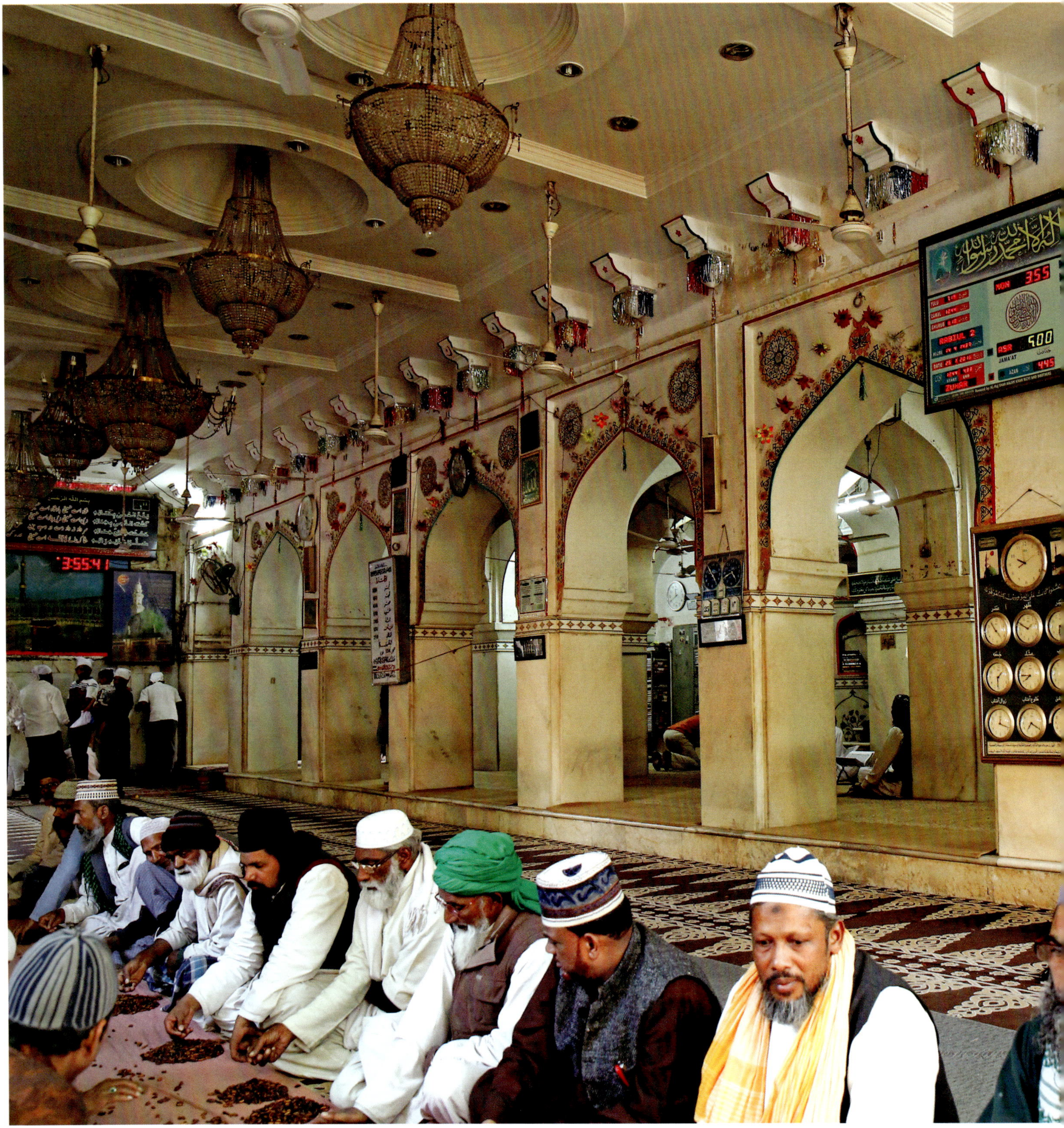

3:55:41
MON 355
RABIUL 2
ASR 500

After Aurangzeb's earliest appearance at the shrine, he paid homage at Muinuddin's doorsill on another three occasions; the last to commemorate his victory over Udaipur.

In 1897 CE, Nawab Mohammad Ishaq Khan Jehangirabad spent an estimated 5,000 rupees to refurbish the Sandal Mosque, associated with powerful monarchs and their reigns. In its present avatar, it is also remembered as Masjid Phoolkhana (Flower Mosque), as petals from the prime sanctum are placed here and once a year, sandalwood powder is prepared in this mosque for the customs of Urs.

Sadly, Sandal Mosque's main entrance is ravaged by modern travesties in the name of preservation—the portico is a clumsy palette of leaf and mint green; the lower domes on both sides are in mint hues, erasing any trace of finer architectural details. Towards its north lie the tombs of Muinuddin's wives.

In stark contrast, close by its side, is a still reticent Auliya Masjid, Mosque of Saints—Khwaja Muinuddin's first stop in Ajmer. In its first birth, it was a pen for turkeys for Prithviraj Chauhan. *Seeratul Muin* notes that a nobleman from Purnia District, Chaudhary Mohammed Bakhsh laid a brick canopy to shield worshippers from the brutal desert sun. This mosque has a quaint, short walkway lined with arcs and columns in yellowing granite and black and white floor tiles. At its end, a small door in deep green opens into a prayer hall.

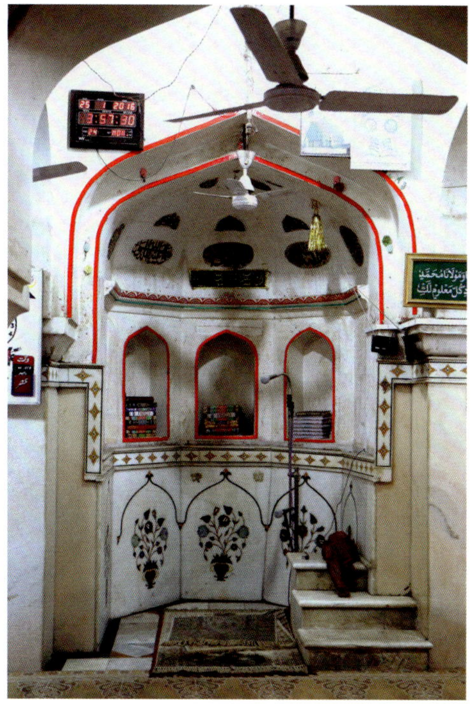

Above: The mihrab (prayer alcove) in Auliya Masjid, Mosque of Saints

Facing page: Inside view of Sandal Mosque

Next page: Qawwali at the Princess Courtyard after Karka

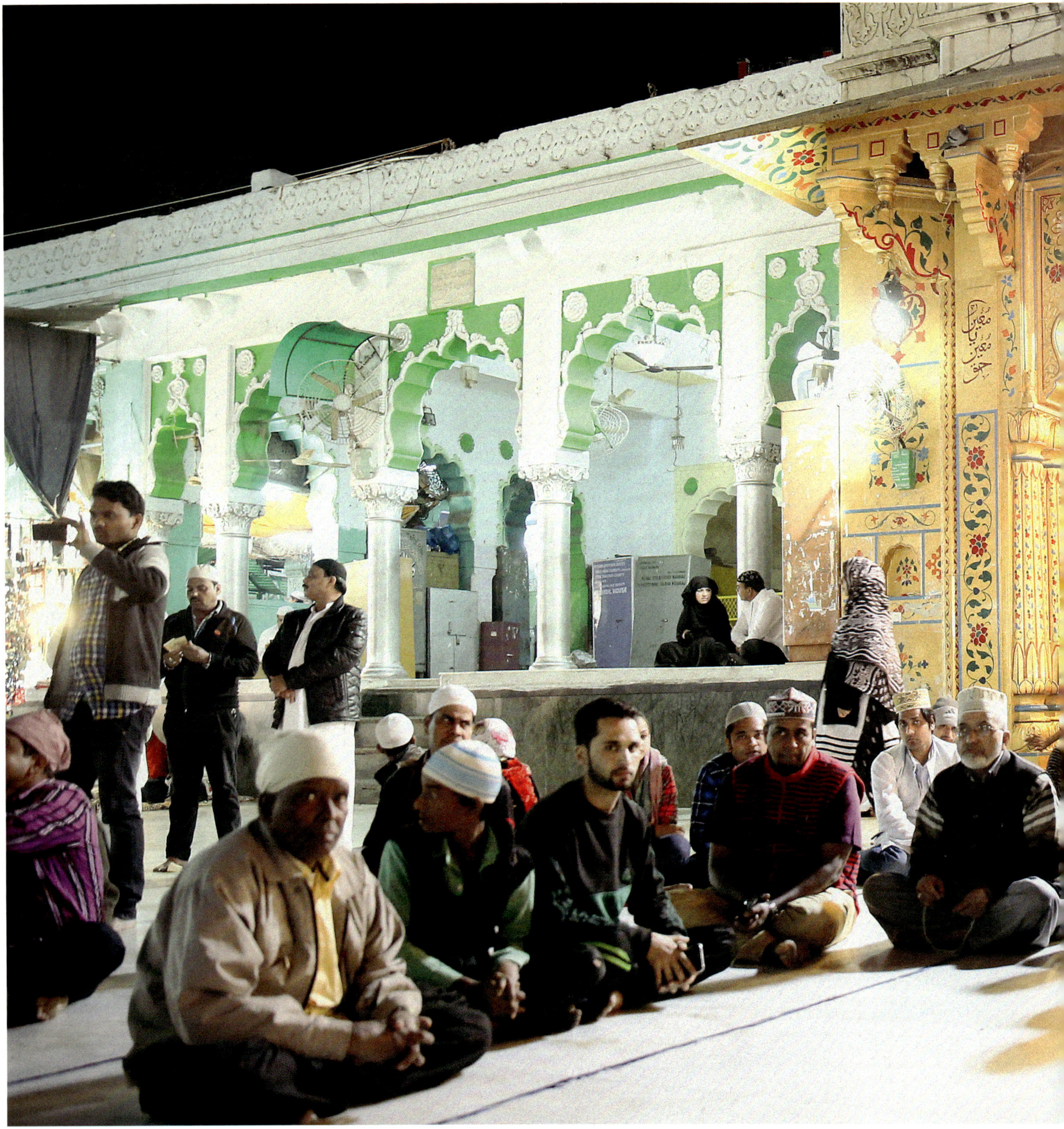

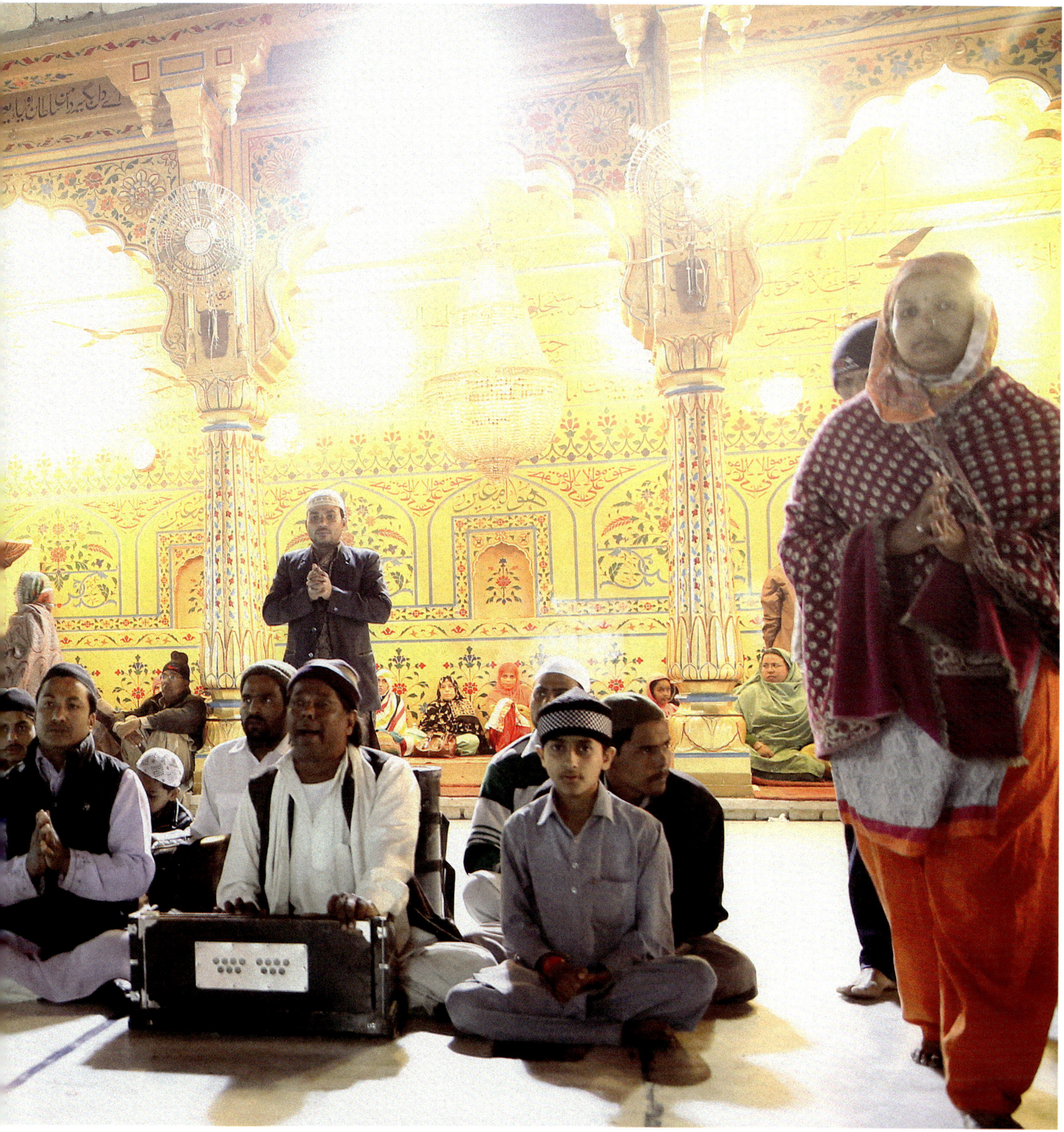

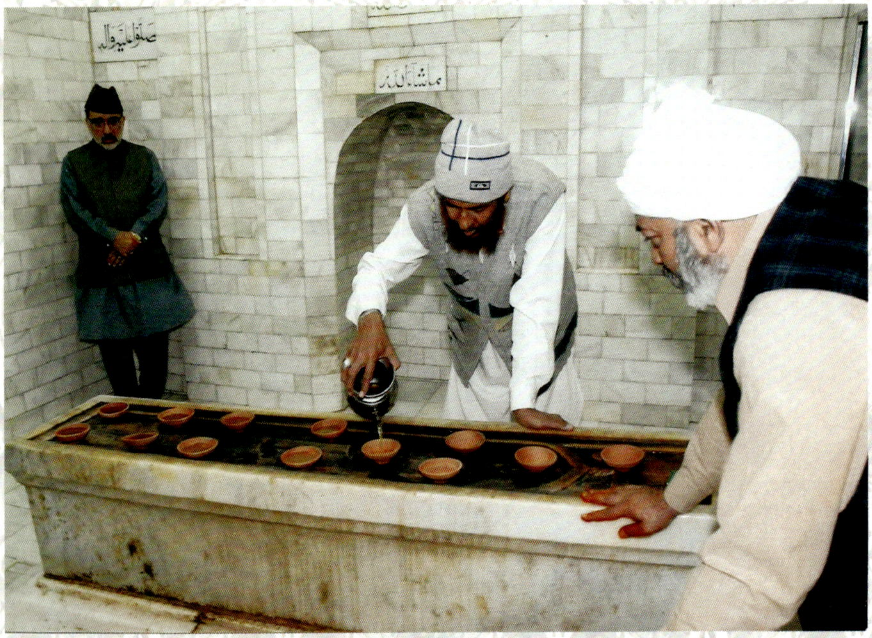

Inside Ganj-e-Shakar chamber, a special ceremony of Koozian (Gulping from a clay cup) is underway

The Well of Sweetness

'Don't dissipate the heat of your work
by engaging in cold conversation with people.'
Baba Fariduddin Ganj-e-Shakar

Adjacent to the tomb of Chammeliwali Bibi and a small gateway, is a tiled wall with an iron gate that conceals Chilla Baba Farid (Fariduddin's Meditation Cavern), close to Sandal Mosque.

One of the more intriguing locations in this revered complex, a steep stone stairwell leads into a dark underground hollow. Bakhtiyar Kaki's principal caliph, Baba Fariduddin Ganj-e-Shakar chose to perform the mandatory practice for Sufi induction—a 40-day seclusion—in the heart of the Chishti Sufi Order. The iron grille to the cell stays locked for most of the year and opens on the fifth day of Muharram, the first month of the Muslim lunar calendar.

Many accounts and followers aver that Farid's cavern is adjacent to Khwaja Muinuddin's authentic resting place, sealed with a wall. But chief custodian, Syed Salman Chishty, denies the presence of another sepulchre of the saint other than the one in the sanctum. Fariduddin, as successor to Bakhtiyar Kaki, was dear to Muinuddin who bestowed the title of 'Ganj-e-Shakar' (The Sweetened Well), upon him.

Today, revered as Baba Farid of Pakpattan Sharif, near Multan in Pakistan, the mystic master spent a few years in Delhi with his teacher, Bakhtiyar Kaki. Baba then chose the quieter, deeper recesses of Punjab as his station. Shaped by his mother, Maryam Bibi and Bibi Fatima bin

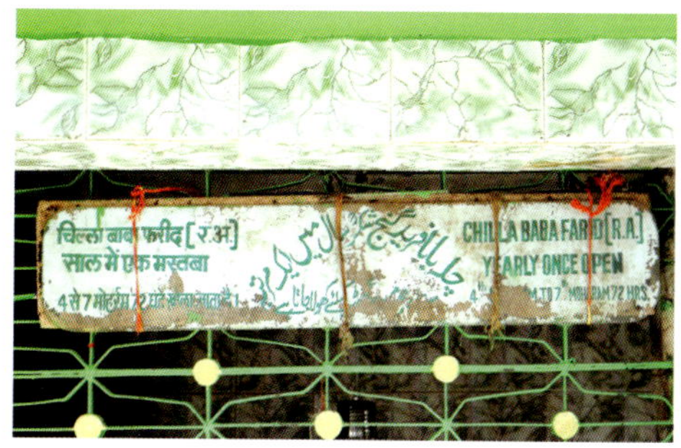

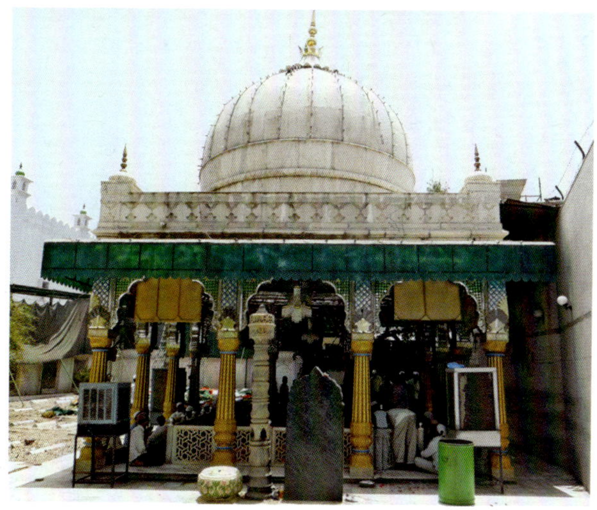

Top: Grilles of the stairway to Baba Farid's seclusion cavern

Above: Bakhtiyar Kaki's Dargah in Mehrauli, Delhi

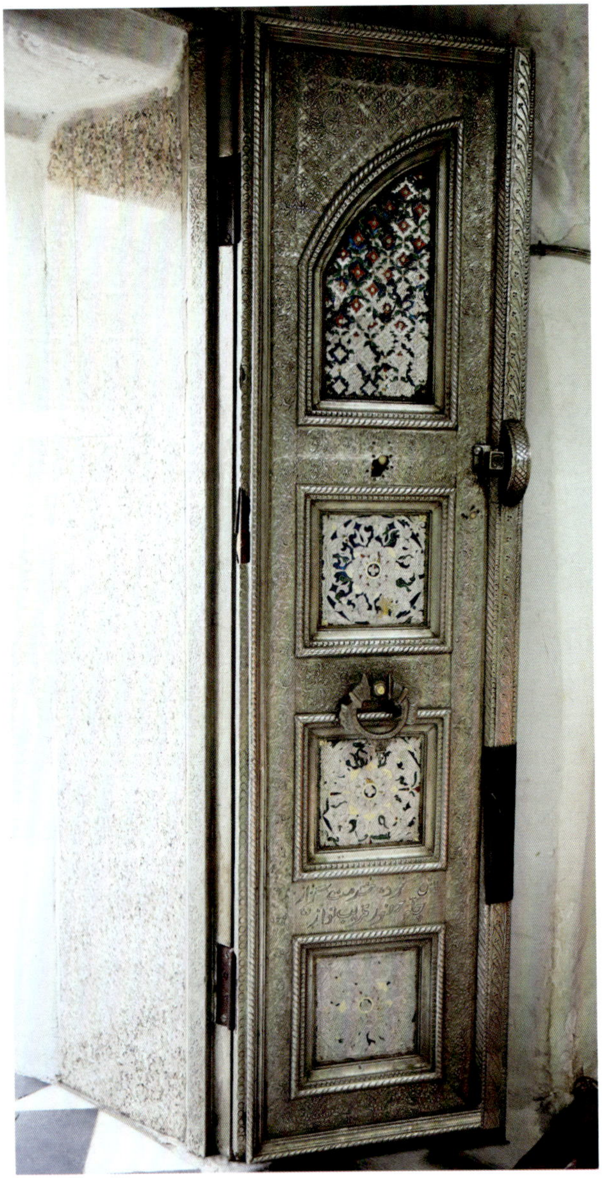

Silver doors in the shrine complex

Sam, his adopted sister, remembered by a modest 800-year-old memorial in Delhi, Farid fasted throughout the year and led a life of poverty.

Fariduddin was also a poet and according to renowned scholar K.A. Nizami's account of his life, many of his verses are included in the *Guru Granth Sahib:*

Farid return thou good for evil
Bear no revenge in thy heart
Thus will thy body be free of maladies
And thy life blest.

Baba Farid selected Nizamuddin Auliya as his primary caliph and the latter's unwavering loyalty to him is extensively documented in *Fawaid al-Fuad* (*Morals for the Heart*), considered the last word on Nizamuddin.

A small patch of ashen granite, Kochak Sang Safed (Nook of White Stone), on the east of the plane facing Sandal Masjid, houses a few vaults—those of an old disciple, Sheikh Tajuddin Bayazid, his wives and relatives. Legend has it that a strand of Prophet Muhammed's white hair, was brought from the Hazratbal Shrine in Kashmir, and preserved at this spot on the orders of Aurangzeb. Some years later, the relic was sent back to its home in Srinagar.

Jannati Darwaza (Gateway to Paradise), located to the west of the sanctum sanctorum, and next to the grave of Princess Gaiti Ara (Shah Jahan's granddaughter) is, after Shah Jahan's edifices, easily the most abundantly crafted specimen of superior workmanship in these grounds. Sheets of finely inscribed silver form its main door and it stays bolted except on the four fetes of the two Eids, the Urs of Muinuddin and the Urs of his spiritual father, Usman Harooni. Devotees believe that seven rounds through the door secure a pilgrim a place in heaven.

Khilji left another most stately mark here in the shape of the Buland Darwaza (the High Gate). Towering over every other monument in

Ajmer Sharif, the gate was built in red stone. Today, austere in pure white, the gateway presides at 85 feet in height, with an overstated ogee pinnacle. Two staircases, cut into its sides, lead to a *burj* (tower) of 2.5 feet with a golden kalasha.

The High Gate opens in the north, with two simple domed, pillared pavilions (*chhatri*s) on either end of the lintel. *Chhatri*s are often used to denote north and south ends. The annual ceremony of hoisting the flag to signify the inauguration of the Urs also takes place at this gateway.

The burial chamber of Muinuddin's caliph, Shamsuddinul Maroof is housed in the gate's foyer. According to *Moeen Al Aulia*, this door represents Mahmud Khilji's gratitude for his victory over Ajmer, whereas H.B. Sarda contests this in *Ajmer Historical and Descriptive*. Sarda mentions the Buland Darwaza as a gift from Sultan Inayatuddin.

A few of the ancient underground chambers in its vicinity have been preserved for storage. Two mammoth metal containers tower on either side of the Buland Darwaza as its majesty opens out to taupe, cream and black tones of Sehan Chiragh (Lamp Terrace). A delicate octagonal lamp pavilion on a tan granite pedestal, fenced in grilles with a mint plastered cone, graces the centre. The historic, tiered golden lamp-stand is one of Akbar's multiple donations.

The Chittor Kusha Degh (Chittor Victory Cauldron), installed in 1527 CE is another. The colossal vessel has a circumference of 36.10 feet and is 11.50 feet in diameter. Akbar removed his crown for his walk to the shrine and left this timeless bequest. For centuries, it has doled out 100 mounds of sweetened rice to feed over 55,000 people of all creeds, each passing day.

Akbar's son, Nuruddin Jahangir's smaller replica vessel, crafted in Agra, faces his. Jahangir supervised its first meal in Ajmer in 1613, feeding 5,000 pilgrims. This cauldron holds up to 80 mounds of grain; it is 25.8 feet in circumference, with a diameter of 8.2 feet and five semicircular steps are built on two sides of both containers. Beside

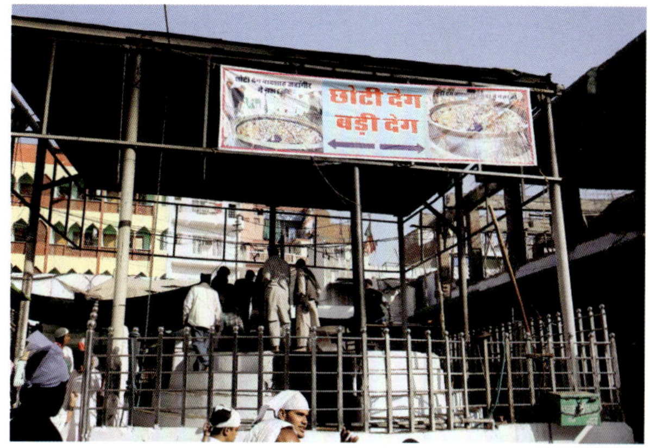

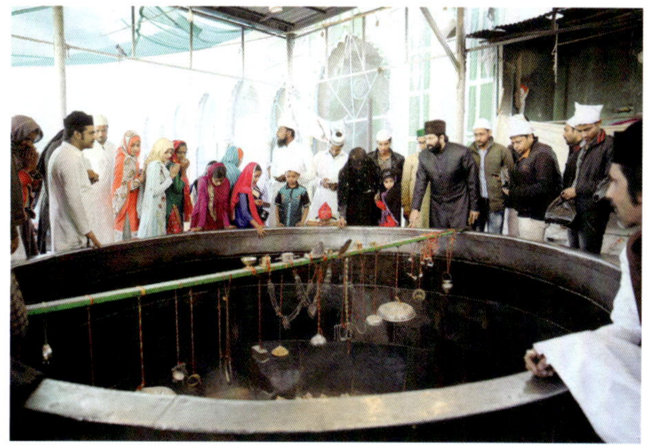

Top: The steps leading to Jahangir's smaller replica of his father's cauldron

Above: Akbar's Chittor Kusha Degh has an array of wish symbols across it

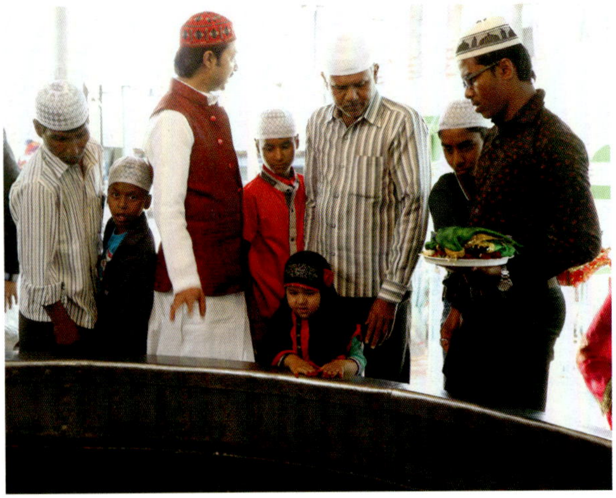

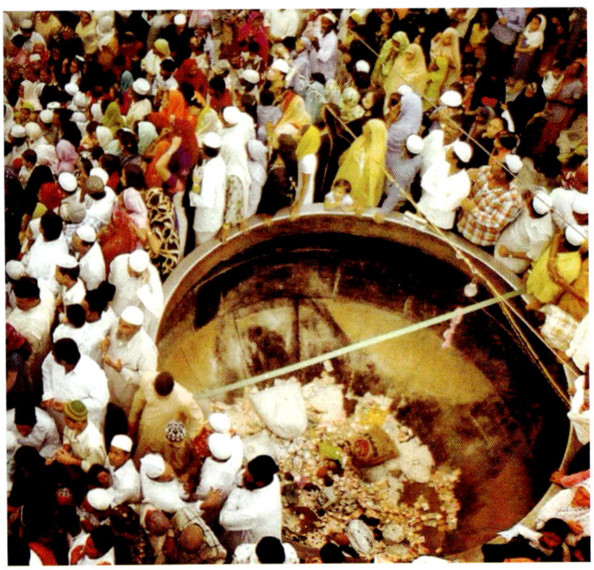

Top: Pilgrims around Akbar's Degh

Above: Akbar's Degh filled with offerings during Urs festivities

Jahangir's vessel was a large pond, 21.2 feet in length, which has been covered for conservation. Centuries of use later, Ishaq Wazir of Hyderabad (Deccan) repaired Akbar's container and Nawab Nawaz Jung reconstructed Jahangir's dilapidated cauldron.

After Akbar's last homage at Ajmer Sharif, Jahangir breathed new life into the Chishti shrine's bonds with the Mughal Empire. As mentioned in *Tuzuk-e Jahangiri* (*Memoirs of Jahangir*), the Emperor was cured of a deadly affliction after he meditated at Muinuddin's door. He spent the next three months in Ajmer, and went nine times to the shrine where he fed the poor, led many ceremonies of the Urs, and built monuments in the town of Ajmer; the degh and the first fence around the tomb of the saint, placed in 1615 CE have been his enduring stamps on collective memory. He had also vowed to have his ears pierced upon recovery to wear earrings as symbols of slavery to Khwaja, and kept his word. Jahangir also released a golden coin embossed with *'Ya Muin'* (Hail Muin).

Jahangir's earliest visit to Ajmer is recorded in 1613 CE, when he stayed in the city for three years, returning to Agra in 1616 CE. In this duration, he found himself at Muinuddin's threshold nine times.

In *Memoirs of Jahangir*, the monarch writes:

> *My father, when he made a vow respecting my birth, had gone on foot from Fathpur to Ajmir on a pilgrimage to the shrine of the great Khwaja Mu'inuddin Chisti, a space of 120 kos, and it would therefore be nothing great if I were to go this short distance upon my head or eyes. When I had obtained the good fortune of visiting the tomb ...I did not find it to my liking. My intention was that it be so exquisite that travelers of the world could not say they had seen one like it...*
>
> *While the work was in progress...I was obliged to march towards Lahore. The builders had built according to their own taste, and had altered the original design at their discretion. The whole money had been expended, and the work had occupied three to four years. I ordered clever architects...should pull down the objectionable parts...By degrees, a very large and magnificent building was raised, with a nice garden...entered by a lofty gate, consisting of minarets made of white stone.*

Another souvenir from Akbar, the Langarkhana (communal kitchen), is on the eastern side of the terrace. Painted in white with hints of pale aquamarine on curves and borders, an inner door leads to a small porch where enormous iron pots bubble with porridge for the hungry. Until a few years ago, the Nizam of Hyderabad sponsored one meal of the day.

Tareekhi Chhatri (Historic Kiosk), appears in the kitchen porch. An ancient, decrepit parasol-like Mughal structure with a wide dome, bordered with curved edges, is held up by short poles in green. Akbar once arrived in the compound in the guise of a beggar and waited his turn for the barley dish. The king's earthen bowl escaped his grip and split into two. The episode was immortalised by him with this charming token.

In the northern end of the main kitchen portico is a Bijli Ghar (Light House), from 1920. Its ancient engine came from Sir Karim Buoy in Bombay to keep the compound ablaze. However, at present Ajmer city's powerhouse performs this function.

Situated between the saint and the Jama Masjid, west of Sehan Chiragh, is the magnificent, Mehfil Khana (Celebration Hall) perennially immersed in devotional energy. It shimmers with chandeliers, the quivers of oil lamps and is fragrant with generous whiffs of rose. Most festivities of the Urs are played out here, such as the qawwali that resounds through the night to end before dawn prayers. Raised in 1891 by Nawab Bashirud Daulah Osman Jah of Hyderabad (Deccan), the plane is a gesture of reverence on the birth of Muinud Daulah, scion born to the noble at the age of 80. The hall is spread over approximately 46 sq feet, with a 14 feet gallery around it. Earlier, the area was occupied by a school, Darul Uloom Moeenia Osmania, which was sealed after 1947.

The western wall of the Mehfil Khana connects it through an indiscernible door to the Khanqah, a devotional cubicle. Built in 1570 CE by Akbar, the rites of bathing Khwaja Muinuddin's body before his burial were conducted at the site. It is also believed that his family resided in these quarters.

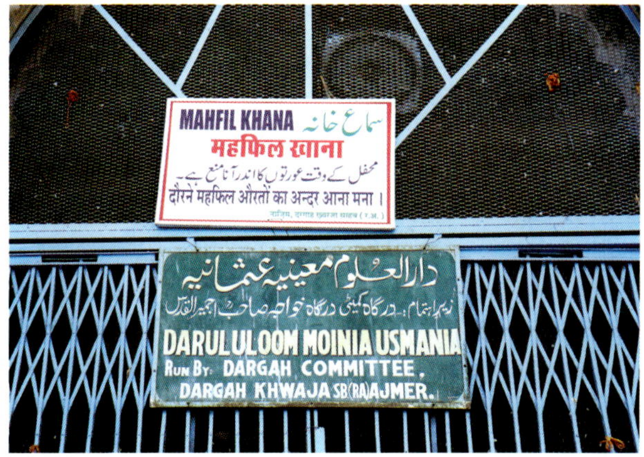

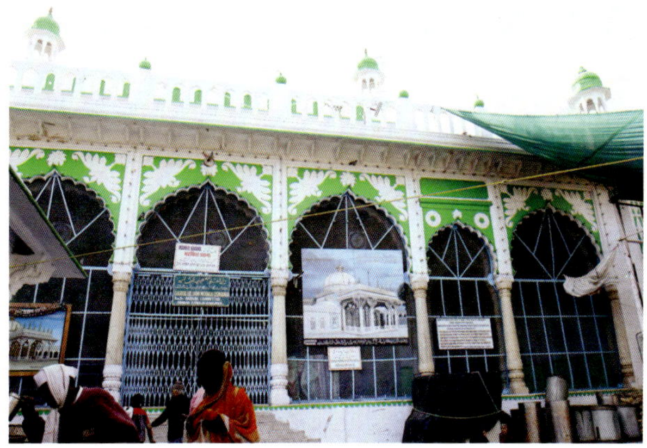

Top: The Mehfil Khana (Celebration Hall) in the shrine complex

Above: The Mehfil Khana hosts qawwali sessions during the Urs

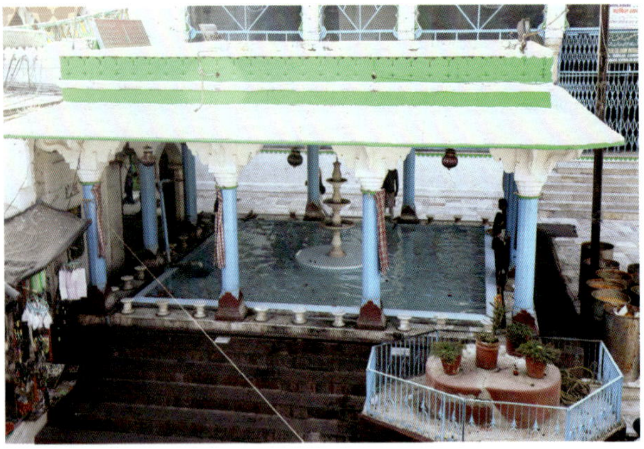

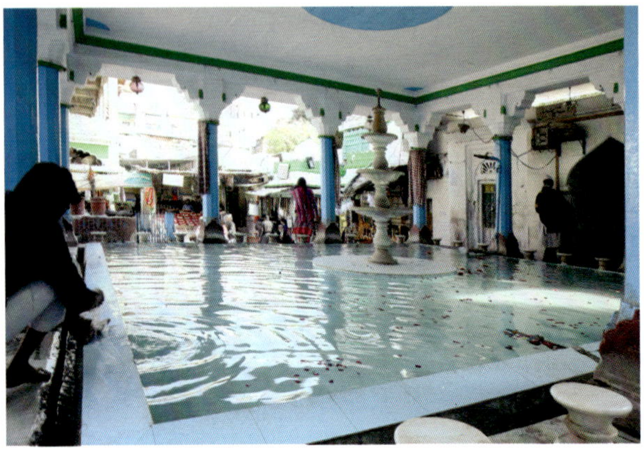

Top: Hauz O Hamaal Khana (Cleansing Pond) provides cool relief

Above: The cleansing pond where pilgrims wash away the dust of travel

The enclosure finds an ardent mention in *Akbarnama: Akbar ne ek masjid aur iss ke mutsal ek khanqah banai'* (Akbar raised a mosque and a *khanqah*—building for Sufi gatherings and spiritual retreat—near it). Every year, in the late afternoon hours of the first day of the Urs, the chief custodian, Dewan Zainul Abedin, leads a special gathering here.

Hauz O Hamaal Khana (Cleansing Pond), ripples in the north-west direction of the Mehfil Khana. Arcs and pillars in hues of turquoise and green frame the blue pond from all sides. Used for ablution practices, it bears a reminder of Queen Mary's historic visit in 1911. She left 500 rupees for a remembrance to be placed on her behalf. A large part of the donation went into the construction of one of the canopies above the pond, and the remaining was invested in rituals of the shrine. Beside the pool is a water tank, Sabeel Sanjari from 1941. Water carriers fill their leather bags here to serve the thirsty as their livelihood. Two crypts of governors, appointed by Daulat Rao Scindia and Madhoji Scindia, in Ajmer are in its vicinity.

Hauz Jama Masjid (Pool of Jama Mosque), displays remains of Mughal grandeur. Built by Shah Jahan, its stone curved bordered roof, embossed in a distinct vine design, is painted with lime. The inner arches and pillars are green and visitors pay their salutations by filling water in exchange for remunerations for the water bearers.

The Arcot Verandah opens out near the pool and close to the main sanctum. Named after the viceroy, it was laid out in white granite in 1793. A taupe, polished stone pavilion, opulent with filigree, arcs, posts and niches is set along a boundary.

To the south of the mausoleum complex is a dramatic scene of moist rock and damp air. A wide craggy cut through the hill travels to the stream of Jhalra. Estimated to be thousands of feet in depth, its sacred waters have flowed through epochs to feed many neighbourhoods in Ajmer. A long stairwell dips into it from a platform within the shrine; water carriers use this access to fill tanks and serve devotees in the premises. Another

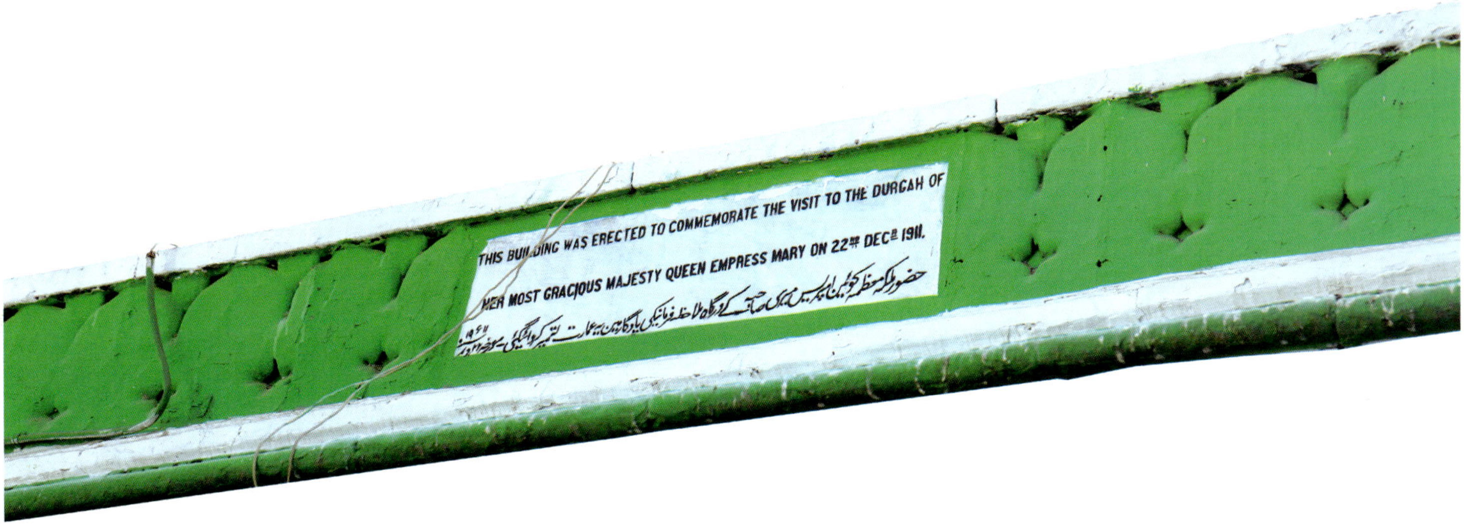

stairway pours into the rivulet from the Sola Khamba and a third is close to the sanctum.

In his true imperial style, Emperor Shah Jahan wrapped an impenetrable wall around the main torrent as a barrier to the lost Abudi, which spilt into Jhalra during the monsoon. The ancient tributary's course changed with a dam by Akbar and it turned towards Ajmer Bazaar, leaving Jhalra to surge in solitary splendour.

Ensconced between Jhalra, Arcot Courtyard and the pond is the short stretch of Shahi Ghat or Saaya Ghat (Royal Shore). The patina of its onyx awning throws shadows on the memorial of Muinuddin Chishti's son, Hisamuddin, and Abu Saleh, Bibi Ummatullah's brother.

Ajmer attracted many lesser-known pilgrims from royal households who devoted monuments of ardour for Muinuddin Chishti.

Maya Bai, the wet nurse of Aurangzeb's daughter, Zebunissa, constructed a mosque in red sandstone, as did Bai Tilokdi, the daughter of Akbar's prized musician Tansen. Both mosques sit along the path to the dargah and of the two, the nurse's structure is more impressive. Built from 1643 CE to 1644 CE, it bears an unusual similarity to Shah Jahan's mosque at the shrine—five arched entryways on delicate piers shape its facade. Maya Bai Mosque's priest alcove, is a modest version of its imperial counterpart.

Chishti Chaman, close to the Madari Gate, is an expansive park rolled out by a Maratha chieftain, Santoji, in 1756 CE.

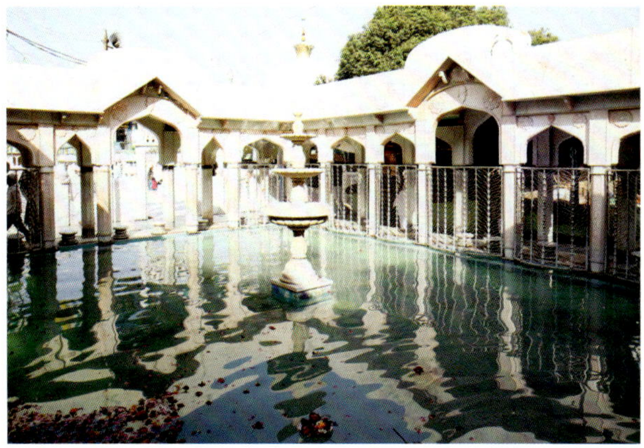

Top: The canopy over the cleansing pond commemorates Queen Mary's visit in 1911

Above: Soothing waters within the shrine complex

Next page: Intricately carved marble pillars at the shrine entrance

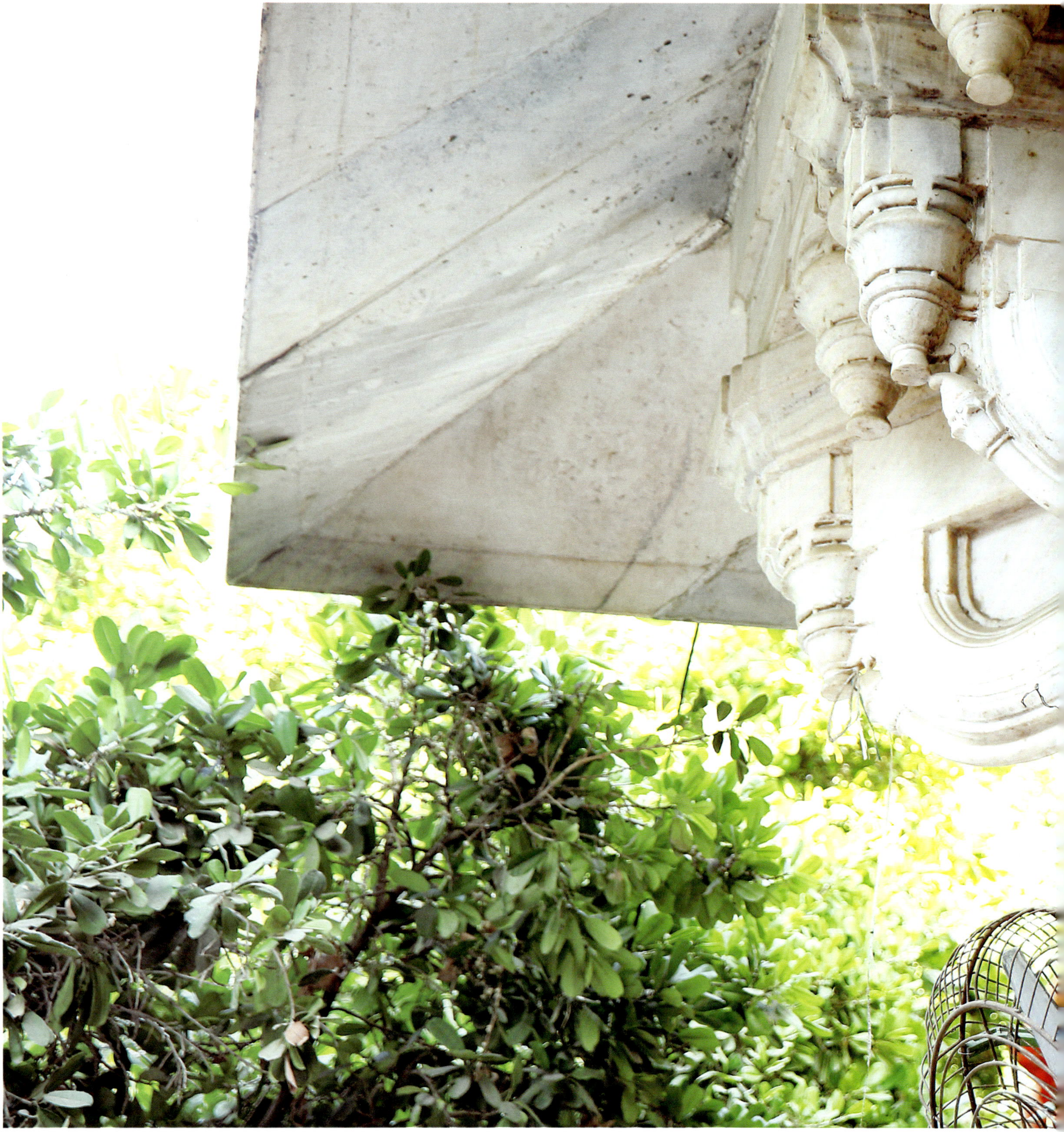

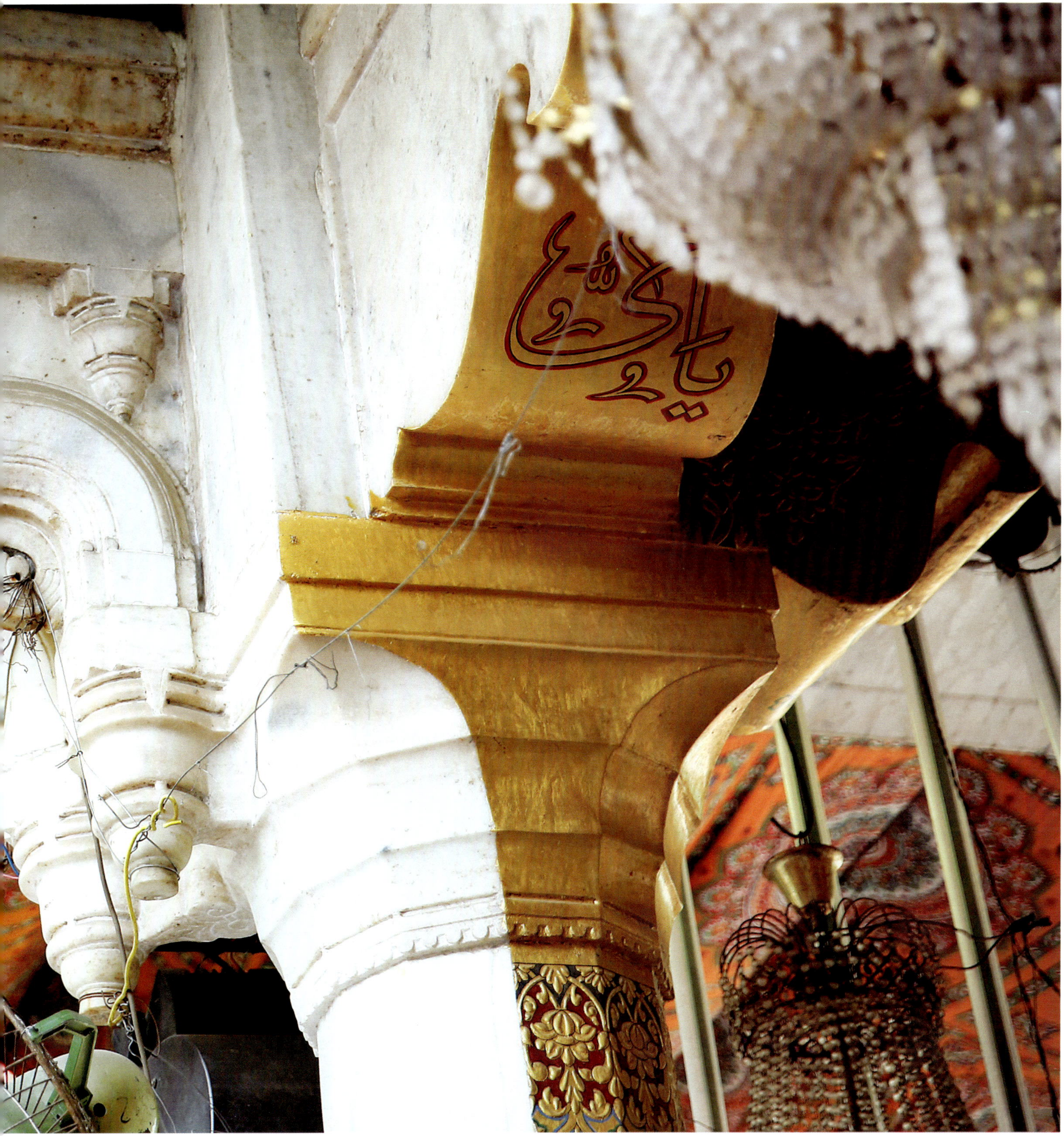
یا علی

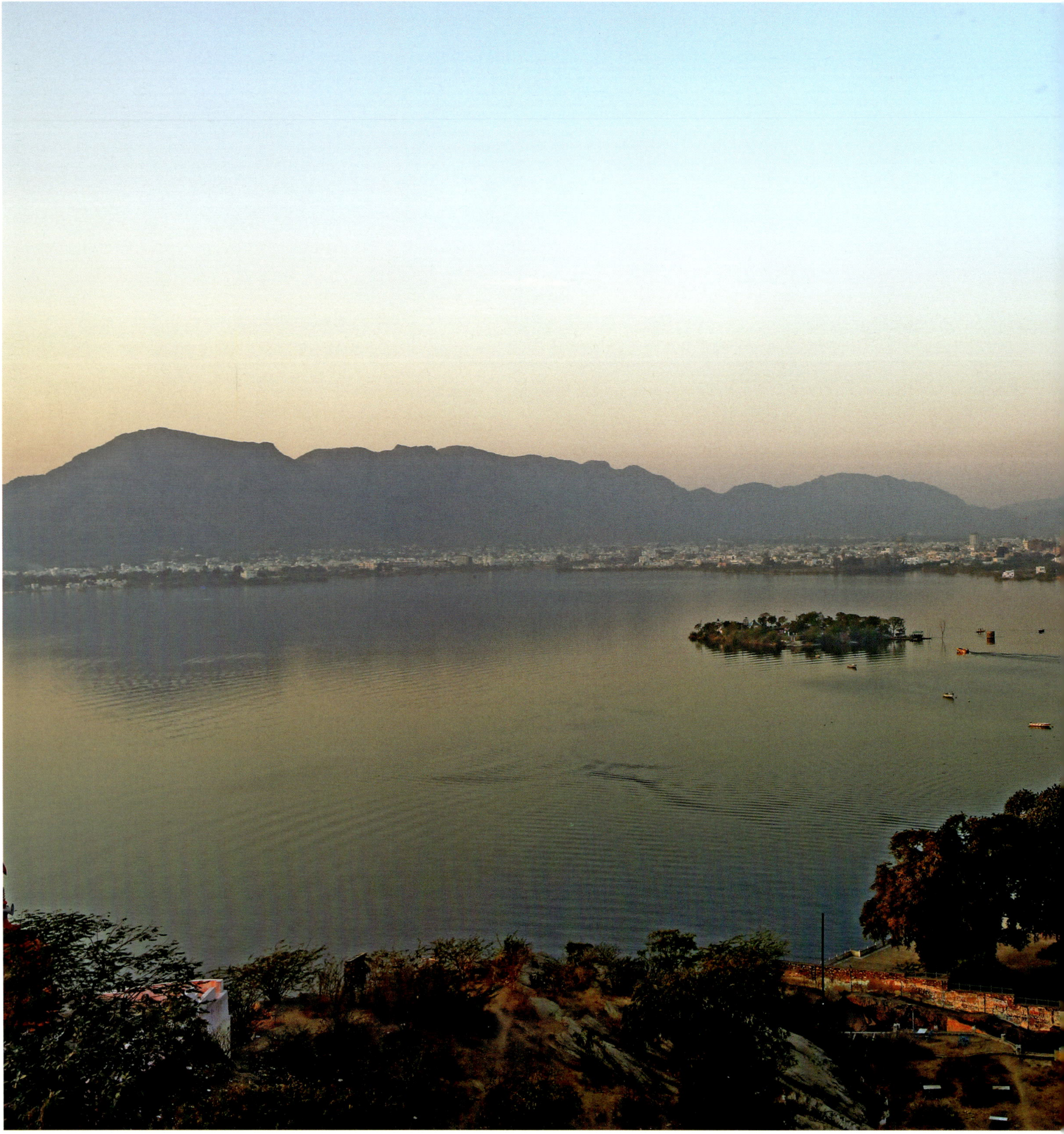

Ana Sagar Lake

Moist with Devotion

Almost still in placid, molten silver, shades of the sky glide over the stream. Raja Ana Dev carved it out in 1180 CE. Its banks are saturated in devotional history, beginning with the Cave of Muinuddin Chishti who, upon his arrival in Ajmer, spent 40 days in spiritual isolation here. Embedded in the Sada Bahar Hill, a rough orifice with a raised platform at his seating place is secured by an inscribed door. Marked as Gharib Nawaz Chilla Sharif, it can accommodate up to 10 people. At the peak of the hill, stands a small, domed structure with the grave of Masood, a soldier and a disciple of the saint. His is one of many vaults and meditational cells of dervishes and devotees scattered on the hillside.

In 1638 CE, Shah Jahan encamped at Jahangir's palace by the lake, which at the time was an onyx building with gardens. He ordered many additional structures, such as the Jharoka, a ceremonial balcony. Today, there is no trace of Jahangir's bequests along the scenic stream. However, four of his son's delicate gifts live on in gleaming marble—a few arched pavilions with small porticos and spires, overlooking calm waters are at a distance from the banks.

On the southern tip of the hill, twin pavilions face each other. Faceted pillars with multi-lobed brackets are carved in ivory marble, Shah Jahan's preferred fabric. Two others differ in design—one turns towards the lake and the other to the embankment. Grooved posts separate it into two concentric portions. A three-door, modest mosque with emerald green interiors, constructed on the design of the Qalandari Mosque still abides in the area.

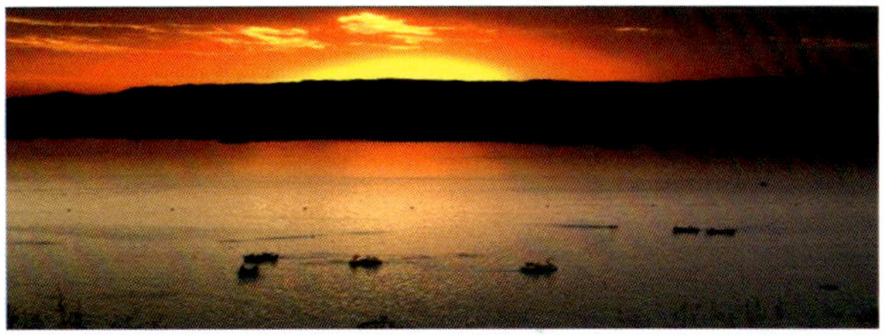

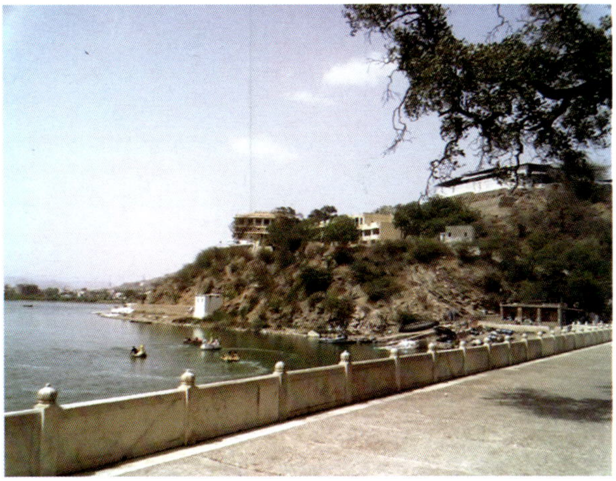

Top: Shades of spirituality—sunset at Ana Sagar Lake

Above: Daulat Bagh gardens at Ana Sagar Lake

Facing page: The tranquil vista of Ana Sagar Lake

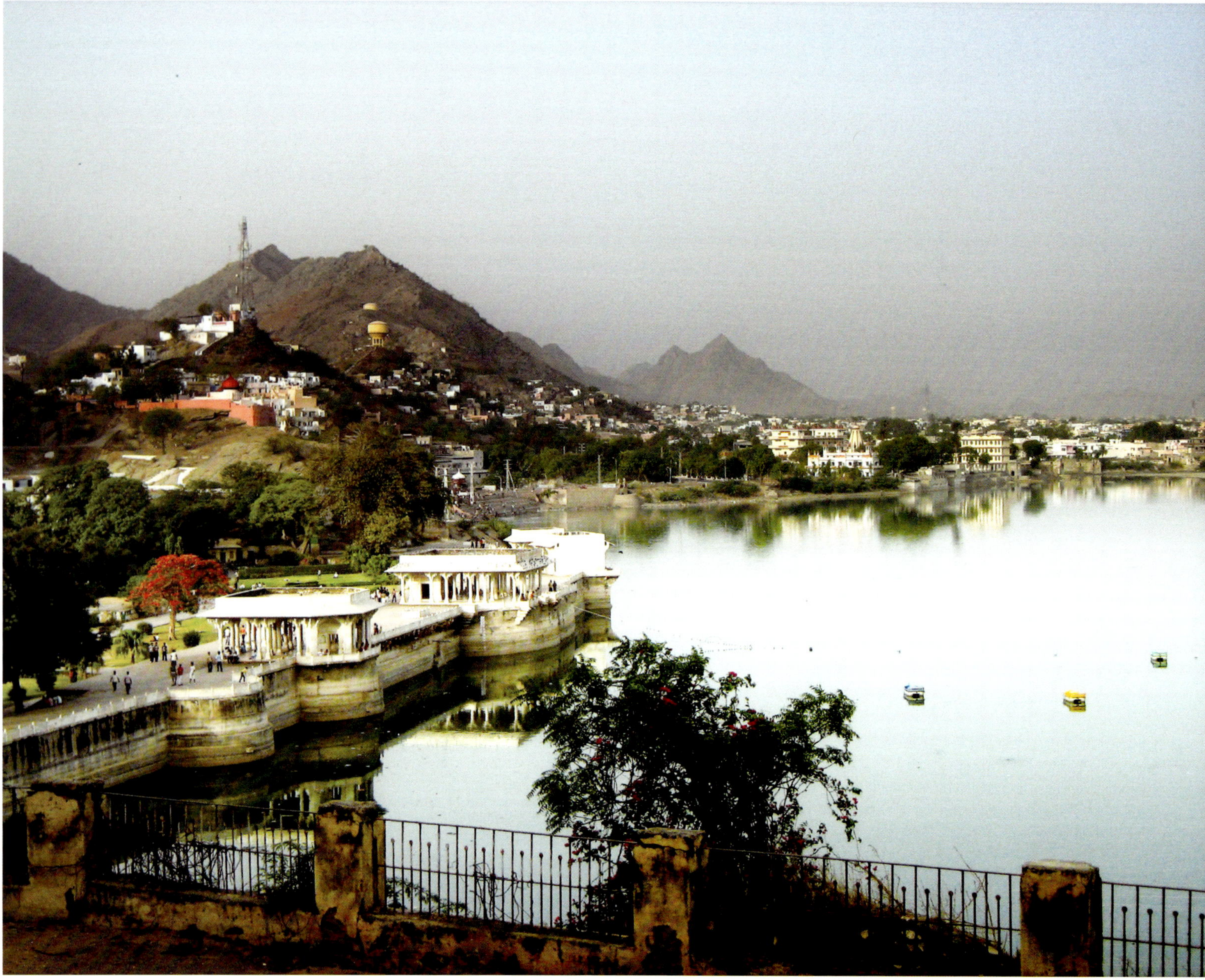

Near Muinuddin's cave is a domed portal; a plain, square-framed colonnade runs around it. This is Muinuddin's rite of avowal to his spiritual mentor, Usman Harooni, who was buried in Mecca. Harooni's belongings are preserved in this chamber and a flag goes up with a presentation of other devotional fare, on the day of his death anniversary ceremony at the Ajmer shrine.

The eastern end of the hill is studded with Bakhtiyar Kaki's seclusion cell where Muinuddin's foremost companion and caliph prayed for 40 days. A diminutive mosque stands in the outer terrace, with a faint Persian verse on its door. The engravement indicates that Daulat Khan, a revenue collector of Ajmer, rebuilt it on the occasion of his ascension as governor of Ajmer. Sadly, frequent renovations of the Chilla Khana have reduced all signs of its 17th century version to an indiscernible degree.

On the day of Kaki's Urs at his shrine in Delhi, keepers and devotees from the Ajmer sanctuary uphold age-old traditions of reverential customs at the cave. To the west of the hill, beside the ruins of Jahangir's loved smaller palace, Nur Chashma (Spring of Light), constructed in 1616 CE, is Bibi Hafiza Jamal's deified cove. Muinuddin's daughter and caliph followed her father's practice and went into loneness. The cavern is close to Jahangir's legacy of the verdant Daulat Bagh that stretches near the lake. The monarch built it when he came to power in 1605 CE.

I stood under a tree to stare at the Ana Sagar Lake, the kind of place where one conjures up visions. The khadim narrates supernatural episodes—evil being destroyed, angels swooping down—as routine incidents.

These waters beg for reflection. The mind lets in images of one's own who must have prayed here fervently. Then of the searching sightless, madmen and dervishes, lives knotted in threads, shoe-minders, and bare feet. If only this march of humanity in deference and difference, fixed in acceptance, could be unleashed into the world.

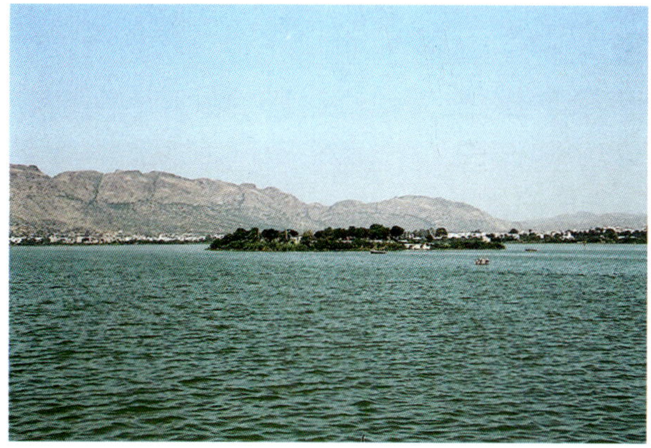

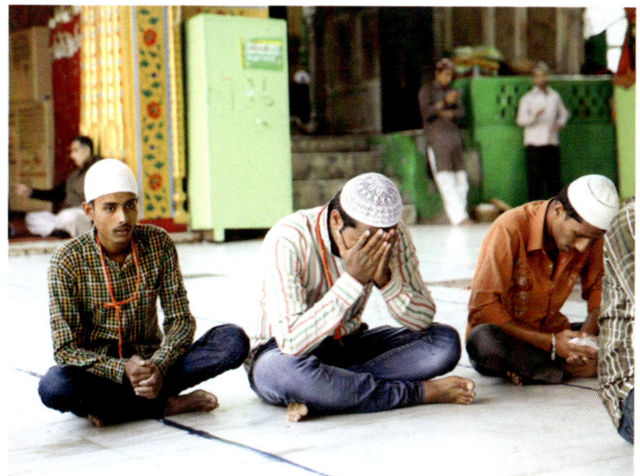

Top: Serene waters of Ana Sagar Lake

Above: Seekers of solace at the shrine

Facing page: Baradari or marble pavilions built by Shah Jahan on the banks of Ana Sagar Lake

Next page left: Sunset over still waters—view from the marble pavilions

Next page right : Visitors at the silver sheet of Ana Sagar

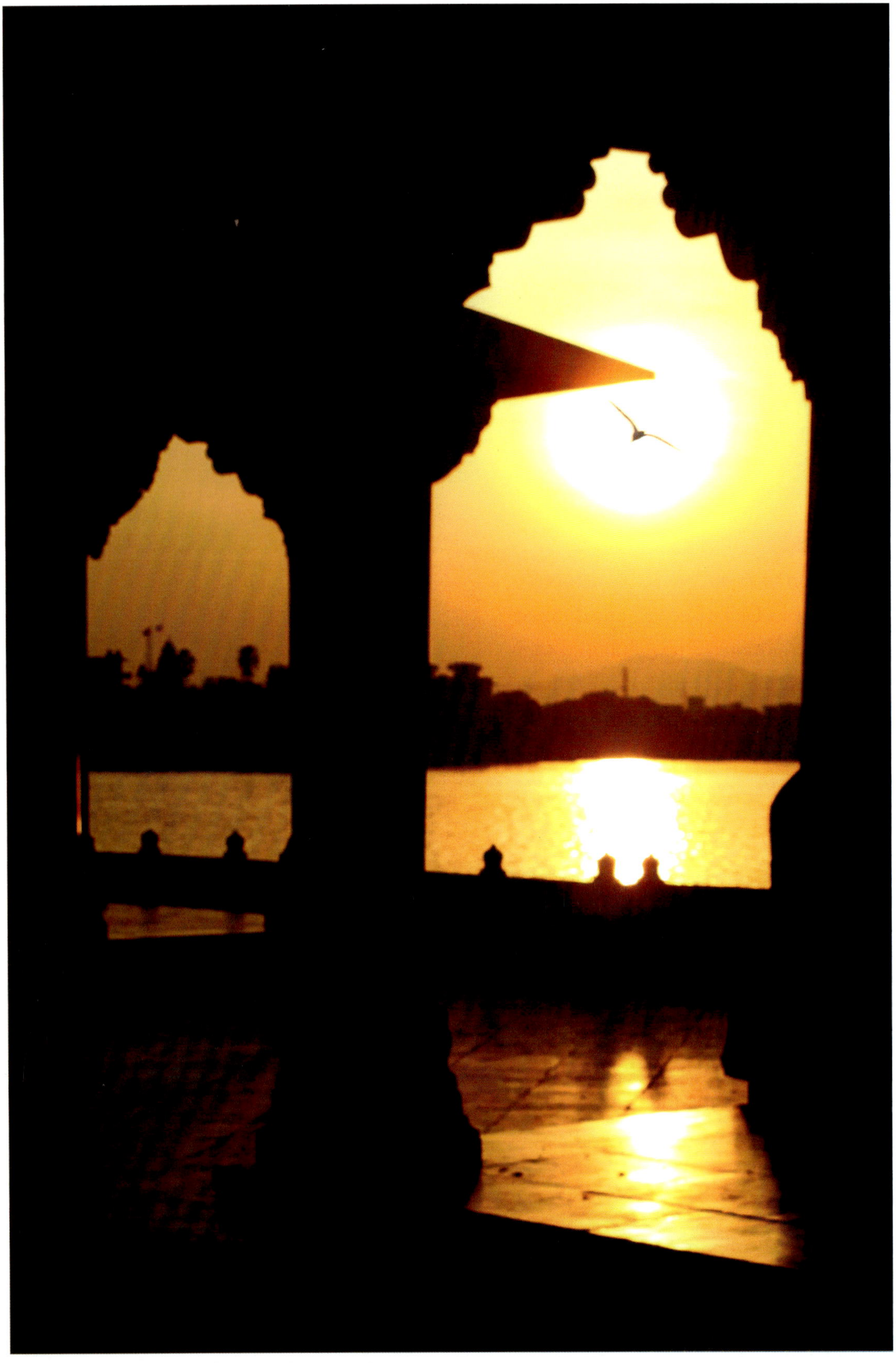

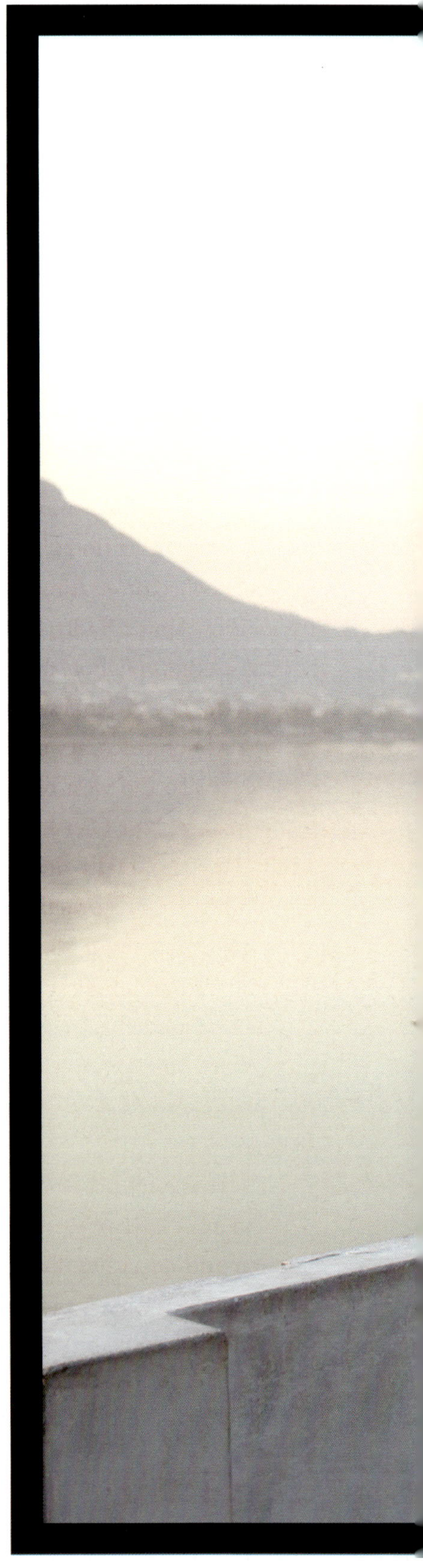

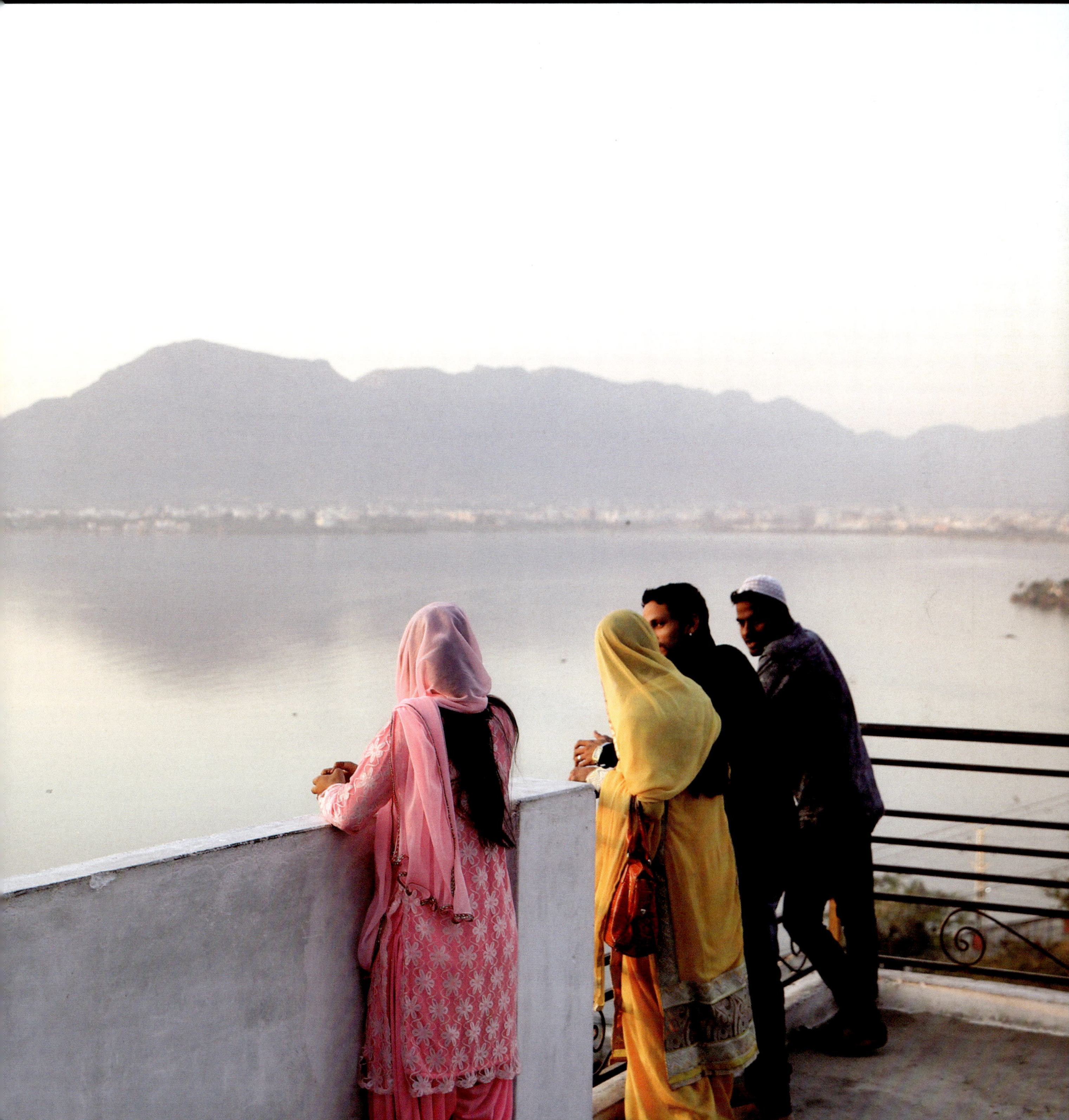

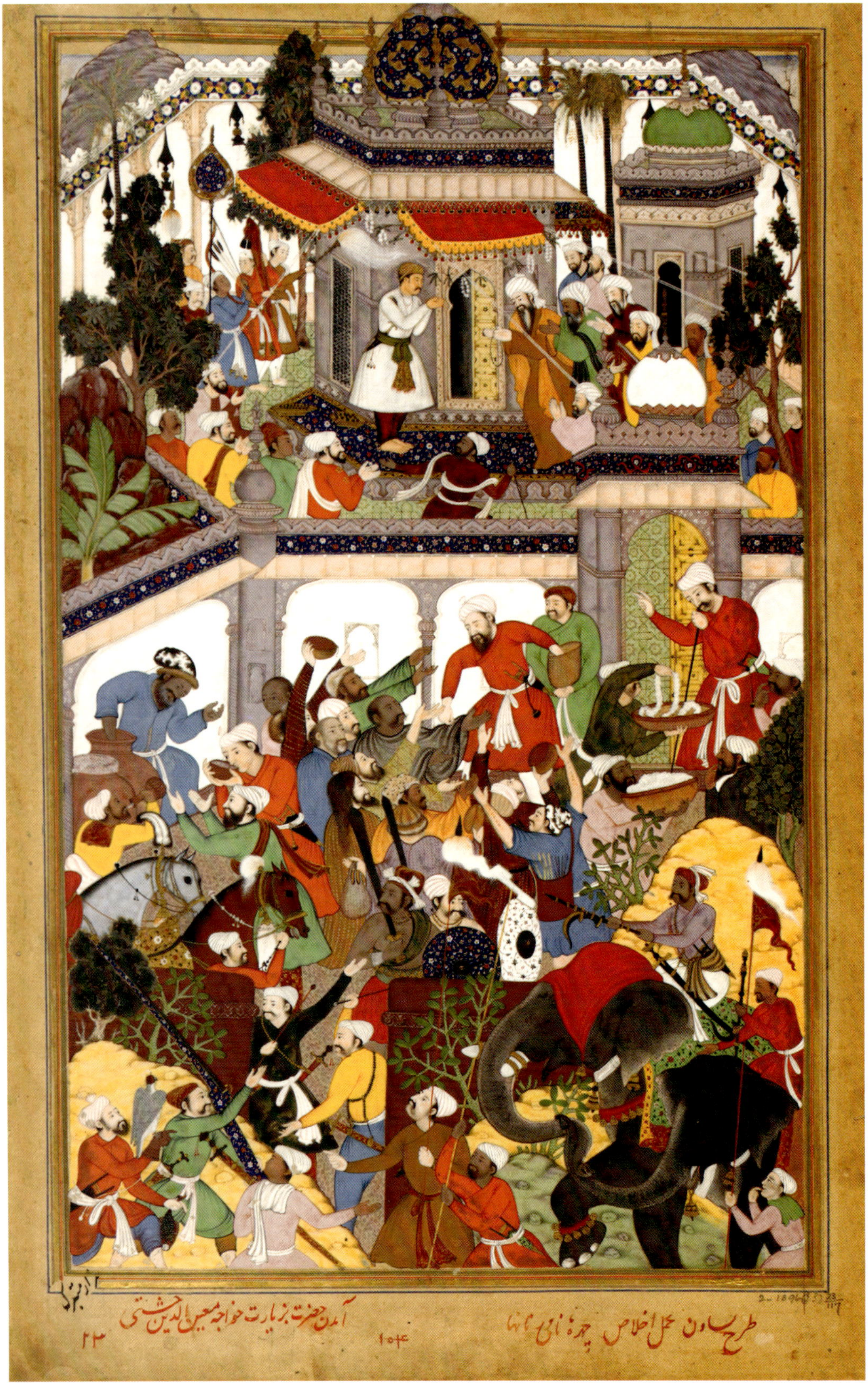

'Akbar visits the tomb of Khwaja Muinuddin Chishti at Ajmer', painting by Basawan (c. 1595)

Akbar
Bow of Power

'Akbar the king, illumines India's night,
And is as a lamp in the court of the House of Timur'
Abul Fazl, Akbarnama

Muinuddin's most powerful and historic devotee was the secular emperor, Jalaluddin Mohammed Akbar, who often paid homage at the shrine, for sons and conquests.

The sovereign's first introduction to Sufism was through his tutor, Abdul Latif, which led him to Salim Chishti, a Sufi sage in Fatehpur Sikri. Chishti, a devotionalist of Muinuddin, lived a lonesome life in the wilderness of Fatehpur's hillside. Akbar confided about his fear of never having an heir, to his spiritual master. When his wife Jodha was with child, Akbar sent her to stay close to Salim Chishti's sacrosanct dwelling. In 1559 CE, the royal couple was blessed with a son who was christened Salim, in honour of the Fatehpur Sikri sage. Some years on, the young prince became Jahangir, 'the one who seizes the world', a title from his father.

Akbar looked after Salim Chishti for as long as the saint lived. In his last moments and on his deathbed, Chishti was listening to one of the king's *nauratans*, the musician, Tansen. Salim Chishti lies in a pristine white marble tomb built by Akbar in 1580 CE, in the courtyard of the Fatehpur Mosque. A colonnaded portico, topped with a white dome, is a closed, intricate latticed gallery.

When Jahangir was three years old, in 1562 CE, Akbar covered 360 kms from Agra to Ajmer on foot, with head bowed, and feet naked.

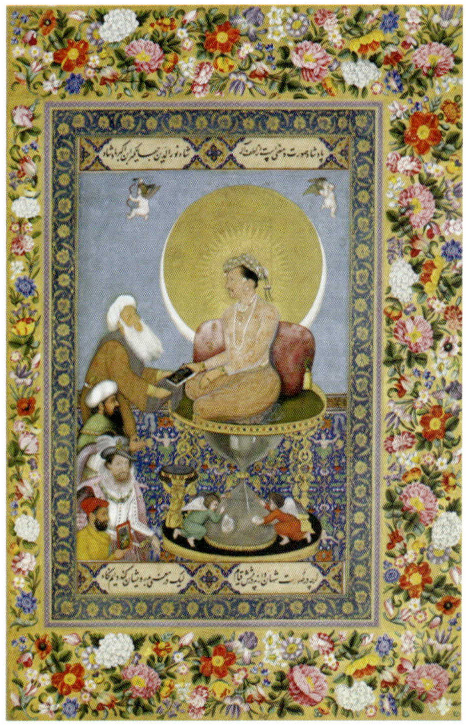

'Jahangir Preferring a Sufi Shaikh to Kings', opaque watercolor by Bichitr (c. 1615-1618)

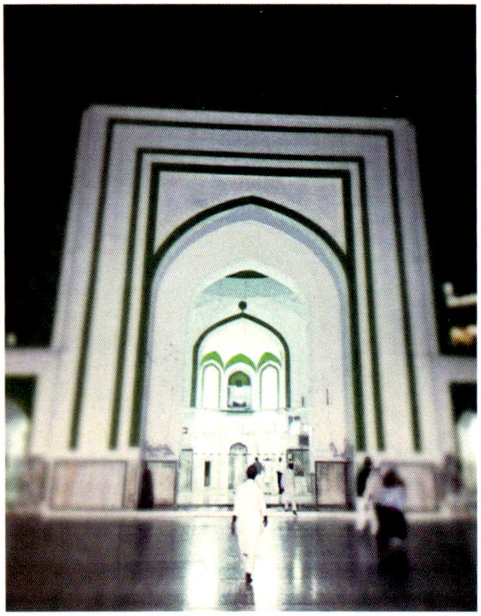

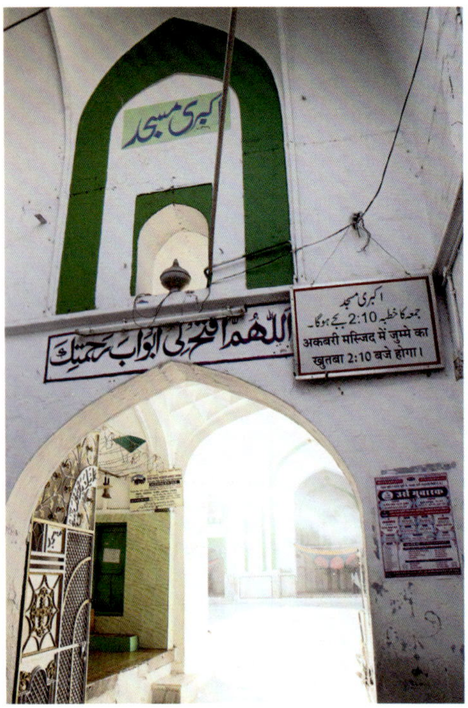

After this pilgrimage, he initiated the plan for a road from Fatehpur to Ajmer, replete with conical markers of kos minars, at every two miles (approx.). Some of these have survived the ravages of time and exist till date.

Akbar's acts of acquiescence, redolent with ardour, were regular, the last being in 1579 CE. He was also the first monarch to inscribe his signature gold coins with 'Ya Muin' and the only one to issue a new Muini coin.

However, Akbar's most regal imprint at Ajmer Sharif is Akbari Mosque, constructed in 1562 CE as a token of gratitude for his heir. According to historians, he ordered its lofty gate some six months after Jahangir was born. Smug in majesty, cast in red sandstone with onyx arches, the mosque square is 140 feet, its mihrab is 56 feet high, with a majestic dome and marble minarets. Its courtyard pond and a tank have been filled up. The reservoir had a plaque dated 1568 to 1569 CE—the time of its construction by Gesu Khan, an employee in the town of Merta, in present-day Rajasthan, and the chief of Akbar's regal kitchen.

The mosque, on the immediate west of the southern gate, is entered through a large courtyard, its centre presenting a Timurid architectural influence. It has a recessed, curved entry with coloured bands in sea-green and spandrels reminiscent of Humayun's tomb in Delhi. A dominant, high arc *pishtaq* forms the defining feature of the prayer hall's facade. The eastern facade in stark granite, is engraved with geometric inlay and its interior has net pendentive corbeling. Some centuries later, Nawab Ghaffar Ali Khan Danapuri carried out the area's renovation. At present an educational institution for children operates within the mosque's confines.

It is the hour to leave a place where the world of man blurs; when man and divinity are close. As the rickshaw lurches towards a dying sun, a geography of Sufi power and human zeal lies behind me. A confluence of Arab, Persian, Turkish and Indian rituals, it is extravagant, yet spiritually electric.

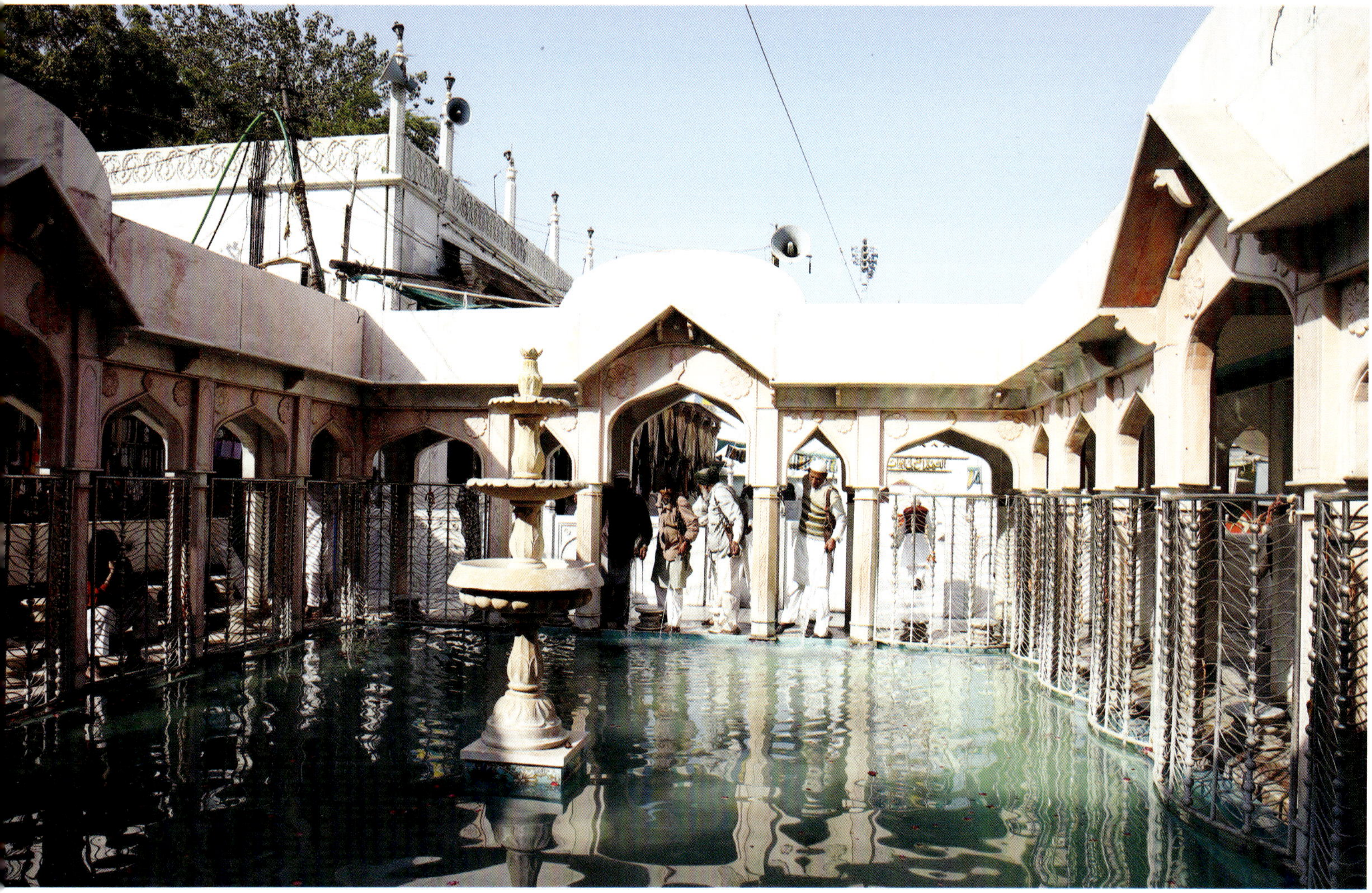

Even today, diversity flourishes here. This is where any seeker has a measure of peace.

Ya mujhe afsar-e-shahana banaya hota
ya mera taj gadayaana banaya hota

(Either You should have created me the King of kings
Or granted me a crown like the beggar's bowl)

—Bahadur Shah Zafar, the last Mughal who came to Muinuddin in 1708 and 1710 CE.

Above: Carved colonnade around a water feature in the shrine

Facing page above: The lofty entrance to Akbari Mosque

Facing page below: Inner view of the entrance to Akbari Mosque

Next page: Sheltered by faith—devotees under a colourful canopy in the shrine courtyard

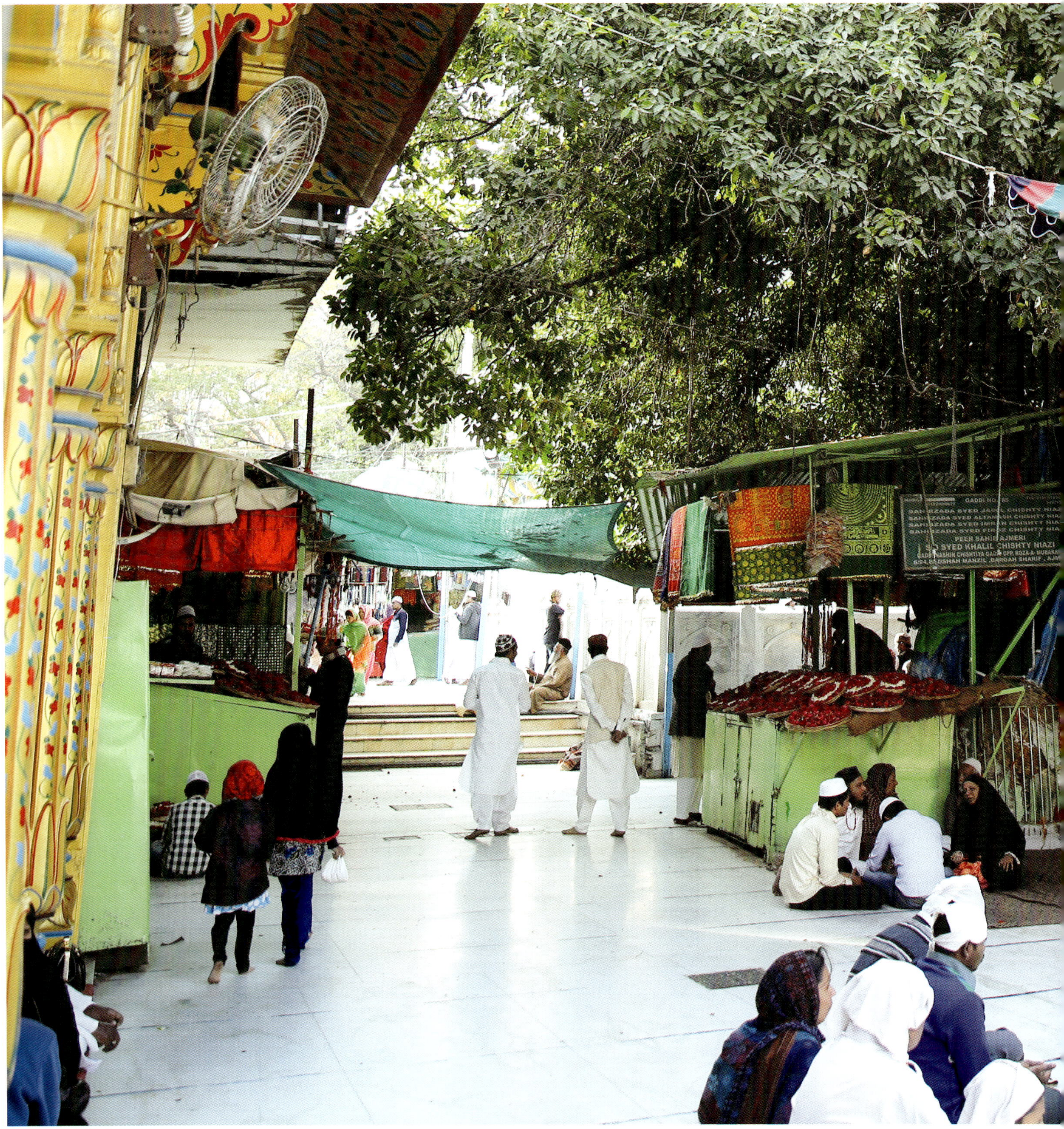
GADDI NO.
PEER SAHIB AJMERI
SYED KHALIL CHISHTY NIAZI

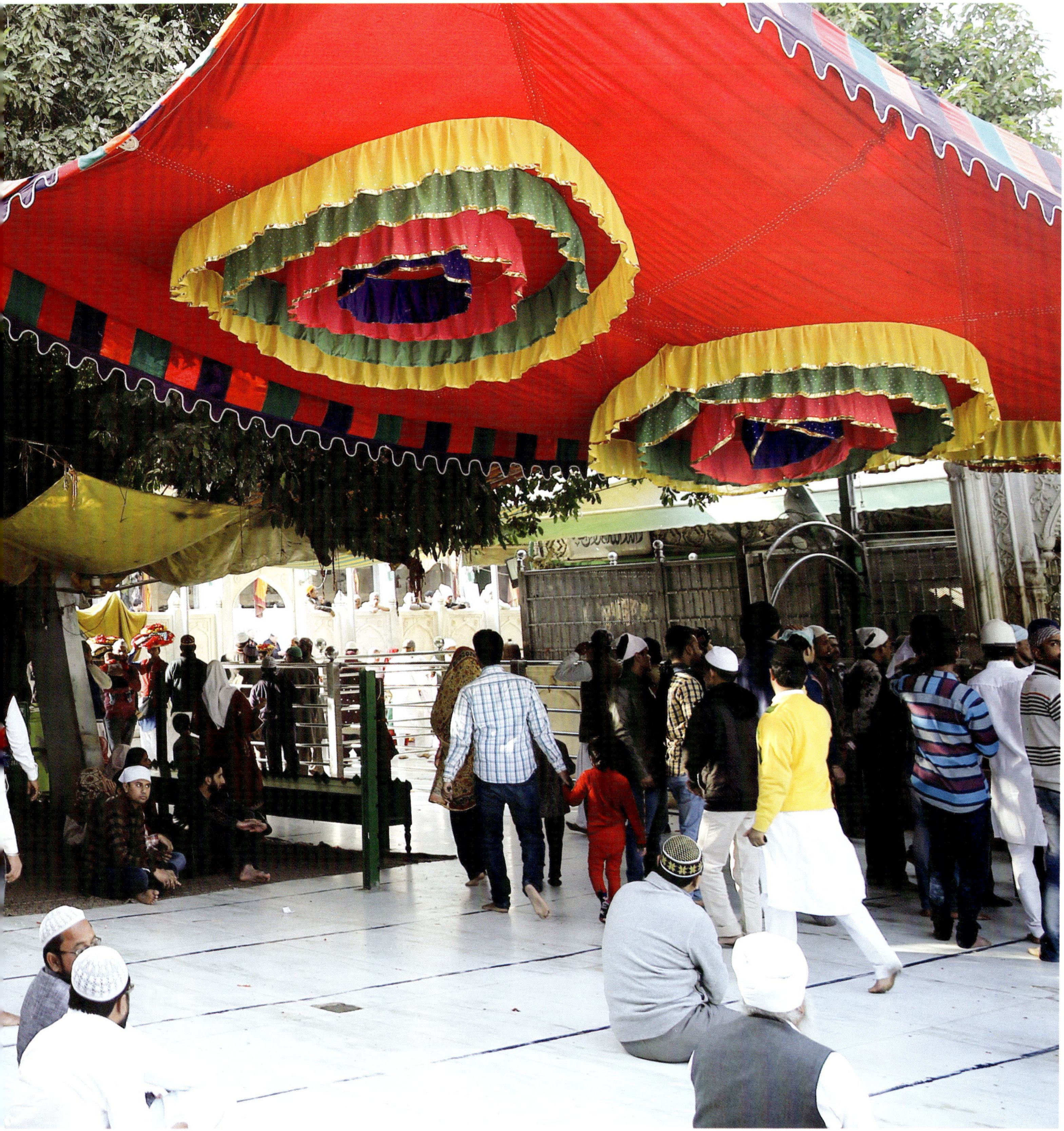

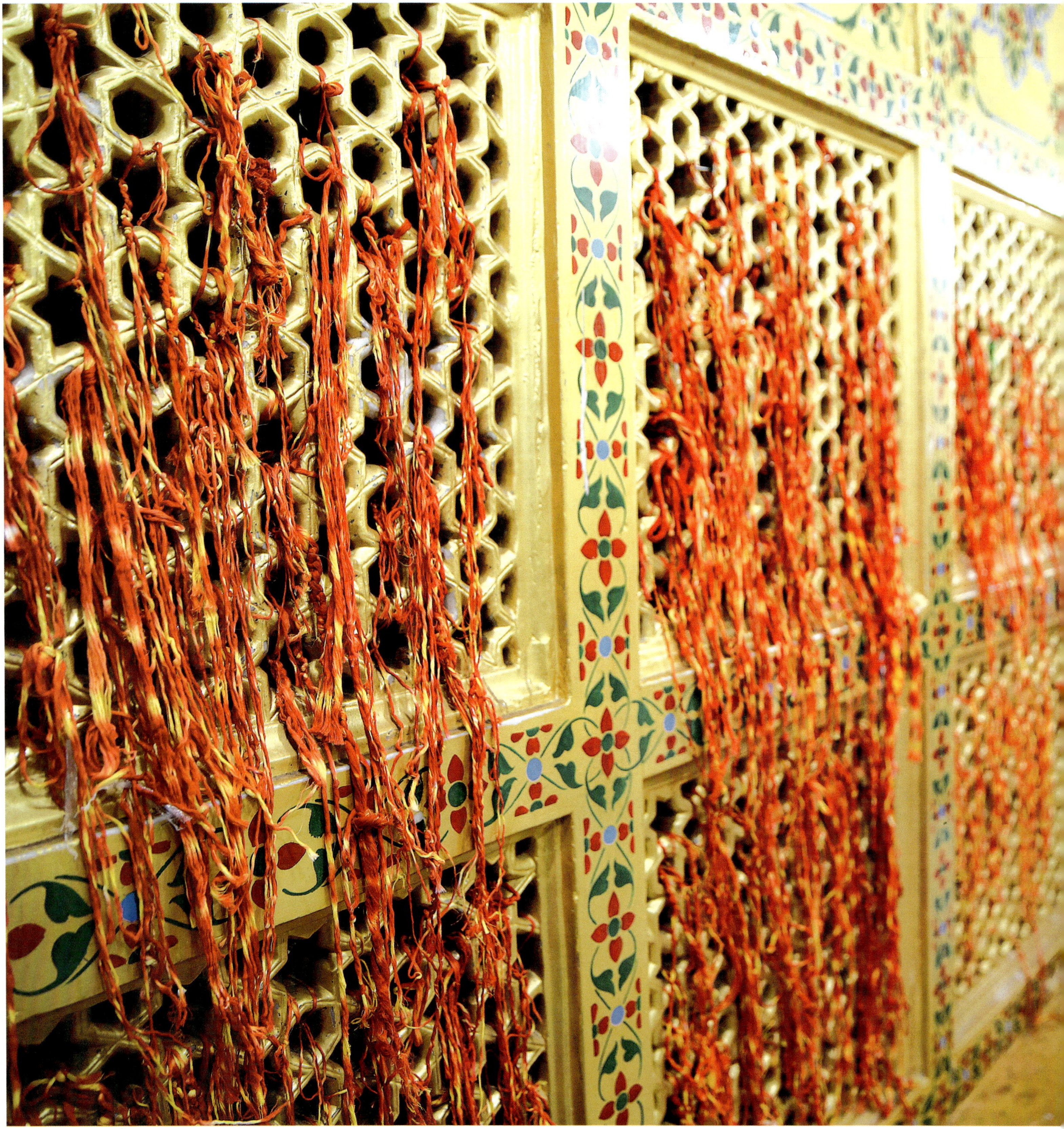

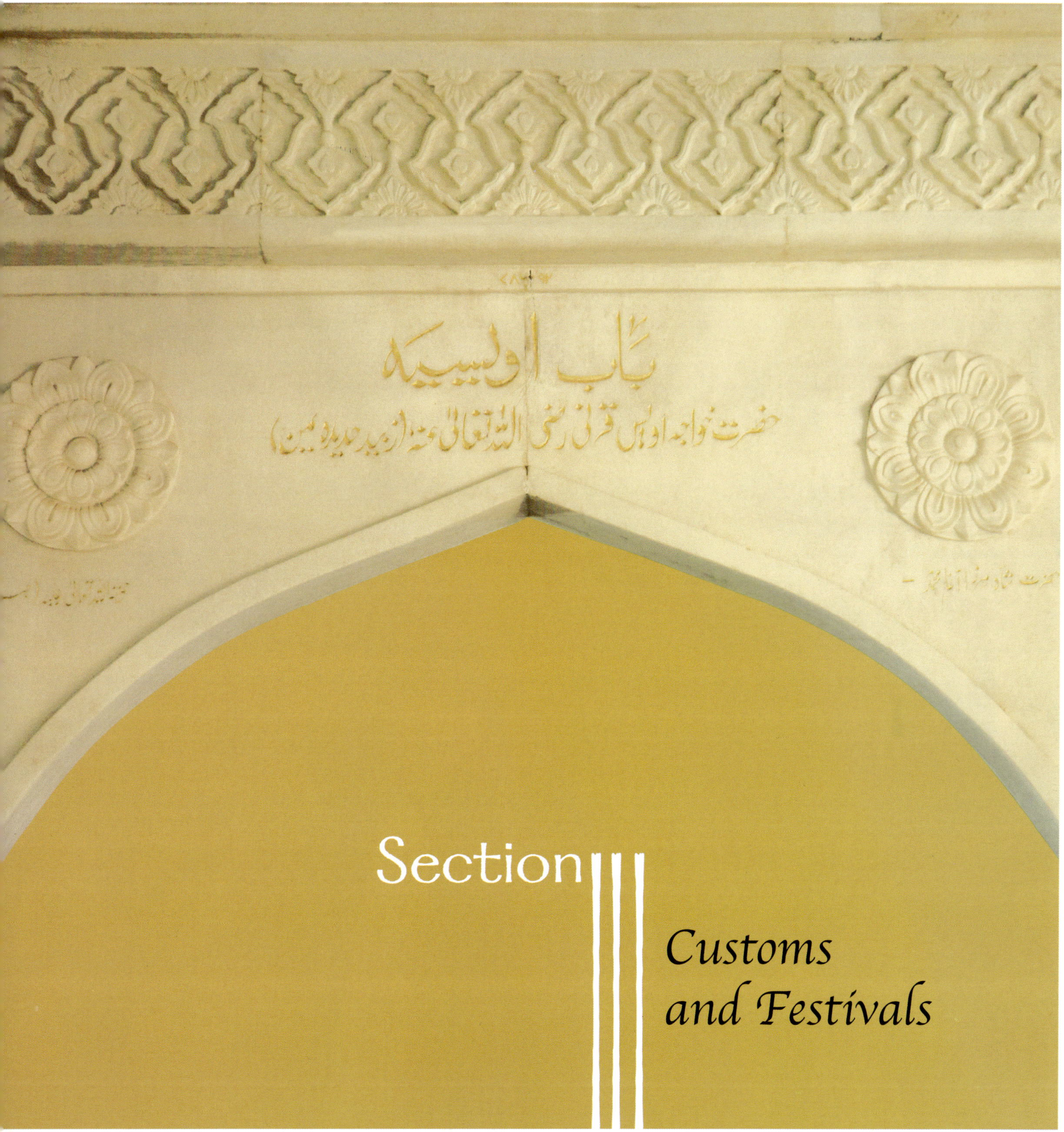

Section III

Customs and Festivals

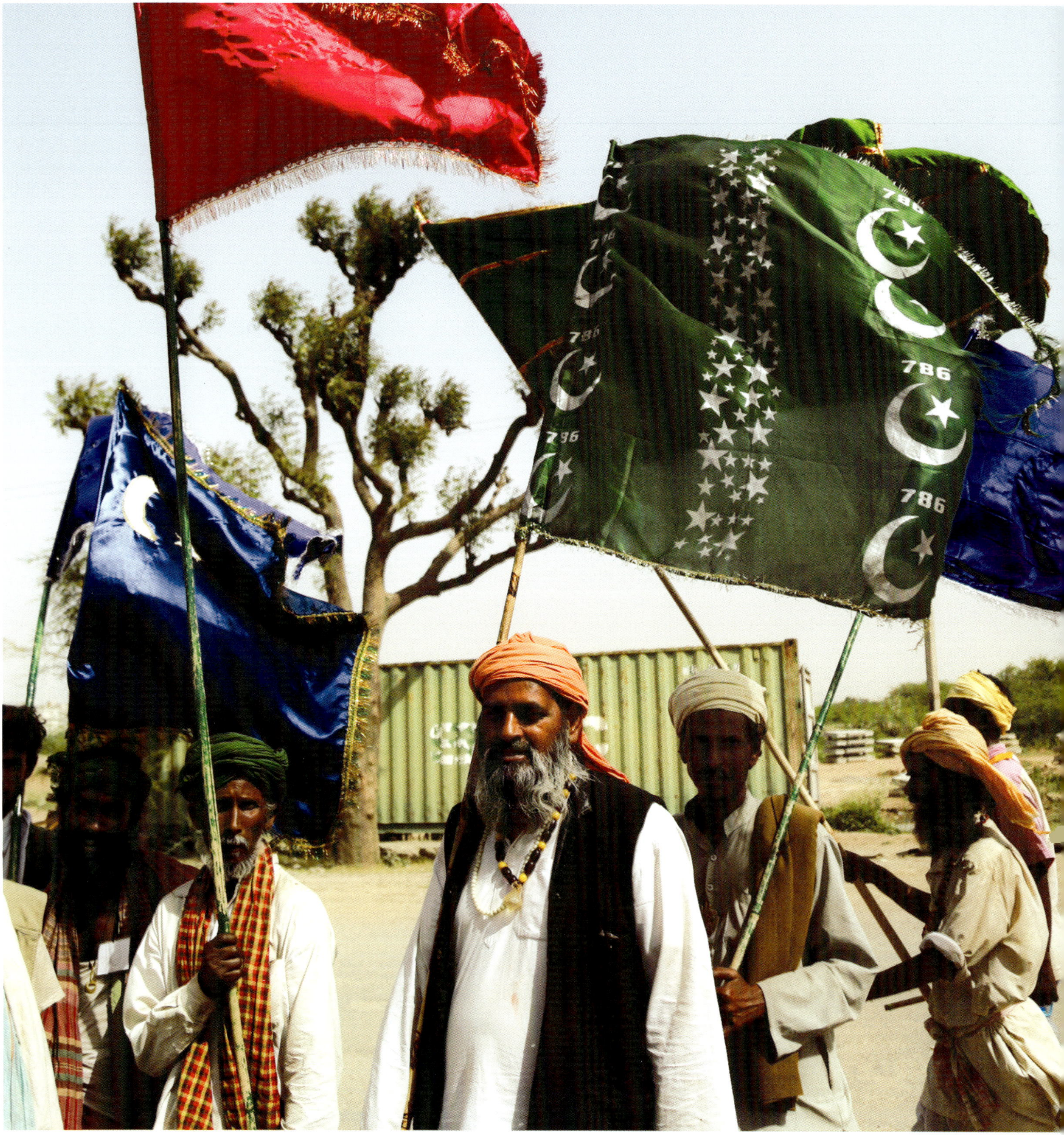
786
786
786
786
786
786

Rites of Love

Introduction

Come, come, come again
Whoever you may be,
Come again, even though
You may be a pagan or a fire worshipper.
Our centre is not one of despair.
Come again, even if you may have
Violated your vows a hundred times
Come again.
Mevlana Rumi

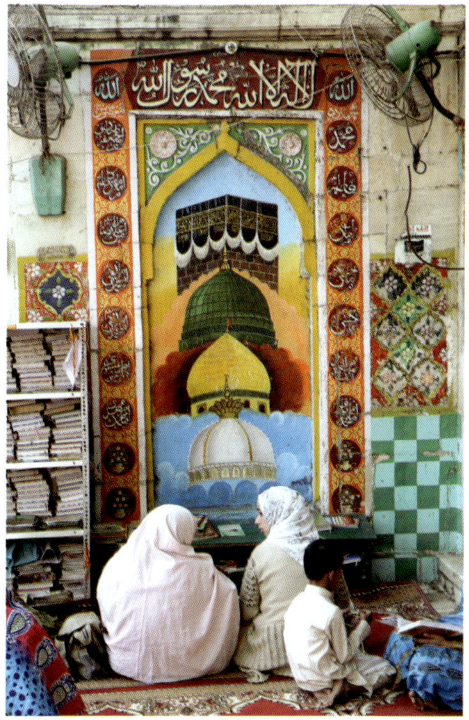

Above: In quiet contemplation—
women in the Ladies' prayer terrace

Facing page: Vagabond love—
ascetics and dervishes make
their journey of passion from Delhi to Ajmer

Previous spread left: Hopes tied in red and saffron

The longing for pilgrimage is universal and ancient. Each faith or belief comes with a prescribed set of rituals, but pilgrimage is deeper. The heart is the catalyst. A tourist traverses a route; the pilgrim's is an inner journey to a place of sanctity, a sanctuary. Sufis see the Way as the path to God.

The liturgy of Sufism grew from the grassroots over epochs, pulling multitudes in chase of simplified faith to venerable Sufi saints. In return, sages interpreted rigid doctrines for the unlettered with values of unity, love, and relief. In South Asia, the sway of the philosophy was a barricade to clerical domination.

Sufi Islam entered the region with Muinuddin and the Chishti Order. Music set the order apart from the other three schools—Naqshbandi, Qadiri and Suhrawardi. Layered with meanings, relatable, the inclusive flavour of its musical renditions has survived the eras and their vicissitudes. Muinuddin wove Iranian customs into indigenous Indian devotional

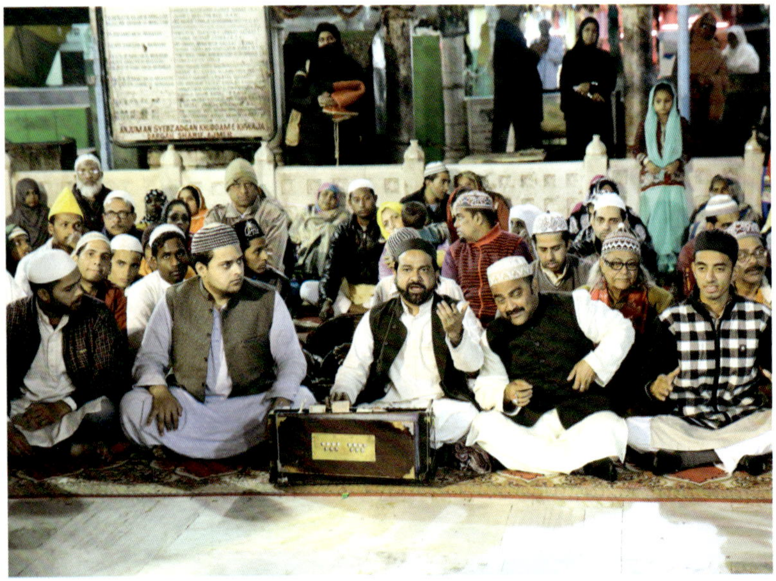

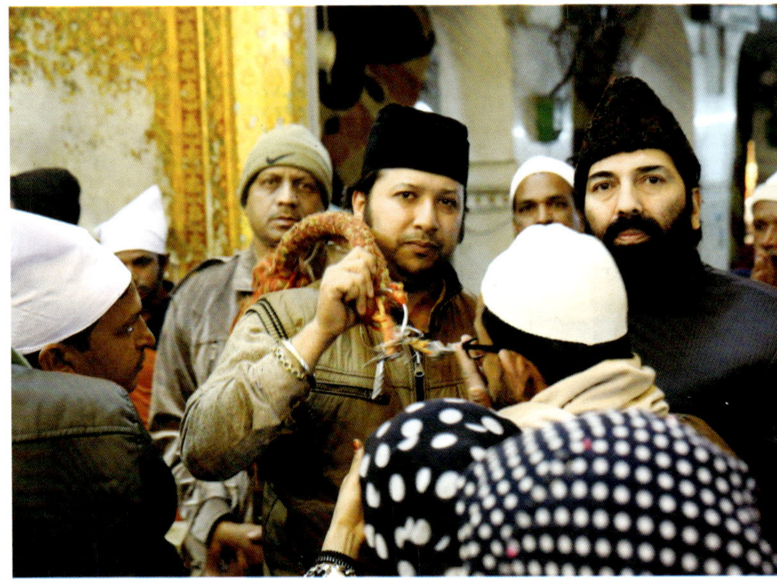

traditions. Therefore, *sama* (atmosphere) and qawwali are structured on *qaul*, 'saying' in Arabic. The raconteur is a 'qawwal', a sayer.

Thus far a male discipline, mystical verses have been carried forward by descendants of various lineages, such as Qawwal Bachche, who trace their origins to Amir Khusrau. A Qawwali performance is infused with Persian in abundance, played out in a sequence of allegiance. It often turns to native languages—Urdu, Hindi, Punjabi, Purbi, Sindhi and other dialects.

Purists aim for *haal*, an altered state of consciousness. An ecstasy where the self is beyond restraint. For a performer, this state is the ultimate influence or reward for his art. At Ajmer Sharif's shrine, varied rituals evolved under the patronage of Mughal, Rajput and Maratha regimes, creating a cross-pollination of cultures and creeds.

The custom of *baridari* (key custody) blends with Meccan practices and *haft chauki* (seven clans), combines an arrangement of the Mughal kings with traditions at iconic temples. At Ajmer Sharif, *Dalbadal*

Above: Qawwali is an essential ritual at the shrine

Above right: A pilgrim kisses the sacred keys in the presence of custodians Khalid Hashmi and Haji Farrokh

(a special canopy reserved for dignitaries) the presence of torchbearers, and macebearers dressed in Mughal garb, are aspects from the resplendent courts of the Mughals. Thursday nights at Chishti mausoleums radiate with the high voltage energy of qawwali, as does the prime week of the Urs.

Other than ceremonial elements, many Persian terms from Mughal darbars live on in the routine jargon at the mausoleum. *Ghulam gardish*—an exclusive passageway for keepers; *farrashas*—unique, handwoven bouquets of peacock feathers to bless devotees, and *bangla*—fastening a rose netting over the cenotaph, are some samples.

As Lyaqat Moini, a scholar at Aligarh Muslim University, records in *The Dargah of Khwaja Gharib-un-Nawaz of Ajmer*, that, in the 18th century, *kesaria bhat*, sweetened saffron rice, infused Maratha and Rajput aromas into Mughal customs. It is cooked in the two Mughal cauldrons to the present day.

Moini, in his counter-narrative to P.M. Currie's tome on Ajmer, also serves up the most relevant feature of a pluralistic sanctuary—the induction of non-Muslims to significant offices and their fixed share in the communal feast.

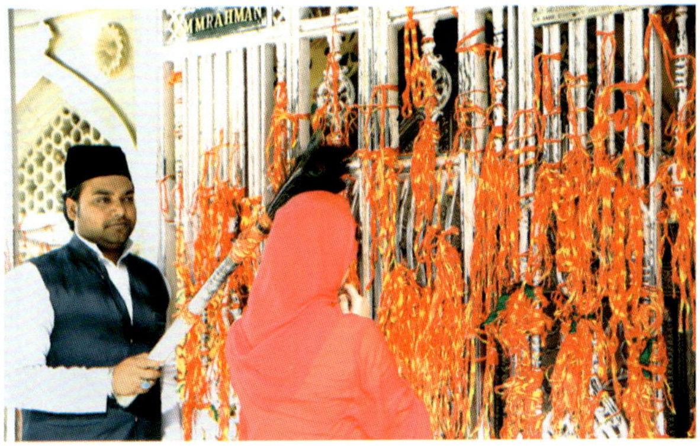

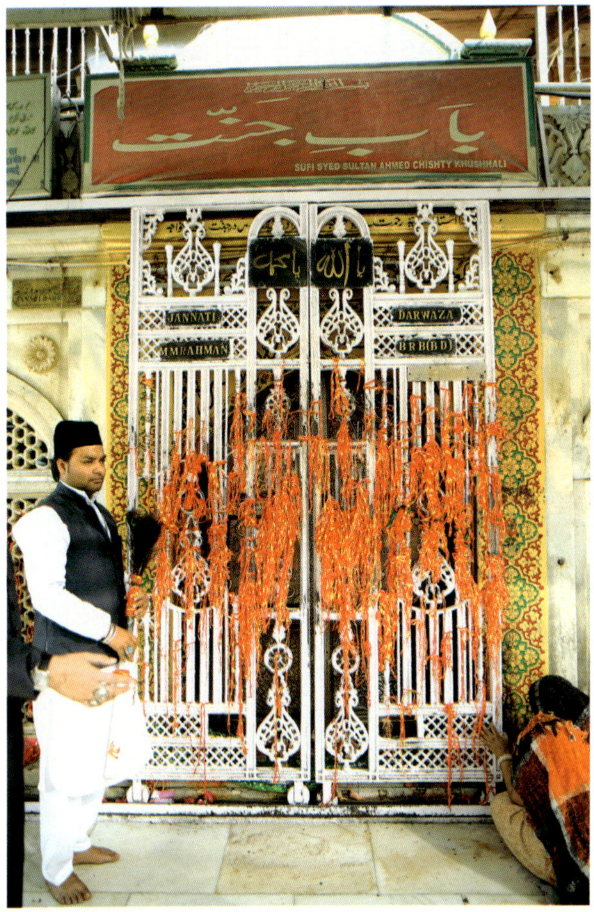

Top right: Peacock feathers provide blessings of hope at the Jannati Darwaza

Right: A Khadim watches over the Jannati Darwaza (doorway to paradise)

Next page: Surge of devotion after Karka

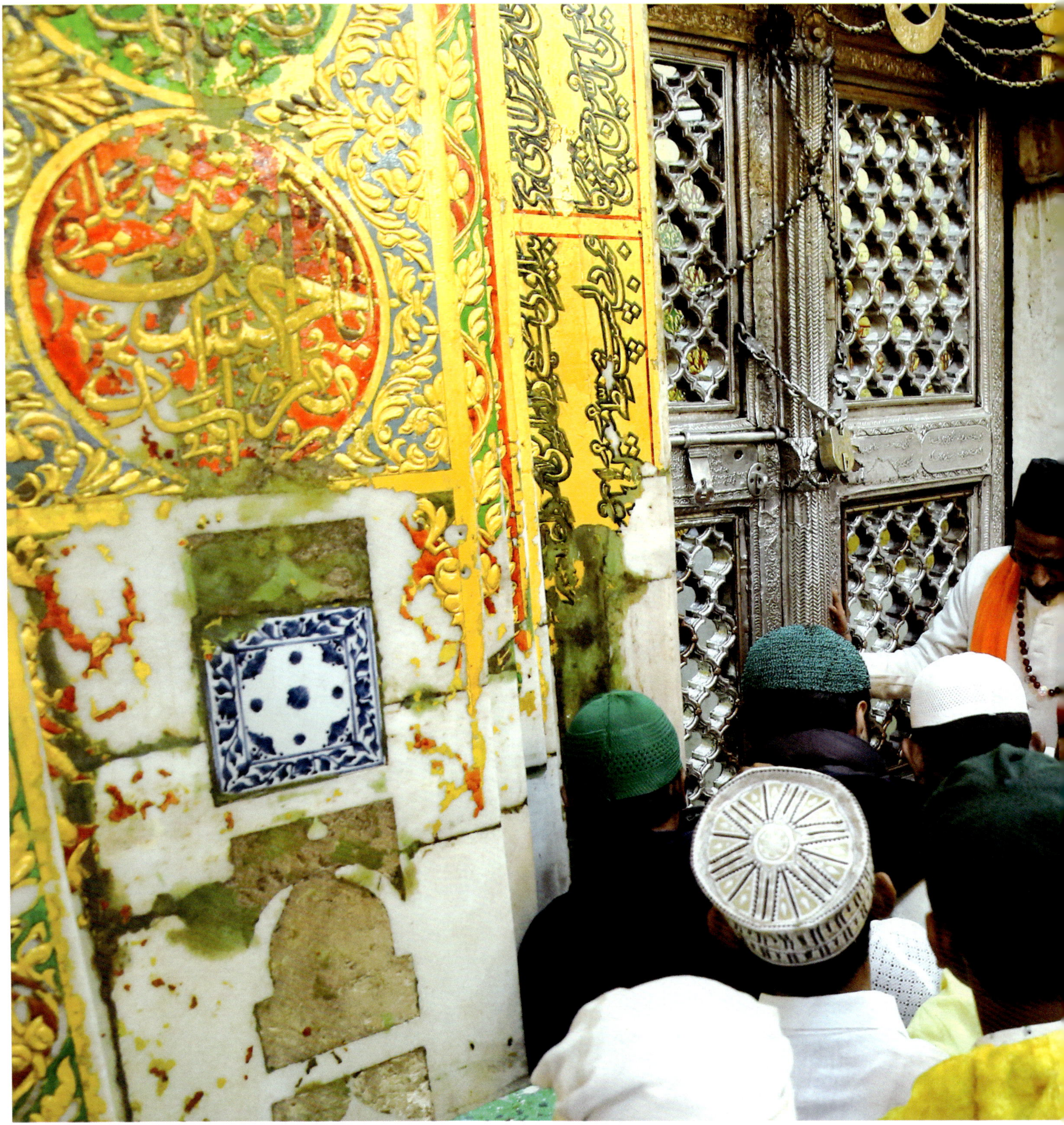

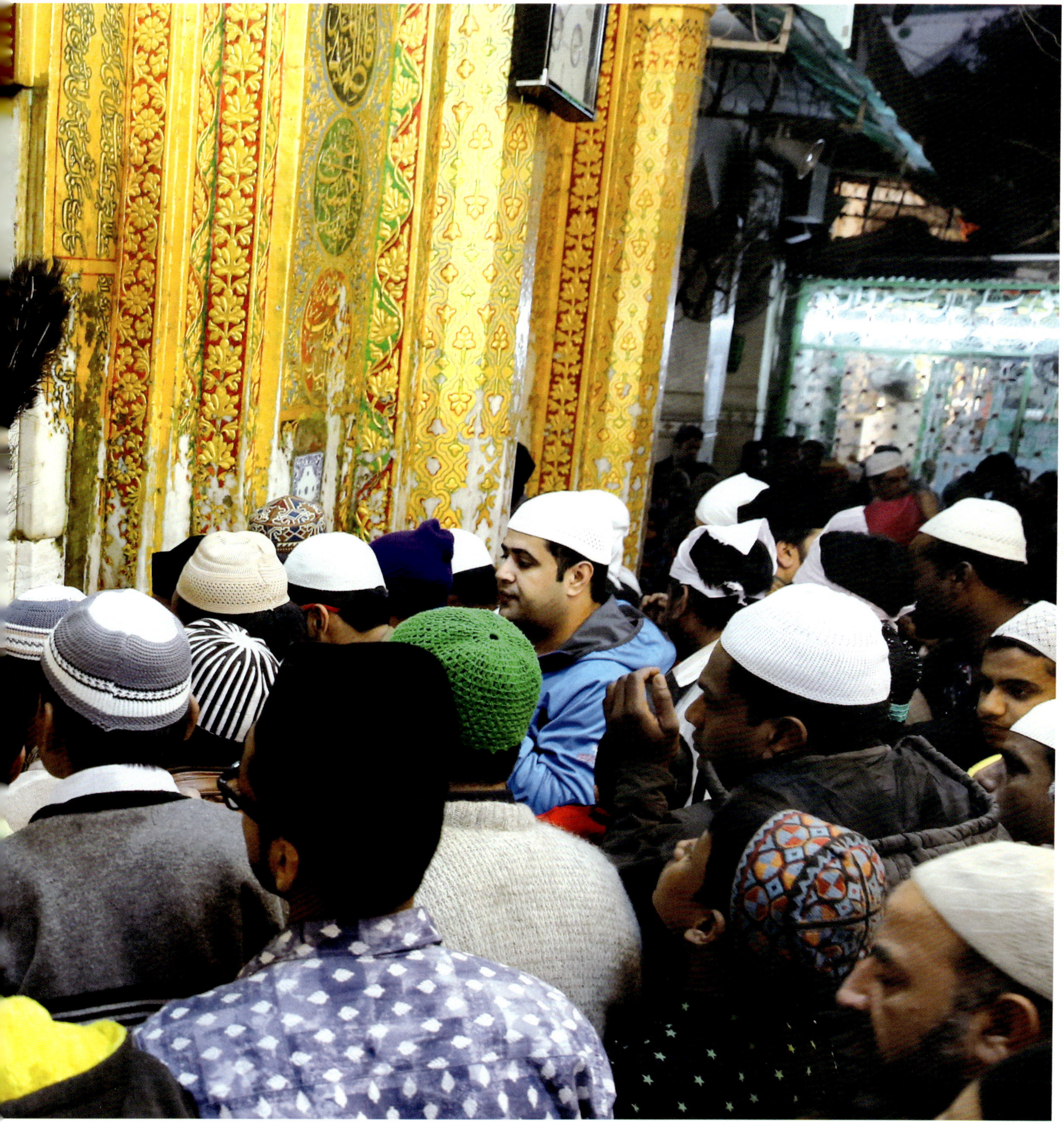

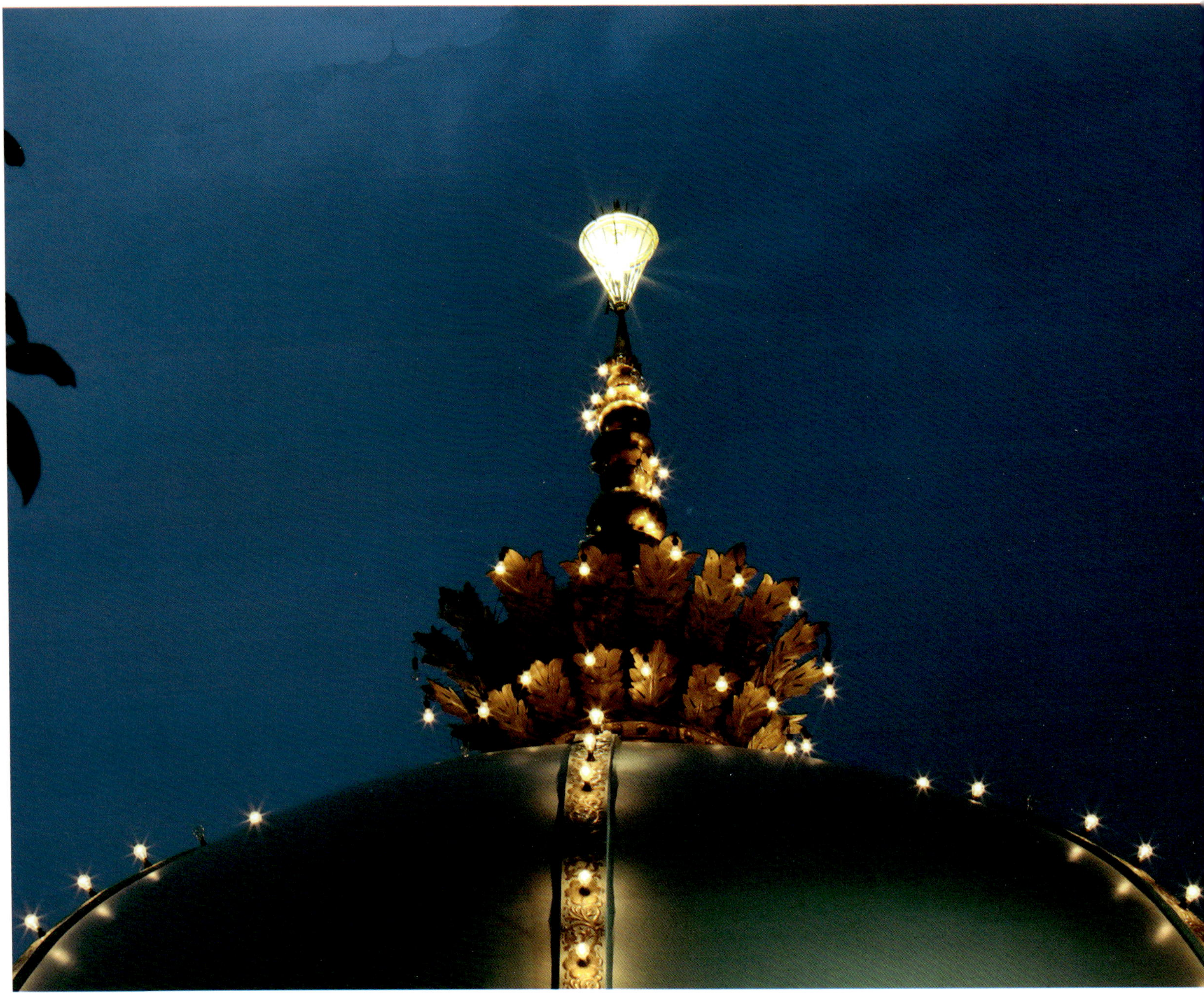

The Concert of Belief

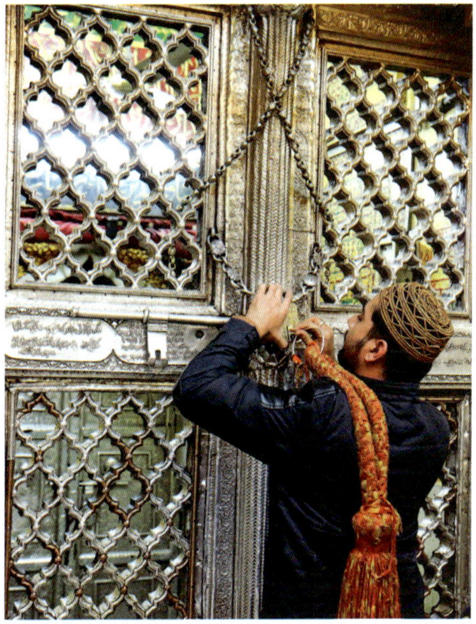

One is struck by the semblance between Muinuddin's shrine and his life in a hut, where none were turned away. Ajmer Sharif, as it exists today, is a place where I saw faith as organic and living.

In the sunny hours before the primary ceremonies, snug passages to the gates are thick with devotees—on foot, in carts and rickshaws. Some already consumed by the energy of belief—a frail, old lady circling in ecstasy; brides laden with henna, jewels and silken clothes walking briskly to the door with starched grooms; mendicants breaking into husky chants. Others clutching the sick and the distressed, in the hope of absorbing blessings and prayers through the night.

Passing a spectrum of these nests of activity, the first glance at the courtyards witnesses an otherworldly mood. Keepers assure one that the saint's spirit is palpable to the earnest.

Sunrise and mid-afternoon hours make for the most redolent time—the front door closes and a black curtain falls on the back door, where I stand obstinately to witness a dramatic, moving ritual of Khidmat (service). An hour before first light, the main silver door of the sanctum is unbolted by the custodian with the key; an elder recites the call to prayer, performs varied forms of devotional greetings, and other keepers pour in and the door shuts behind them.

By the back door, senior khadims in black and green robes enter the prime sanctum; the sepulchre is rinsed in sandalwood, saffron and rose water, as the heady fragrance wafts out to the ardent. Oil lamps and candles cut dancing silhouettes in corner niches, and across the spreading

Above: A custodian secures the sacred chamber

Facing page: The lotus finial and the light of faith

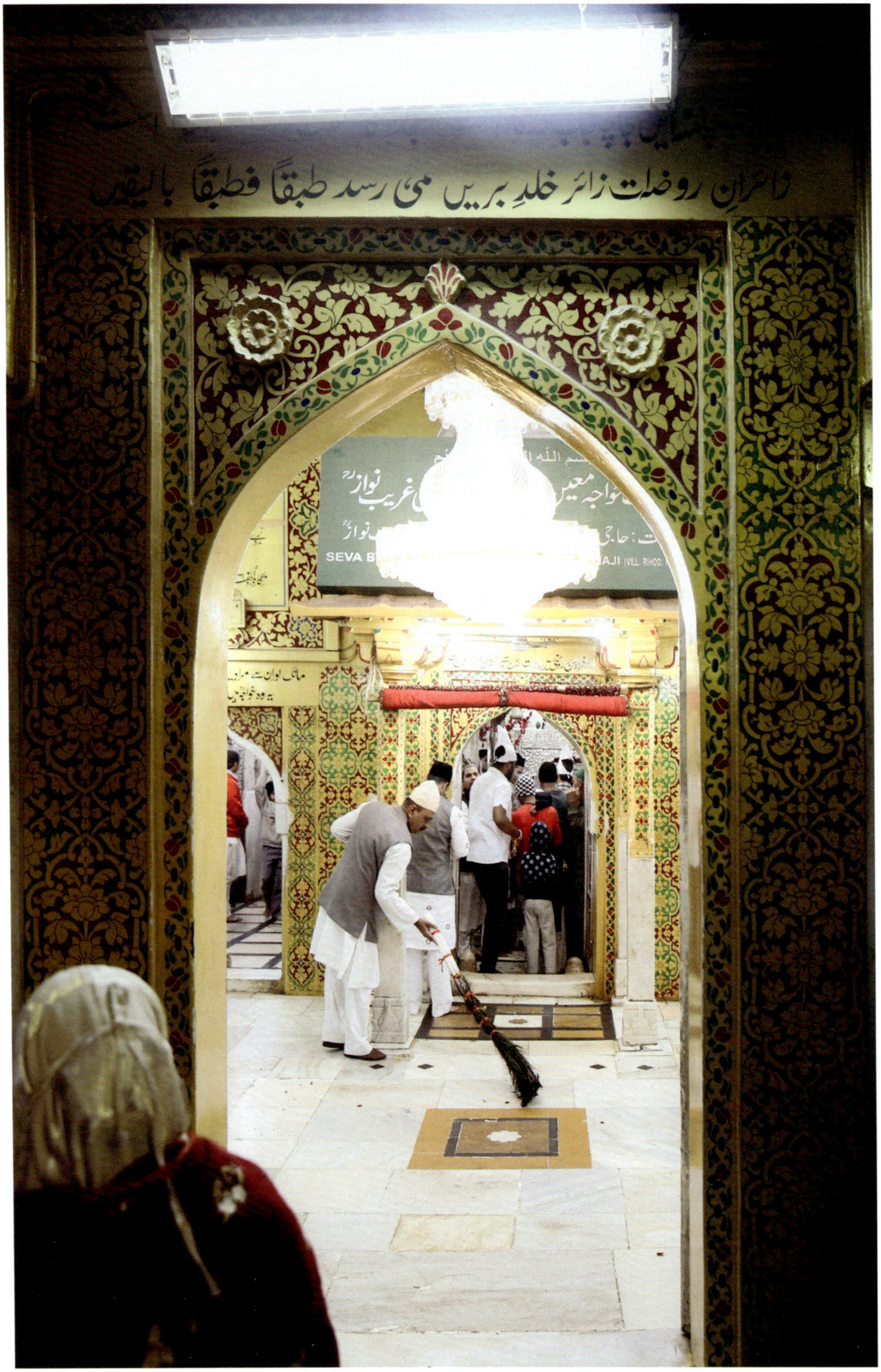

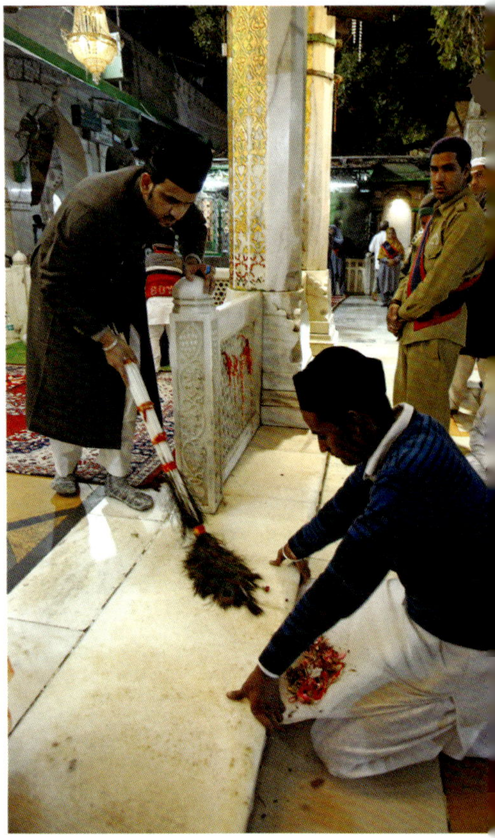

Above: The rose petals from the tomb are carefully gathered to be distributed among the faithful

Left: Dusk rites of the Illumination Ceremony (Roshni) inside the sanctum

dome. A chosen server removes the *sej*, a finely knit shroud of flowers, from the tomb. It is deposited in a basket with care and covered with a special cloth. Another carries it to the tomb of Bibi Hafiza Jamal, where, following her bathing rituals, her father's flowers swaddle her grave.

Two custodians enter the inner fence around Muinuddin's tomb, and sweep towards the smaller doorway by the footstone. Petals are scooped into containers and distributed among pilgrims and visitors. Once the cleaning rituals conclude, the same keeper recites verses from the holy book and a drape is spread over Khwaja's vault. A fresh, dewy sej covers it with a sprinkling of attar; the darbar is declared open for homage.

In the afternoon, the ritual is begun anew, however, with an alteration—the area perceived to be the saint's chest is plastered with a coat of sandalwood paste. New drapes replace drenched morning wear, and the sanctum key is passed on to the custodian in line for the ensuing 24 hours. Peacock feathers sweep the outside porches; khadims begin to spill out, tearful, their hair and robes soaked.

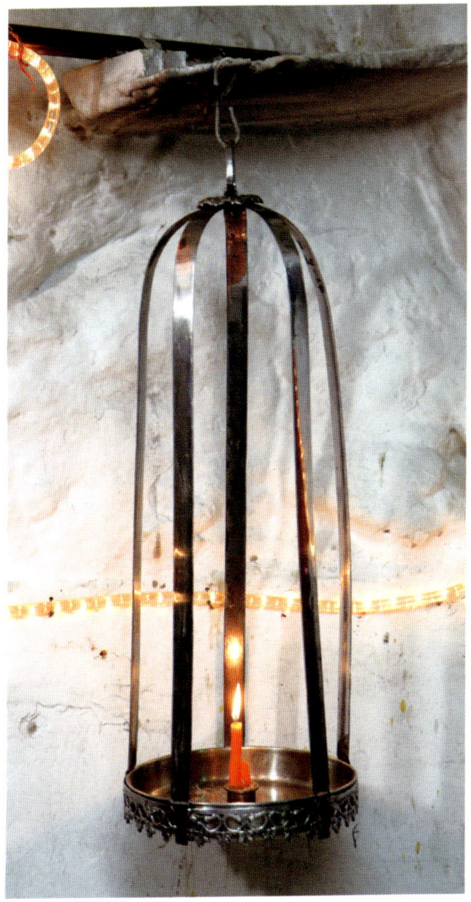

Above: The steady flame of faith—a candle-stand in the shrine

Next page: A glittering chandelier lights the pilgrims' path

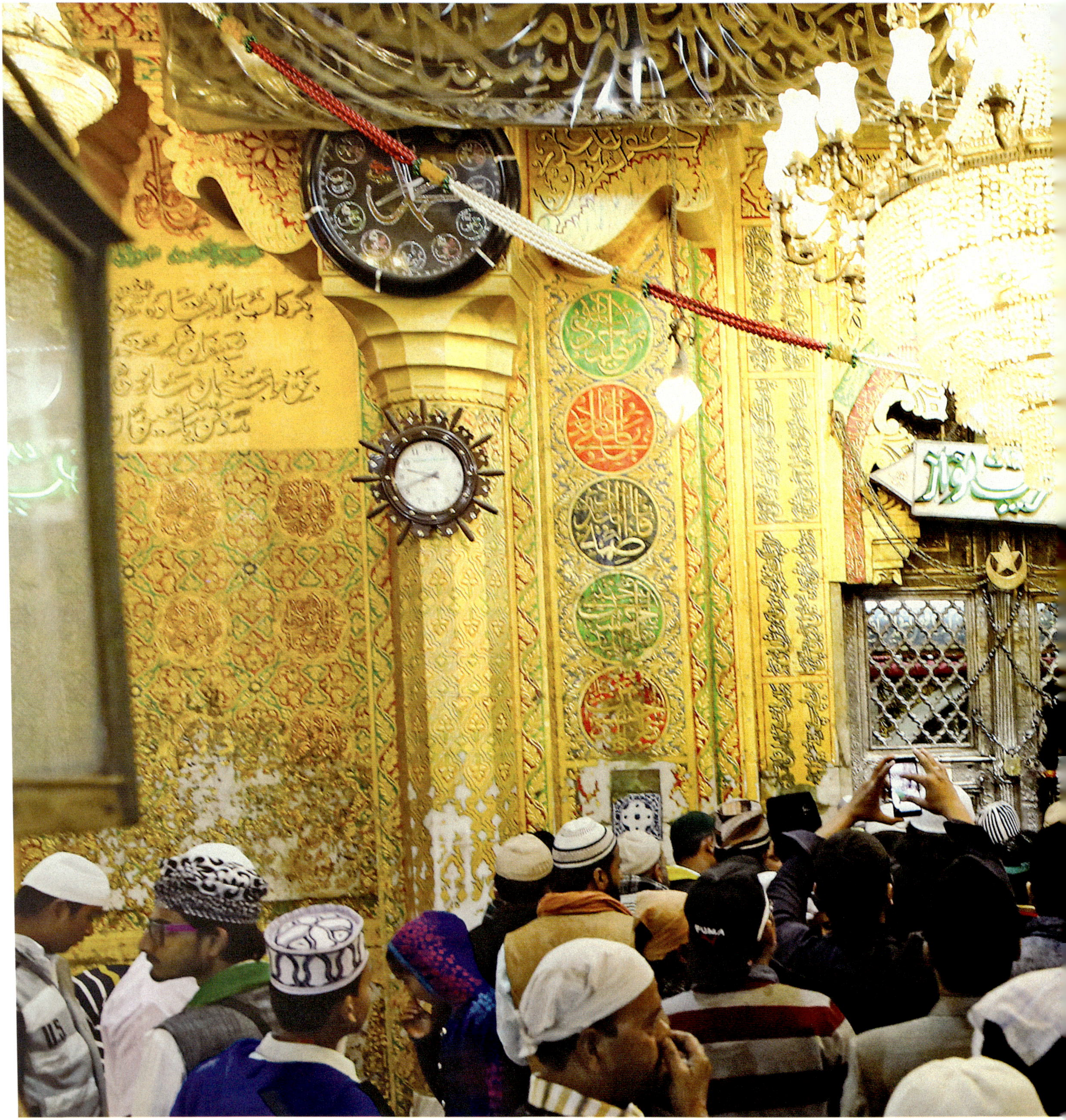
PUMA

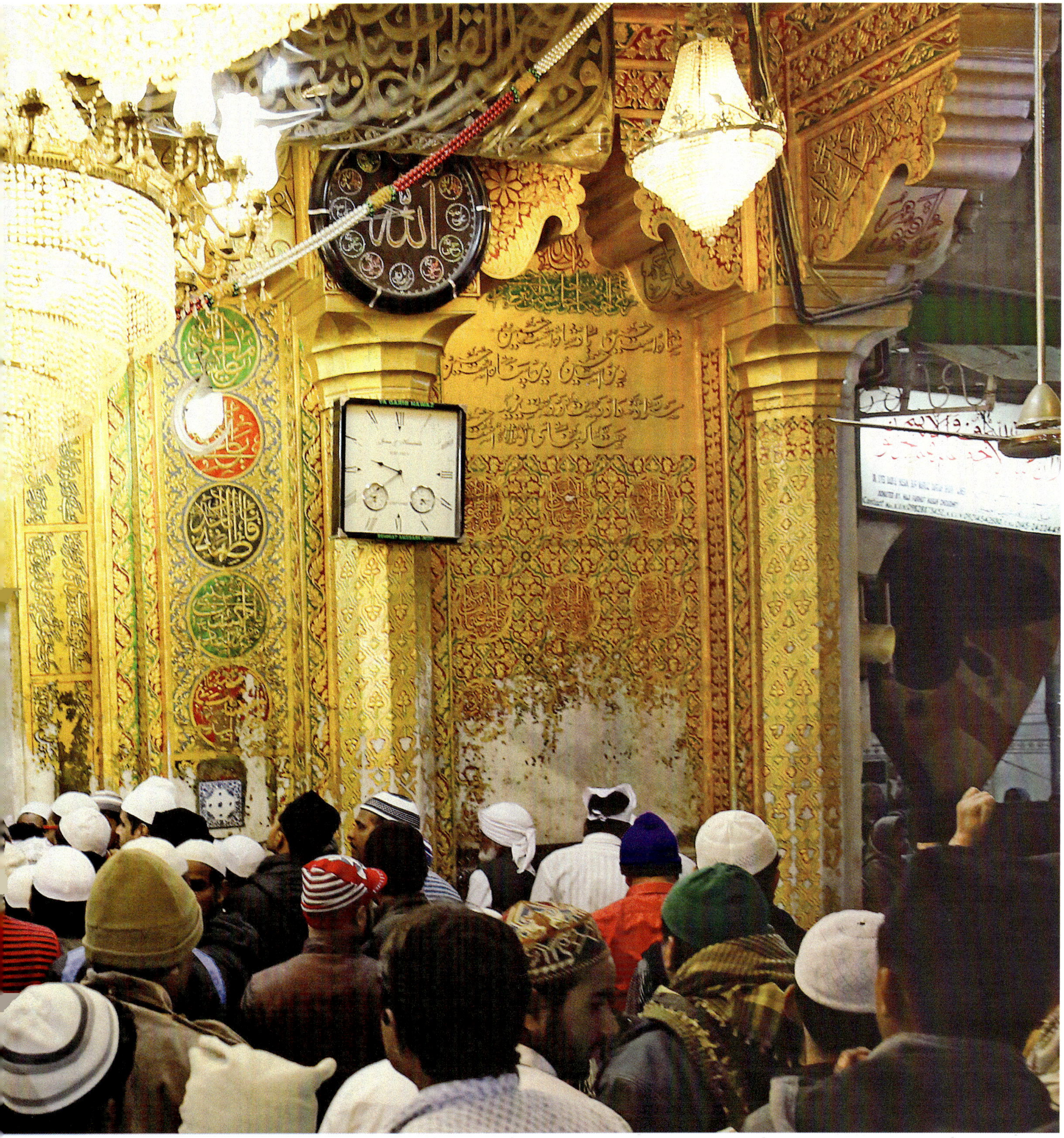

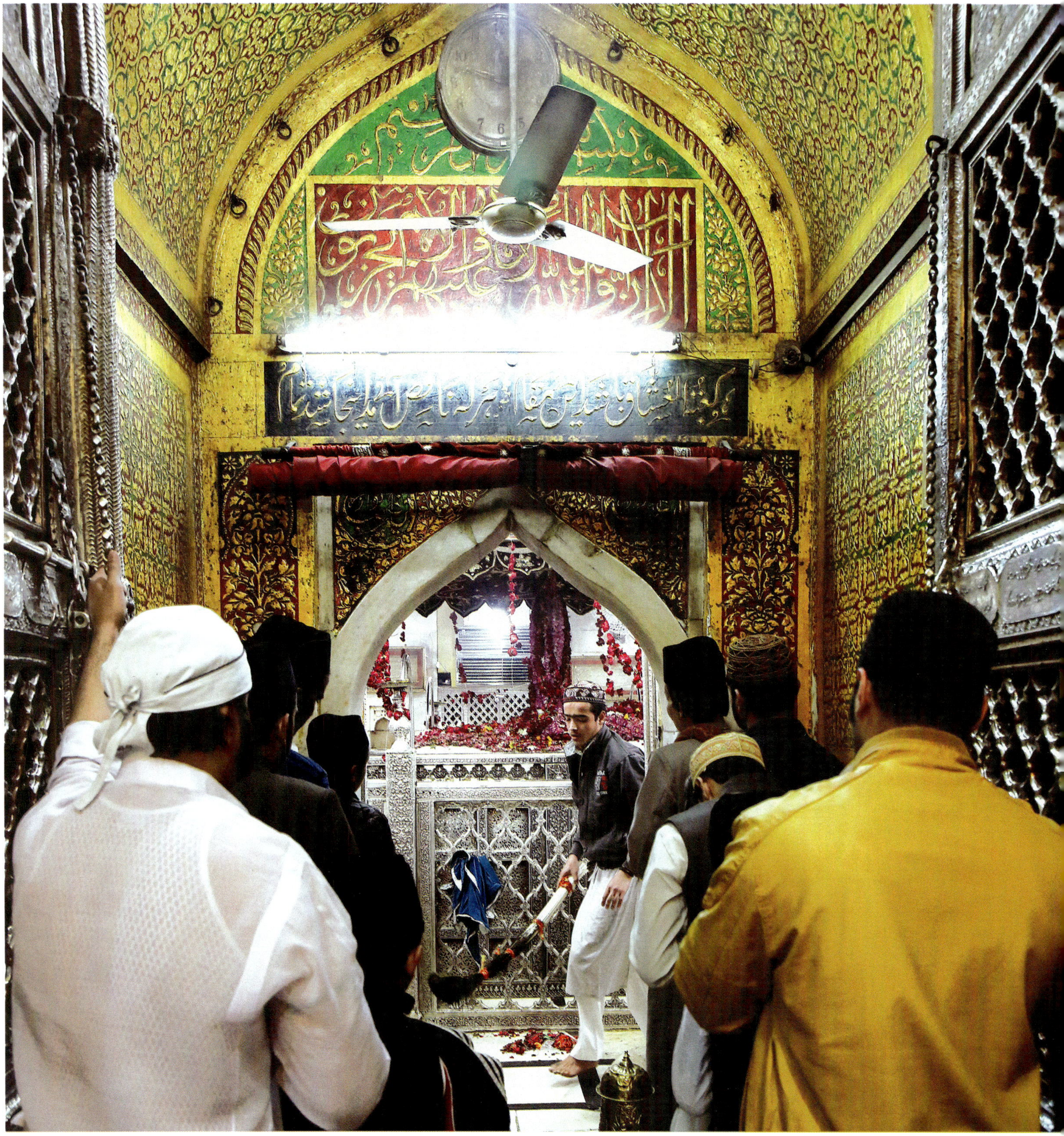

Roshni (Light)

In the failing light, as the sun slides behind the dome, another replay of cleansing commences 15 minutes before *Maghrib* (sunset prayers). Roshni, the ceremony of illumination in Muinuddin's sacred chamber, is the most ancient of customs. Unshared by another Sufi order, it follows a distinct sequence of lyrical acts.

Incense sticks and chunks of *oud* (aloe wood), arranged in a holder are placed in the middle of the western side of the railing, perhaps to symbolise Maghrib—both dusk and west. Four large *shamadans* (candle-stands), rest on all four sides, facing the incense burner; four keepers facing the tomb stand at the corners, suggesting that they have been granted the right to elevate these stands above their heads.

Outside, in the focal portico, three khadims with candles emerge from an enclosure near the communal kitchen, where sanctum candles are stored. As they begin their walk to the shrine, drums resound from kiosks above gates, a powerful background score for the stirring ceremony. Khadims cross the Sandal Mosque, enter the sanctum from the eastern doorway, and male pilgrims gather inside the chamber.

Candle bearers approach the candle-stands; the first lights the one in his hand and another passes candles to others by the stands. A few candles are handed over by the last keeper to the candle maker who fixes them in the silver holders attached to the tomb's posts. The first keeper to enter, lights all four candles raised by custodians. One of the wardens beside a post sets off a narration of Persian verses, odes to Khwaja, most likely compiled by Hamiduddin Nagauri.

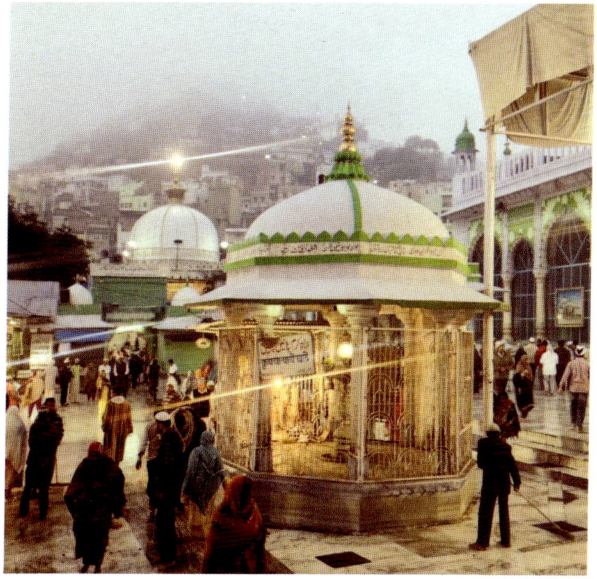

Above: Lit up Sehan Chiragh

Facing page: The heart of the shrine—a glimpse of the Khwaja's tomb

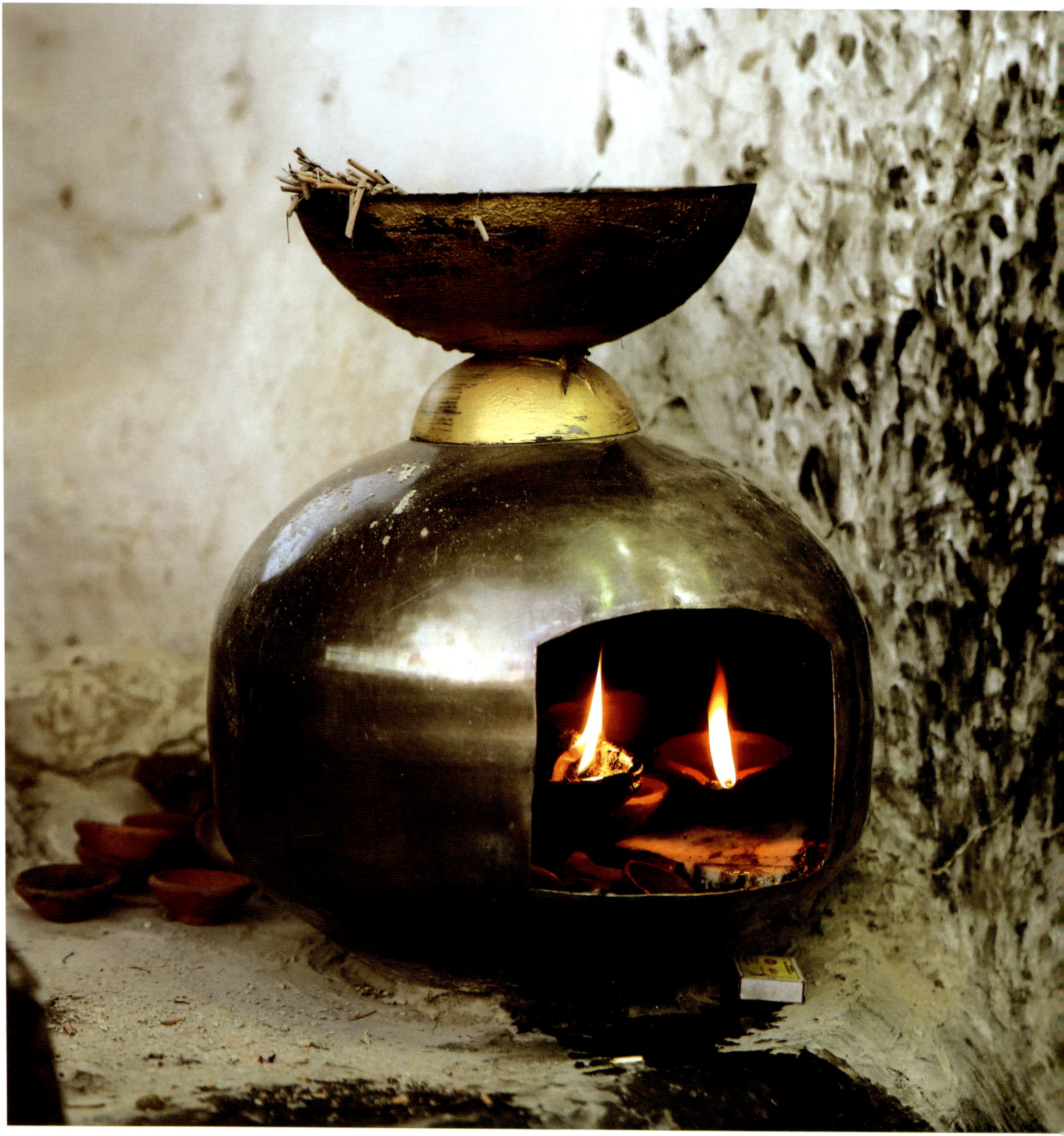

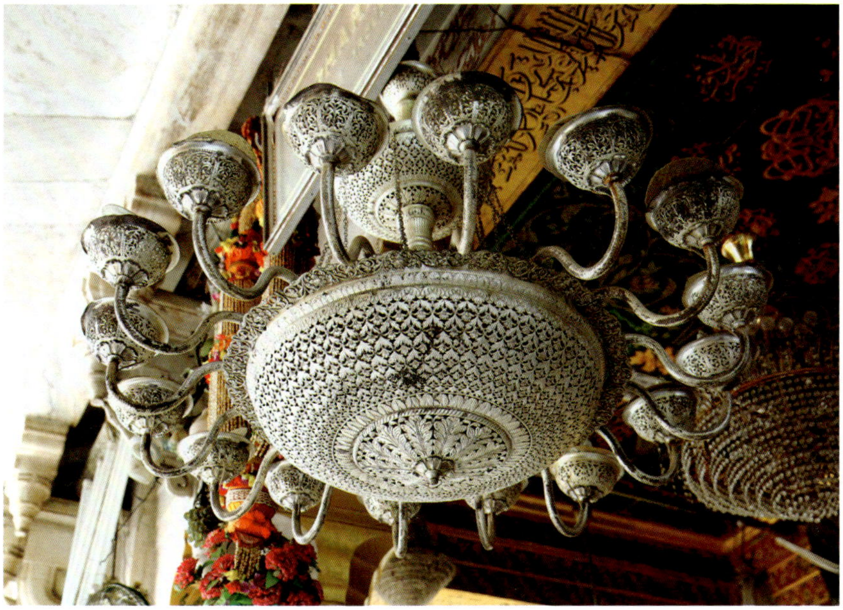

As the reading culminates, lamp-stands are taken to the four sides and candle-stands atop poles and in all corners shimmer with miniature flames. The entourage departs from the southern door, beside Bibi Hafiza Jamal's enclosure. A candle is then lit at her abode and droves of women amble into the shrine, bringing Roshni to a close.

Above: An intricate silver filigree chandelier illumines the way of the seeker

Right: An oil lamp cone in the Princess Courtyard

Facing page: Flames of faith

Next page: A view of Shah Jahan's delicate archway and the majesty of Moinuddin's dome

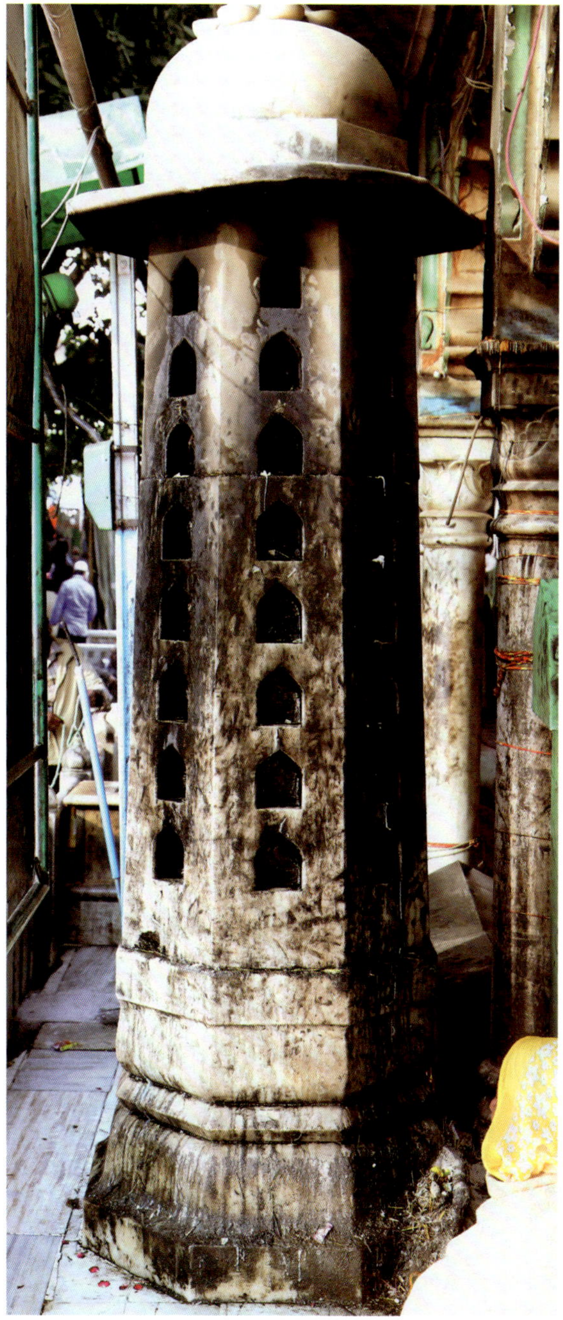

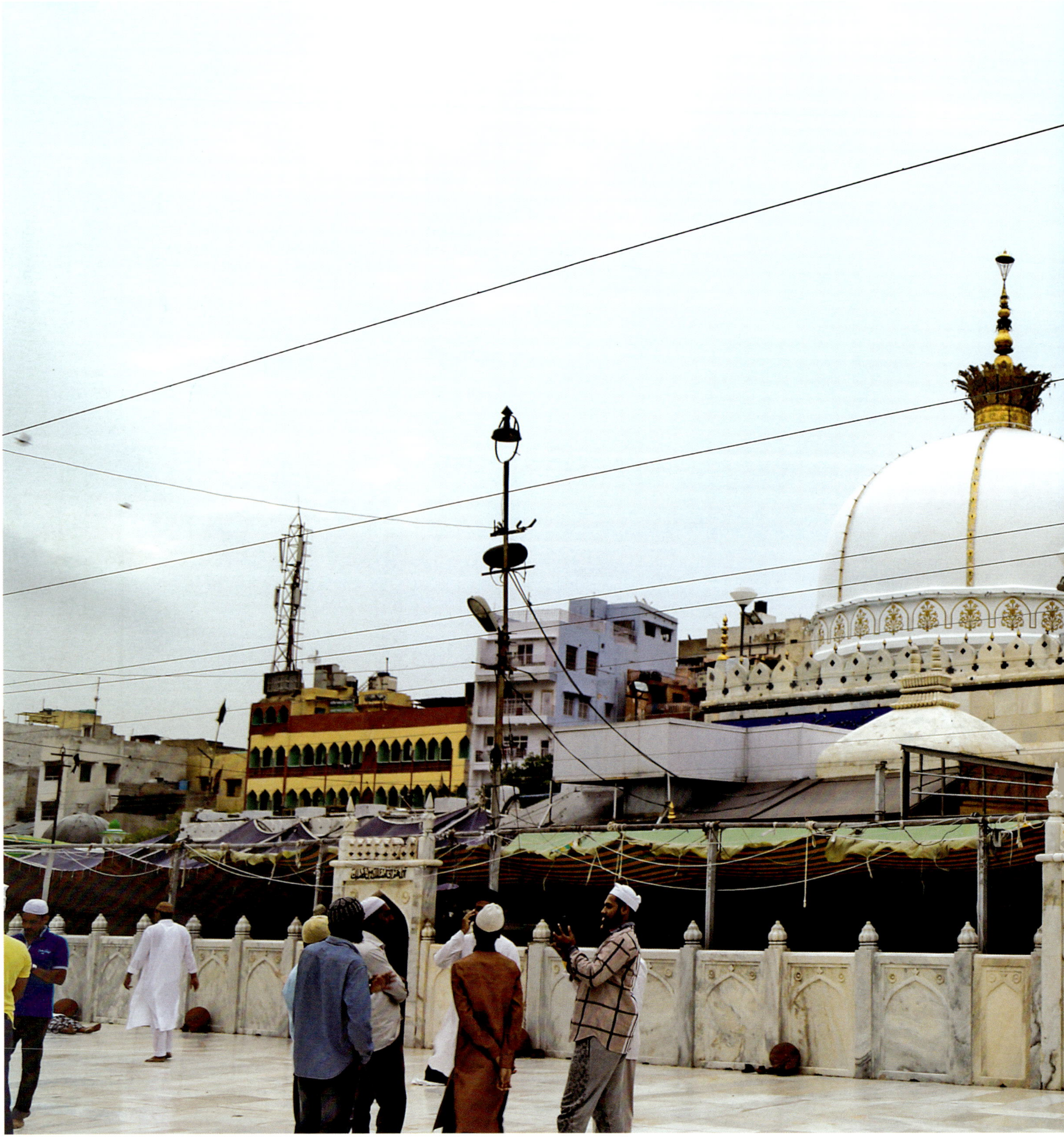

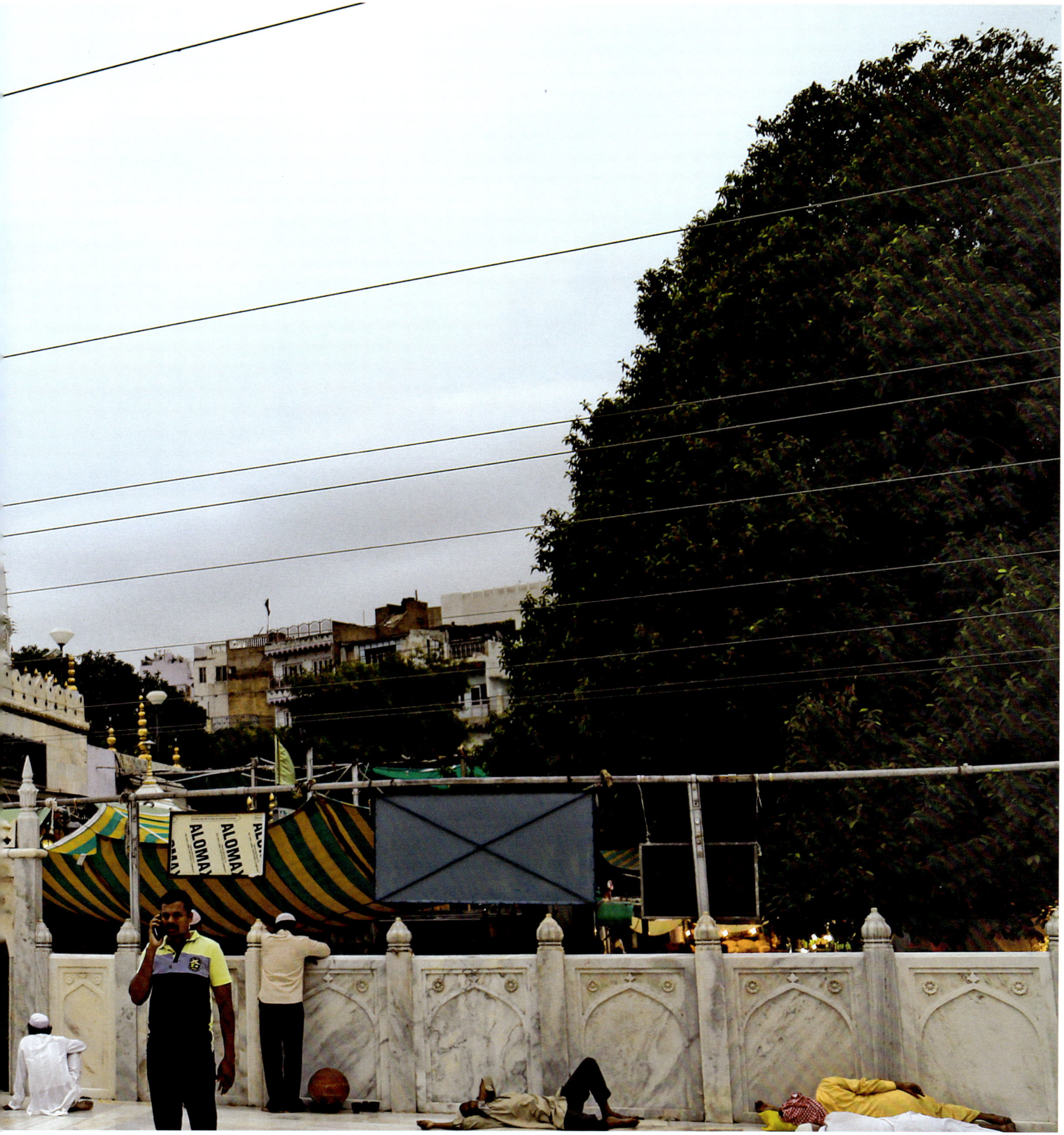

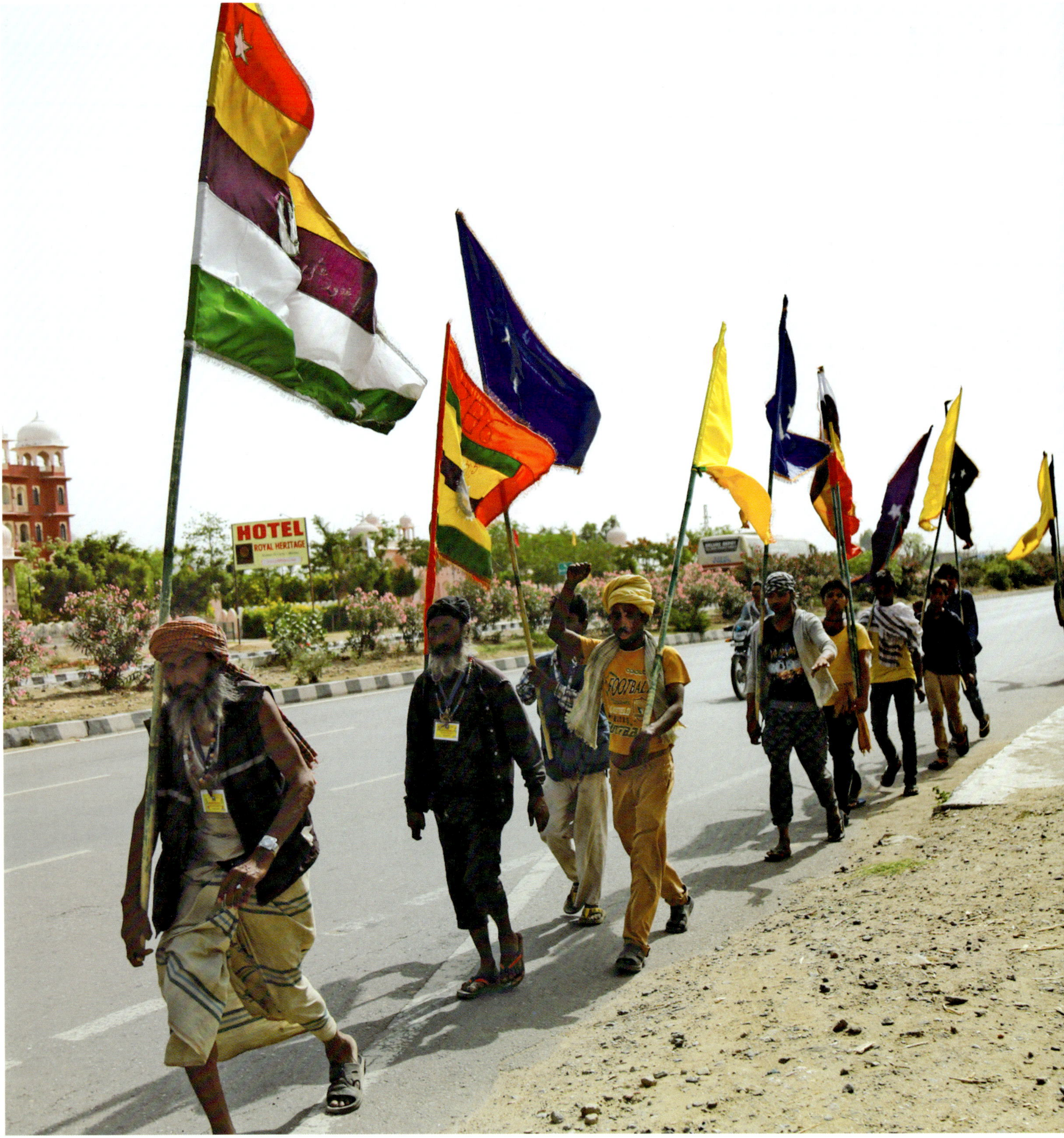
HOTEL
ROYAL HERITAGE

Karka (War Song)

Oh ye Muinuddin, truly lord protector, who graces fortunes,
You have lit the Chishti lamp the world over.
Oh ye Muinuddin, truly lord protector who graces fortunes,
The spiteful came with brutal trickery,
Their 52 attempts vanquished,
They scattered in the air at thy orders,
You the pillar for here and hereafter,
The saint of India, the Light and Beloved of God, a door to Divinity,
Such a master of masters, your shrine has a splendour its own,
It brightens the four ends of the universe.
The pillar of virtue,
Cast a glance, bestow gnosis upon me.
The great emperor, hazrat-e-Chishti
Oh Muinuddin, Khwaja, the tower of Compassion.

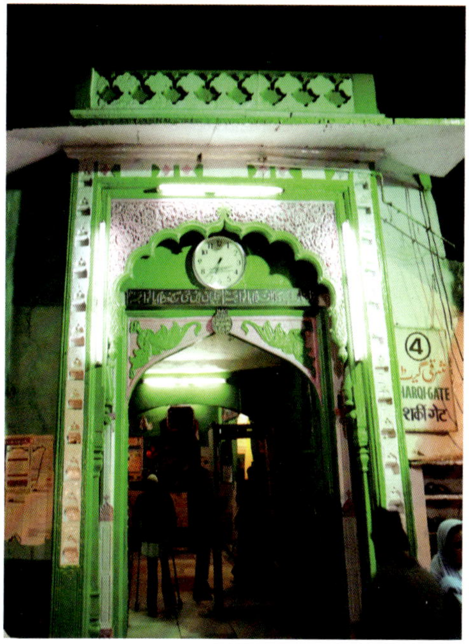

Karka, originally an ancient Rajput war song to motivate soldiers, has met assimilation here as a reminder for devotees to battle evil with abiding grace. The Karka stanza is composed in Bhojpuri, and is claimed to be the work of either Shaikh Mitha, a devotee, or Roora Mithu, a musician in the court of Jahangir.

At 10 pm, the ceremony, pitched on the verses above, scripts the completion of the sanctum's journey through the day. Three keepers follow each other at intervals to purify the area outside the inner fence.

Above: Devotees at the entrance to Sharqi Gate

Facing page: Armed by faith—pilgrims on the long trek to Ajmer Sharif

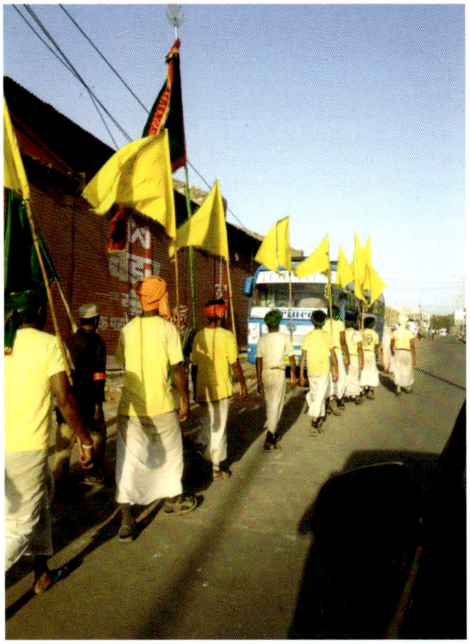

Above: All roads lead to Ajmer Sharif

Facing page: Moved by faith to make mystical journeys

Pilgrims file in rows of two by the eastern entryway; none are permitted inside. Khadims step out one after the other and gently dust bowed heads with their farrashas, as they walk towards the Sandal Mosque to place flowers and dusters in a particular container.

Each silhouette in the complex rises when Karka is underway, and the shrine's qawwals, descendants of families employed by the Mughals, belt out cantos in the saint's honour. Once the last keeper departs, the *gharyaali* (timekeeper), pronounces the passage of six *gharis*. In ancient times, one *ghari* was 24 minutes in duration. The door is barred at last and a teeming sea of heads bow in supplication.

A sole woman of a slight frame, has been motionless, not even heaving with breath; her head against a far corner of the sanctum wall. She looks up at the sound of the bolt on the door. Her swollen, blood-shot eyes, desperate and searching, emit an intensity that gives me gooseflesh.

Other than these customary ceremonies, *naubat*, at sunrise and at sunset, pierces every nook of silence through the complex as well as the bazaar; a communal meal of a barley dish is supplied twice to pilgrims, tourists and dervishes as an early breakfast and an early evening repast.

On Thursday nights, the Ehaata Noorani (the Courtyard of Light), sets the stage for a qawwali in the presence of the Dewan. After the night prayer, he arrives in Mughal regalia, escorted by torchbearers. The recital begins with devotional verses, followed by a distribution of special sweets prepared for the occasion. Qawwals launch into 'qauls' in praise of the saint, and continue till the curtain rings down on Karka customs. I stand still and let the atmosphere of praise wash over me.

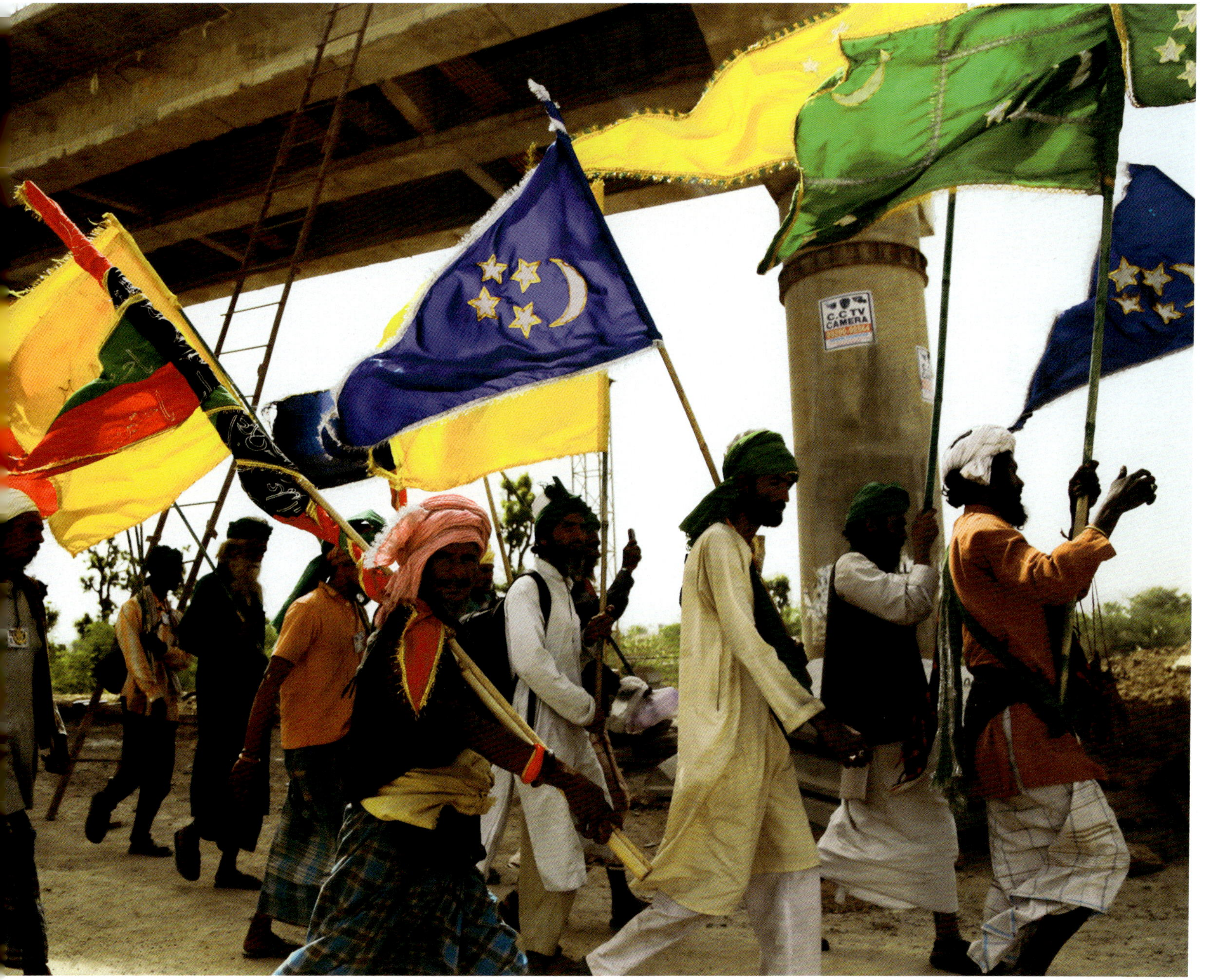
C.C TV
CAMERA

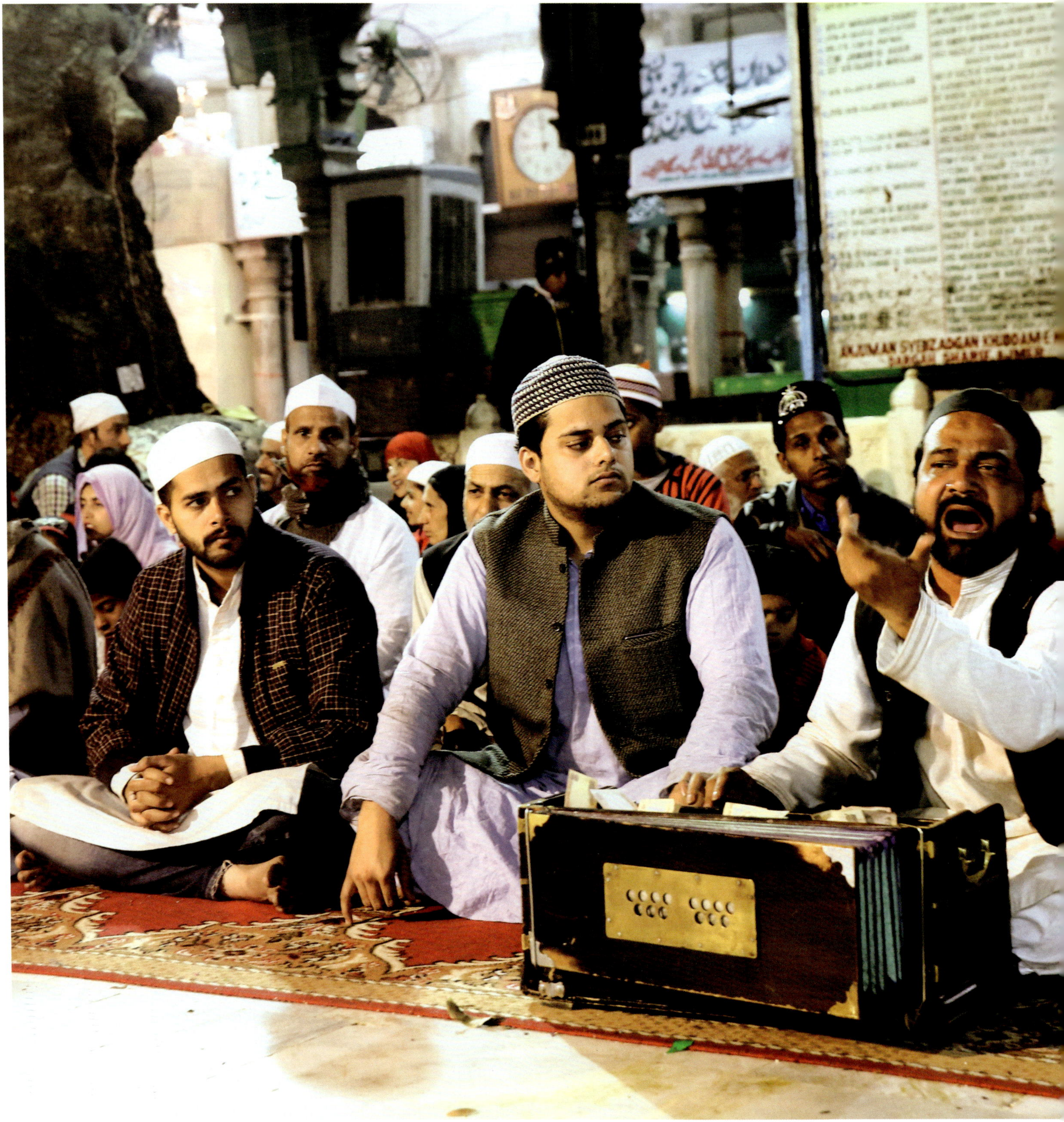

Chhati Sharif (The Sixth Day)

The sixth day of each month of the Muslim lunar calendar is honoured as Chhati Sharif, with a similar assembly to commemorate Muinuddin's departure for his Divine Beloved—*wisal* in Sufi terms, death in the material context.

The same courtyard hosts a reading from the Holy Book at 9 am; a keeper delivers the spiritual pedigree of the Chishti Order, along with verses from ancestors of the present custodians. Blessings are sent to every devotee in attendance; jaggery, sweetmeats, and *batasha* (sugar pellets) make rounds as bequests of a sanctified day.

Besides Chhati Sharif, the shrine observes death anniversaries of celebrated saints throughout the year with analogous fanfare. One such occasion is the Urs of Muinuddin's spiritual tutor, Usman Harooni. The Jannati Darwaza is thrown open in his honour, to venerate Bibi Hafiza Jamal, and Hisamuddin, offspring of Khwaja entombed in his grounds. Qawwalis, an elaborate langar and an endless flow of sweets for visitors, persist throughout the assigned days.

Recitations from scriptures after early evening prayers, replaces qawwali in Ramadan (the month of fasting), and its hum envelopes the hall by the Buland Darwaza.

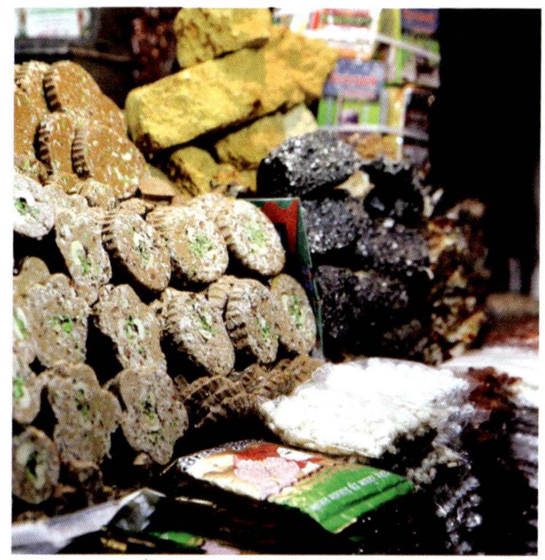

Above: Ritual offerings—sweets for visitors

Facing page: Immersed in qawwali—a group of Sufi singers at the shrine

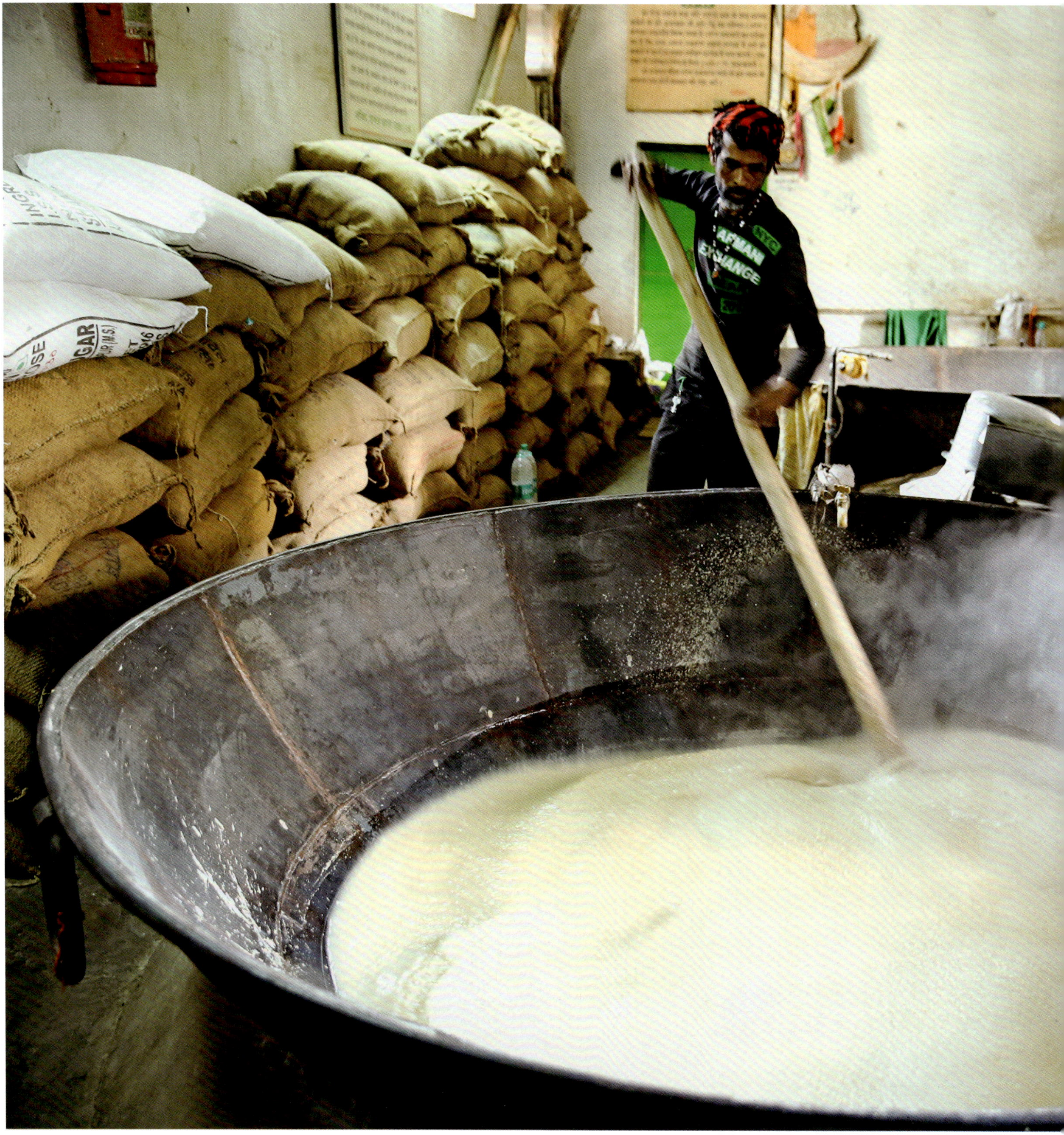

Rasm-e-Basant
(Festival of Spring)

Basant was first introduced to Chishti customs by Amir Khusrau, the renowned mystic poet and Nizamuddin Auliya's beloved disciple. Its first celebration was at Nizamuddin's Dargah in Delhi. Tradition recounts that after the loss of his loved nephew, the saint went into deep depression for months and much labour failed to bring cheer to him.

On Basant Panchami, Khusrau saw a procession in saffron, orange and red stride out in glee towards a Kalka temple. He borrowed a shirt, garland, and a *dhol* (drum) from the merrymakers, and danced into Nizam's chamber. The act brought a smile to Khusrau's master and with that beam, the festival became synonymous with the Chisti Order.

At Muinuddin's Shrine, Basant means colour and elation. On Holi, devotees gather at the Buland Darwaza chanting verses in Khwaja's honour and smear its steps with *gullal* (red powder). Similarly, the shrine glitters in a sea of oil lamps on Diwali, with the main communal kitchen serving purely vegetarian fare.

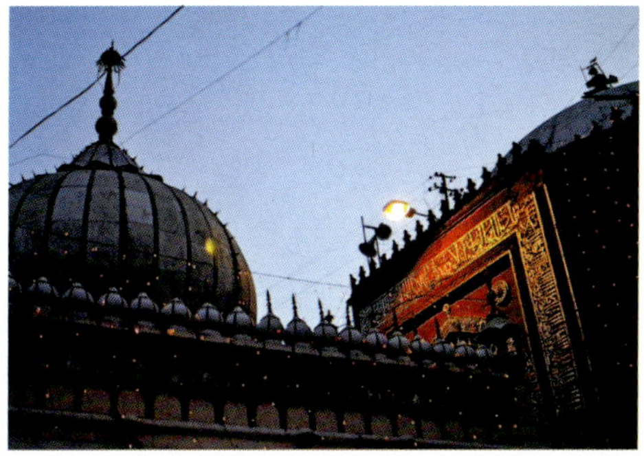

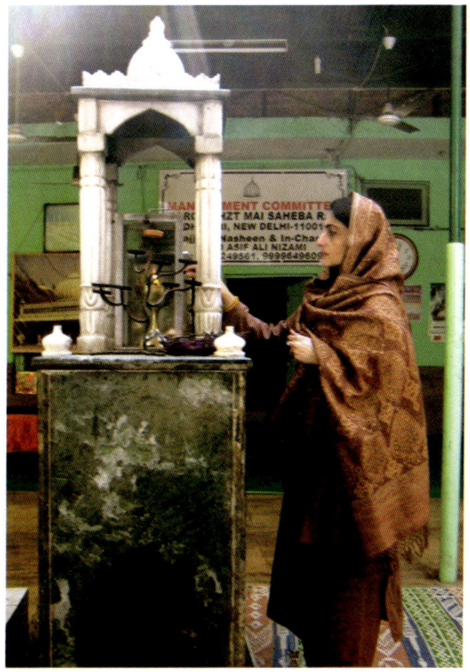

Top right: Nizamuddin's Dargah in Delhi

Right: Shaykha Amat un Nur lights a lamp at Nizamuddin Auliya's mother, Mai Saheba's tomb in Delhi

Facing page: In the Langarkhana, a cook prepares the barley meal, served in the morning and early evening

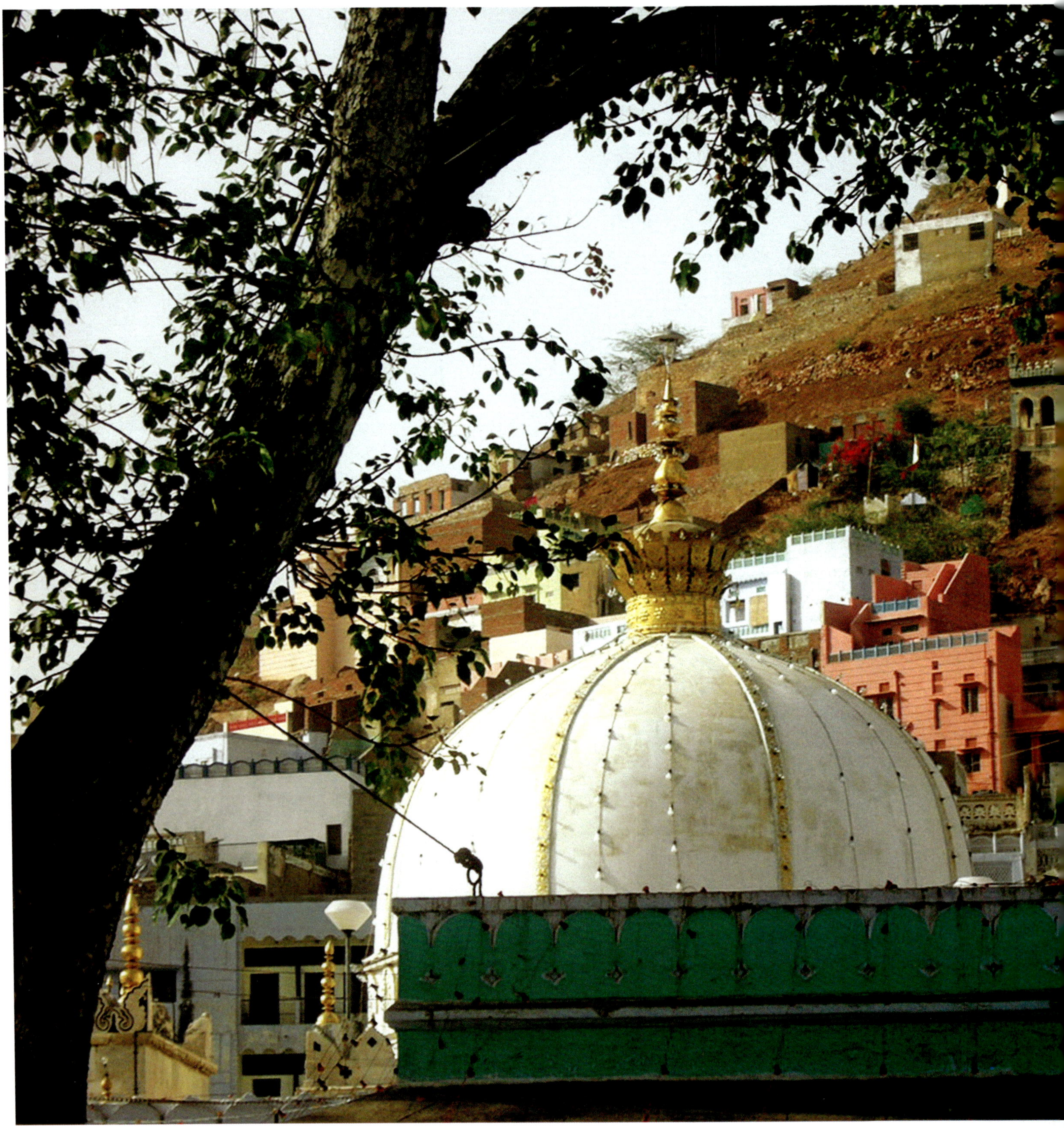

Urs—Meeting with Divinity

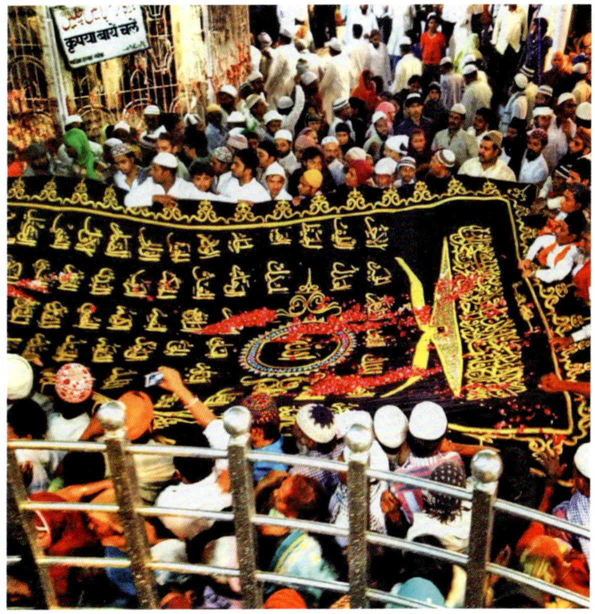

Above: A colossal chaddar offering from Pakistan bears 99 names of God

Facing page: Strings of lights cover the dome for the week of Urs festivities

The opening of the most evocative rite of passion is held at Qutub Minar's Hauz-i-Shamsi. This is where Baba Farid carried buckets of sand to build his spiritual mentor, Qutubuddin Bakhtyar Kaki's early grave. Today, it forms the backdrop of the ceremony where *charri*s (flags) from Kaki's shrine are handed to the procession making its way to Ajmer Sharif.

A fortnight before Muinuddin Chishti's death anniversary, the tradition at the historical venue heralds the beginning of their journey. The custom preserves the memory and ardour of Kaki, who walked with a flag to Ajmer, accompanied by his followers.

'The quality of people has degenerated; now the tradition continues but the piety and cleanliness have evaporated. Qutub sarkar would arrive in Ajmer as the moon of Gharib Nawaz's month rose,' says Rabbani sahib, the custodian and a charming flag-bearer of the past. Hailing from Bokhara, aged and genteel, his sophistication is from a finer age.

A caravan of *qalandar*s, dervishes, devotees and mendicants sets out on foot from the memorial of Qutubuddin Bakhtiyar Kaki, the saint whose funeral prayers were led by Iltutmish, in the Delhi suburb of Mehrauli. Some five days prior to the Urs, the old walls of the alleys are unable to contain the torrent of mankind; the *nishan*, or flag, rises at the Buland Darwaza. People cram in Sehan Chiragh, the qalandar caravan shuffles in with flags and a procession of khadims greets them and their musicians outside the gate.

The Walking Iron Man, is a model of mendicant passion. Eagle-eyed, dishevelled, reed thin, he knows little of the world outside. Windswept,

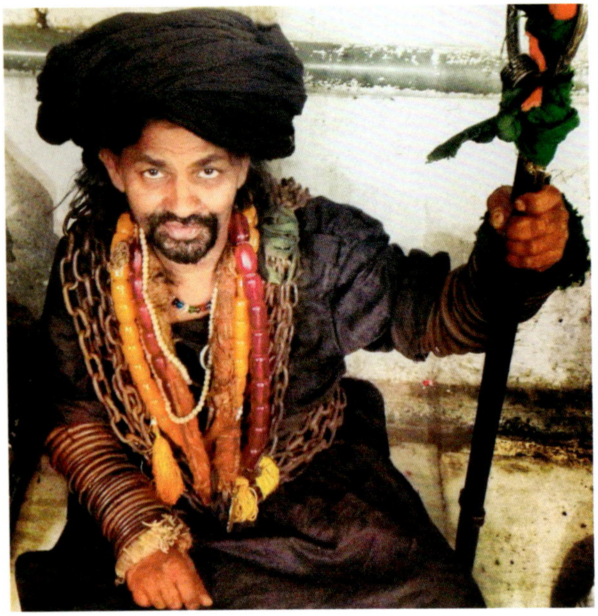

The Walking Iron Man or Iron Dervish at the end of his journey

rainbow-filled, spiritual, he walks with 60 kgs of iron fastened to his wrists, waist and ankles.

This day, the smaller door at the foot-end, named jhijri, is barred. As the moon of the sixth month lightens the skies, drums roll to announce the onset of anniversary celebrations. The permanent band of qawwals arrives at sunset, settles before the front porch, and recites the couplets below:

Bar tui mehfil shahana
mubarak zindabad.

(Hail, the grandest gathering,
long live this grandest gathering.)

Illahi tabaabd astaan iyar rahe,
yeh asra hai gharibon ka, barqarar rahe

(O Lord, grant eternity to this sacred abode,
May the sanctuary of the poor and weary, never cease.)

For these days, routine practices of the shrine are changed in time; the tomb is cleansed twice in the night, and the *ghusl* (bath), of the central cenotaph is carried out in dark hours.

Before the doors let visitors in, khadims conduct cleaning amid holy verses. The second service is after midnight, in the presence of the Dewan, the seven representatives of the keepers, and the key holder. Once they leave, the shrine is closed till sunrise. These scenes are replete with hints and echoes of the numinous, however intangible.

Strains of qawwalis from the Celebration Hall, flow through the compound for all six days. The Dewan arrives in the same pomp and circumstance as the *Punjshamba*; the two mace bearers flank him to maintain order and to carry out various duties.

The shrine qawwals inaugurate the gathering and troupes from within and outside India, follow. After midnight, the Dewan leaves for the sanctum, and returns by 3 am, the last touch to the day's festivities. Persian and Bhojpuri verses are read in chorus in various areas of the complex, as eulogies to saints.

The Paradise Gate stays unlocked for all six days of the Urs, and multitudes collect around it in anticipation of their turn to make seven rounds. The endless deluge of devotees reaches blurry levels, becoming a hazy collision of forms. Some carry an array of bequests, some shave their heads, and others weigh themselves in jaggery, coins, sugar, or dry fruits to offer that much in weight as gestures of devotion.

A new dimension to the most venerated week in Ajmer Sharif, is the arrival of a large delegation from Pakistan, carrying a vast velvet shroud, stamped with 99 names of God.

The Roshni plays out at the eastern Begami Courtyard, and the entire complex, from the dome downwards is lit in streams of fairy lights, oil lamps and candles. The communal breakfast is prepared by *anderkotis* (residents of the fort) and its cost is borne by one whose circle of prayer, or the fulfillment of a wish, is complete.

The final ceremony of *Qul* (invocation), falls on the night of the fifth day as celebrations reach a crescendo; the music gathers a feverish pace, with qawwalis, songs, drum rolls, communal feasts, elaborate ceremonies and an ocean of humanity in the campus and across Ajmer, grow to a climax.

On the morning of the sixth day, the prime sanctum is closed to the public. Keepers in ceremonial robes, with turbans, gush in with flowers, incense, sweets.

They recite the spiritual lineage of the Chishti Order and verses christened *faryad* (a plea). Pledging adherence to the saint, they perform other rites of dedication, repentance and blessing.

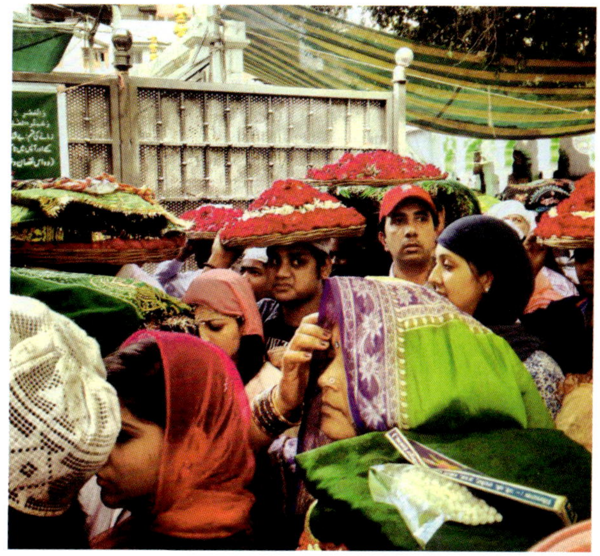

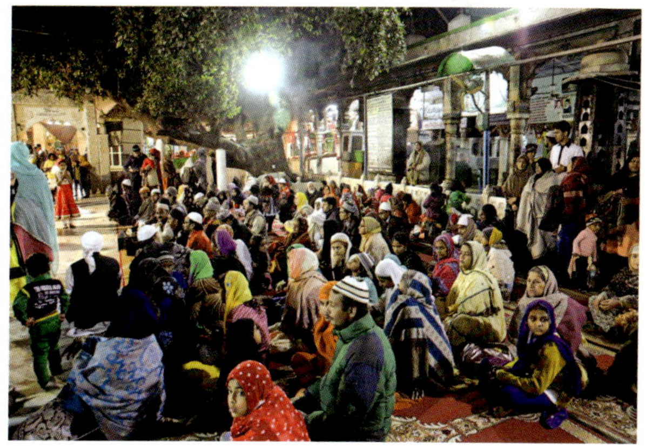

Top: Devotees bring offerings to the shrine

Above: Pilgrims wait for the blessings of grace

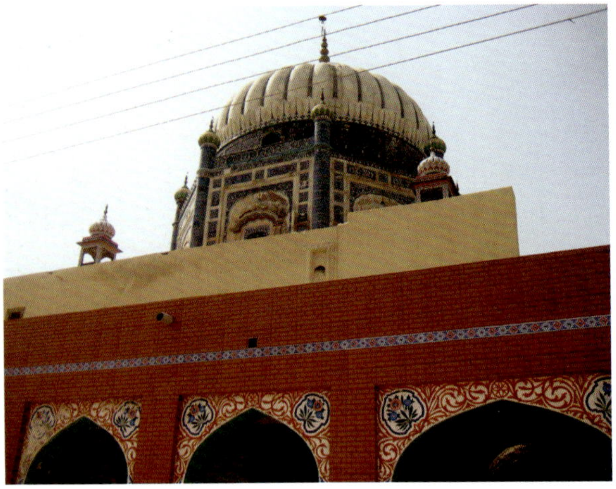

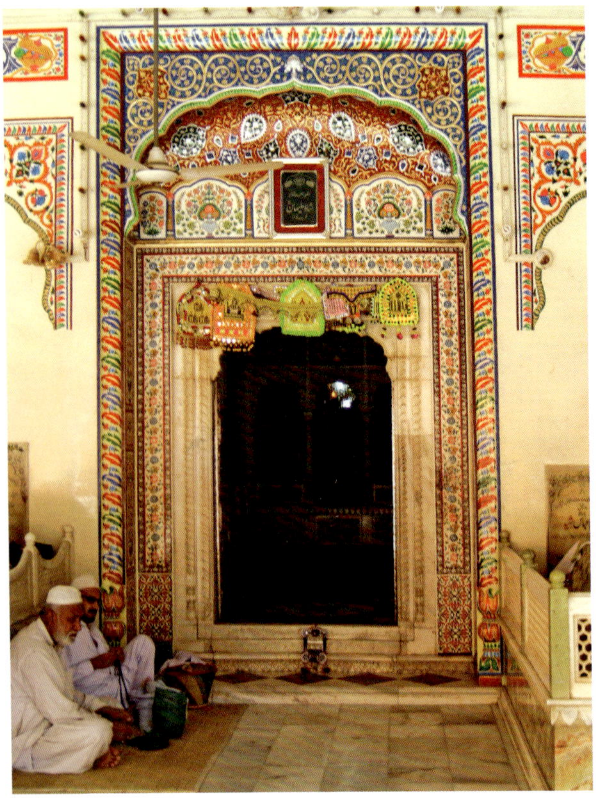

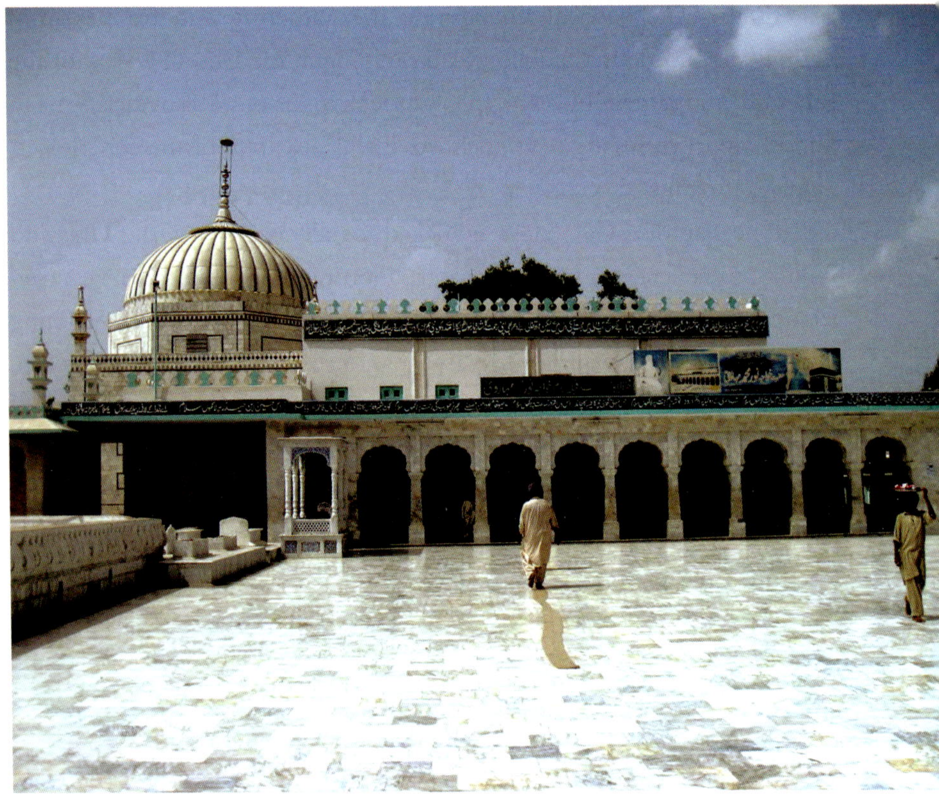

At the Gathering Hall, the shrine qawwals open *sama* at 11 am, ending in *rang*, and as their instruments fall silent, *badhawa* (a presentation of praise), is sung with synced clapping.

Here is an extract of a badhawa verse:

Both universes be sacrificed
at your behest o' Khwaja.
My rounds of the dome in deep devotion,
the splendour cascades from the balcony above, you survey the world.

Cannons fire from nearby hills and drumbeats mark the closing of the Urs and the Jannati Darwaza. Everything comes to a final halt, in perfectly orchestrated harmony. Interestingly, the rituals of the Urs are enshrined in the constitution of the Chisti Order and have seen centuries in their original form. Some hark back to the early Chishtis and many were introduced by the Mughals.

Among the five remaining Chishti seats in Pakistan, led by Baba Farid Ganj-e-Shakar in Pakpattan, Punjab, distinctive rituals of the order flourish with both fervour and regularity at three seats.

Pakpattan Sharif stays doused in the system to its core. Pir Zahir Chishti, a prominent custodian of the shrine attests: 'Daily and weekly rituals of the Chishti Order and anniversaries of Baba Farid's spiritual ancestors are celebrated with zeal and reverence.'

The next seat is of Noor Maharvi, an 18th century Sufi saint, in Chishtian, near Bahawalnagar in Punjab. More popularly known as Qibla-e Alam, this lesser-known spiritual place enjoys a significant station in the Sufi Order's line, as the 13th century saint Khwaja Tajuddin Chishti brought the town into being in 1275 CE. A foremost guardian, Asim Maharvi, maintains that the shrine's setting in the remote recesses of southern Punjab impedes the pursuit and dissemination of Sufi practices.

> *There's a madrassah, and a mosque attached to the shrine. But we persevere with Chishti rituals and anniversaries of the Order's saints. We have regular qawwali but it has been toned down sans loud speakers. The complexion of the area was altered by Zia-ul-Haq and is still in recovery.*

Maharvi also explains that despite two suicide bomber attacks and an immense wave of fear, devotees pour in undeterred. 'Khwaja Gharib Nawaz's Chhati Sharif and death anniversary are observed with devotion; without him we lose all meaning,' he concludes.

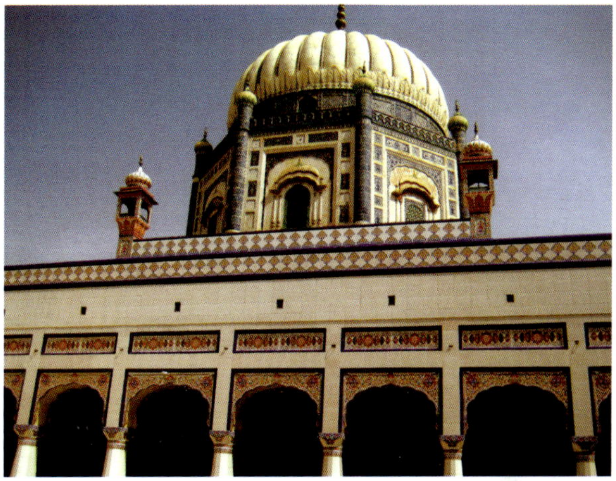

Top: Taunsa Sharif, Pakistan

Facing page above left: The main dome of Taunsa Sharif

Facing page above right: Noor Maharvi, Pakistan

Facing page below: Entrance to the memorial chamber of Taunsa Sharif, Pakistan

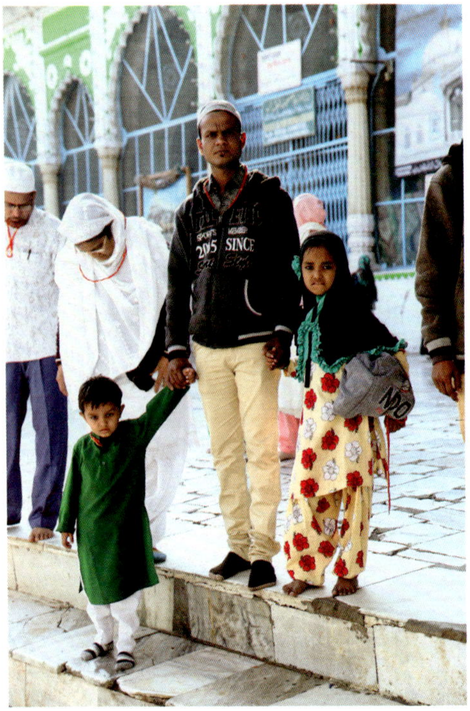

Pir Zahir Chishty and Asim Maharvi agree that another revered mausoleum steeped in Chisti culture, is of Muhammad Suleiman Taunsvi. He lies in Taunsa District near Dera Ghazi Khan in Punjab. Taunsa Sharif stands on the Indus Highway by the Indus River. The sage's death anniversary falls in the first week of the second month in the Muslim lunar calendar.

Maharvi avers that this beautifully maintained shrine is free from any of the restrictions he has to contend with. 'Taunsa Sharif has not entered the jurisdiction of the Auqaf Department. Hence, it maintains the essence of our Orientalist history and the Chishti Order. Non-Muslims are embraced; in fact they are engaged in activities to serve the cause of interfaith harmony.'

However, at the end of this story, little is clearer than a singular, stabbing message—no one has the power to halt another's path. And if we do, then in the name of which interpretation of divinity?

All of this is the history and legacy of a man in a mud hut. He was guided not by prophecies or the logic of an empirical science. But by humanity and by kindness. That alone should make every difference.

'Let us go and visit the dwelling place of these ascetics, who have consumed their ego completely.'

Shah Abdul Latif Bhittai, mystic and poet.

Above: Seeking the saint's blessings for their young ones—a family visits Ajmer Sharif

Facing page: Dispeller of darkness—the dome of Ajmer Sharif, decorated for Urs festivities

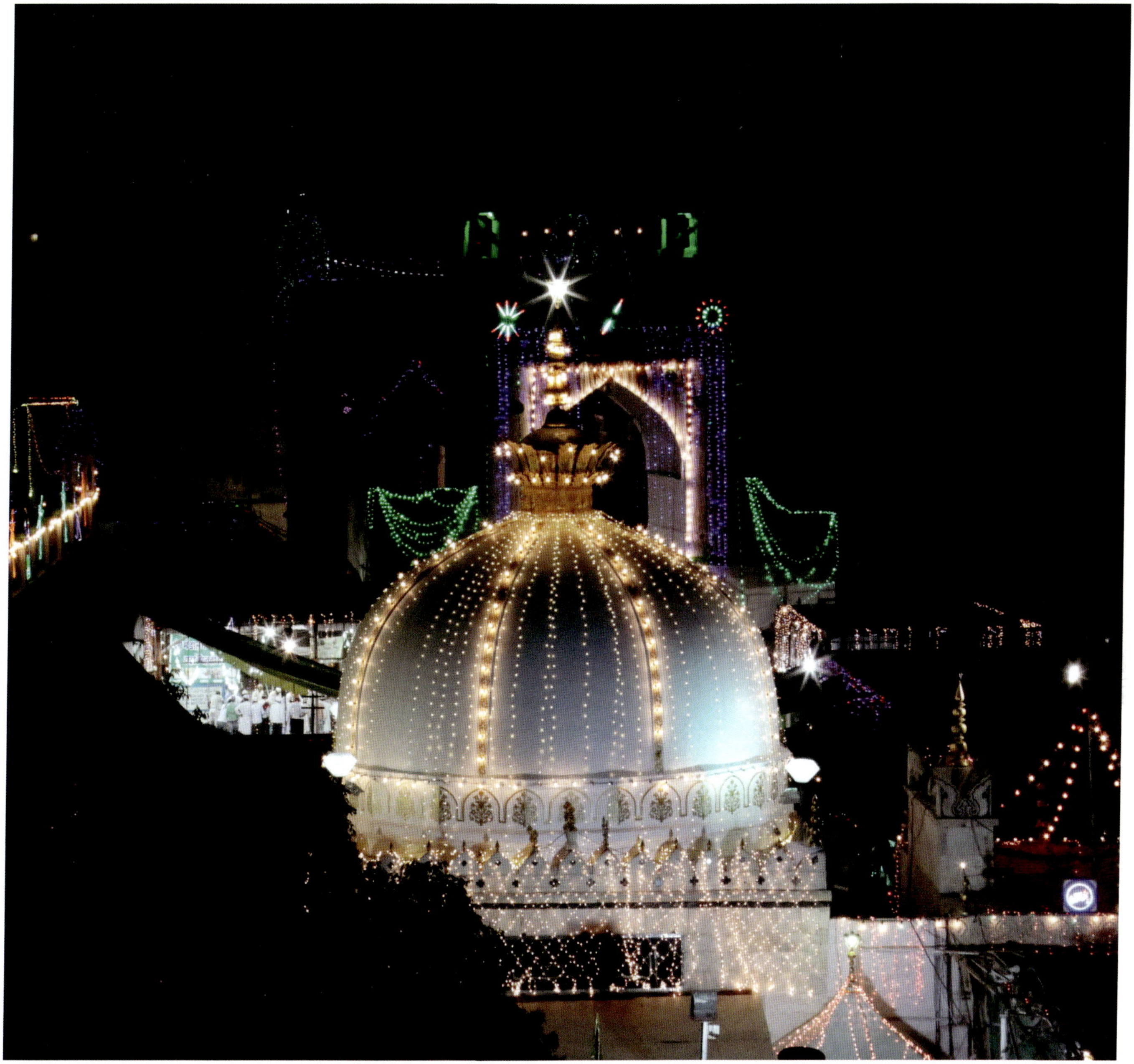

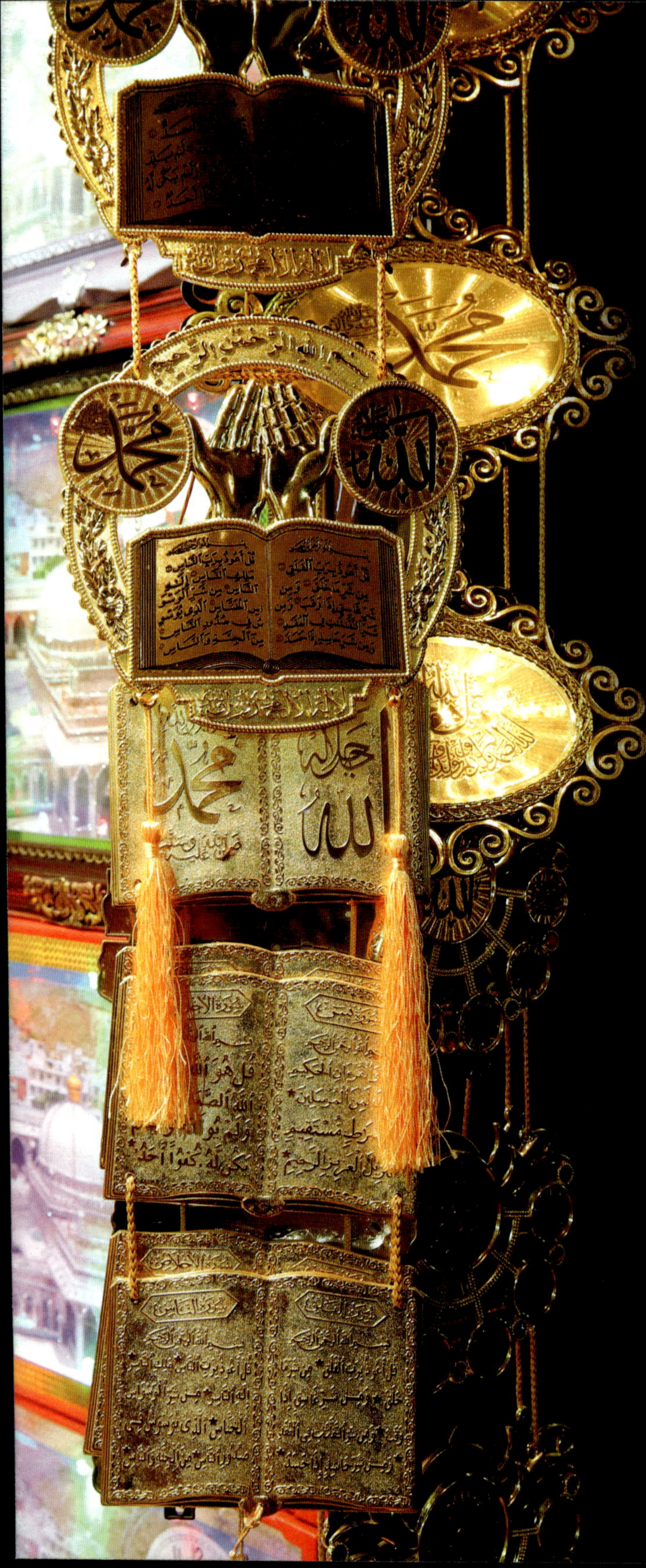

Acknowledgmen

Syed Salman Chishty
For continued facilitation and guidance

Rabbani Sahib
Bakhtiyar Kaki Shrine, Delhi, India

Farid Nizami
Nizamuddin Shrine, Delhi, India

Shaykha Naila H. Tiwana
(Amat un Nur), Pakistan

Pir Zahir Chishti
Pakpattan Sharif, Pakistan

Asim Maharvi
Maharvi Sharif Shrine, Pakistan

Liyaqat Moini
Aligarh Muslim University, and author, India

Ahtisham Ahmad Nizami
Aligarh, India

Dr F. S. Shirana
Director GEC, Kennedy Auditorium, Aligarh Muslim University, India

Khalid Hashmi and Haji Farrokh
Ajmer Sharif, India

Hameed Haroon
CEO, Pakistan Herald Publications Ltd (Dawn)

Aamer Ahmed Khan
My former editor and renowned journalist

Nawabzada Farrukh Said Khan Chhatari
Aligarh, India

Imad Jafar
New York University. Assistance in extensive research on the Chishti Sufi Order in Pakistan

References

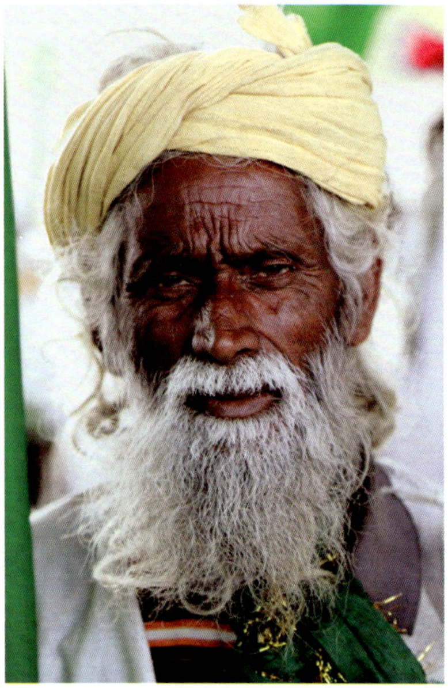

Asher, Catherine B. *Architecture of Mughal India (The New Cambridge History of India)*. Cambridge, UK: Cambridge University Press. 2008.

Aslan, Reza. *No God but God: The Origins, Evolution, and Future of Islam*. Random House, 2005.

Begg, W.D. *The Holy Biography of Hazrat Khwaja Muinuddin Chishti*. Tucson, Arizona: Chishti Sufi Mission of America, 1977.

Berinstain, Valérie. *Mughal India: Splendours of the Peacock Throne*. Trans. Paul Bahn. London: Thames & Hudson, 1998.

Boyle, J.A., ed. *Cambridge History of Iran – Vol 5 (The Seljuk and Mongol Periods)*. Cambridge, UK: Cambridge University Press, 2008.

Butenschon, Andrea. *The Life of a Mogul Princess Jahanara Begum: Daughter of Shahjahan*. Lahore: Sang-e-Meel Publications. 2004.

Chaghatai, M. Ikram., ed. *Babaji: The Life and Teachings of Farid-ud Din Ganj-i Shakar*. Lahore: Sang-e-Meel Publications, 2006.

Currie, P.M. *The Shrine and Cult of Mu'in al-din Chishti of Ajmer*. Oxford: Oxford University Press, 2007.

Elliot, Sir H.M. *Memoirs of Jahangir*. Ed. Prof. John Dowson. Lahore: Islamic Book Service, 1975.

Embree, Ainslie T., ed. *Sources of Indian Tradition*. New York: Columbia University Press, 1958.

Ernst, Carl W., and Bruce Lawrence. *Sufi Martyrs of Love: The Chishti Order in South Asia and Beyond*. New York: Palgrave Macmillan US, 2002.

Fazl, Abul. *Akbarnama Vols I, II, III*. Trans. H. Beveridge. Lahore: Book Traders, 1986.

Haeri, Muneera. *The Chishtis: A Living Light*. New York: Oxford University Press, USA, 2000.

Jaffer, Mehru. *The Book of Muinuddin Chishti*. New Delhi: Penguin, 2006.

Jahangir. *The Tuzuk-i-Jahangiri Vols 1 & 2*. Trans. Alexander Rogers, Ed. Henry Beveridge. London: Royal Asiatic Society, 1909.

Lewisohn, Leonard and David Morgan. *The Heritage of Sufism (Volume III)*. London: Oneworld Publications, 1999.

Moini, Prof. (Dr) Syed Liyaqat Hussain. *The Dargah of "Khwaja Gharib-un-Nawaz" of Ajmer*. New Delhi: DK Agencies, 2015.

Mukhia, Harbans. *The Mughals of India*. New Jersey: Wiley-Blackwell, 2004.

Nicholl, Fergus. *Shah Jahan - The Rise and Fall of the Mughal Emperor*. New Delhi: Viking/ Penguin, 2009.

Sarda, Har Bilas. *Ajmer: Historical and Descriptive*. Ajmer: Fine Art Printing Press, 1941.

Schimmel, Annemarie. *Islam in the Indian Subcontinent*. Lahore: Sang-e-Meel Publications, 2003.

Shah, Idries. *The Sufis*. New York: Anchor Books/Doubleday & Co Inc, 1964.

Suvorova, Anna. *Muslim Saints of South Asia: The Eleventh to Fifteenth Centuries*. Oxford: Routledge, 2004.

Weisgrau, Maxine and Carol Henderson, eds. *Raj Rhapsodies: Tourism, Heritage and the Seduction of History*. Oxford: Routledge, 2007.

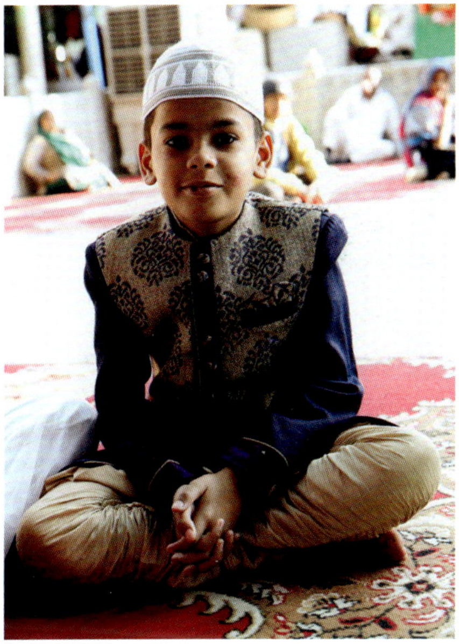

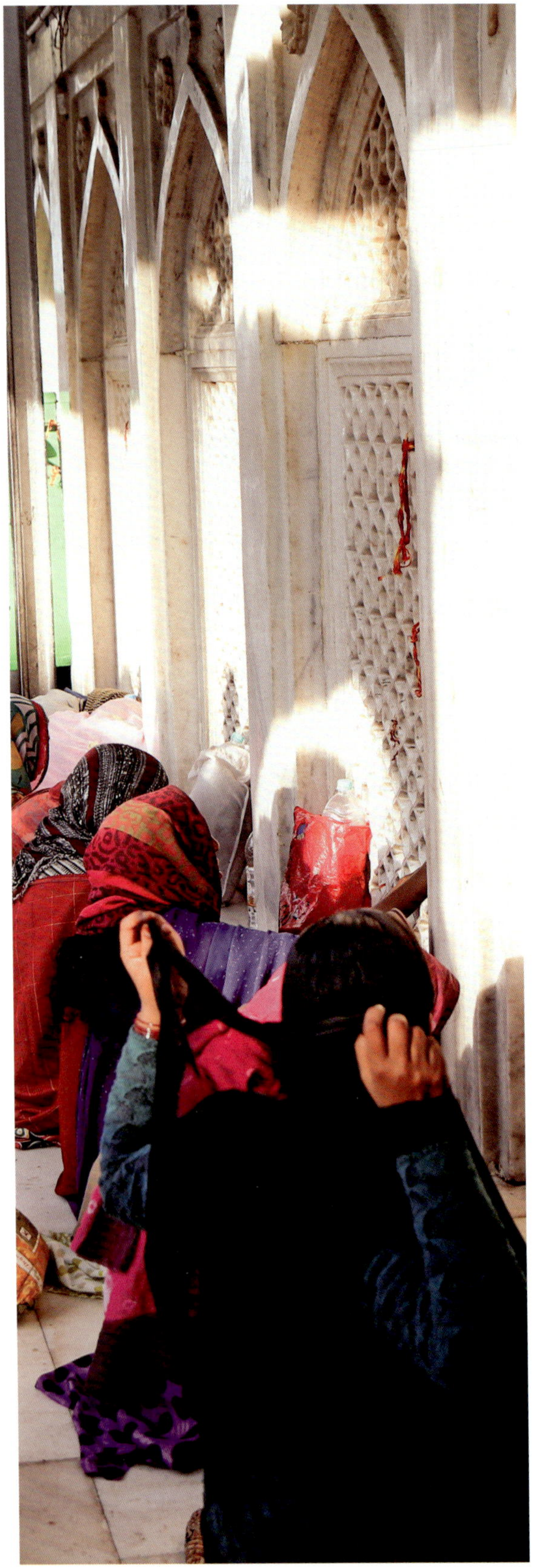

Image Credits

P. 60. The high arch of the screen wall at Adhai din ka Jhonpra, Ajmer: Billyakhtar, CC-BY-4.0, *https://commons.wikimedia.org/wiki/File:Adhai_Din_Ka_Jhonpra.jpg*

P. 61. The interior of the mosque's dome at Adhai din ka Jhonpra, Ajmer: Varun Shiv Kapur, CC-BY-2.0, *https://commons.wikimedia.org/wiki/File:Adhai_Din-ka-Jhonpra_Dome_decorative_work_(6134499928).jpg*

P. 62. Ajmer—a silver lake nestled amidst rocky hills: Shahrukhalam334, CC-BY-4.0, *https://commons.wikimedia.org/wiki/File:A_view_of_ajmer_city.jpg*

P. 64. Mihrab dome and arcade at Adhai din ka Jhonpra, Ajmer: Varun Shiv Kapur, CC-BY-2.0, *https://commons.wikimedia.org/wiki/File:Adhai_Din-ka-Jhonpra_Arcade_and_mihrab_dome_(6134506218).jpg*

P. 64. Decorated ceiling of the mosque arcade at Adhai din ka Jhonpra, Ajmer: Varun Shiv Kapur, CC-BY-2.0, *https://commons.wikimedia.org/wiki/File:Adhai_Din-ka-Jhonpra_Arcade_and_ceiling_detail_(6133962667).jpg*

P. 64. The screen wall at Adhai din ka Jhonpra, Ajmer: Varun Shiv Kapur, CC-BY-2.0, *https://commons.wikimedia.org/wiki/File:Adhai_Din-ka-Jhonpra_Screen_wall_(6133975257).jpg*

P. 65. Tomb of Balban at Mehrauli Archaeological Park, Delhi: Harvinder Singh, CC-BY-4.0, *https://commons.wikimedia.org/wiki/File:Tomb_of_Balban,Mehrauli_Archaeological_Park,New_Delhi,India.jpg*

P. 70. Sunset over Sambhar Lake, Rajasthan: Nawanshu91, CC-BY-3.0, *https://commons.wikimedia.org/wiki/File:Sambhar_lake_sunset_scene.JPG*

P. 71. Chilla Nizamuddin, the residence of Nizamuddin Auliya: Varun Shiv Kapur, CC-BY-2.0, *https://commons.wikimedia.org/wiki/File:Chilla_Nizamuddin,_residence_of_Nizamuddin_Auliya,_near_Humayun%27s_tomb,_Delhi.jpg*

P. 72. Devotees at the tomb of Qutubuddin Bakhtiyar Kaki: Varun Shiv Kapur, CC-BY-2.0, *https://commons.wikimedia.org/wiki/File:Qutbuddin_Bakhtiyar_Kaki%27s_tomb.jpg*

P. 73. Entrance to the grave enclosure in Qutbuddin Bakhtiyar Kaki's tomb: Varun Shiv Kapur, CC-BY-2.0, *https://commons.wikimedia.org/wiki/File:Entrance_to_grave_enclosure_within_Qutbuddin_Bakhtiyar_Kaki%27s_dargah_compound.jpg*

P. 76. Taragarh Fort stands proudly over the city of Ajmer: Hemant Shesh, CC-BY-3.0, *https://commons.wikimedia.org/wiki/File:The_Fort_Wall_of_Taragarh,_Ajmer.JPG*

P. 84. Grand gates lead into the shrine complex: Ajkumar, CC-BY-3.0, *https://en.wikipedia.org/wiki/File:Dragah_Sharif_-_Buland_Darwaza.jpg*

P. 90. Princess Jahanara's tomb: Varun Shiv Kapur, CC-BY-2.0, *https://commons.wikimedia.org/wiki/File:Nizamuddin_Dargah_and_Jamaat_Khana_Masjid,_Delhi.jpg*

P. 91. Princess Jahanara: Image from *Histoire générale des Voyages*, l'Abbé Antoine François Prévost and Jacques-Nicolas Bellin, (Paris, 1746-1759; 15 volumes), *https://commons.wikimedia.org/wiki/File:Jahan-ara.jpg*

P. 102. Aurangzeb's tomb in Khuldabad: PP Yoonus, CC-BY-3.0, *https://commons.wikimedia.org/wiki/File:TOMB_aURANGAZEB.JPG*

P.103. Emperor Aurangzeb on horseback (ca. 1690–1710); The Cleveland Museum of Art, public domain, *https://commons.wikimedia.org/wiki/File:The_Emperor_Aurangzeb_on_Horseback_ca._1690%E2%80%931710_The_Cleveland_Museum_of_Art.jpg*

P. 108. Inside Ganj-e-Shakar chamber a special ceremony of Koozian (Gulping from a clay cup) is underway: Raisuddin Shaikh

P. 109. Bakhtiyar Kaki's Dargah in Mehrauli, Delhi: Varun Shiv Kapur, CC-BY-2.0, *https://commons.wikimedia.org/wiki/File:Tomb_of_Sufi_saint,_Qutbuddin_Bakhtiyar_Kaki_in_Mehrauli,_Delhi.jpg*

P. 119. Sunset at Ana Sagar Lake: Singh92karan, CC-BY-3.0, *https://commons.wikimedia.org/wiki/File:Overlooking_beautiful_Anasagar_lake.jpg*

P. 119. Daulat Bagh gardens at Ana Sagar Lake: Fatehrawkey, public domain, *https://commons.wikimedia.org/wiki/File:The_Anas%C4%81gar_Lake_1_PHOTOGRAPHED_BY_FATEH.RawKEy.jpg*

P. 120. Baradari or marble pavilions on the banks of Ana Sagar Lake: Hemant Shesh, CC-BY-3.0, *https://commons.wikimedia.org/wiki/File:Anasagar_Lake_in_Ajmer.JPG*

P. 121. Serene waters of Ana Sagar Lake: Debabrata Ghosh, CC BY-SA 3.0, *https://commons.wikimedia.org/wiki/File:Anna_sarobar-2-ajmir.jpg*

P. 122. Sunset over still waters—view from the marble pavilions: Logawi, CC BY-SA 4.0, *https://commons.wikimedia.org/wiki/File:Ana_Sagar_pavilion_sunset_2016.jpg*

P. 124. 'Akbar visits the tomb of Khwaja Muinuddin Chishti at Ajmer', painting by Basawan (c. 1595): Victoria and Albert Musuem, public domain, *https://commons.wikimedia.org/wiki/File:Basawan_-_Akbar_visits_the_tomb_of_Khwajah_Mu%27in_ad-Din_Chishti_at_Ajmer_-_Google_Art_Project.jpg*

P. 125. 'Jahangir Preferring a Sufi Shaikh to Kings', opaque watercolor by Bichitr (c. 1615-1618): The Freer Gallery of Art, Public Domain, *https://commons.wikimedia.org/wiki/File:Bichitr_-_Jahangir_Preferring_a_Sufi_Shaikh_to_Kings,_from_the_St._Petersburg_album_-_Google_Art_Project.jpg*

P. 157. Nizamuddin's Dargah in Delhi: Divya Gupta, CC-BY-3.0, *https://commons.wikimedia.org/wiki/File:Nizamuddin_Dargah_Complex_(Delhi,_India).jpg*

P. 157. Shaykha Amat un Nur lights a lamp at Nizamuddin Auliya's mother, Mai Saheba's tomb in Delhi: Shaykha Naila H. Tiwana (Amat un Nur)

P. 158. Strings of lights cover the dome for the week of Urs festivities: Shahnoor Habib Munmun, CC-BY-3.0, *https://commons.wikimedia.org/wiki/File:Dargah_of_Sufi_saint_Moinuddin_Chishti_Ajmer_India_(3).JPG*

PP. 162-3: Taunsa Sharif images: Shaykha Naila H.Tiwana (Amat un Nur)

P. 162: Noor Maharvi: Ammarkh, CC-BY-3.0, *https://commons.wikimedia.org/wiki/File:KhawajaNoor.jpg*

All other photographs courtesy Syed Salman Chishty.

Facing page: Women pray outside the marble walls of the shrine

Index

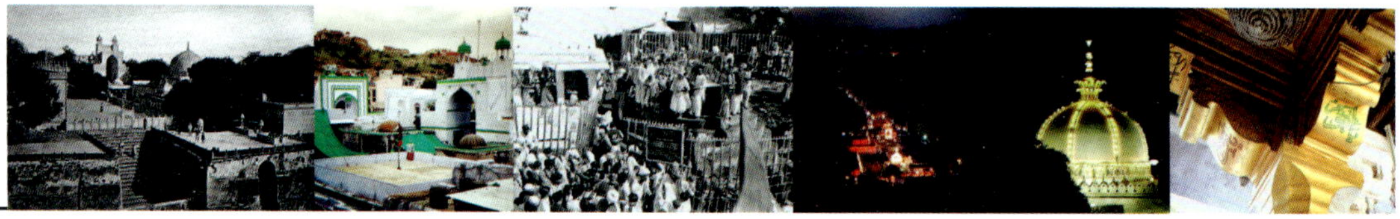

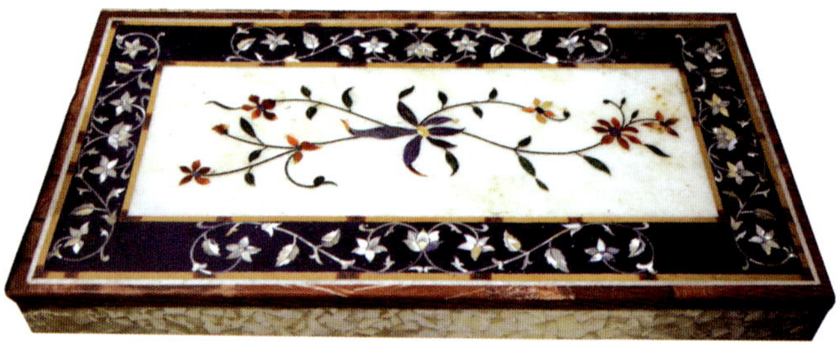

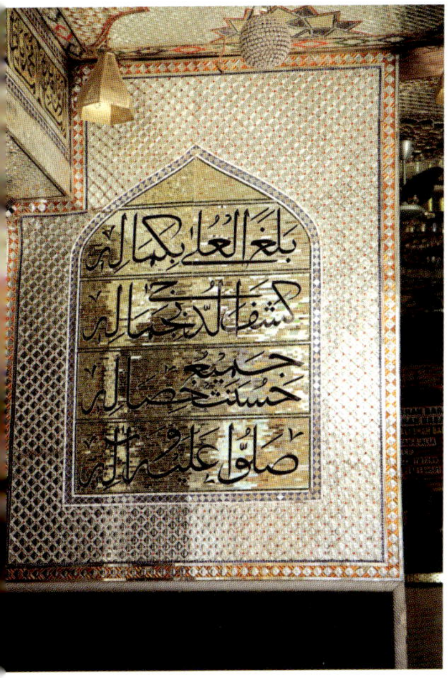

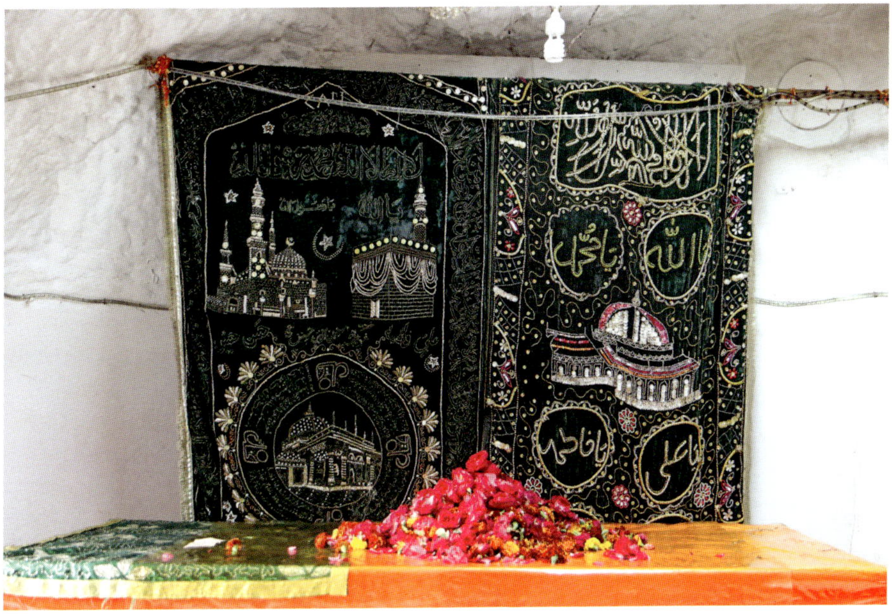

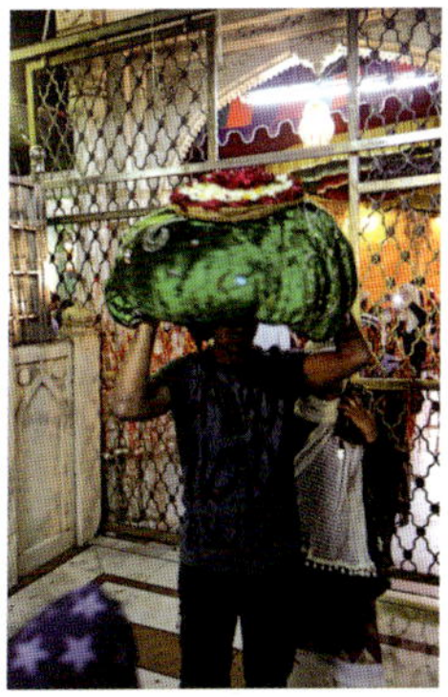

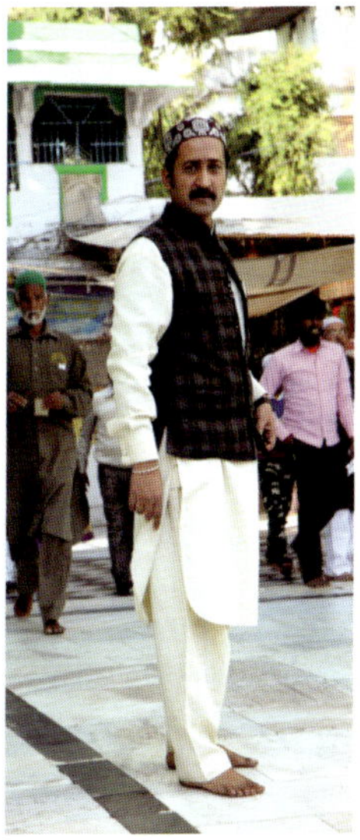

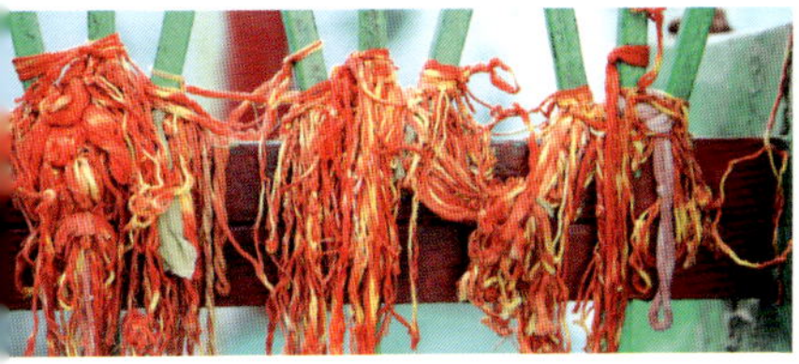

Glimpses of grace—
vignettes of Ajmer Sharif

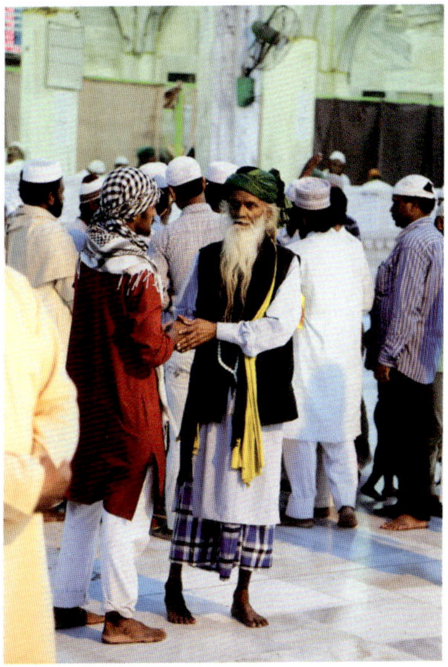

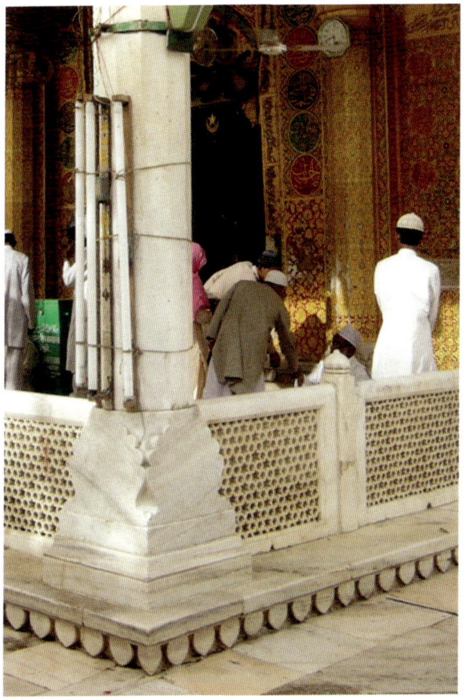

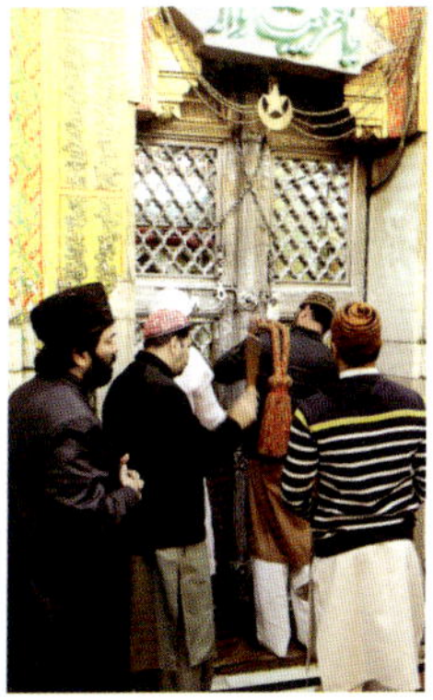

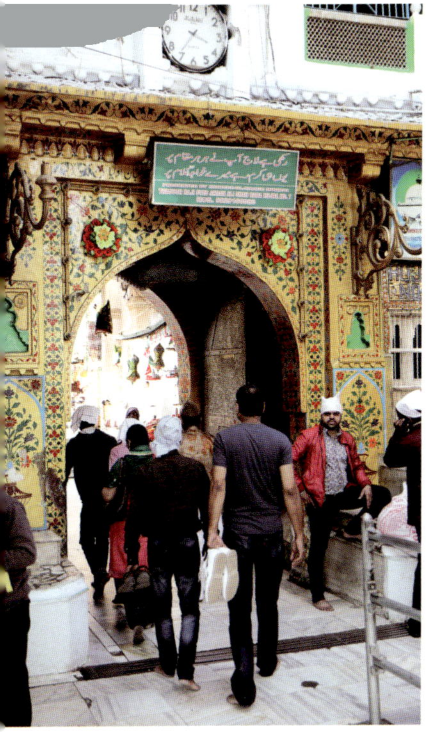

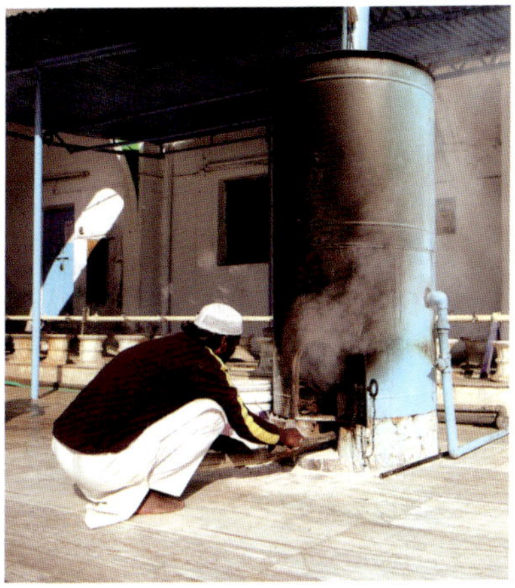

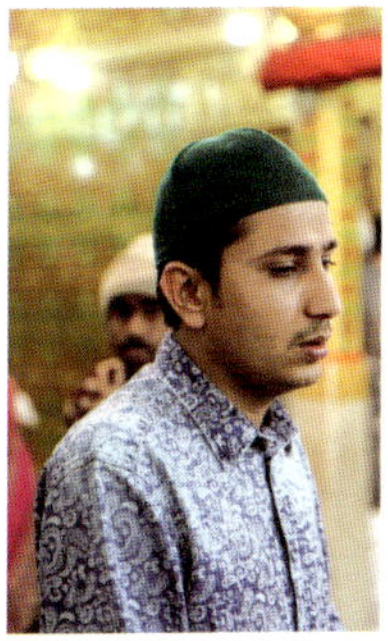

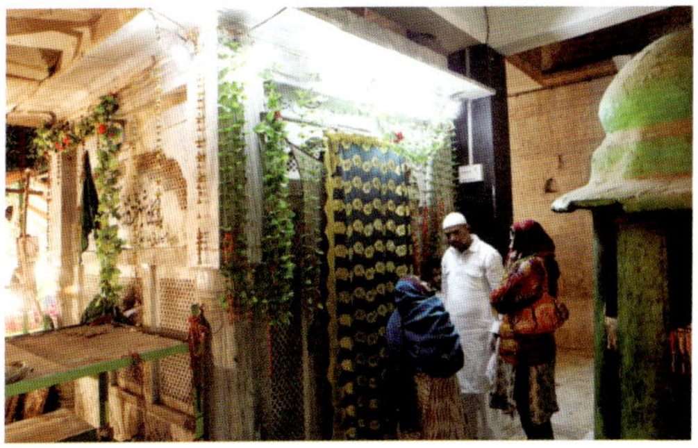

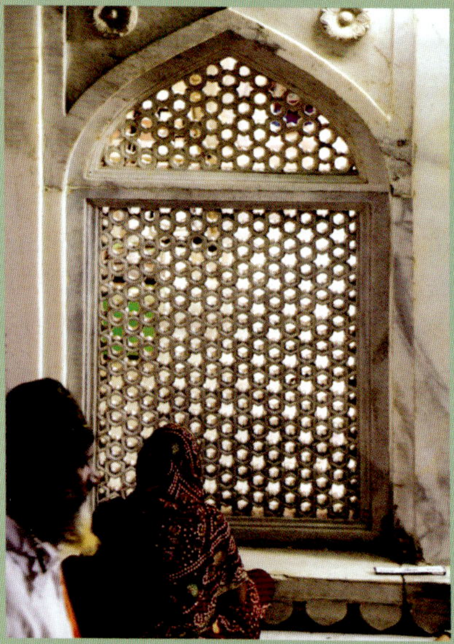